PHILIP'S

STREF̶ ̶ ̶AS

Noɪ ̶ ̶ ̶rland

First published in 2001 as
Tyne & Wear Northumberland by

Philip's, a division of
Octopus Publishing Group Ltd
2-4 Heron Quays, London E14 4JP

First edition 2005
First impression 2005

ISBN-10   0-540-08755-6 (pocket)
ISBN-13   978-0-540-08755-6 (pocket)

© Philip's 2005

Ordnance Survey®

This product includes mapping data licensed from
Ordnance Survey® with the permission of the
Controller of Her Majesty's Stationery Office.
© Crown copyright 2005. All rights reserved.
Licence number 100011710.

Contents

III **Key to map symbols**

IV **Key to map pages**

VI **Route planning**

X **Administrative and Postcode boundaries**

1 **Street maps** at 1⅓ inches to 1 mile

112 **Street maps** at 2⅔ inches to 1 mile

186 **Index** of towns and villages

188 **Index** of streets, hospitals, industrial estates, railway stations, schools, shopping centres, universities and places of interest

Digital Data

The exceptionally high-quality mapping found in this atlas is available as digital data in TIFF format, which is easily convertible to other bitmapped (raster) image formats.

The index is also available in digital form as a standard database table. It contains all the details found in the printed index together with the National Grid reference for the map square in which each entry is named.

For further information and to discuss your requirements, please contact Philip's on 020 7644 6932 or james.mann@philips-maps.co.uk

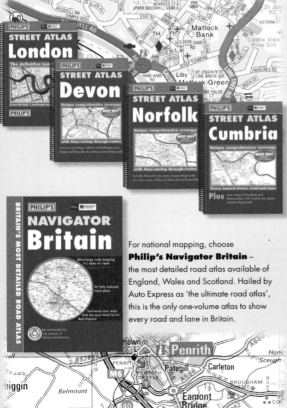

(22a)	**Motorway** with junction number
	Primary route – dual/single carriageway
	A road – dual/single carriageway
	B road – dual/single carriageway
	Minor road – dual/single carriageway
	Other minor road – dual/single carriageway
	Road under construction
	Tunnel, covered road
	Rural track, private road or narrow road in urban area
	Gate or obstruction to traffic (restrictions may not apply at all times or to all vehicles)
	Path, bridleway, byway open to all traffic, road used as a public path
	Pedestrianised area
DY7	**Postcode boundaries**
	County and unitary authority boundaries
	Railway, tunnel, railway under construction
	Tramway, tramway under construction
	Miniature railway
Walsall	**Railway station**
	Private railway station
South Shields	**Metro station**
	Tram stop, tram stop under construction
	Bus, coach station

◆	**Ambulance station**
◆	**Coastguard station**
◆	**Fire station**
◆	**Police station**
✚	**Accident and Emergency entrance to hospital**
H	**Hospital**
+	**Place of worship**
i	**Information Centre** (open all year)
🛒	**Shopping Centre**
P P&R	**Parking, Park and Ride**
PO	**Post Office**
⋀	**Camping site**
🚐	**Caravan site**
▶	**Golf course**
✕	**Picnic site**
Prim Sch	**Important buildings, schools, colleges, universities and hospitals**
River Medway	**Water name**
	River, weir, stream
	Canal, lock, tunnel
	Water
	Tidal water
	Woods
	Built up area
Church	**Non-Roman antiquity**
ROMAN FORT	**Roman antiquity**
94 164	**Adjoining page indicators and overlap bands** The colour of the arrow and the band indicates the scale of the adjoining or overlapping page (see scales below)

Acad	**Academy**	Inst	**Institute**	Recn Gd	**Recreation Ground**
Allot Gdns	**Allotments**	Ct	**Law Court**		
Cemy	**Cemetery**	L Ctr	**Leisure Centre**	Resr	**Reservoir**
C Ctr	**Civic Centre**	LC	**Level Crossing**	Ret Pk	**Retail Park**
CH	**Club House**	Liby	**Library**	Sch	**School**
Coll	**College**	Mkt	**Market**	Sh Ctr	**Shopping Centre**
Crem	**Crematorium**	Meml	**Memorial**	TH	**Town Hall/House**
Ent	**Enterprise**	Mon	**Monument**	Trad Est	**Trading Estate**
Ex H	**Exhibition Hall**	Mus	**Museum**	Univ	**University**
Ind Est	**Industrial Estate**	Obsy	**Observatory**	W Twr	**Water Tower**
IRB Sta	**Inshore Rescue Boat Station**	Pal	**Royal Palace**	Wks	**Works**
		PH	**Public House**	YH	**Youth Hostel**

■ The small numbers around the edges of the maps identify the 1 kilometre National Grid lines

■ The dark grey border on the inside edge of some pages indicates that the mapping does not continue onto the adjacent page

The scale of the maps on the pages numbered in blue is 4.2 cm to 1 km • 2⅔ inches to 1 mile • 1: 23810

0 ¼ ½ ¾ 1 mile
0 250m 500m 750m 1 kilometre

The scale of the maps on pages numbered in green is 2.1 cm to 1 km • 1⅓ inches to 1 mile • 1: 47620

0 ¼ ½ ¾ 1 mile
0 250m 500m 750m 1 kilometre

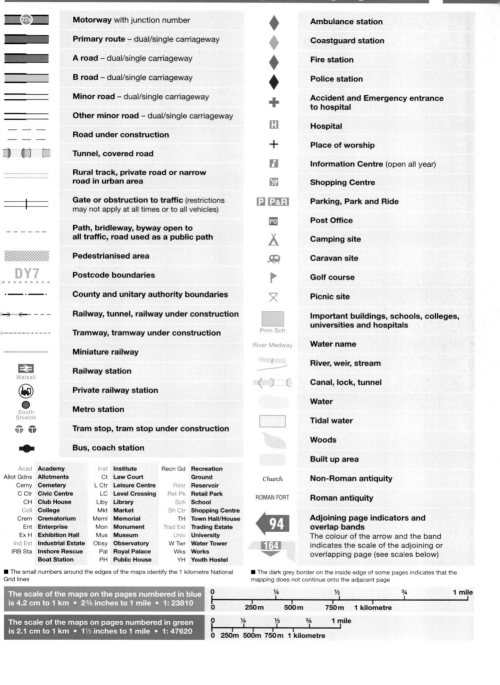

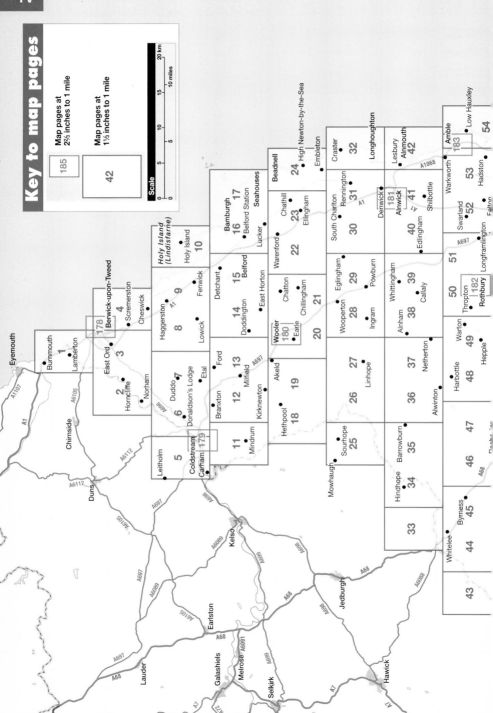

Key to map pages

Map pages at
2⅓ inches to 1 mile

185

Map pages at
1⅓ inches to 1 mile

42

Scale

0   5   10   15   20 km

0   5   10 miles

V

Hemscott Hill
Cresswell
112 113
Lynemouth
66
Widdrington
65
Woodhorn
Newbiggin-by-the-Sea
Widdrington Station
114 115 116 117 118
Hebron
Pegswood
Ashington
64
Longhorsley
Stakeford
Cambois
Morpeth
119 120 121 122 123
Blyth
128 129
New Delaval
134 135
Whitley Bay
144 145
Marden
Tynemouth
South Shields
Whitburn
Sunderland
Seaham
Easington Colliery
Trimdon

Forestburn Gate
Wingates
63
Netherwitton
62
Pigdon
76
Molesden
Whalton
85
Milbourne
Stannington
124 125
Nedderton
Bedlington
126 127
Shotton
130 131
132 133
Seghill
Seaton
Delaval
142 143
Killingworth
Wideopen
138 139
140 141
Newcastle International
Ponteland
148 149
Throckley
Whickham
Felling
Washington
Houghton-le-Spring
Murton
Sherburn
Coxhoe
Sherburn
Durham
A1(M)
Bowburn
A167
Ferryhill
Spennymoor
Bishop Auckland

Widdrington
66

Otterburn Camp
58 59
Otterburn
West Woodburn
72
Ridsdale
Redesmouth
71
184
Bellingham
Birtley
80 81
Wark
Gunnerton
Simonburn
90
Newbrough
Haydon Bridge
158 159
Hexham
160 161
Whitley Chapel
98
Sinderhope
106
Sparty lea
105
Carrshield
Ninebanks
104
Blagill
185
Alston
Nenthead
110
Wearhead
111
Allenheads

Falstone
69
Greenhaugh
70
Lanehead
Stonehaugh
79
Whygate
78
Edges Green
88
Twice Brewed
Henshaw
154 155
Melkridge
Bardon Mill
156 157
Langley
97
Whitfield
96
Bearsbridge
Allendale Town
Kielder
55
67
68
Churnside Lodge
77
86 87
Gilsland
Greenhead
152 153
Haltwhistle
Coanwood
95
Slaggyford
103
Ayle
102
Tindale
Halton-Lea-Gate
94
150 151
Upper Denton
Brampton
Wetheral
Lazonby
Penrith

Elsdon
60
Raylees
61
Thockrington
82 83
Kirkheaton
Colwell
Ingoe
Matfen
93
Great Whittington
92
Halton
Acomb
91
Humshaugh
Corbridge
162 163
Dilston
Ovington
164 165
Newton
Wylam
146 147
Heddon-on-the-Wall
Stamfordham
136 137
Dalton
Belsay
84
Middleton
75
Cambo
74
Kirkwhelpington
Capheaton
Knowesgate
73

Stanley
Rowlands Gill
168 169
Blaydon
Ryton
Prudhoe
166 167
Riding Mill
Slaley
100
Juniper
99
Blanchland
108
Hunstanworth
107
Spartylea

Stockfield
170 171
Whittonstall
101
Chopwell
172 173
Ebchester
174 175
Consett
Shotley Bridge
176 177
Leadgate
Allensford
109
Castleside
Blackhall Mill
Lanchester
Langley Park
Esh Winning
Brandon
Willington
Crook
Tow Law
Stanhope
Wolsingham
Stanhope

Chester le-Street
Sacriston

Newcastle upon Tyne

Tyne & Wear STREET ATLAS

Cumbria STREET ATLAS

County Durham and Teesside STREET ATLAS

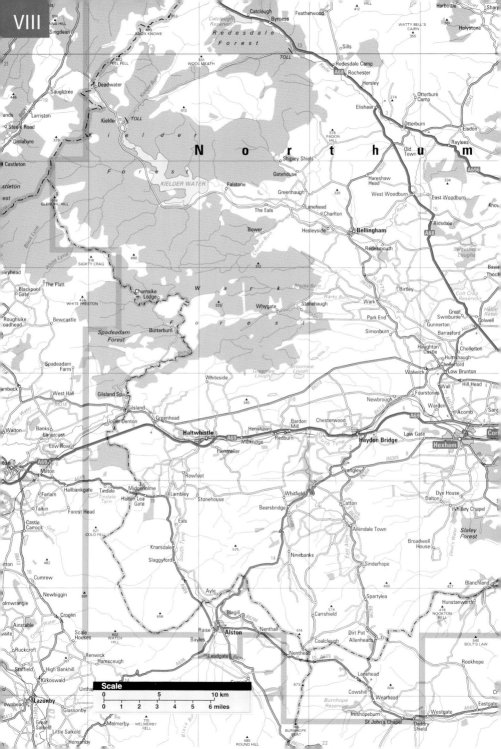

County and unitary authority boundaries

District boundaries

Postcode boundaries

Area covered by this atlas

Scale

| 0 | 5 | 10 | 15 km |
| 0 | | 5 | 10 miles |

East Lothian

Scottish Borders

NT NU

Berwick-upon-Tweed

Horncliffe

Coldstream

Lowick

Holy Island

Belford
Bamburgh

Berwick-upon-Tweed

Seahouses
Beadnell

Wooler
Chatton
Ellingham

Rock
Craster

Eglingham
Longhoughton

Whittingham
Alnwick

Netherton
Harbottle
Alnwick
Amble

Byrness
Rothbury

NT
NY

Kielder

N o r t h u m b e r l a n d

Widdrington Station
Lynemouth

Falstone
Ashington
Newbiggin-by-the-Sea

Cambo
Morpeth

Bellingham

Castle Morpeth

Wansbeck

Belsay

Tynedale
Dinnington
Cramlington

Stamfordham
North Tyneside

Newcastle upon Tyne
Whitley Bay

Corbridge
Prudhoe
South Tyneside

Hexham
Stockfield

Gateshead

Halton-Lea-Gate
Ebchester

Sunderland

Cumbria
Durham

NY NZ

NU
NZ

A　B　C　D　E　F

Mast

Fairnieside

A1 Edinburgh

Burnmouth Hill
PARTANHALL

PH

Chesterbank

Flemington

Burnmouth

Mast

Greystonelees

Ross
Ross Point

COWDRAIT

TD14

Chester Hill

Mast

Ayton Hill

Hilton Bay

Lamberton Shiels

Lamberton Moor

Greenfield Plantations

Greenfield

Lamberton
Maryfield
Mast

Witches Knowe

Deans Hill

Mordington Holdings

TD15

Marshall Meadows

Marshall Meadows Bay

St John's Haven

Woodhills

New East Farm

Folly Farm

Mordington House

Loughend

Needles Eye

Wheatland Burn

West Edge Farm

Clappers

Cemys

A6105 Duns

A6105

Cumberland Bower

Bogend

Conundrum

North Road Ind Est

Grand Loaning

Halidon Hill

Mast
Mast

PH

A1

Sch

178

NEWFIELDS

ST GEORGE'S RD
SEA VIEW
ST MAGDALENE DR

Edrington Mains

Baitstrand

Brow of the Hill

Camphill

HALIDON TERR
MEADOW HILL

178

NORTH RD A1167

High Cocklaw

Sanson Seal

A6105
DUNS RD

A1

A6105

Meadow Hill Ho

White Damhead Burn

94　A　95　B　96　C　97　D　98　E　99　F

8
61
7
60
6
59
5
58
4
57
3
56
2
55
1
54

3

For full street detail of the highlighted area see page 178.

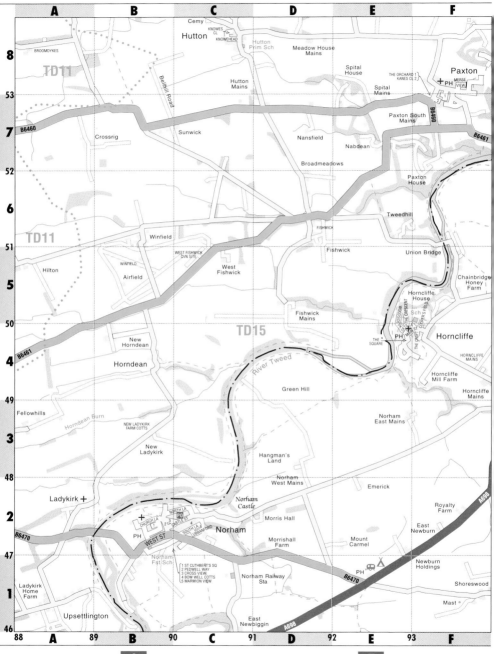

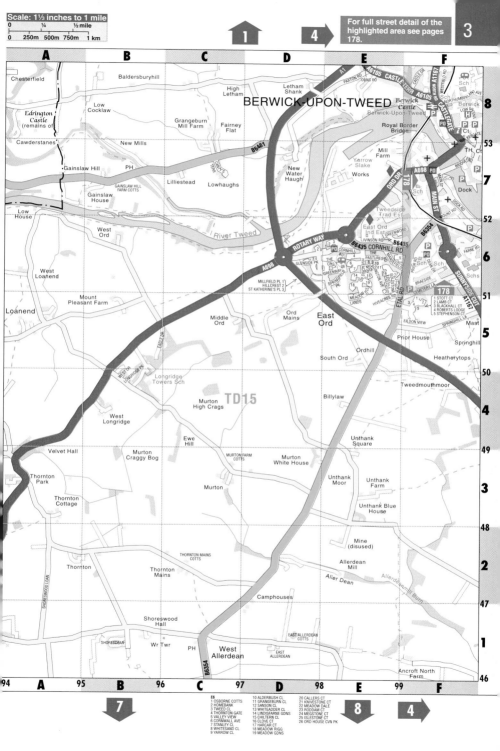

For full street detail of the highlighted area see pages 178.

3

Scale: 1½ inches to 1 mile

| 0 | ¼ | ½ mile |

| 0 | 250m | 500m | 750m | 1 km |

A **B** **C** **D** **E** **F**

8

CH
P

Mus
TA
53 Ramparts
P

PIER RD

7 Pier Meadow Haven

178

52 IRB Sta
P
DOCK RD
BALLENDEAN RD
SANDSTELL RD
Sch
Spittal
6 MAIN ST
ADAMS DR
LC
NORTH LANE

51 COVE RD
P
ELMBANK CVN PK
Bear's Head
178
Seaview Farm
Huds Head

A1167

5

50

DERWENT WATER TERR
4 ST PETERS TERR
RESTORATION COTTS
A1167
A1
Sch
Scremerston
LC
Sea House
CHURCH RD
WEST LANE
INLANDPASTURE

49 1 PRINCE CHARLES ST
2 PRINCE CHARLES PL
3 PRINCE CHARLES CRES
4 PRINCE CHARLES RD
5 NORHAM GN
6 ARMSTRONG CT
Cocklawburn Beach

TD15

3 Woodside Cottage

48 Cocklawburn Dunes
Nature Reserve

Mast
SCREMERSTON TOWN FARM
2 SCREMERSTON HILL FARM
B6525

47 East House
Oxford
Cheswick

1 The Cat Inn
Cheswick House
Ladythorne House
Dowie House
Cheswick Shiel
Cheswick Sands
B6525
Nabhill
A1

46

00 **A** **01** **B** **02** **C** **03** **D** **04** **E** **05** **F**

3
8
9

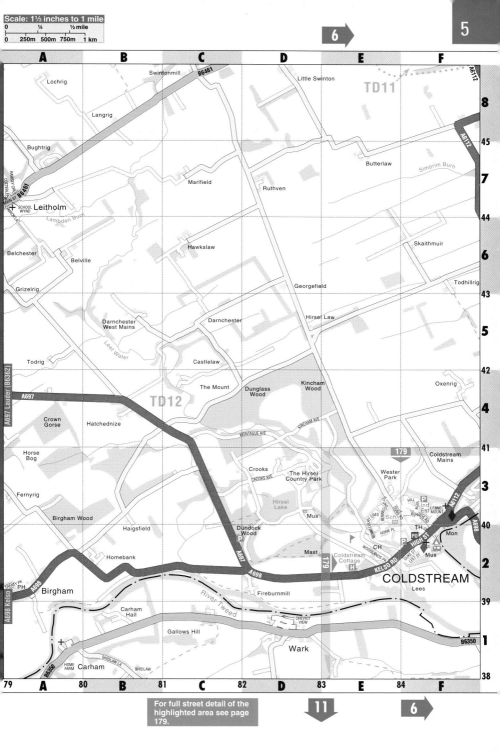

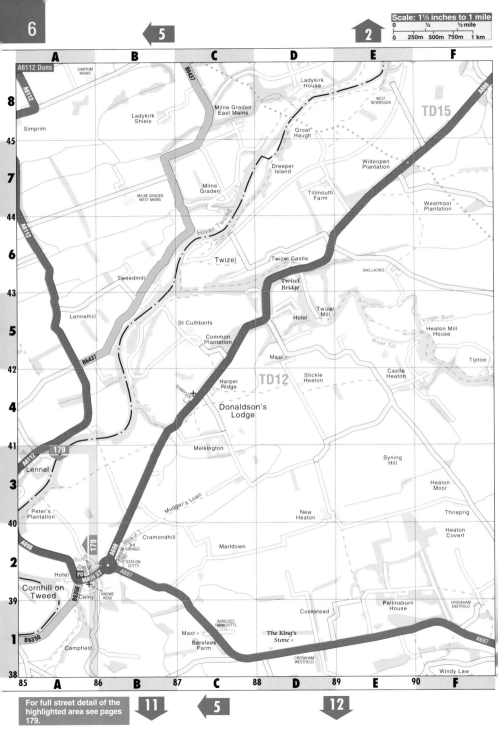

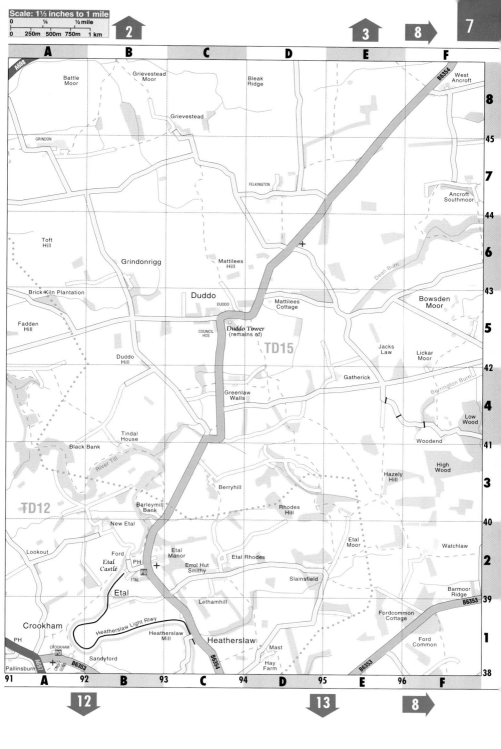

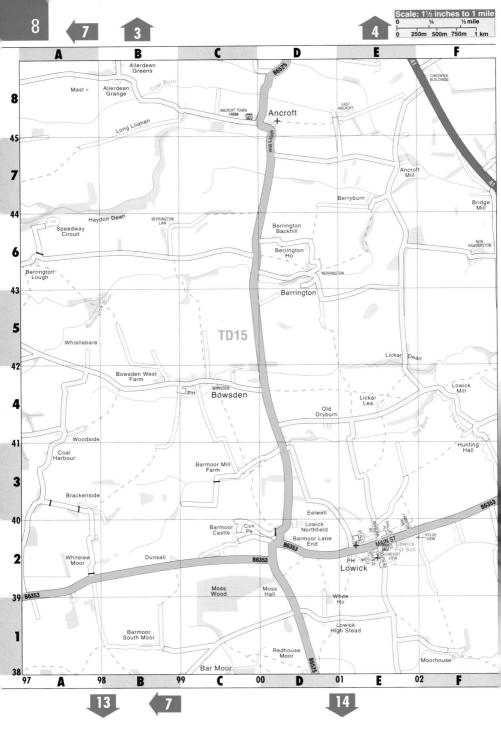

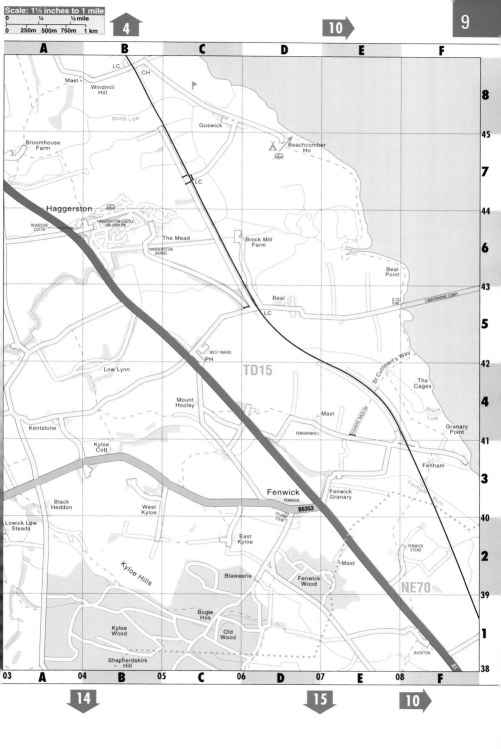

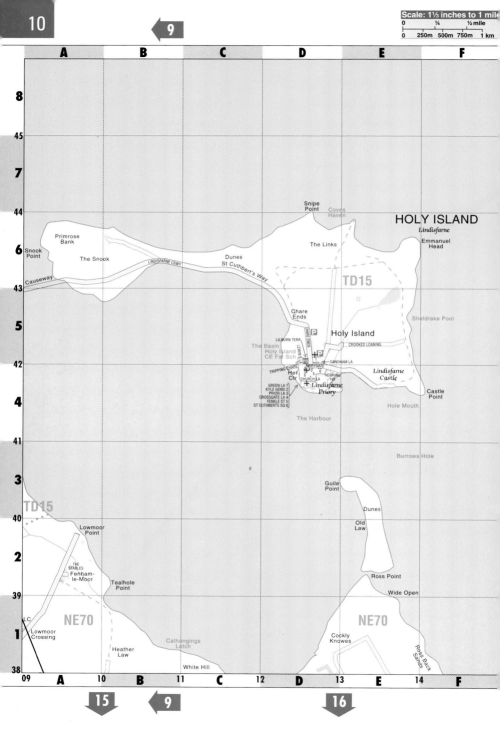

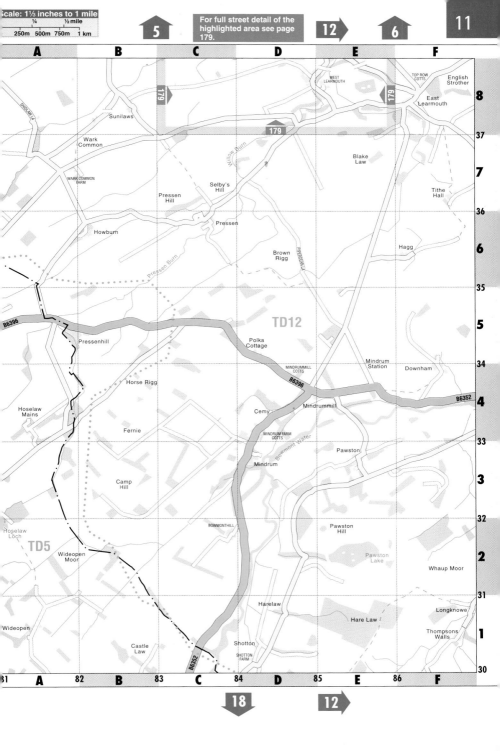

For full street detail of the highlighted area see page 179.

Scale: 1⅛ inches to 1 mile

¼   ½ mile

250m 500m 750m 1 km

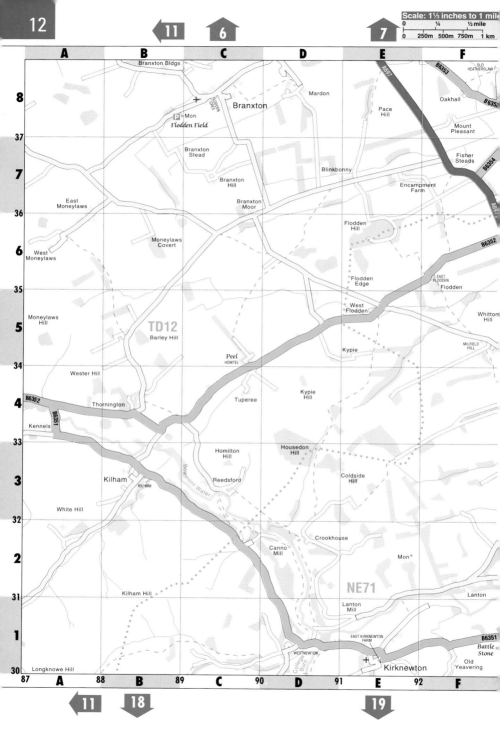

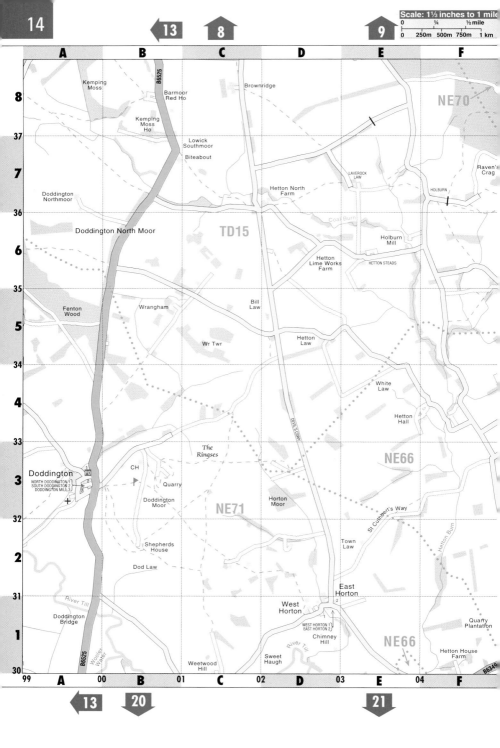

A   B   C   D   E   F

8

37

7

36

Knoxes Reef

The Kettle

Chapel

Little Scarcar

Tower

Inner Farne

6

CH

Bamburgh Castle

Bamburgh

B1342   B1340

RADCLIFFE RD

The Friars

FRIARY FARM

Mus

LUCKER RD

B1341

Hotel

LINDISFARNE AVE

CUTHBERT'S GARTH

LINKS RD

P

35

RADCLIFFE PK
ISLESTONE CT 2
SOUTH VICTORIA TERR 3

Dukesfield

ARMSTRONG COTTS

Red Barns

RED BARNS CRES

5

GREENHILL COTTS

Greenhill

34

NE69

INGRAM CA

MONKS HO

4

Burton Hall

Fowberry

St AIDAN's Dunes

EAST BURTON

New Shoreston

NEW SHORESTON COTTS

Shoreston Hall

33

Humbleton Hill

Quarry

ST AIDAN'S

FARNE CRES

1 CHAPEL ROW
2 CRUMSTONE

Mus

F2

1 DUNSTAN VIEW
2 NORTH ST
3 WEATHERLEY ST
4 GEORGE ST
5 TAYLOR ST
6 UNION ST
7 BRADY ST
8 JUBILEE PL
9 BEECH CROFT
10 MILLSTONE CL
11 CLIFF TOP CVN PK

3

SEAFIELD RD

Seahouses

Springhill

BRIAR RD

Westfield

OSBORNE TERR

Seahouses Fst Sch

Libys

NORTH ST

KING ST

32

NE68

ISLESTONE WK

RIDGE WAY

+

HARCAR

Seahouses Mid Sch

CH   Mast

Snook or North Sunderland Point

2

NE 70

Ct Rickerwood Burn

Cemy
WEST VIEW
THE CROFT

North Sunderland

MAYFIELD 1
JACKSON PL 2
GREENACRES 3
BROWNSMAN CT 4

FIELDS

31

ELFORD FARM COTTS

Elford

Pasturehill

Southfield

Annstead

1

NE 67

NE 67

NE 67

B1340

Linkhouse

30

Burnhouse

7   A   18   B   19   C   20   D   21   E   22   F

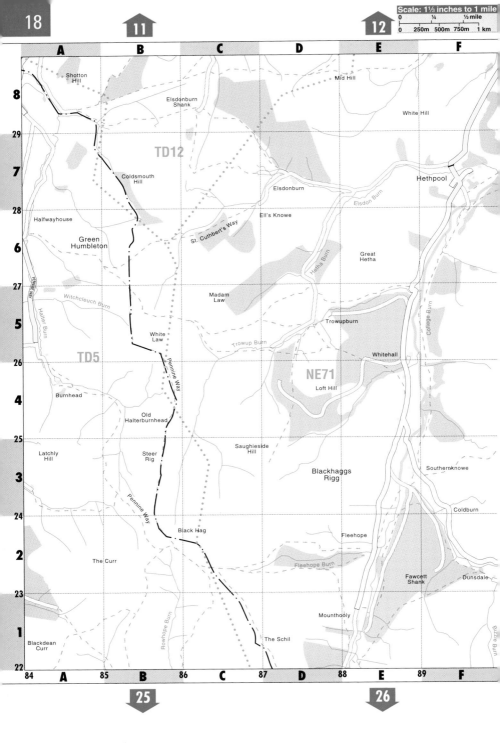

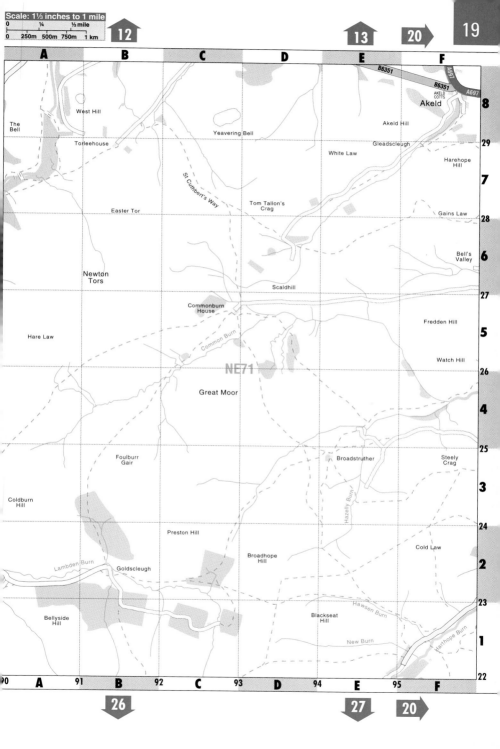

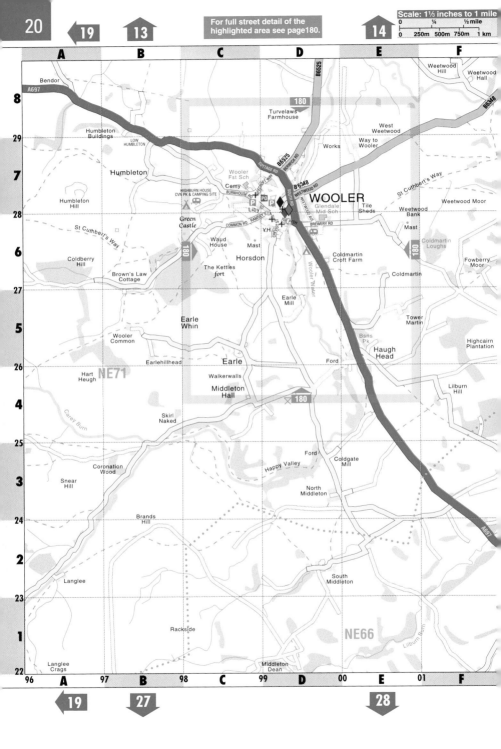

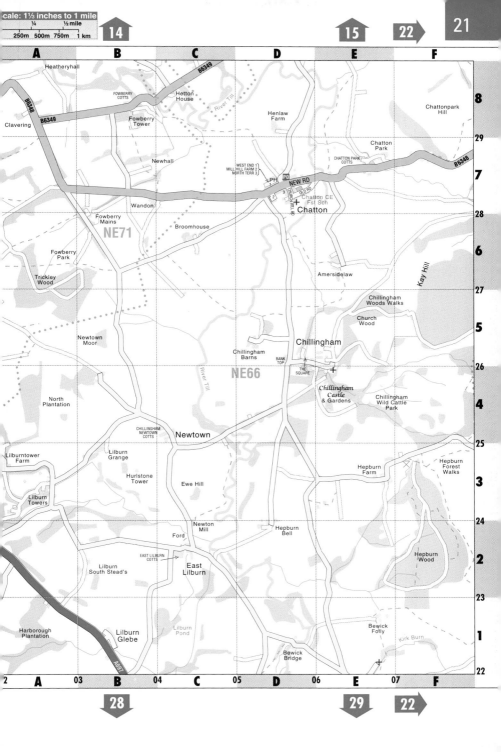

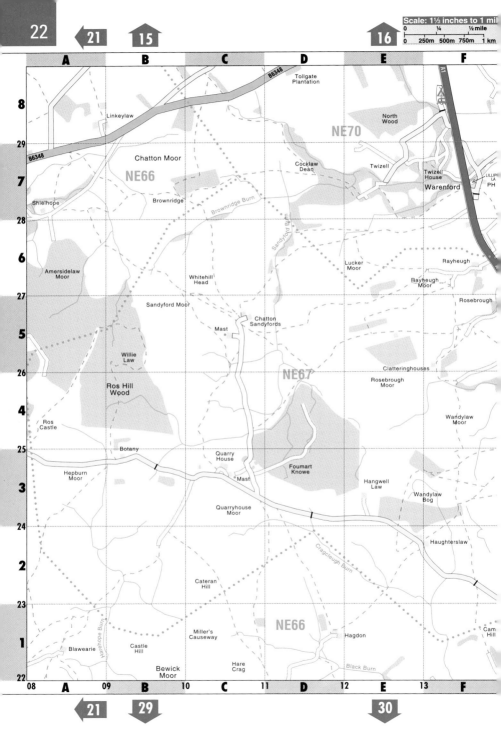

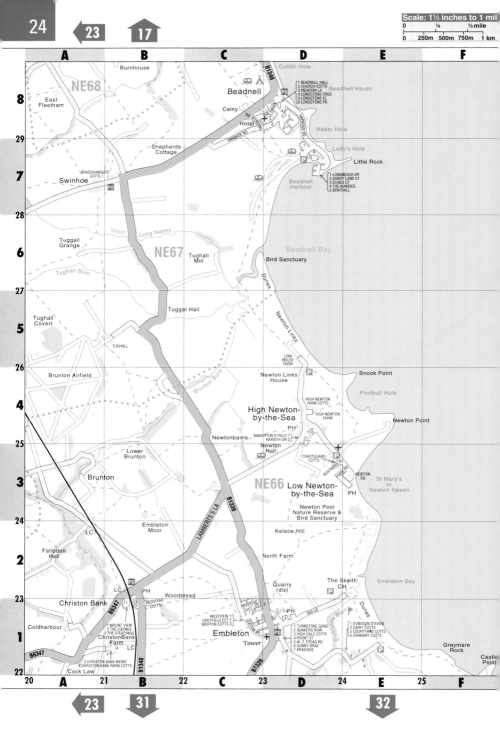

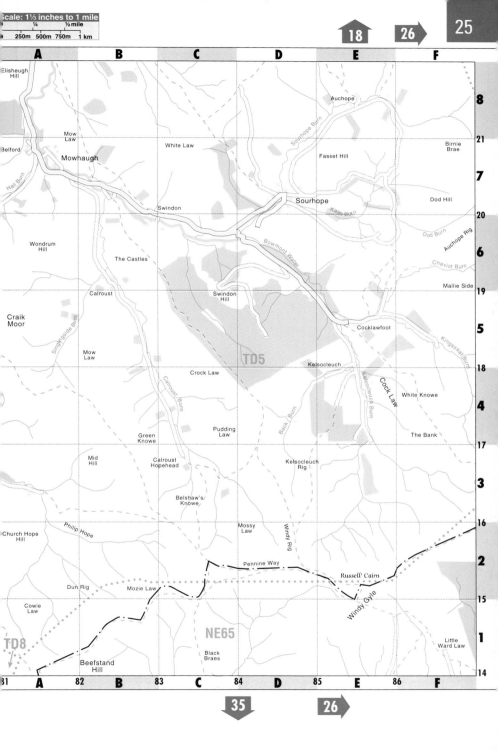

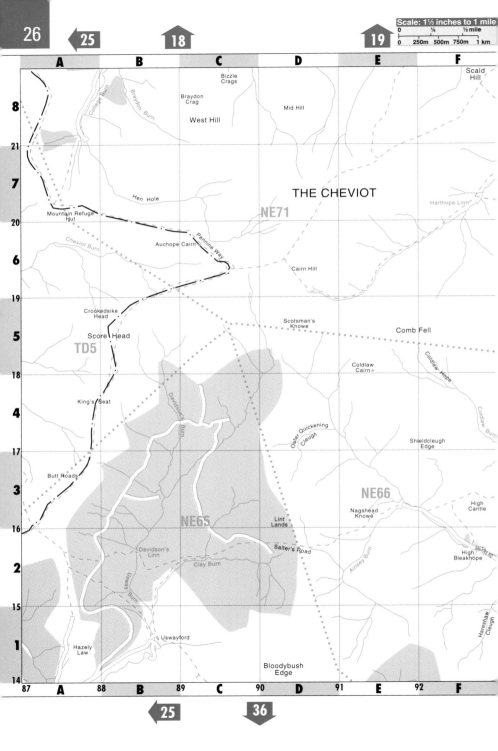

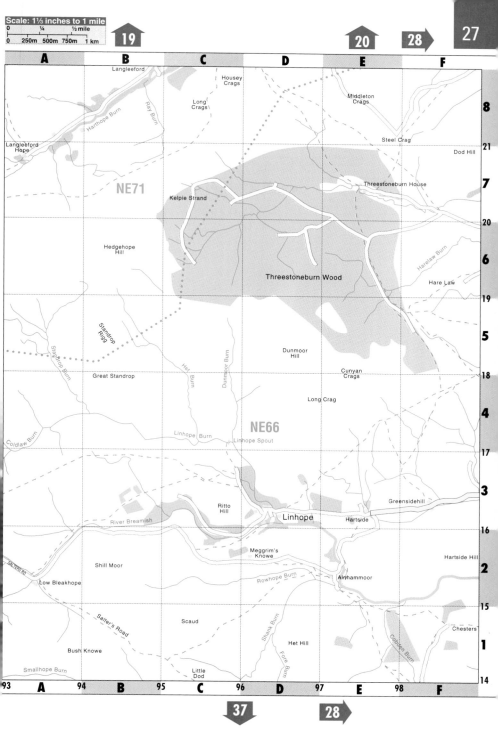

A   B   C   D   E   F

Langleeford

Housey
Crags

Long
Crags

Middleton
Crags

8

Steel Crag

21

Langleeford
Hope

Dod Hill

NE71

Threestoneburn House

7

Kelpie Strand

20

Hedgehope
Hill

Threestoneburn Wood

Harelaw Burn

6

Hare Law

19

Standrop
Rigg

Staindrop Burn

Great Standrop

Het Burn

Dunmoor Burn

Dunmoor
Hill

Cunyan
Crags

5

18

Long Crag

4

Coldlaw Burn

NE66

Linhope Burn

Linhope Spout

17

Ritto
Hill

Linhope

Greensidehill

3

River Breamish

Hartside

16

Meggrim's
Knowe

Shill Moor

Hartside Hill

2

SALTERS RD

Low Bleakhope

Rowhope Burn

Alnhammoor

15

Salter's Road

Scaud

Shank Burn

Chesters

1

Bush Knowe

Het Hill

Fore Burn

Cobden Burn

Smallhope Burn

Little
Dod

14

93   A   **94**   B   **95**   C   **96**   D   **97**   E   **98**   F

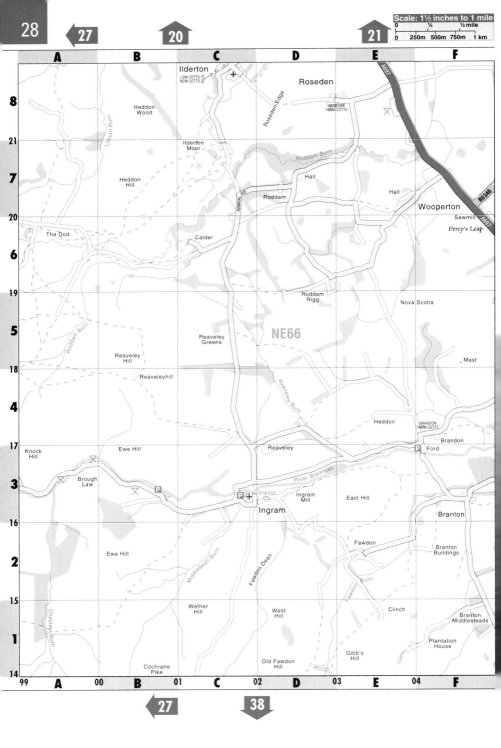

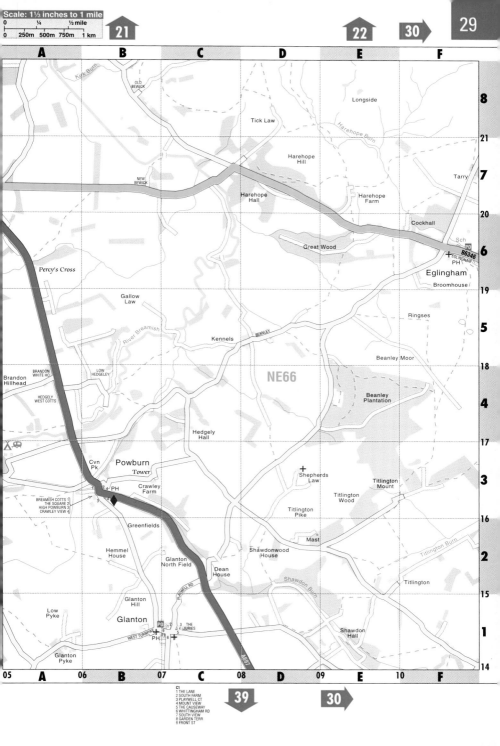

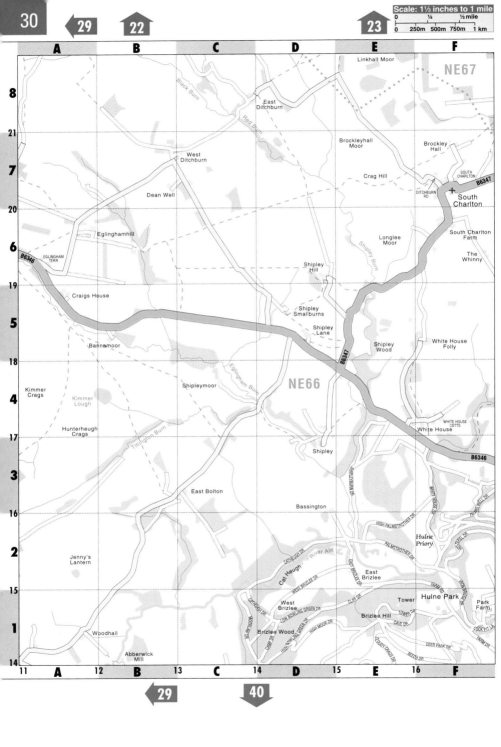

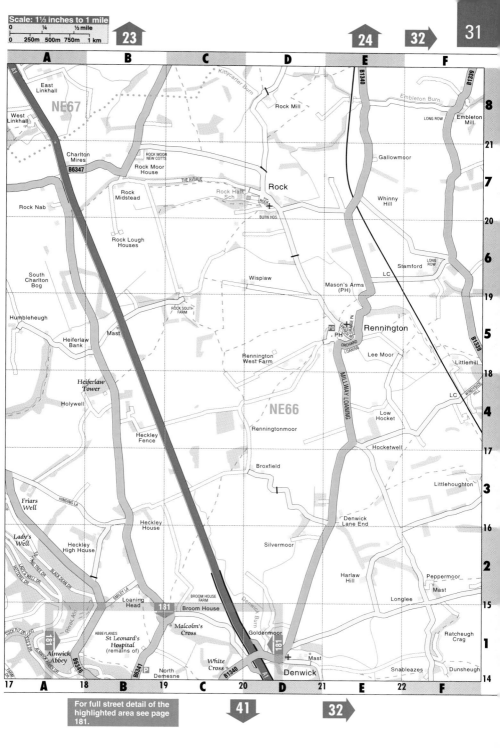

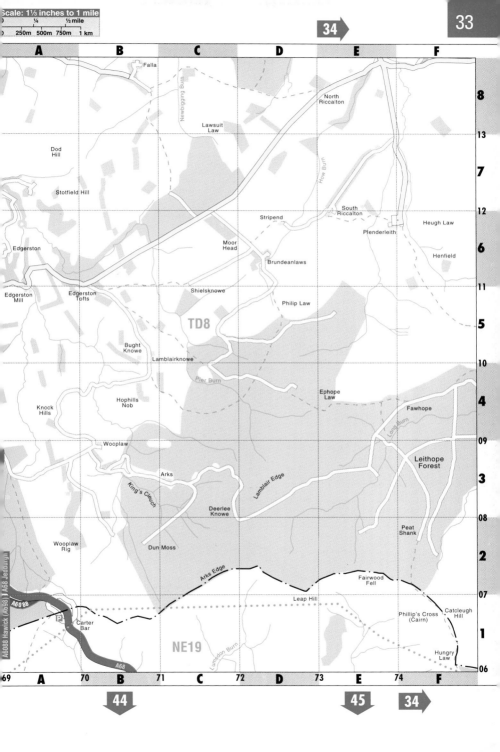

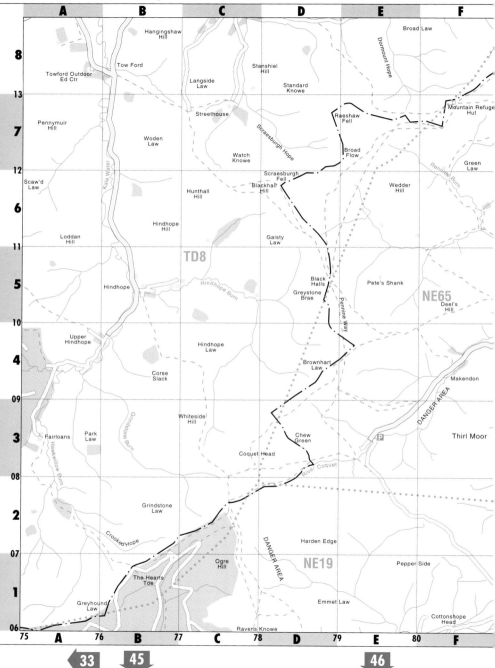

Scale: 1½ inches to 1 mi

0   ¼   ½ mile
0   250m 500m 750m   1 km

A   B   C   D   E   F

8

Broad Law

Dormount Hope

Hangingshaw
Hill

Tow Ford

Towford Outdoor
Ed Ctr

13

Stanshiel
Hill

Langside
Law

Standard
Knowe

Mountain Refuge
Hut

Streethouse

Raeshaw
Fell

7

Pennymuir
Hill

Woden
Law

Scraesburgh Hope

Broad
Flow

Green
Law

12

Scaw'd
Law

Watch
Knowe

Scraesburgh
Fell

Rennies Burn

Hunthall
Hill

Blackhall
Hill

Wedder
Hill

6

Loddan
Hill

Hindhope
Hill

Gaisty
Law

TD8

5

Hindhope

Hindhope Burn

Black
Halls

Pete's Shank

NE65

Greystone
Brae

Deel's
Hill

11

10

Upper
Hindhope

Hindhope
Law

Pennine Way

Brownhart
Law

Makendon

4

Corse
Slack

DANGER AREA

Thirl Moor

09

Fairloans

Park
Law

Whiteside
Hill

Chew
Green

P

3

Grindstone Burn

Coquet Head

River Coquet

Hawkwillow Burn

08

Grindstone
Law

Harden Edge

2

Crooked Hope

NE19

Pepper
Side

07

The Hearts
Toe

Ogre
Hill

DANGER AREA

Greyhound
Law

Emmet Law

Cottonshope
Head

1

06

Ravens Knowe

75   A   76   B   77   C   78   D   79   E   80   F

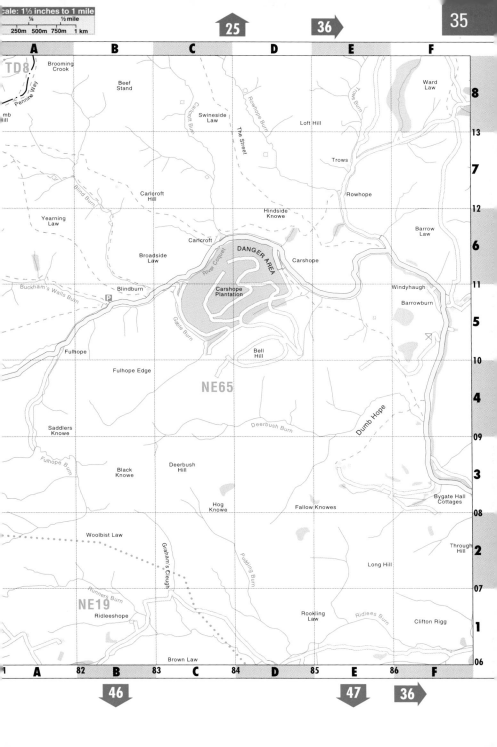

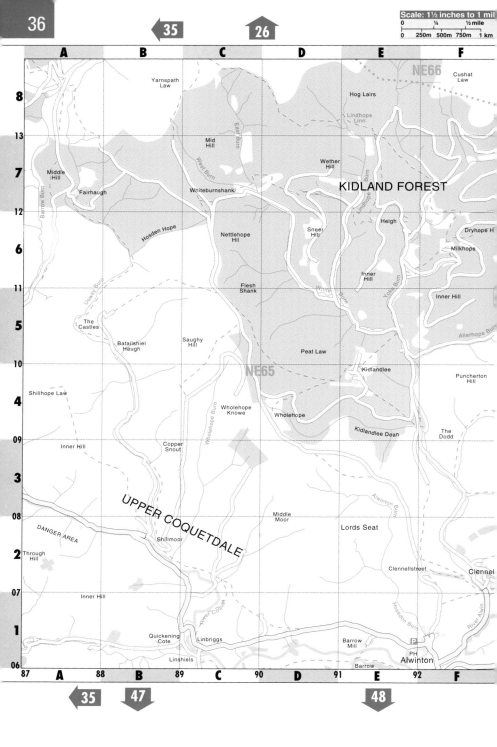

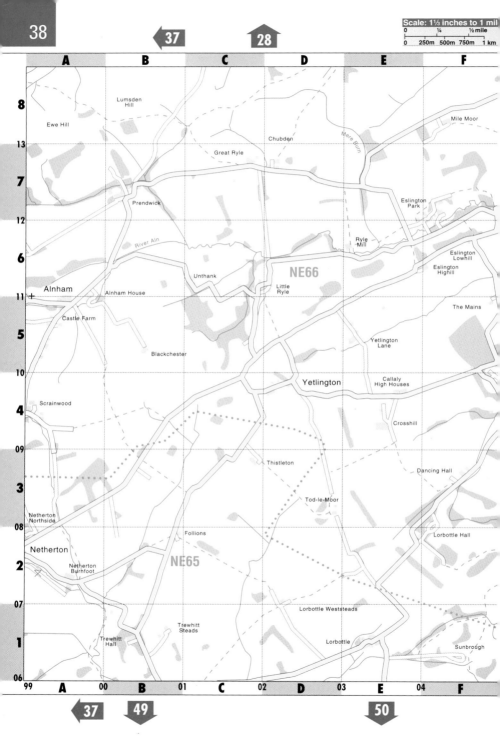

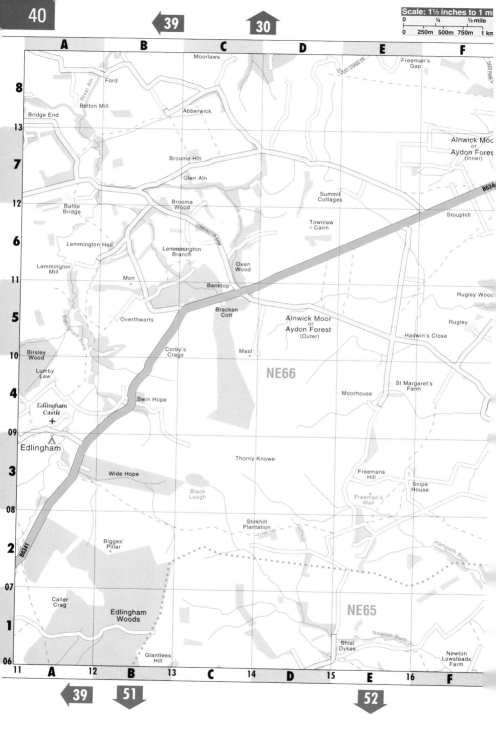

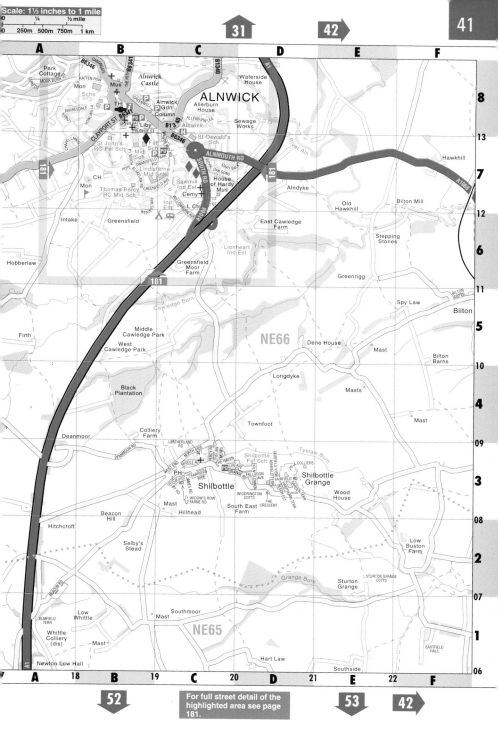

A   B   C   D   E   F

8

13

7

NE66

THE SQUARE 1
ORCHARD TERR 2
GARDEN TERR 3
MEADOWLANDS 4
CROFTLANDS 5
TOWNFOOT STEADING 6
HIPSBURN CRES 7
WILLOW CL 8

Lookout

Field
House

Seaton
House

Boulmer Haven

Seaton Point

Mast

Lesbury

12   PH

B1339   PO

RIVERSIDE

6   THE COPSE

River Aln

Foxbury
House

Foxton Hall
(CH)

FOXTON DR

Cemy

STEPPY LA

Sch

11   SOUTH VIEW

B1338   Hipsburn

Alnmouth
STATION
COTTS   HIPSBURN

A1068

PO

CH

Alnmouth

Alnmouth Bay

5

Waterside
House

Hotel

RIVERSIDE RD

B5
1 SHEPHEARDS HILL
2 FRIARY GDNS
3 ALNWOOD
4 WELLFIELD CL
5 THE WYND
6 THE PINFOLD
7 GROSVENOR TERR
8 LOVAINE TERR
9 RIVER BANK RD
10 NORTHUMBERLAND ST
11 CROW'S NEST LA
12 PROSPECT PL
13 SEA BANK
14 MARINE RD
15 GARDEN TERR
16 PEASE'S LA
17 PEASE'S GDNS
18 ARGYLE ST

10

Wooden
Farm

LC

Dunes

4

09

HIGH BUSTON

3

Northfield

08

Buston
Barns

Shortridge
Hall

NE65

Birling Carrs

BUSTON BARNS
COTTS

2

07

STATION
COTTS

Hermitage
Farm

HERMITAGE DR

Birling

CH

Houndean
Mill

1   LC

River Coquet   Coquet
Lodge   Warkworth

STATION RD

A1068

Cemy

Birling

Coquet
View
CVN PK

06

23   A   24   B   25   C   26   D   27   E   28   F

B1
1 ST LAWRENCE TERR
2 THE BUTTS
3 BRIDGE VIEW
4 BRIDGE ST
5 DIAL PL
6 THE STANNERS
7 YOUNGERS TERR
8 CASTLE ST
9 BREWERY LA
10 HOTSPUR CT

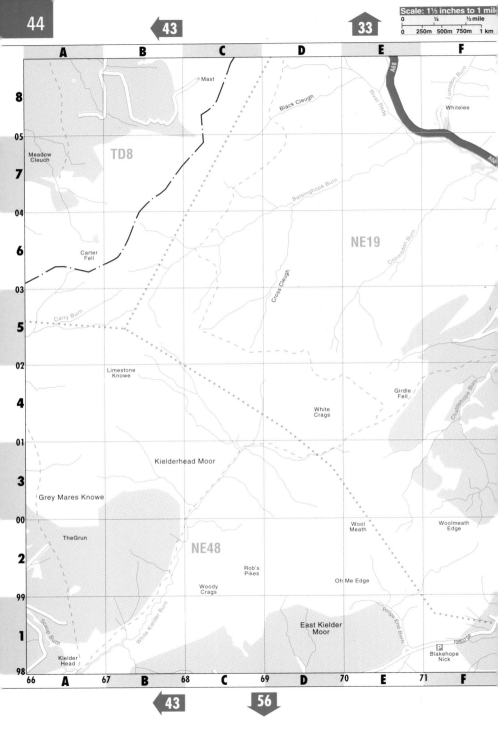

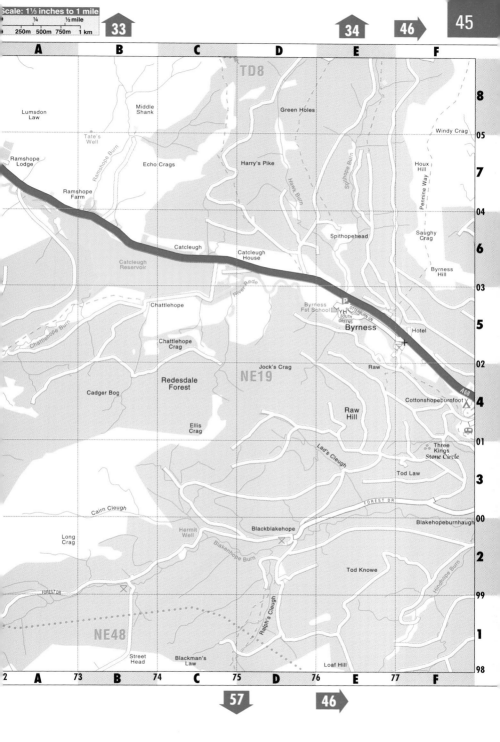

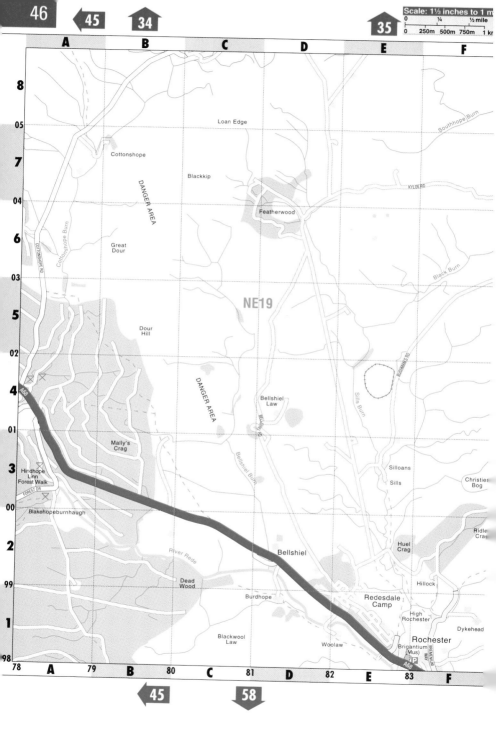

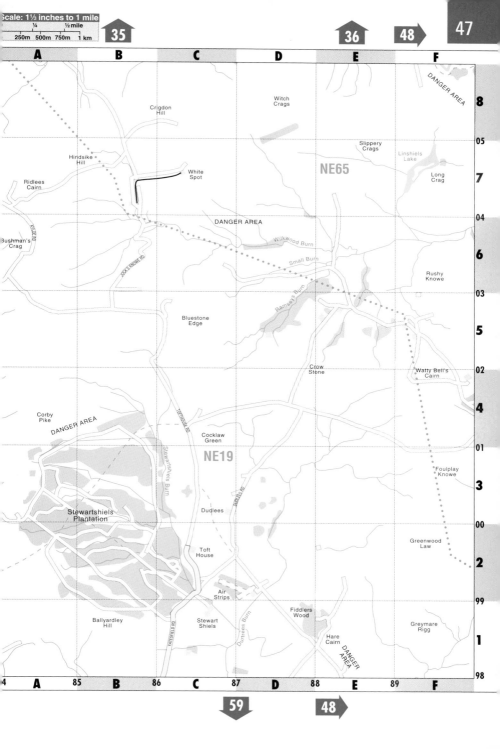

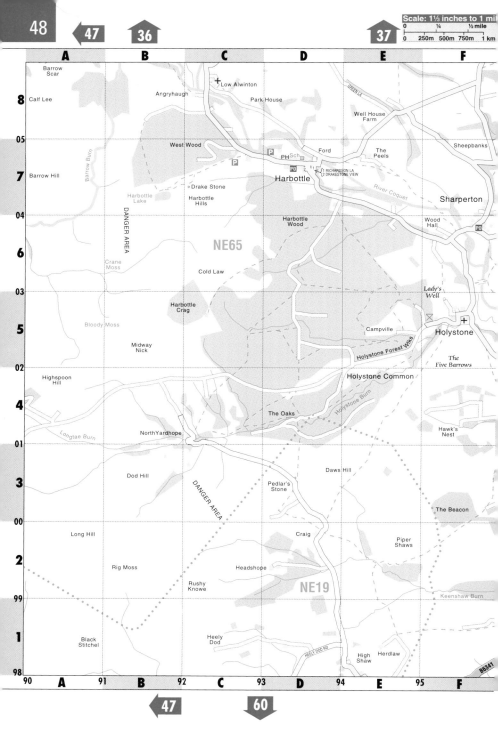

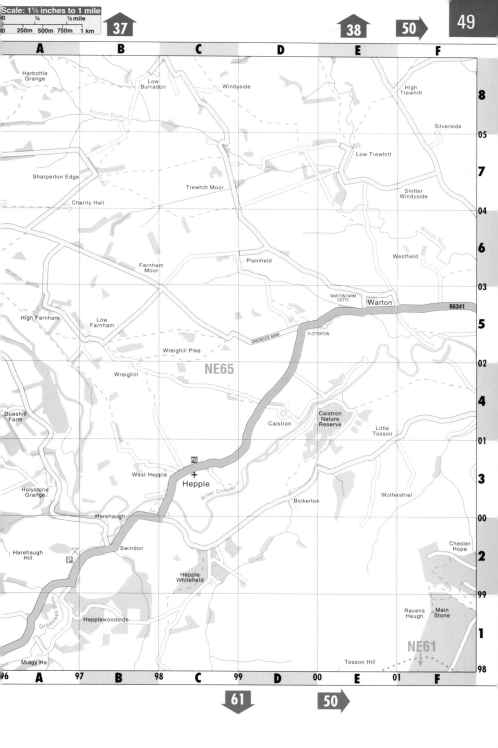

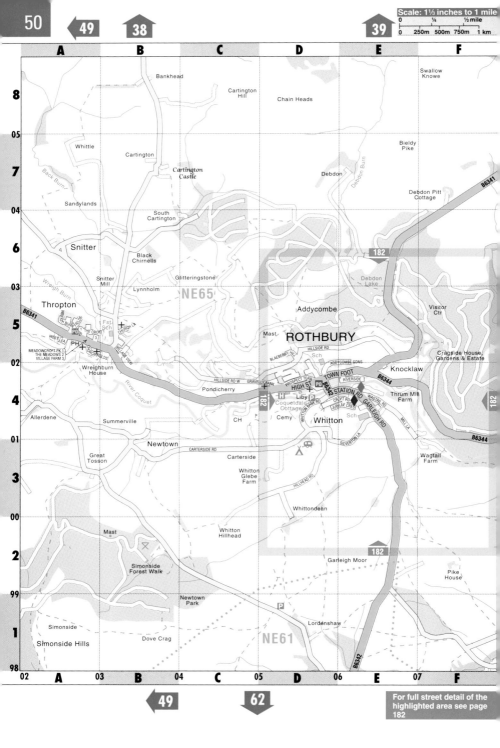

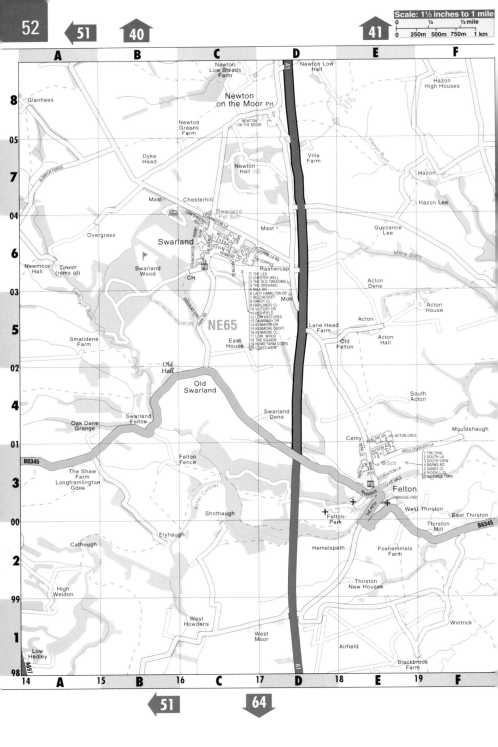

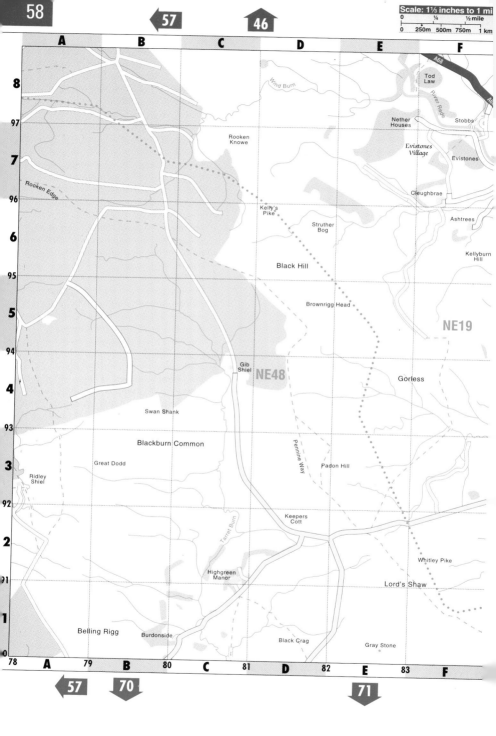

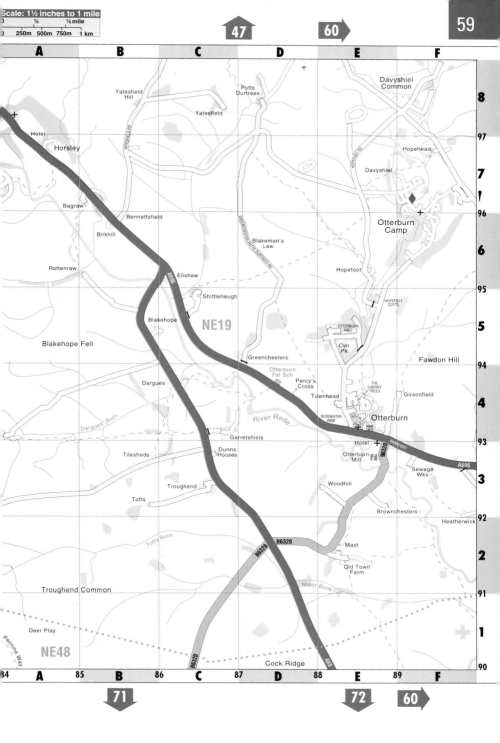

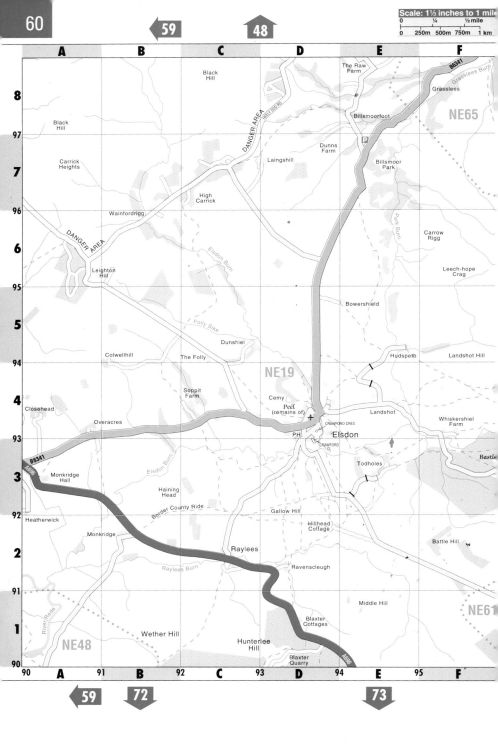

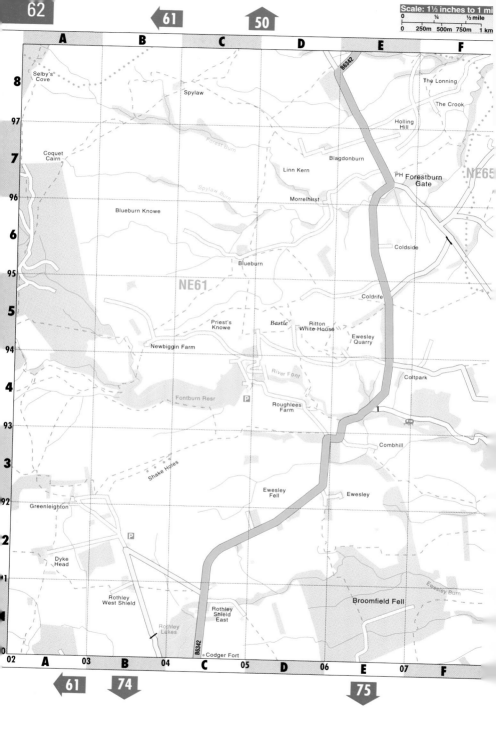

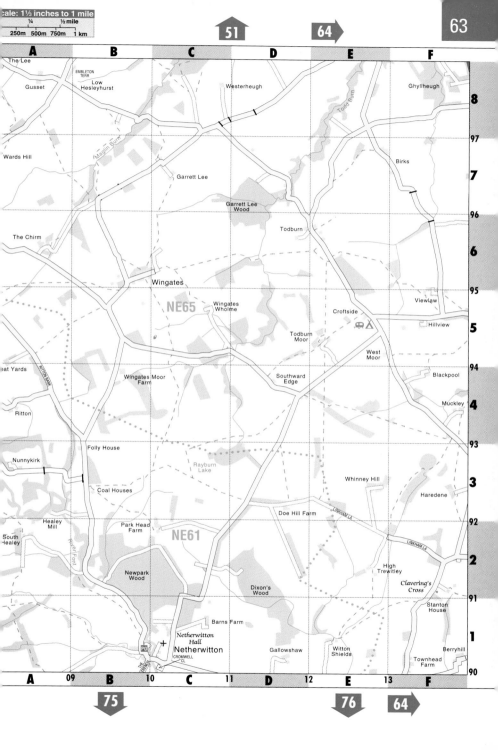

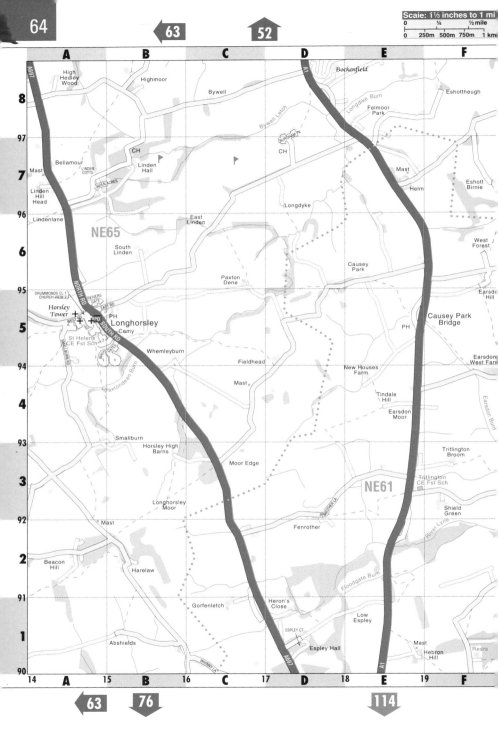

65

54

Scale: 1⅓ inches to 1 mile
0   ¼   ½ mile
0   250m 500m 750m 1 km

A   B   C   D   E   F

8

97

Druridge
Bay

7

Chapel
(remains of)
Low
Chibburn   High
Chibburn

Druridge Bay
Nature Reserve

Druridge   P

96

FARM CT

6

95

Hemscott Hill

5

A1068

Warkworth La

94

112   Blakemoor
Farm

113

NE61

Cresswell

4

Highthorn

93

WARKWORTH LA

Warkworthlane
Cottage

Snab Point

Hagg
House

CROXDALE TERR   CRESSWELL RD   WINDMILL HILL

3

TWEED AVE

Ellington

Linton Burn

PO
Liby
FRONT ST
PH

Ellington
Fst Sch
LYNEMOUTH RD

112

92

ASHINGTON RD

Cresswell Home
Farm

Linton
Fst Sch

Lynemouth

PO
Linton

Lynemouth
Fst Sch

2

West Moor
Farm

DALTON AVE
ALBION TERR
PO   Liby

River Lyne

91

A1068

East Moor
Farm

Haydon Letch

PARK RD

LC

1

A189

Cemy

NE63

A1068

112
A189

NE63

113

90

26   A   27   B   28   C   29   D   30   E   31   F

65   117

For full street detail of the
highlighted area see pages
112 and 113.

118

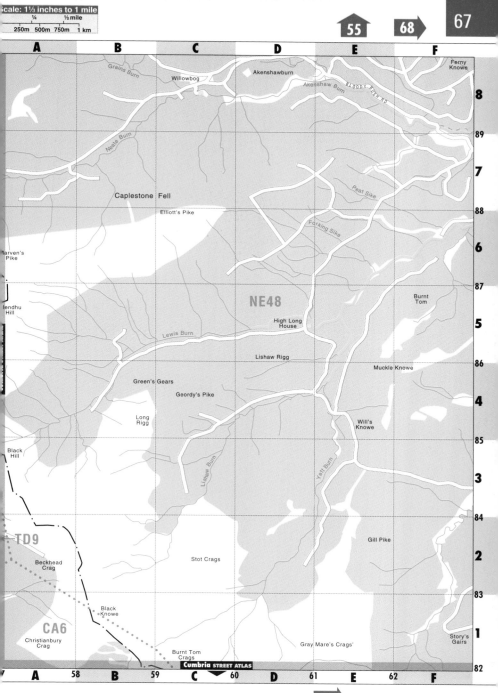

A   B   C   D   E   F

Grains Burn

Willowbog   Akenshawburn   Ferny Knowe

Akenshaw Burn   BLOODY BUSH RD   8

Neate Burn   89

Peat Sike   7

Caplestone Fell   88

Elliott's Pike   Forking Sike

Marven's Pike   6

87

lendhu Hill   NE48   Burnt Tom   5

High Long House

Lewis Burn   86

Lishaw Rigg   Muckle Knowe

Green's Gears   4

Geordy's Pike

Long Rigg   Will's Knowe   85

Black Hill   Lishaw Burn   Yett Burn   3

84

TD9   Gill Pike   2

Beckhead Crag   Stot Crags   83

Black Knowe

CA6   Story's Gairs

Christianbury Crag   Gray Mare's Crags'

Burnt Tom Crags

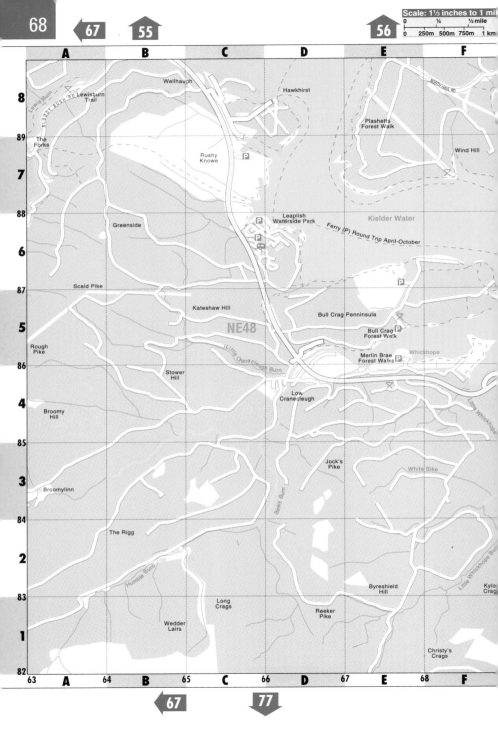

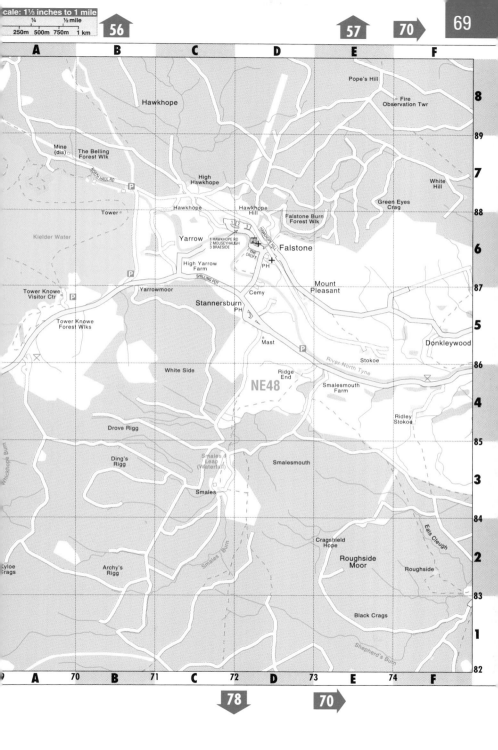

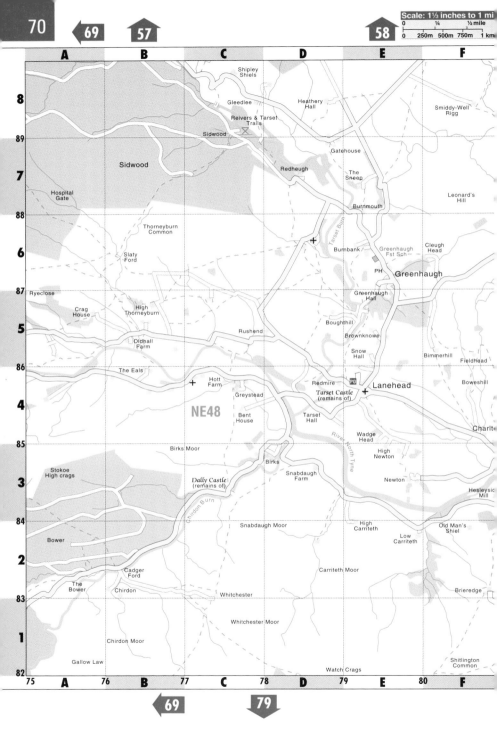

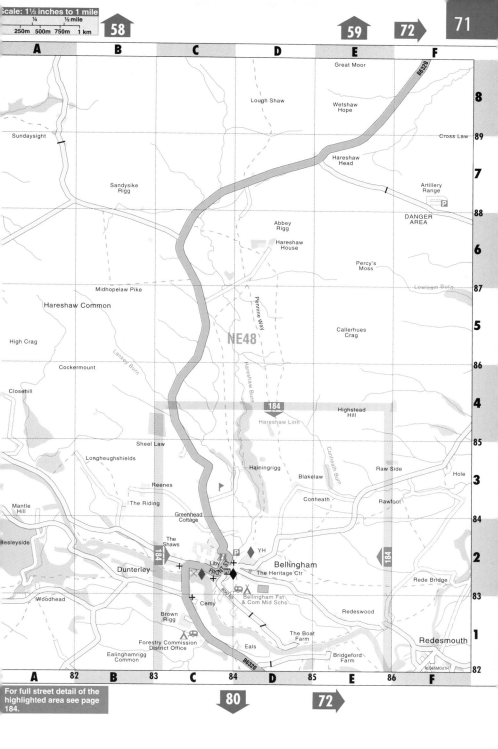

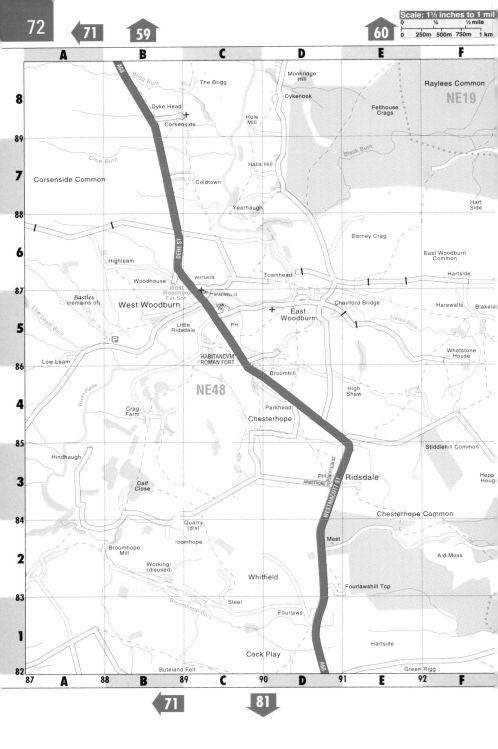

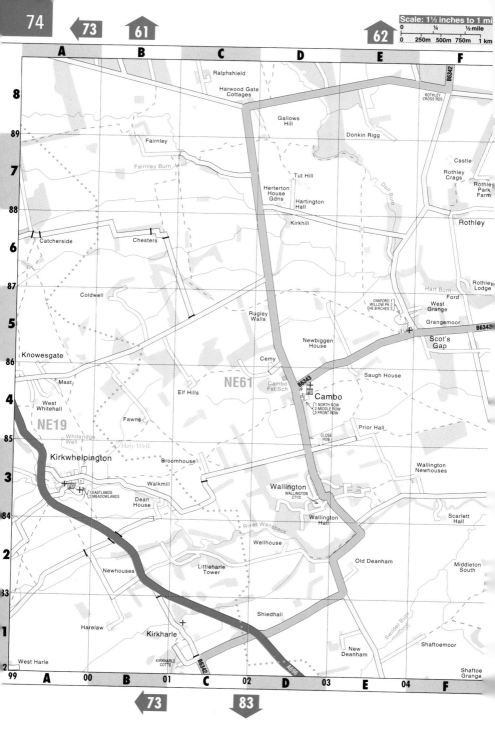

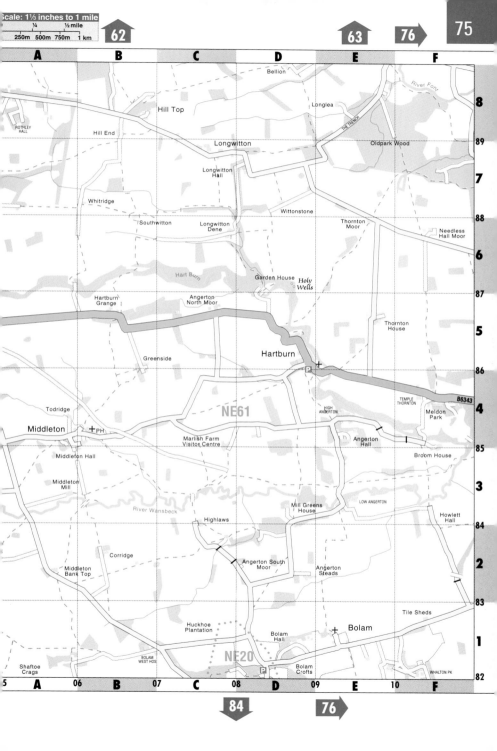

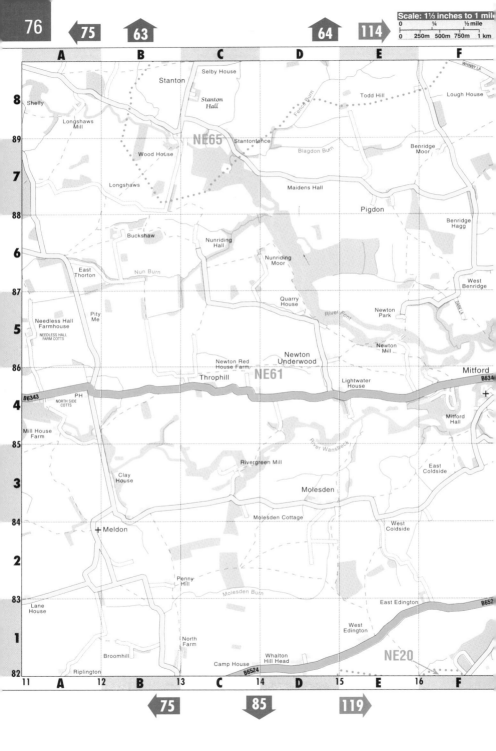

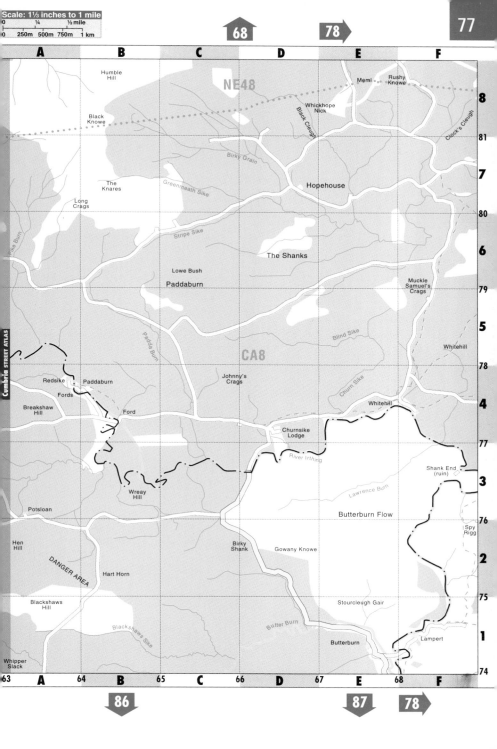

Scale: 1⅓ inches to 1 mile

0   ¼   ½ mile
0 250m 500m 750m 1 km

Cumbria STREET ATLAS

A   B   C   D   E   F

Humble
Hill

NE48

Memi   Rushy
Knowe

Whickhope
Nick

Black
Knowe

Black
Cleugh

Clock's
Cleugh

8

81

Birky Grain

The
Knares

Greenmeath Sike

Hopehouse

7

Long
Crags

80

Pike Burn

Stripe Sike

The Shanks

6

Lowe Bush

Muckle
Samuel's
Crags

Paddaburn

79

Blind Sike

CA8

5

Padda Burn

Johnny's
Crags

Whitehill

78

Churn Sike

Redsike

Paddaburn

Whitehill

4

Fords

Breakshaw
Hill

Ford

Churnsike
Lodge

77

River Irthing

Shank End
(ruin)

3

Wreay
Hill

Lawrence Burn

Potsloan

Butterburn Flow

76

Spy
Rigg

Hen
Hill

Birky
Shank

Gowany Knowe

2

DANGER
AREA

Hart Horn

75

Blackshaws
Hill

Stourcleugh Gair

Blackshaws Sike

Butter Burn

1

Whipper
Slack

Butterburn

Lampert

74

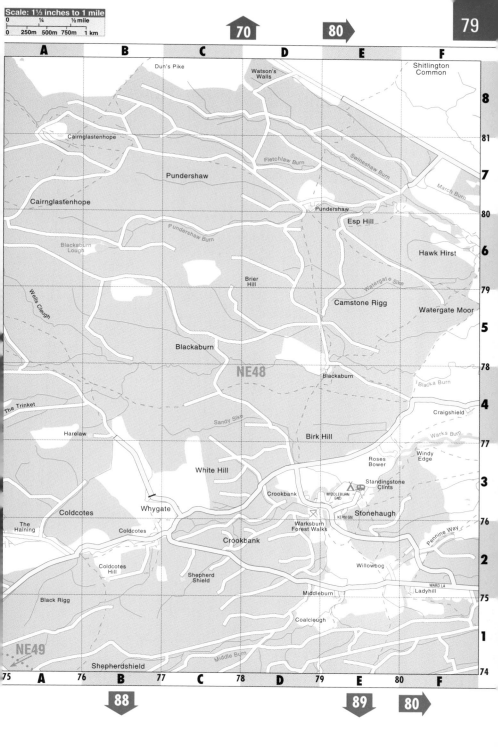

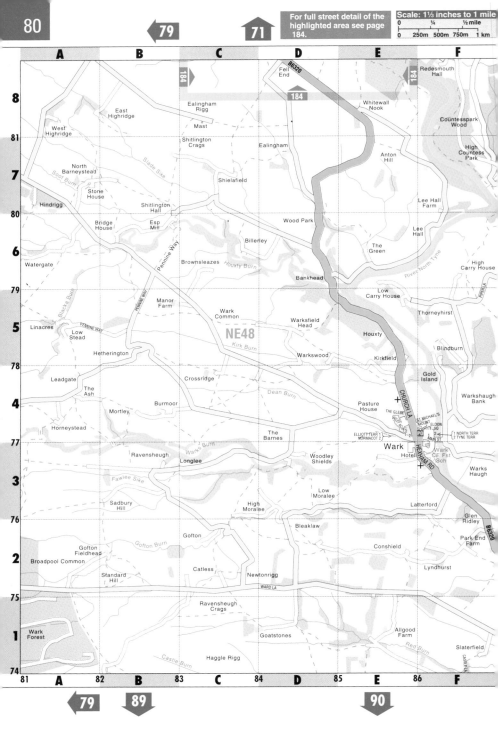

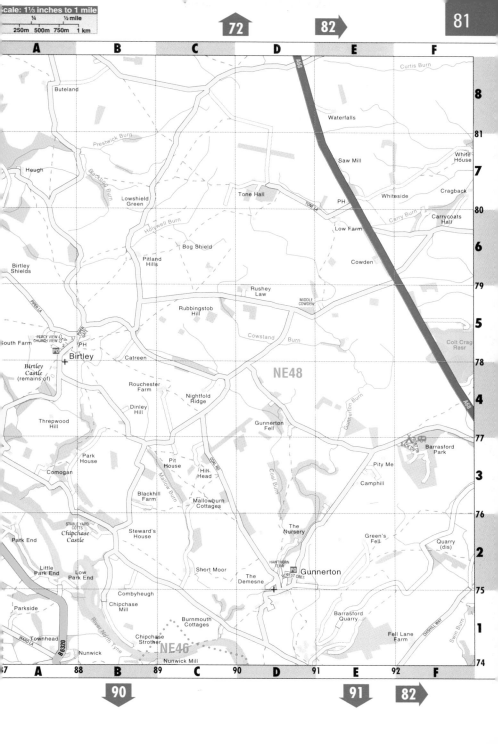

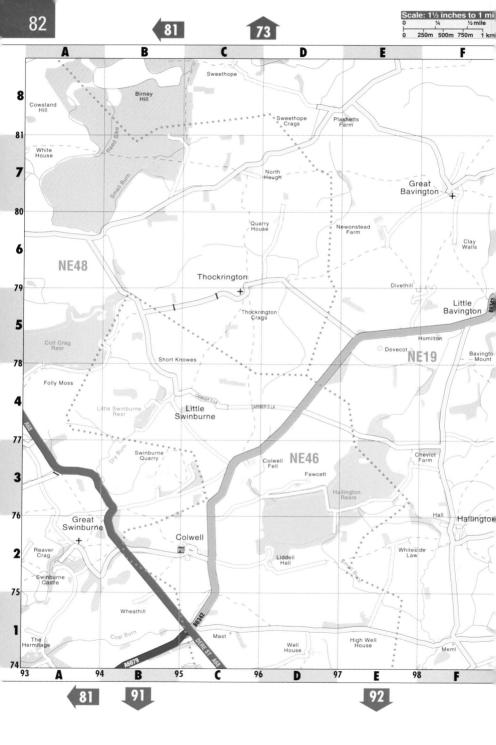

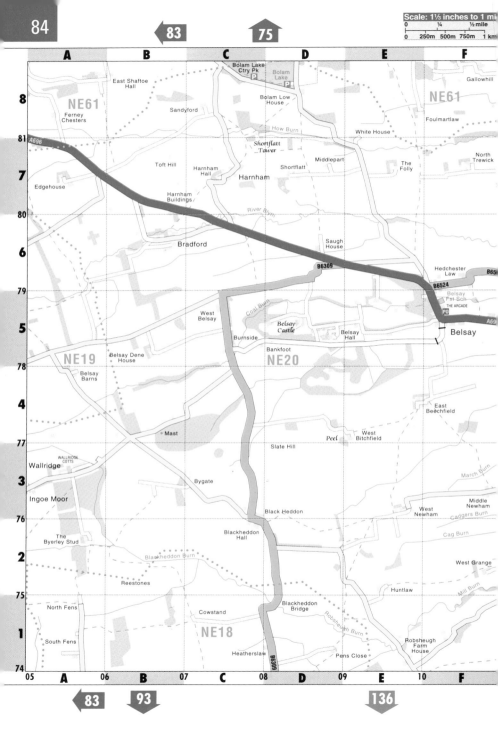

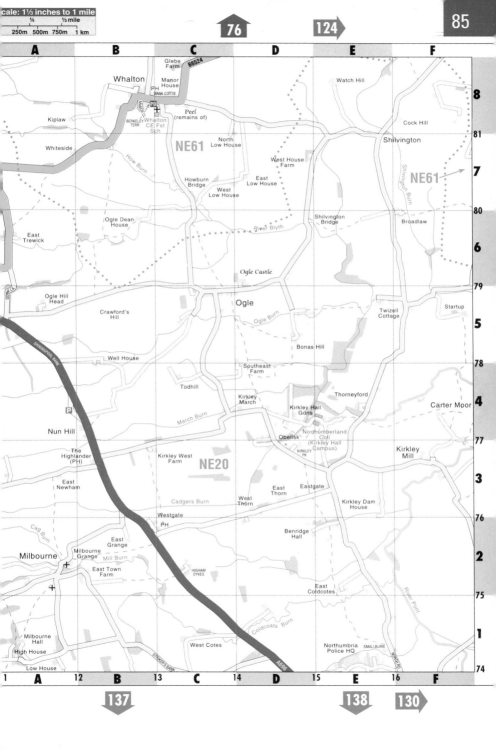

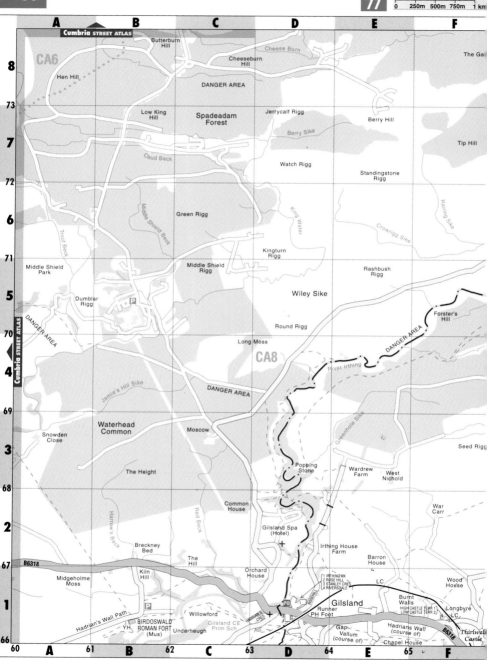

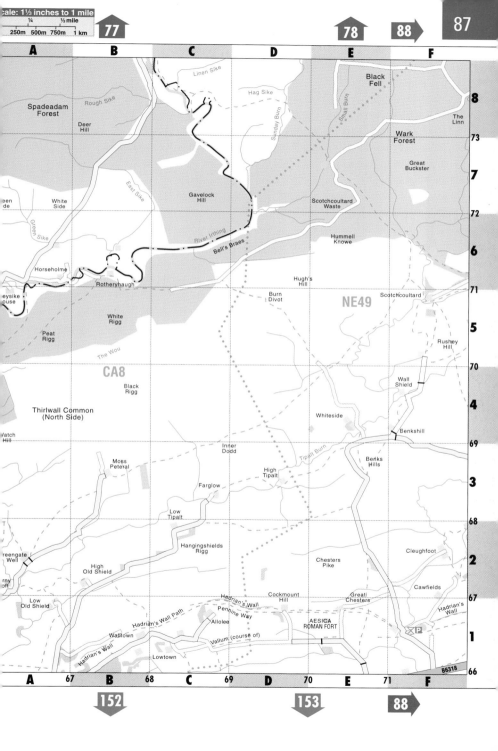

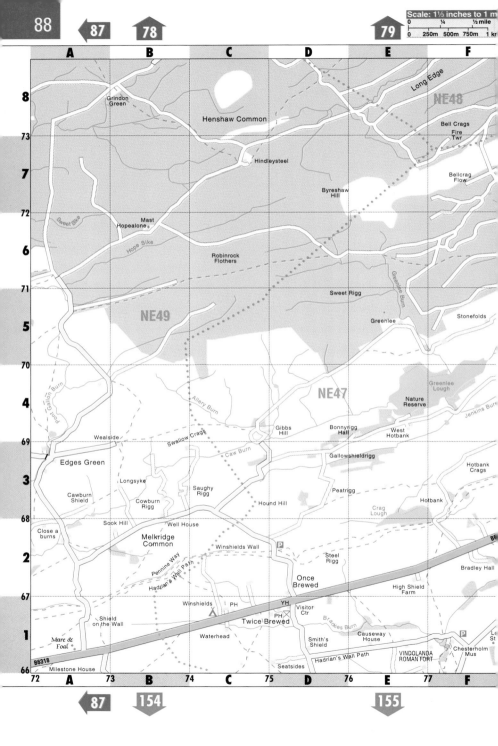

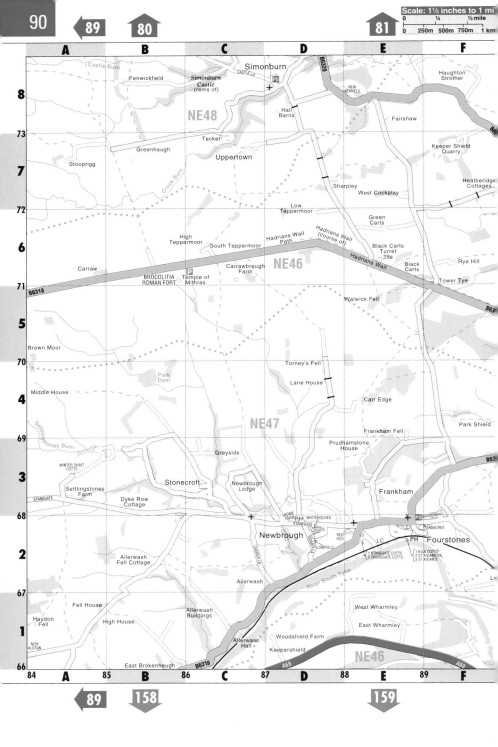

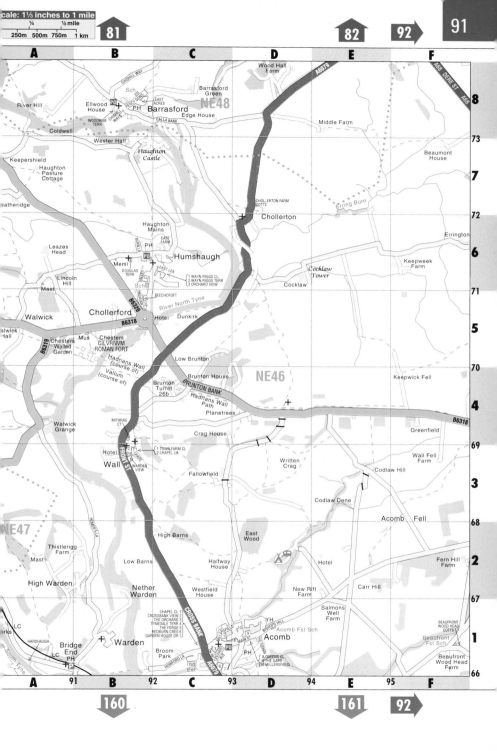

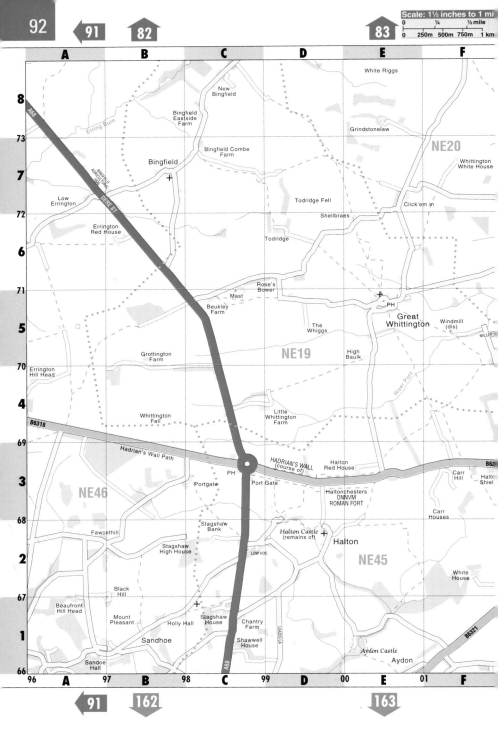

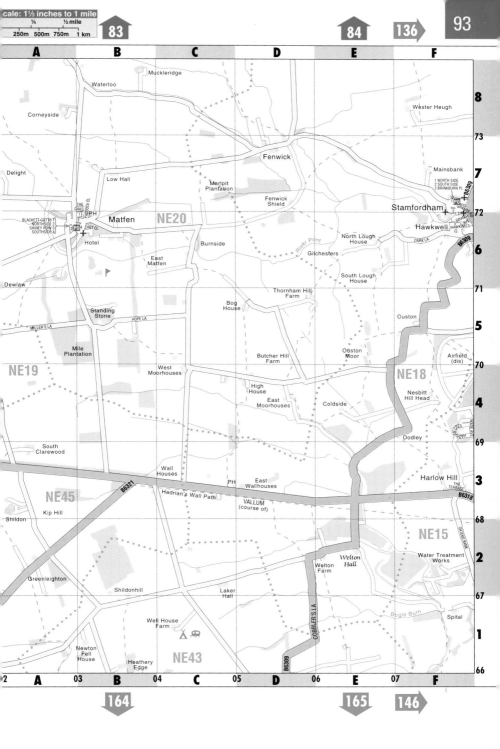

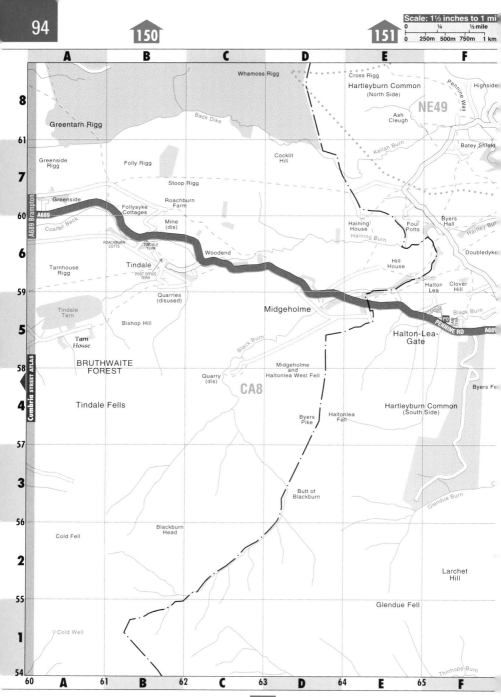

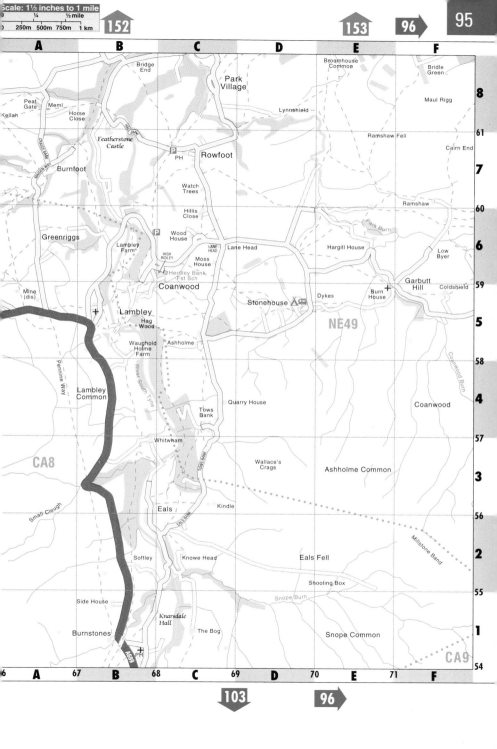

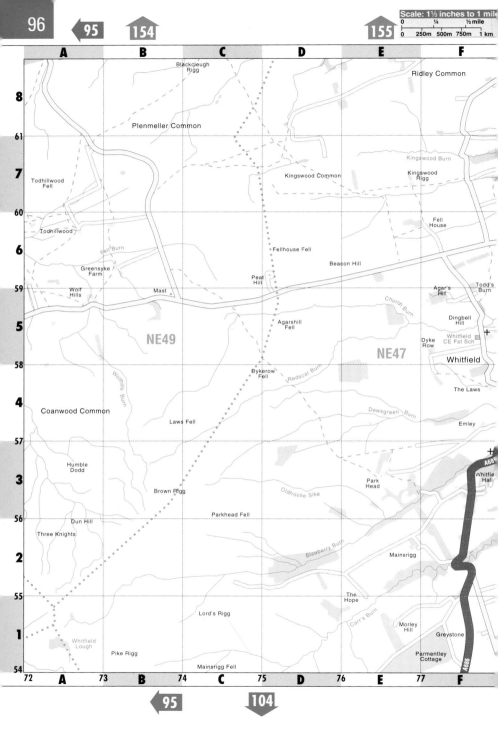

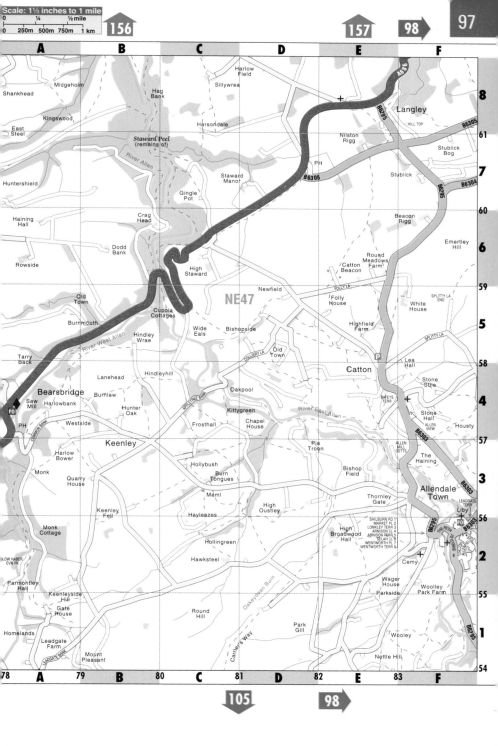

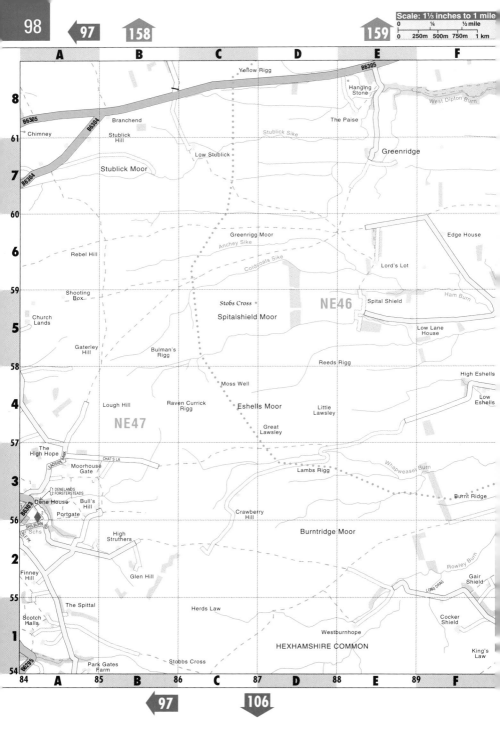

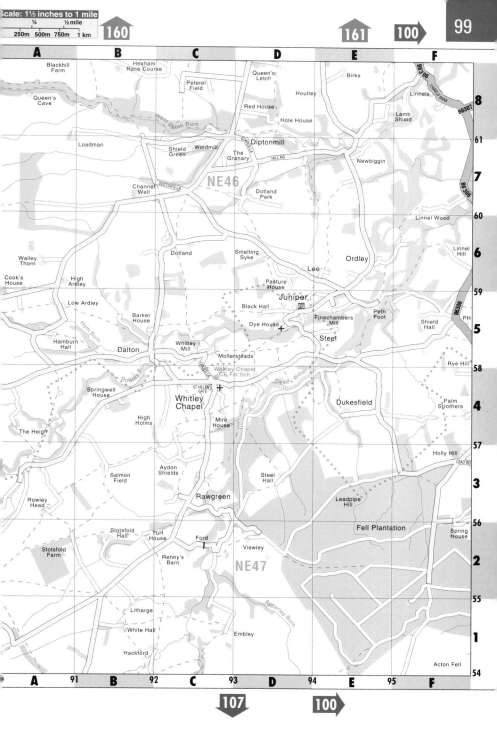

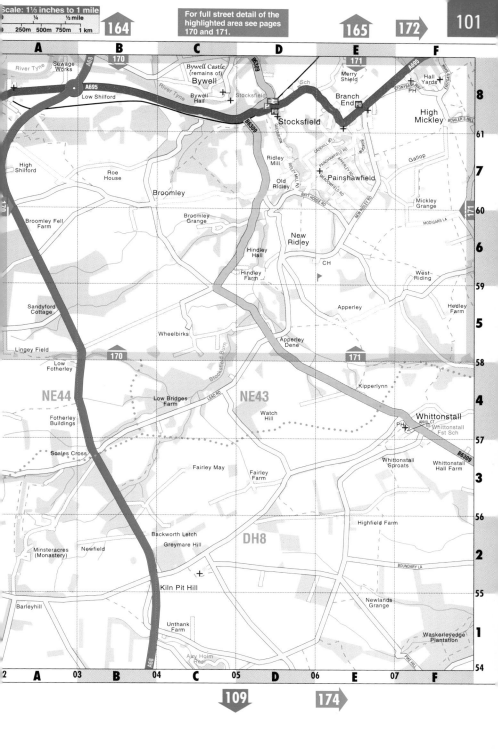

A   B   C   D   E   F

8

Faugh Cleugh

Great Blacklaw
Hill

Thinhope Burn

53

Black Hill

7

Mardy's Cleugh

Knarsdale Forest

Hanging
Shaw

West Dun
Hill

52

Old Water

Crookburn Pike

Hut Burn

6

Geltsdale Middle

Hartchyside

Three Pikes

New Water

CA8

51

Knarsdale Common

5

Gelt Burn

Butt Hill

Guy's Cleugh

50

Knar Burn

4

Green Hill

49

Croglin Fell

CA4

High Shield

3

Lawyer's
Cross

Broad Mea

48

Croglin Water

Farlam Currick

2

Scarrowmanwick
Fell

Peel Dod

47

CA10

CA9

1

Tom Smith's
Stone

Thack Moor

Watch Hill

46

60   A   61   B   62   C   63   D   64   E   65   F

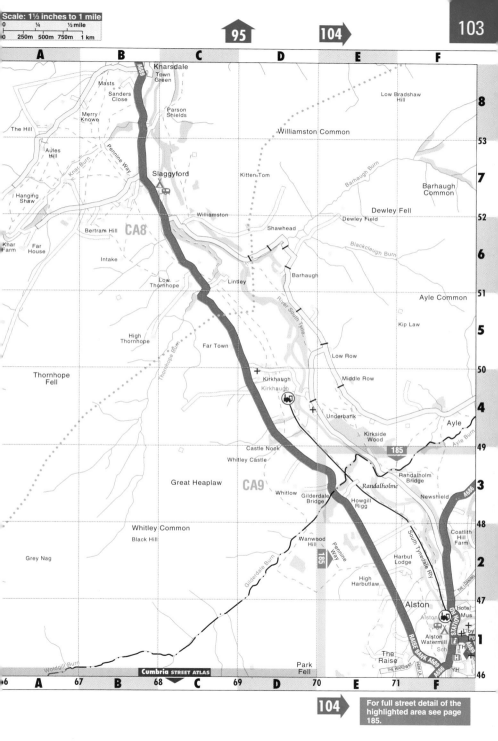

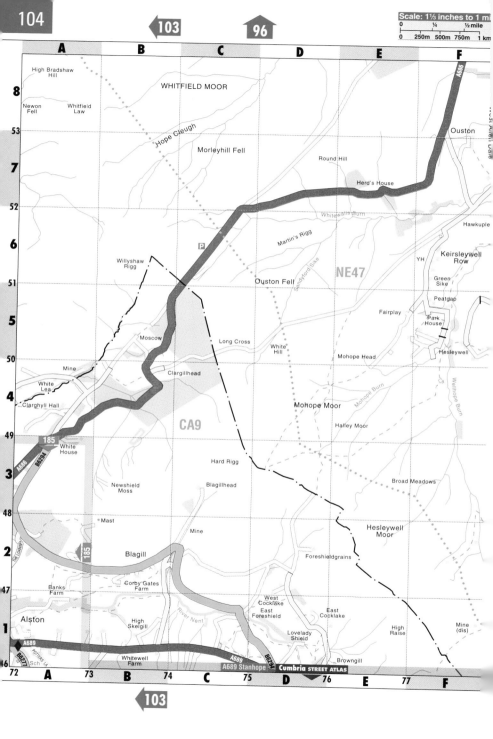

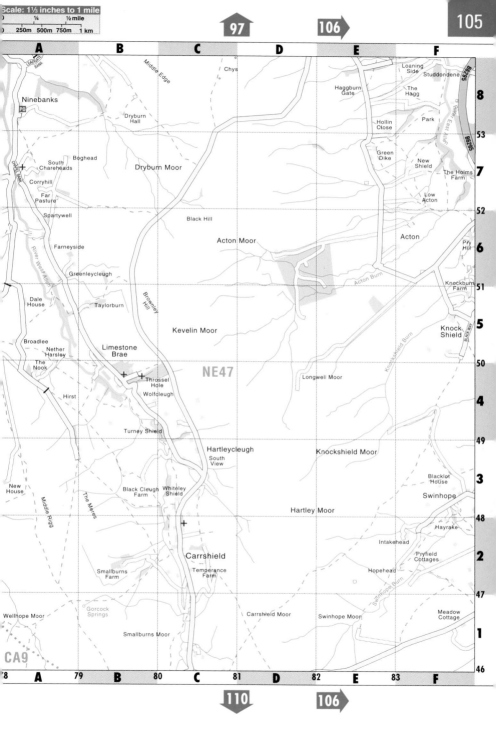

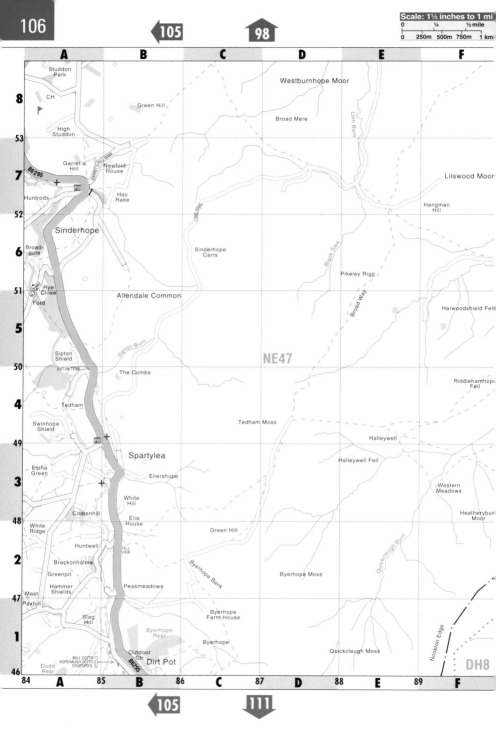

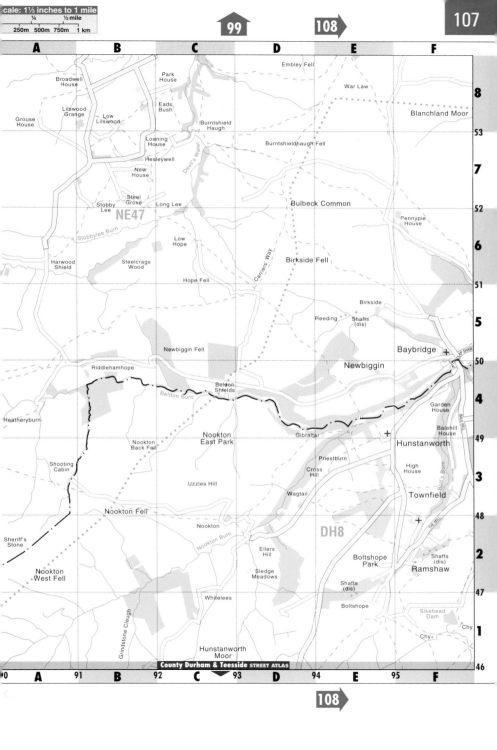

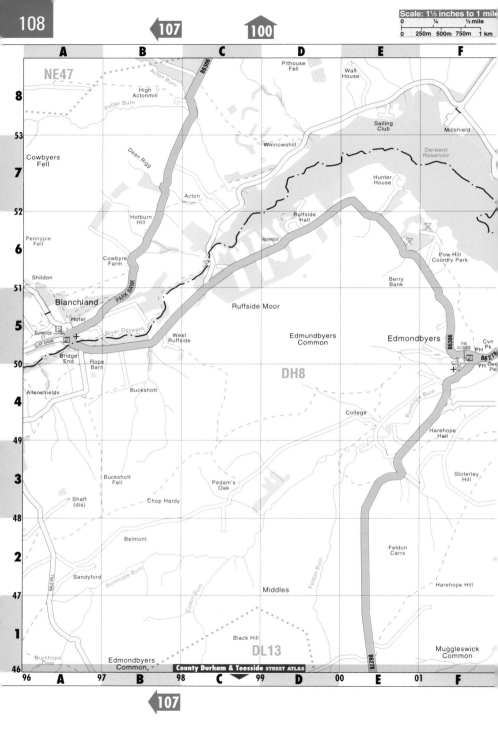

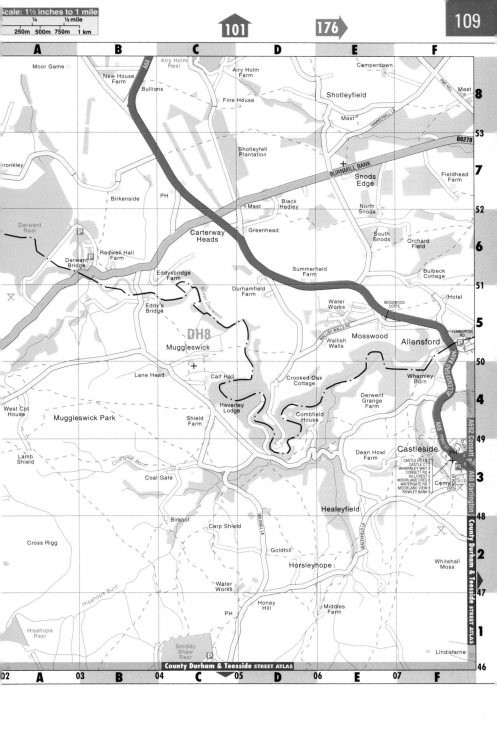

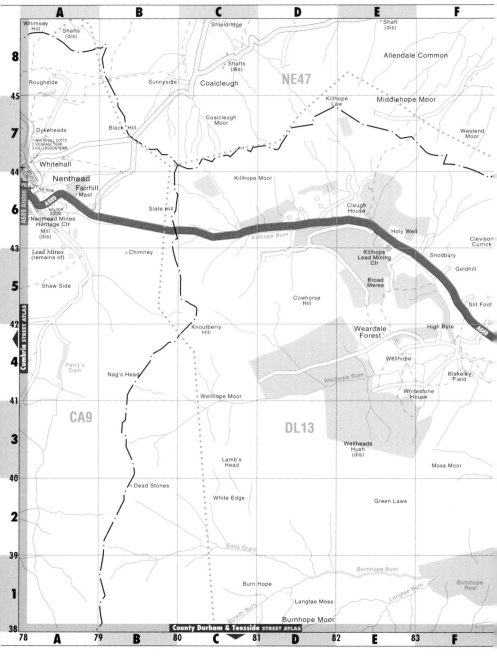

Scale: 1½ inches to 1 mile

0   ¼   ½ mile
0   250m 500m 750m 1 km

| A | B | C | D | E | F |

8

Whimsey Hill
Shafts (dis)
Shieldridge
Shaft (dis)
Allendale Common

45

Roughside
Sunnyside
Coalcleugh
NE47
Killhope Law
Middlehope Moor

7

Dykeheads
Black Hill
Coalcleugh Moor
Westend Moor

1 WHITEHALL COTTS
2 VICARAGE TERR
3 HILLERSDON TERR

Whitehall

44

PO
SPRING ST
THE ROW
Nenthead
Fairhill
Mast
Killhope Moor
Cleugh House
Holy Well
Clevison Currick

6

A689 Alston
A689
HILLTOP COTTS
Nenthead Mines Heritage Ctr
Mill (dis)
Slate Hill
Killhope Burn
Killhope Lead Mining Ctr
Snodbury
Goldhill

43

Lead Mines (remains of)
Chimney
Broad Meres
Slit Foot
A689

5

Shaw Side
Cowhorse Hill
High Byre

42

Knoutberry Hill
Weardale Forest

4

Perry's Dam
Nag's Head
Wellhope
Blakeley Field
Whitestone House

41

Wellhope Moor
Wellhope Burn

CA9

3

Lamb's Head
DL13
Wellheads Hush (dis)
Moss Moor

40

Dead Stones
White Edge
Green Laws

2

Sally Grain

39

Burnhope Burn
Burnhope Resr

1

Burn Hope
Langtae Moss
Burnhope Moor
Langtae Burn
Scraith Burn

38

| 78 | A | 79 | B | 80 | C | 81 | D | 82 | E | 83 | F |

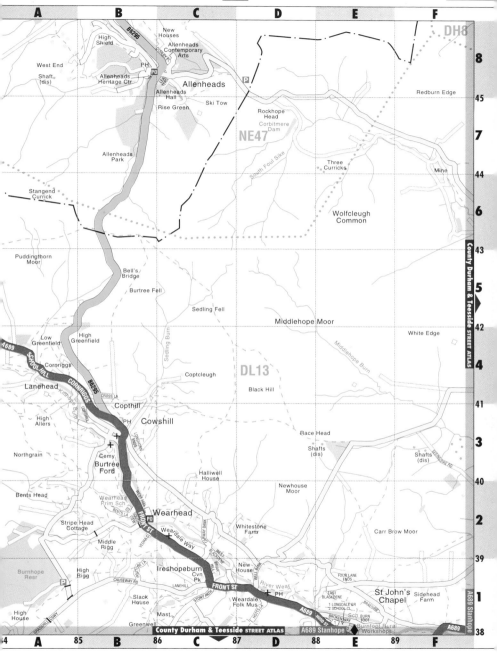

West End

High
Shield

New
Houses

Allenheads
Contemporary
Arts

Shaft
(dis)

PH

PO

Allenheads
Heritage Ctr

Allenheads
Hall

Allenheads

Ski Tow

Rise Green

Rockhope
Head

Redburn Edge

Corbitmere
Dam

NE47

Allenheads
Park

South Foul Sike

Three
Curricks

Mine

Stangend
Currick

Wolfcleugh
Common

Puddingthorn
Moor

Bell's
Bridge

Burtree Fell

Sedling Fell

Middlehope Moor

White Edge

Low
Greenfield

High
Greenfield

Sedling Burn

Middlehope Burn

DL13

Lanehead

Cororiggs

B6295

CROSS LA

Coptcleugh

Black Hill

Copthill

PH

Cowshill

Race Head

High
Allers

Shafts
(dis)

Shafts
(dis)

SEENGSIKE RD

Northgrain

Cemy

Burtree
Ford

Halliwell
House

Newhouse
Moor

Bents Head

Wearhead
Prim Sch

Wearhead

Whitestone
Farm

Carr Brow Moor

PO

Stripe Head
Cottage

Weardale Way

Middle
Rigg

Burnhope
Resr

High
Bigg

Ireshopeburn
Cvn
Pk

New
House

River Wear

FRONT ST

St John's
Chapel

Sidehead
Farm

FOUR LANE
ENDS

PH

East
Blackdene

High
House

Slack
House

Mast

Weardale
Folk Mus

1 LONGDALE GR
2 SCHOOL CL

BRAESIDE

SCTL
BURN
FOOT

BROKENWAY

Greenwell

A689

HIGH ST

A689

Burnfoot Rural
Workshops

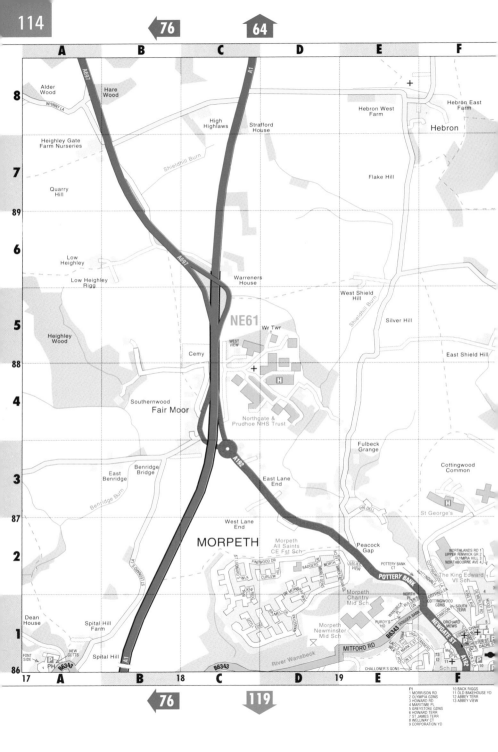

A B C D E F

8

PENDAMOR
CT

Old
Moor

Brocks Burn

LC

Middle
Moor

STATION
COTTS

AGED
MINEWORKERS
HOMES

7

Portland Burn

The Brocks

89

6

Brocks
Hill

Portland
Ind Pk

NE63

Abyssinia
House

5

NE61

88

BOTHAL TERR 1
ELLINGTON TERR 2
DEVON CL 3
DORSET CL 4

NEW

A1068

A197

HIGH MARK

4

LANGWELL
TERR

MORPETH RD

HOME FARM
CL

Bothal
Mid Sch

Bothal
Park

A1068

BOTHAL
COTTS

1 CASTLEWAY
2 DILSTON CL

LINDISFARNE

Sewage
Works

Coney Garth

3

A197

SHEEPWASH RD

Cemy

Road
under construction

Park
Wood

Bothal Burn

WHITEFIELD
FARM COTTS

WANSBEC
RD

87

Bothal
Barns

2

Whitefield

BOTHAL BANK

Bothal
Banks

WELLHEAD DEAN RD

Bothal

Bothal
Castle

NE62

Wansbeck
Riverside Par

WESTWOOD
GDNS

A1063 THIEVES BANK

River Wansbeck

Riding La

1

Welbeck
Wood

River Wansbeck

Bothalhaugh

86

23 A B 24 C D 25 E F

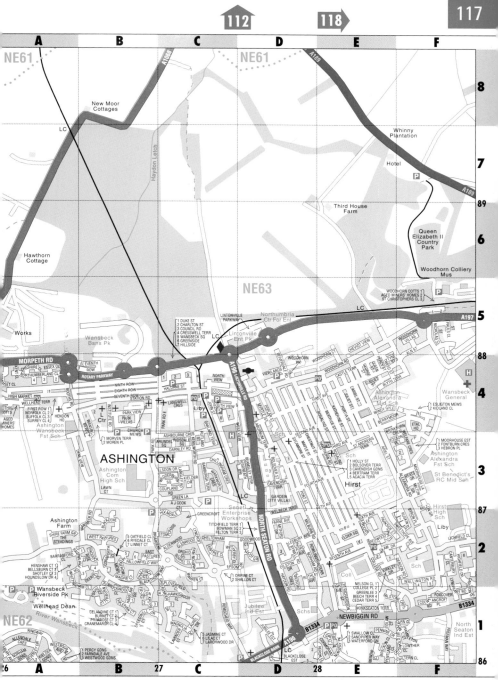

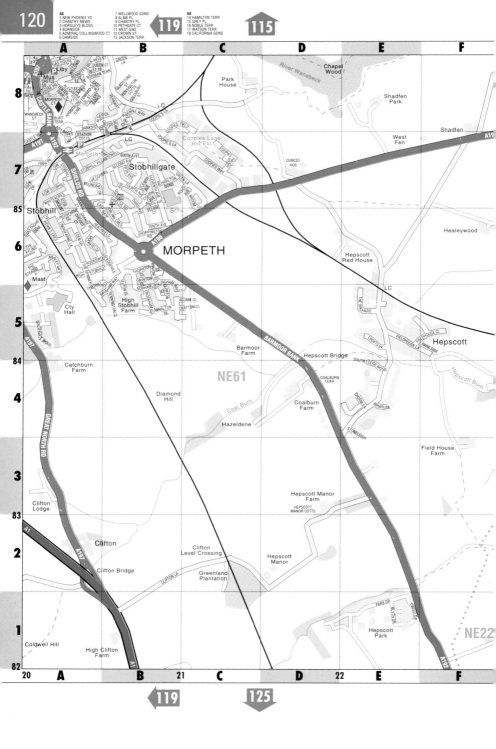

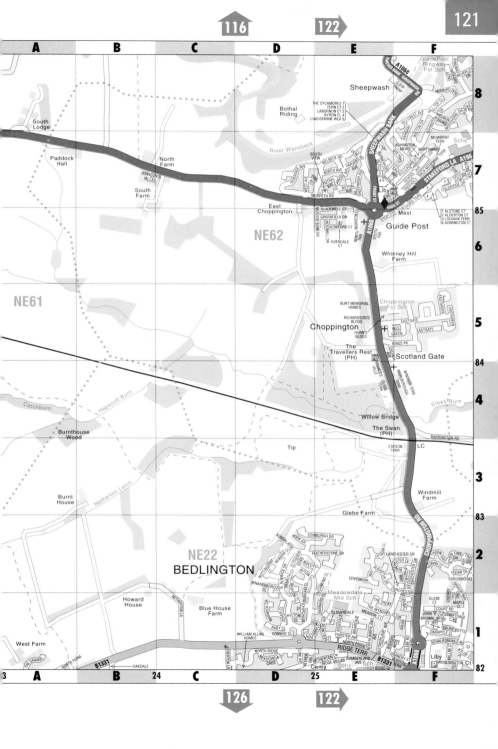

A   B   C   D   E   F

8

NE22

NE63

Ind
Est

LINKS
VIEW

WANSBECK ST

SEA VIEW

SANDY BAY
CVN PK

River Wansbeck

7

Works

Sewage
Works

THE
PADDOCKS

85

SOUTH VIEW

NORTH VIEW

P

LC

WEMBLEY GDNS

WEMBLEY TERR

6

Sleekburn
Bsns Ctr

NE24

5

Cow Gut

Refuse
Tip

Cambois

LC

NE22

Cambois
Fst Sch

84

East
Sleekburn

NORTHFIELD

SANDFIELD RD

WATERFIELD RD

WEIR AVE

HARBOUR
VIEW

+

1 UNITY TERR
2 ADLEY TERR
3 AGED MINERS HOMES

SELBOURNE TERR

4

Sleek Burn

WEST
BRIDGE ST

3

NE22

83

Factory
Point

River Blyth

North
Beach

2

Jetties

North
Blyth

WIMBLEDON ST

DALE ST

DRAY ST

Mast

Sewage
Works

Kitty Brewster
Ind Est

GRASMERE WAY

THIRLMERE WAY

CONISTON RD

BUTTERMERE WAY

DARLEY RD

SPENCER RD

SPENCER RD

TA Ctr

NE24

BLYTH

PORTLAND ST 1
THOMPSON ST 2
BALFOUR ST 3
GRIEVE ST 4

MAYFIELD GDNS

CRANTON AVE ROW

LIME ST

WILLOW ST

CHESTNUT ST

MULBERRY ST

CRANTON AVE

B1329

B1329

BEECHER ST

5 ARGYLE ST
6 THE CLOSE
7 THOMPSON ST
8 ARGYLE MEWS
9 GOSCHEN ST

North
Blyth

1

A193

COWPEN RD

B1329

HODGSON'S RD

1 BUTTERMERE WAY
2 BEECHER ST

82

29   A   B   30   C   D   31   E   F

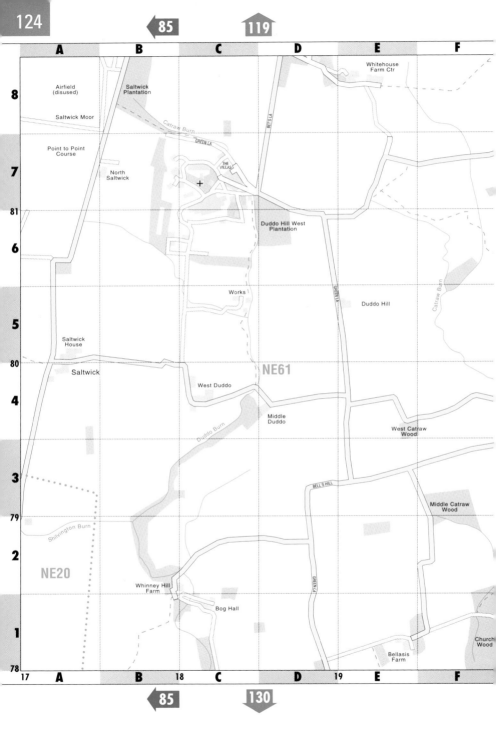

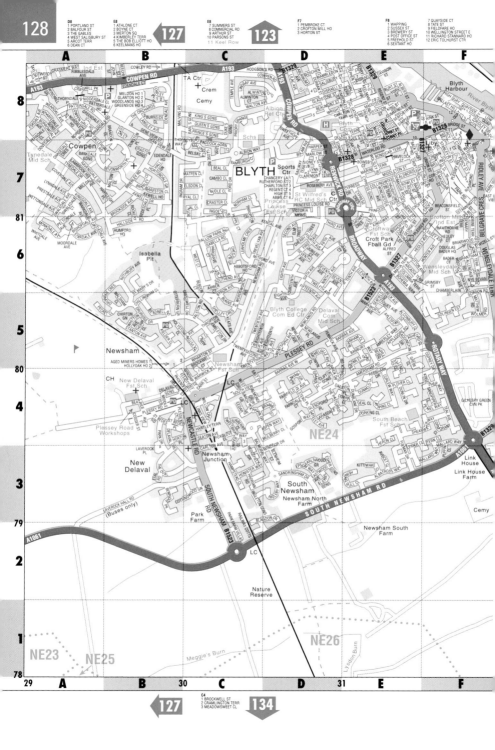

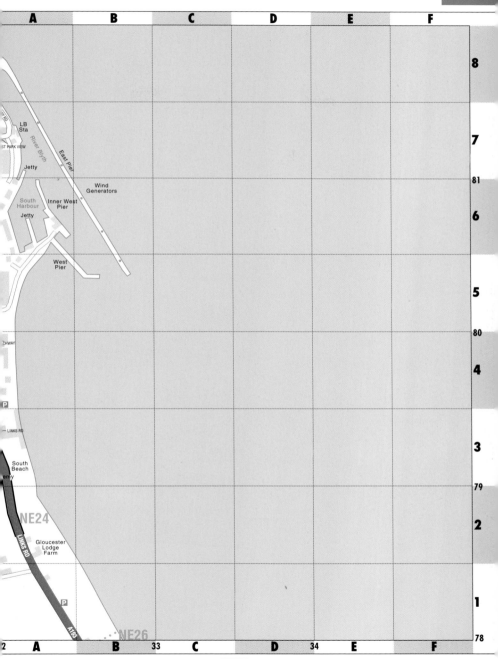

135

85
124

NE61

Bellasis
Bridge

River Blyth

Make me Rich

Berwick Hill
Low House

Low Horton
House

Ewe Hill

River Pont

Pont Ends
Plantation

Gravel La

NE20

NE13

Old Horton
Grange

West End
Farm

East
Farm

BERWICK HILL
COTTS.

New Hor
Grang

NEW HORTON
GRANGE COTTS

South East
Farm

Carr House

Berwick Hill

Park House Farm
Cottages

Park
House

Fox
Cove

PONT PK

DANGER AREA

Rifle
Range

Blackpool Drain

Carr
Plantation

85
139

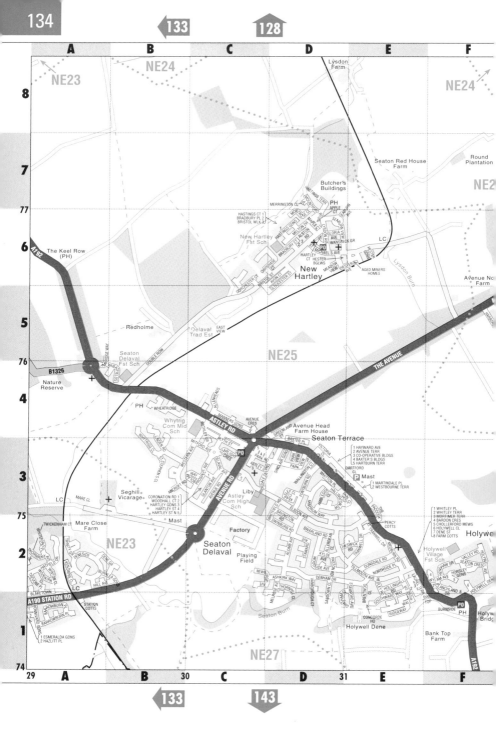

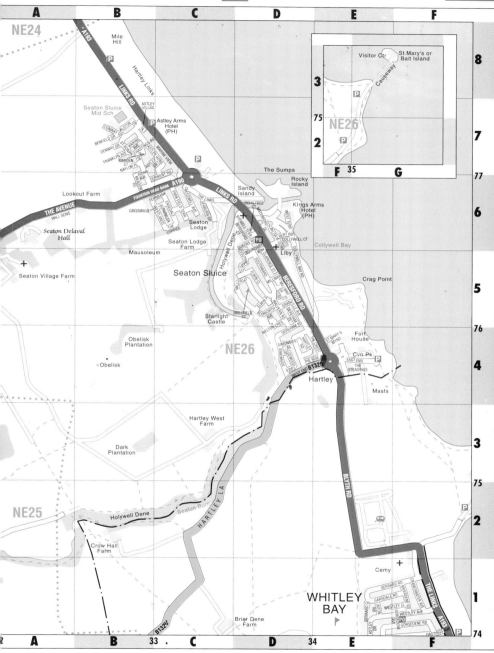

NE20

A B C D E F

8

Heugh
7
The
Heugh
73
Dyke
House

Hillhead
Plantation

Silverhill

6

Brixter
Hill

Dalton
Hillhead

Dalton Sike

5

Chapel
Farm

Dalton
Farm

72 Sch

NE18

THE OL
Sewage
Works
Stamfordham

Nettley
Bank

Windy
Walls

4 B6309

Lane
House

Whinney
Brae

Broomy
Hall

Bridge
End

BRIDGE
END COTTS

The Mill
House

River Pont

Warlage
Hill

3

Bog
Plantation

Cheeseburn
Grange

Eachwick
Red House

Swarden Burn

71

The Park

Street
Houses

Bullshaugh
Plantation

2

Richmond
Hill

Streethouses
Plantation

Grange
House

Kyloe House
Farm

Mast
Stob
Hill

Hilltop
Plantations

Lowfell
Plantations

1

Airfield
(dis)

NE15

Med Burn

70 08 A 09 C 10 E F
B D F

85
138

A B C D E F

STRIKER'S BANK

Botany Bay
Wood

South East
Farm

Bate's
Plantation

8

Larch
Wood

Small Burn

Thorny
Covert

7

73

Redhouse
Farm

Forster's
Plantation

Redhouse
Plantation

6

Cairn
House

Field
Houses

LIMESTONE LA

Dissington East
Houses

Long
Plantation

5

Dalton

PADDOCK LA

72

NE18

NE20

East
Lodge

Benacres
Plantation

4

Dissington
Hall

Dissington Park

3

Donkins
Houses

Eachwick
Hall

River Pont

Eachwick

Eachwick
Bridge

Farrick
Hill

71

Bridge House
Farm

Dissington
Bridge

Swalden Burn

2

THE AVENUE

Medburn

THE RUGERY

Dissington
Old Hall

Med Burn

1

South
Dissington

A B C D E F

12 13 70

147
138

PONTELAND

Eland Green

South Coldcoats

West Smallburn Bridge

Coldcoats Moor

Keepers Cottage

West Farm

Northumbria Police Headquarters

Mast

Eastfield House

Woodside Farm

Collingwood Cotts

Limestone La

West Houses

THE BEECHES WEST RD MAIN ST PONTELAND RD

Meadowfield Ind Est Cattle Mkt

Richard Coates CE Mid Sch

Louisville

Meadowfield Pk 1
Castle Ct 2
Merton Way 3
Bradbury Ct 4

Ponteland Bridge

Ponteland L Ctr

Ponteland Mid Sch

Ponteland Com High Sch

NE20

Coat Hill

Richmond Fields

River Pont

Runnymere Rd

Darras Rd

Darras Hall

Darras Hall Fst Sch

Sandringham Way

Windsor Pl

B6545 ROTARY WAY B6524

CALLERTON LA

High Callerton

Hold House Farm

Brough Hill

Braid Hill

Callerton Hall

Bog Nursery

NE15 NE15

B6323

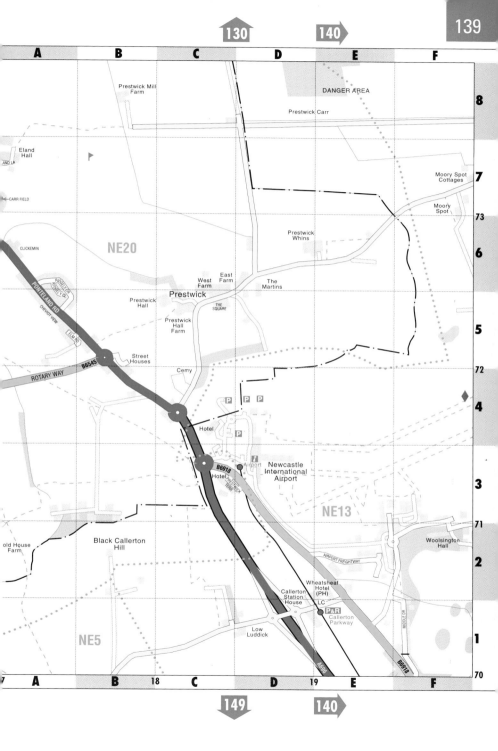

8
Prestwick Mill
Farm

DANGER AREA

Prestwick Carr

Eland
Hall

AND LA

←CARR FIELD

7

Moory Spot
Cottages

Moory
Spot

73

CLICKEMIN

NE20

Prestwick
Whins

6

West
Farm

East
Farm

The Martins

Prestwick

5

PONTELAND RD

Prestwick
Hall

Prestwick
Hall
Farm

THE
SQUARE

CREVID VIEW

ELM RD

B6545

Street
Houses

Cemy

72

ROTARY WAY

P   P   P

4

Hotel

P

Airport
i

Newcastle
International
Airport

B6918

Hotel

3

NE13

71

old House
Farm

Black Callerton
Hill

AIRPORT FREIGHTWAY

Woolsington
Hall

2

Wheatsheaf
Hotel
(PH)

NE5

Callerton
Station
House

LC

Low
Luddick

P&R
Callerton
Parkway

MIDDLE DR

1

A6085

B6918

70

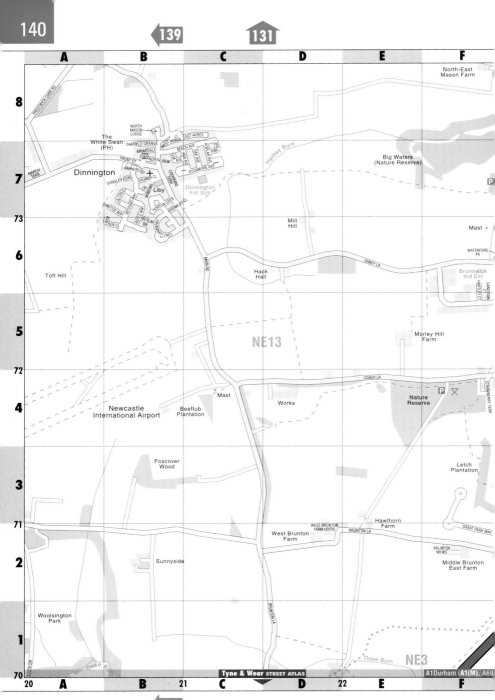

North-East
Mason Farm

8

North
Mason
Lodge

The
White Swan
(PH)

OAKFIELD GRANGE

WEST ACRES   EAST ACRES

BRIARDALE

FRONT ST   NORTH VIEW
FARNDN

BEECH AVE   POPLAR AVE   PINE

Hartley Burn

Big Waters
(Nature Reserve)

Dinnington

DUNSLEY GDNS

WADDING

CHURCH CL

Liby

COPPINE

OAK AVE

ELM AVE   SYCAMORE AVE

ASH AVE

Dinnington
Fst Sch

P

7

HARTSIDE WAY

WILLOW

ASH

WITTON

NORTON CRES

BREWLEY CL

73

EAST   MERLAY
DR

BRACKEN CL

WHINBRAY CRES

Mill
Hill

Mast

WATERFORD
PK

Brunswick
Ind Est

6

Toft Hill

MAIN RD

Hack
Hall

SANDY LA

HARTLEY CT

SANDISON

NE13

5

Morley Hill
Farm

72

COACH LA

Newcastle
International Airport

Mast

Beeftub
Plantation

Works

Nature
Reserve

STRAWBERRY TERR

P

4

Foxcover
Wood

Letch
Plantation

3

WEST BRUNTON
FARM COTTS

Hawthorn
Farm

GREAT PARK WAY

71

West Brunton
Farm

BRUNTON LA

BRUNTON
MEWS

Sunnyside

Middle Brunton
East Farm

2

BRUNTON LA

Woolsington
Park

SOUTH DR

1

Ouse Burn

Ouse Burn

NE3

70

Tyne & Wear STREET ATLAS

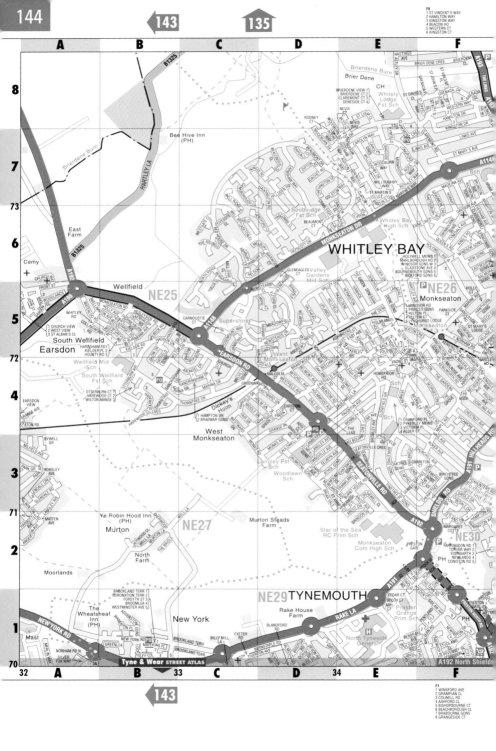

Whitley

MONKSEATON DR

THE LINKS

Northern Promenade

NE26

1 EASTBOURNE GDNS
2 ILFRACOMBE GDNS
3 MARINE CT W
4 MARINE CT E

PROMENADE

A193 PARK RD

PARK AVE

A193

Central Lower Promenade

PARK TERR

Liby

Southern Promenade

1 KITTIWAKE HO
2 SOUTHLEIGH
3 ESPLANADE AVE
4 LINDEN TERR
5 TREWIT RD
6 VICTORIA MEWS
7 MAFEKING ST

84
1 STATION SQ
2 ALBANY GDNS
3 CLARENCE CRES
4 ALEXANDRA TERR
5 ALBERT TERR
6 WATERFORD TERR
7 DEVONSHIRE TERR
8 GLADSTONE TERR
9 STANLEY CRES

1 GORDON TERR
2 ROCKCLIFFE

1 ROCKCLIFFE GDNS
2 GUARDIAN CT
3 GORDON HO
4 ROMNEY CL
5 WESTMINSTER CL
6 COLLINGWOOD TERR
7 ST MARGARETS CT

Whitley Bay

Sch

Brown's Bay

PROMONTORY

Brown's Point

Mast

SOUTHCLIFF
NORMA CRES
CLIFF RD

HILLHEADS RD A191

A193 MARDEN RD S

Sports Ctr

CRESCENT VALE

PLESSEY CRES

CHEVIOT CT

NATERS ST

IRB Sta

NE25

Cullercoats Bay

1 VICTORIA CT
2 DOVE ROW
3 DOVE HO
4 WEST VIEW BLDGS
5 BEVERLEY VILLAS
6 BILGE RD

Tynemouth North Point

Liby

Cullercoats Prim Sch

Cullercoats

1 BRAESIDE CL
2 SHADEN PARK RD 2

THE BROADWAY

NE30

1 EDENGARTH
2 NEWLANDS
3 CONISTON RD
4 BLENCATHRA

1 EGLINGHAM AVE
2 RENNINGTON AVE
3 AYDON CL
4 SEACREST APARTMENTS

Marden

Marden High Sch

Monkhouse Prim Sch

Blue Reef Aquarium

LOUGHBOROUGH AVE

1 THE DRIVE
2 PARKSIDE CRES

BEACH RD

A1058

A193

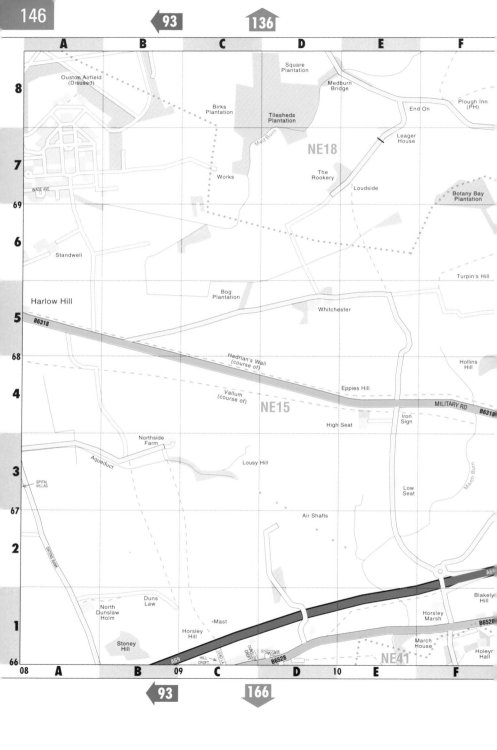

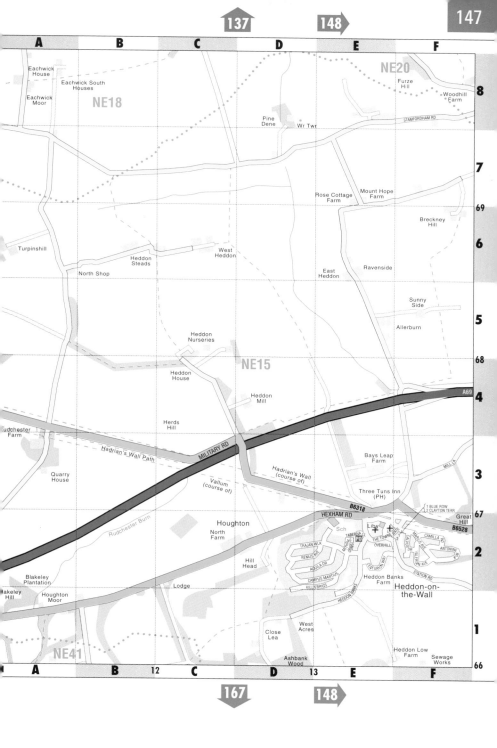

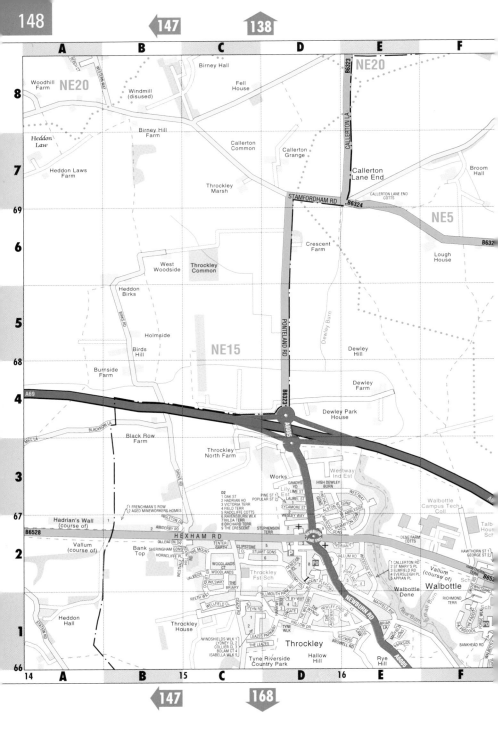

C1
1 ANGRAM WLK
2 ASKRIGG WLK
3 AUDLAND WLK
4 AUSTWICK WLK
C2
1 HANOVER WLK
2 HANOVER CL
3 ELGAR AVE

E1
1 BIRKSHAW WLK
2 BICKERTON WLK
3 KNARSDALE PL
4 HIGHWELL LA

E3
1 WHORLTON PL
2 AGED MINERS HOMES
3 MARSHAM RD
4 COUNDEN RD
5 KENSINGTON VILLAS

F2
1 FRANKHAM ST
2 BARENTS CL
3 FAIRSPRING
4 FENTON WLK
5 FORESTBORN CT
6 FORESTONES
7 FORDMOSS WLK

F3
1 WIMBOURNE GN
2 BUXTON GN
3 CHATSWORTH GDNS
4 PILTON WLK
5 BOYD TERR
6 BELMONT COTTS
7 RAPPERTON CT

A   B   C   D   E   F

8

Lawn Top

CH

B6318

THIRLWALL VIEW

P

MILLBURN TERR

Greenhead

STATION COTTS

YH

GLENWHELT BANK

Wardoughan

Banktop Farm

GREENHEAD BANK

PH

7

B6318

Greenhead Cleugh

A69

65

Gapshield

6

Measlings Cleugh

Windy Law

Mast

5

Gap Shields Fan

Todholes

CA8

Mast

Thirlwall Common (South Side)

Reay Crag

64

Black Hill

Blenkinsopp Common

Mast

4

Small Burn

Hot Moss

Pennine Way

3

Blackpool Rigg

63

Wain Rigg

Middle Hill

2

Cooper's Cleugh

Galloping Rigg

Little Rigg

Featherstone Common

1

Cow Rigg

Glencune Burn

NE49

Round Hill

62

A   B   64   C   D   65   E   F

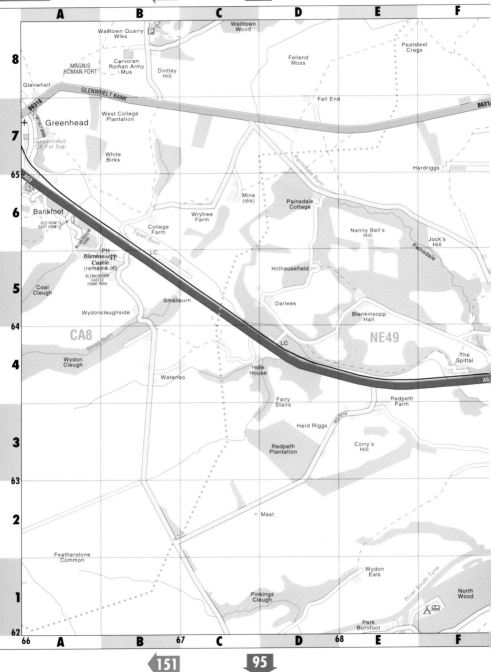

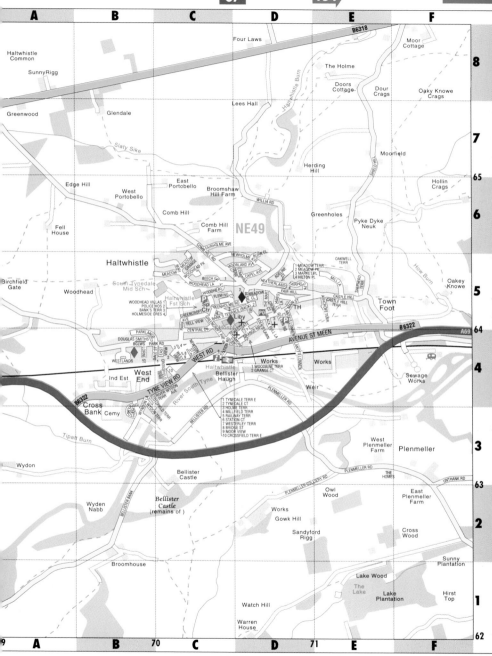

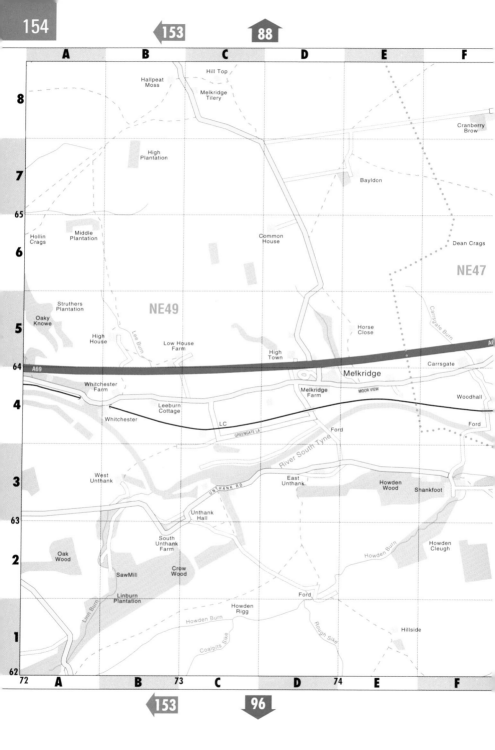

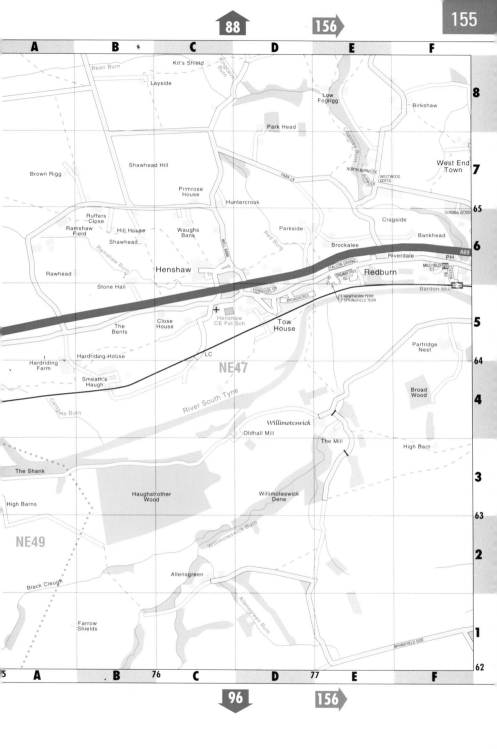

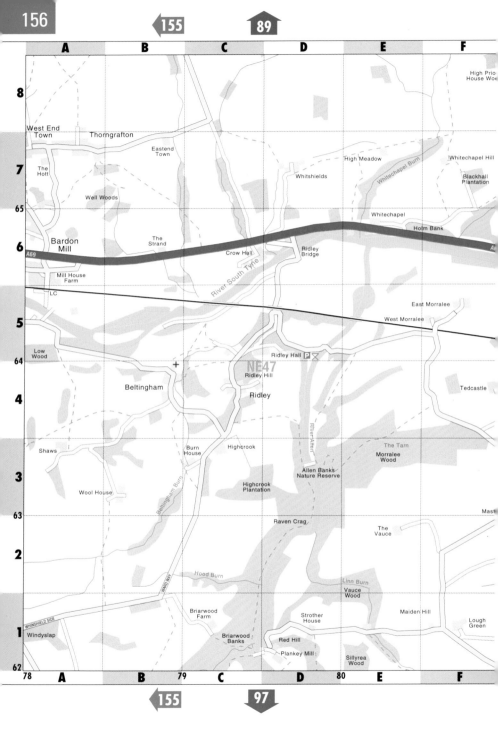

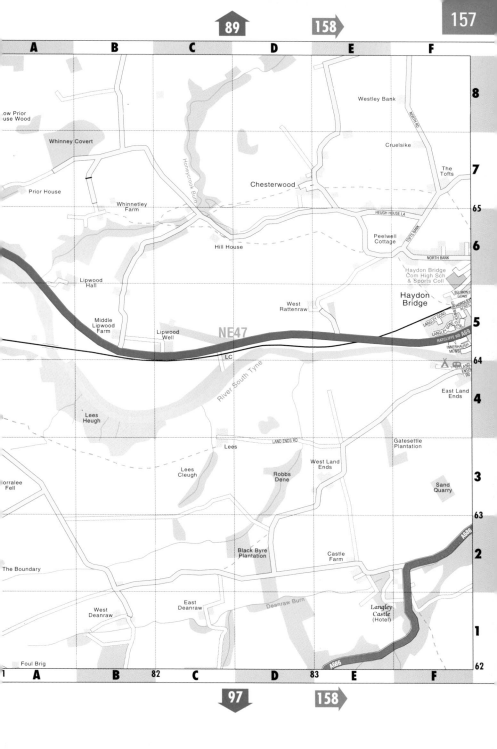

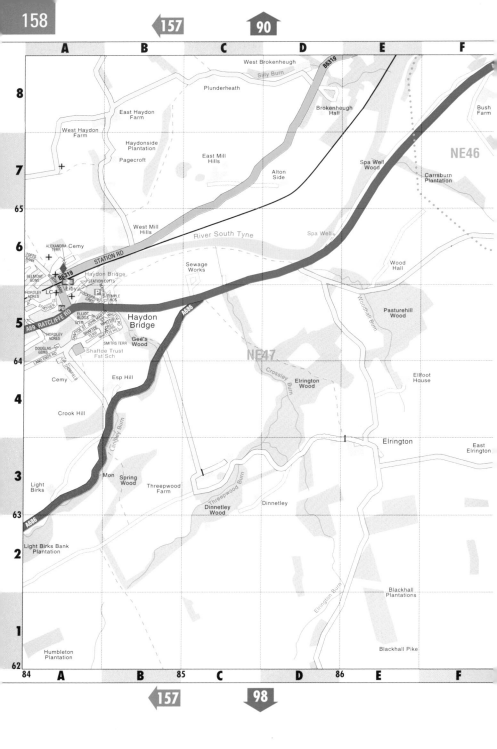

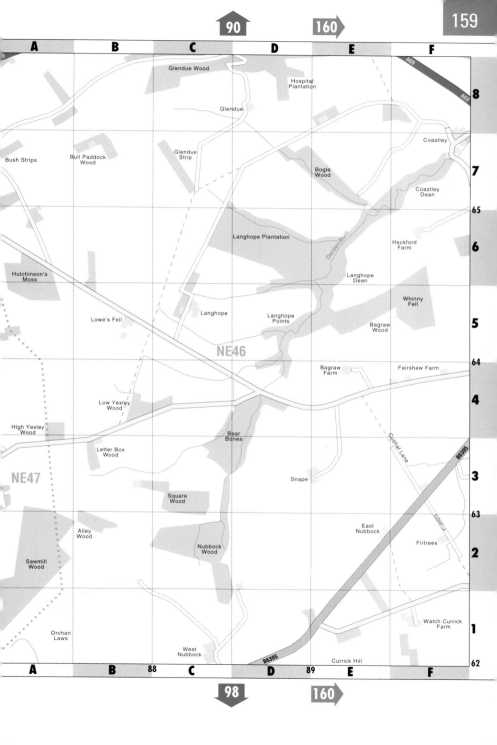

A B C D E F

A69

8

Glendue Wood

Hospital
Plantation

Glendue

Coastley

Bush Strips

Bull Paddock
Wood

Glendue
Strip

7

Bogle
Wood

Coastley
Dean

65

Langhope Plantation

6

Hackford
Farm

Darden Burn

Hutchinson's
Moss

Langhope
Dean

Langhope

Lowe's Fell

Langhope
Points

Whinny
Fell

Bagraw
Wood

5

NE46

Bagraw
Farm

Fairshaw Farm

64

Low Yexley
Wood

4

High Yexley
Wood

Cushat Lane

NE47

Letter Box
Wood

Bear
Bones

B6305

3

Snape

63

Square
Wood

East
Nubbock

Firtrees

2

Alley
Wood

Nubbock
Wood

Sawmill
Wood

Watch Currick
Farm

1

Orchan
Laws

West
Nubbock

B6305

Currick Hill

62

A B 88 C D 89 E F

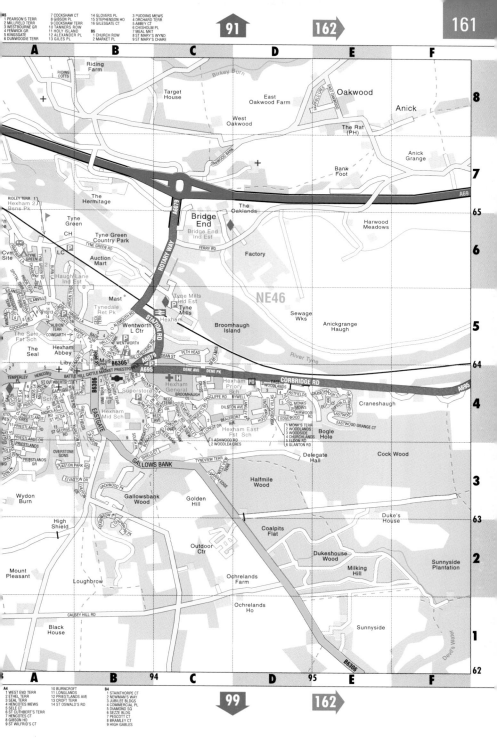

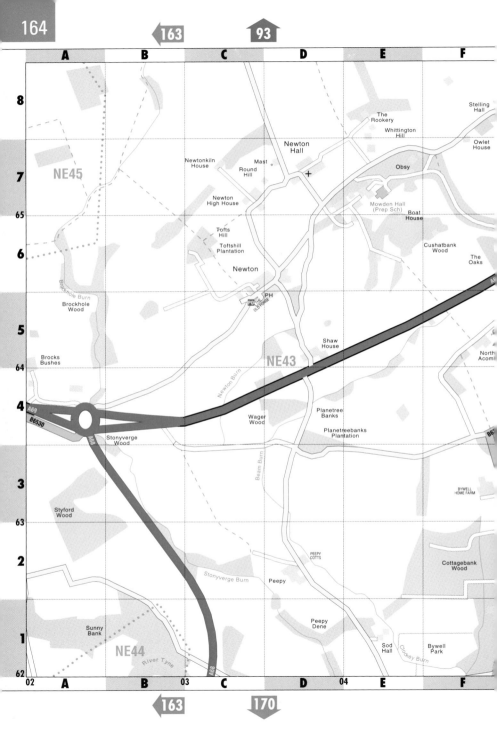

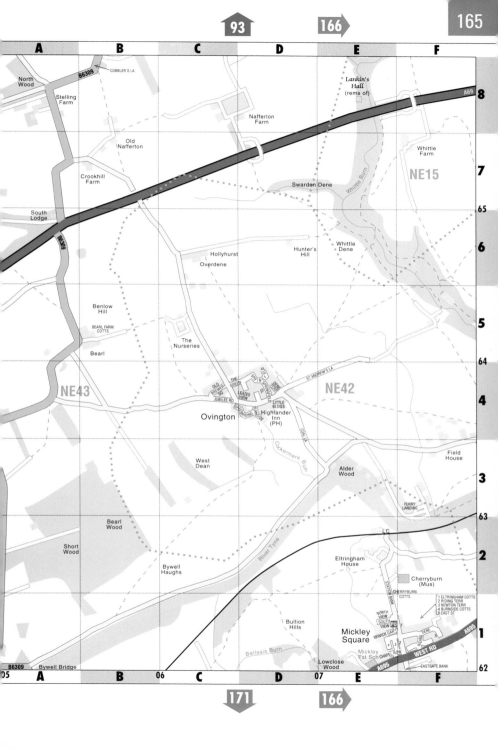

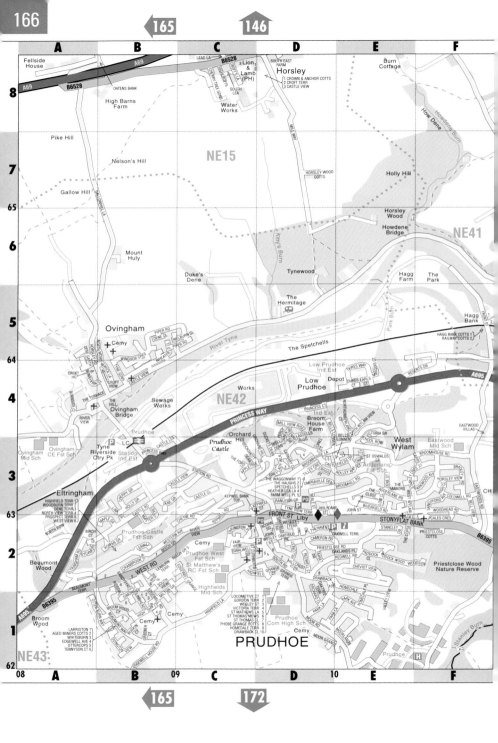

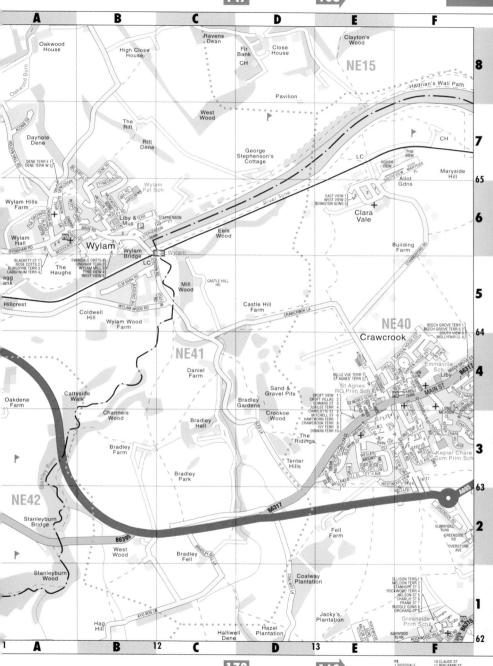

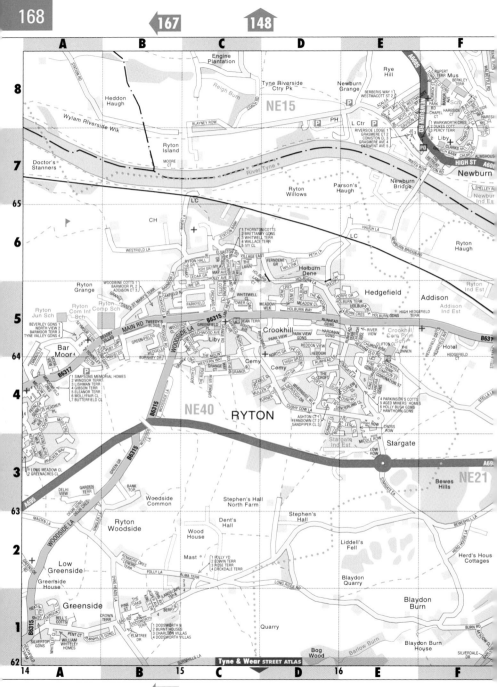

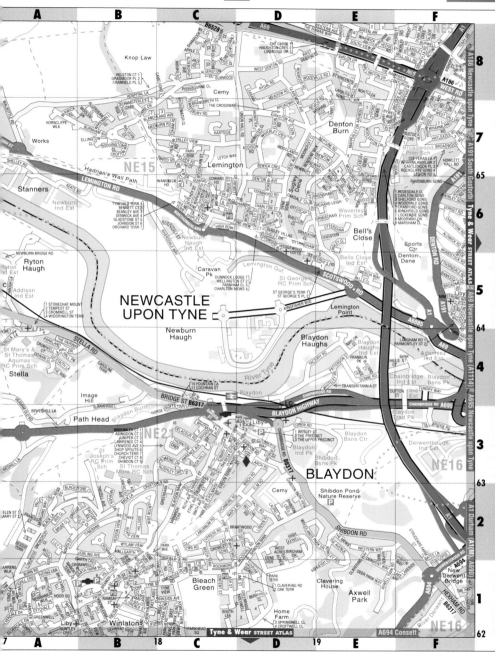

B1
1 LITCHFIELD
2 LITCHFIELD CRES
3 LITCHFIELD TERR
4 OLDWELL AVE
5 MOUNT PLEASANT
6 ROOKSLEIGH
7 THE GARTH
8 THORNBURY
9 COMMERCIAL ST

10 GARDEN TERR
11 NORTH LODGE APARTMENTS

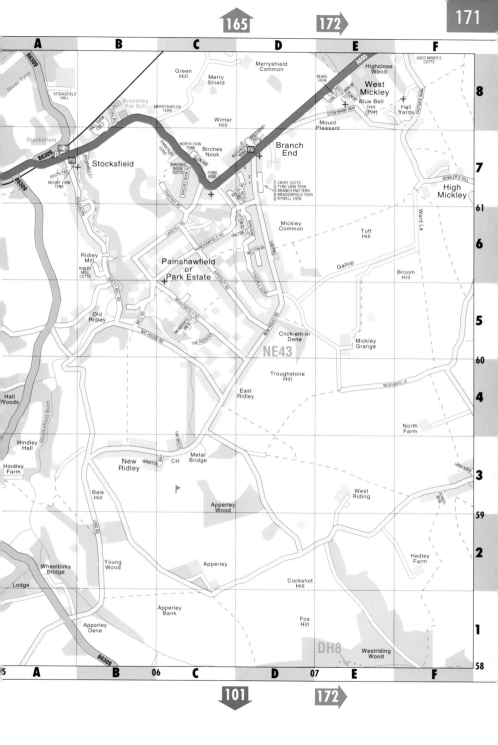

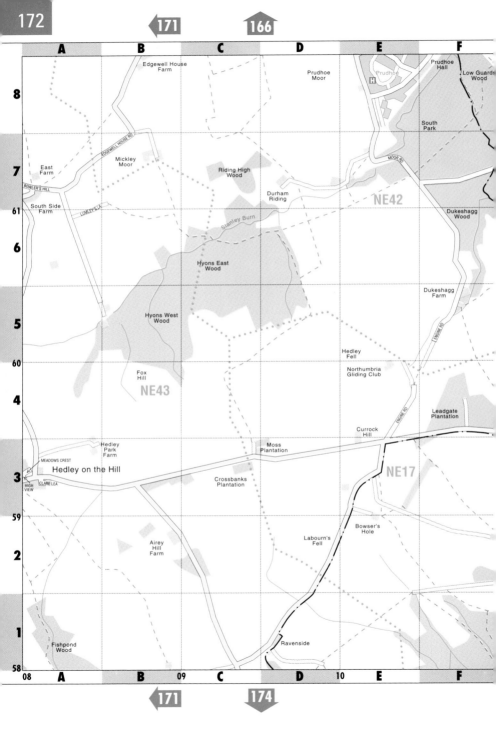

Tyne & Wear STREET ATLAS

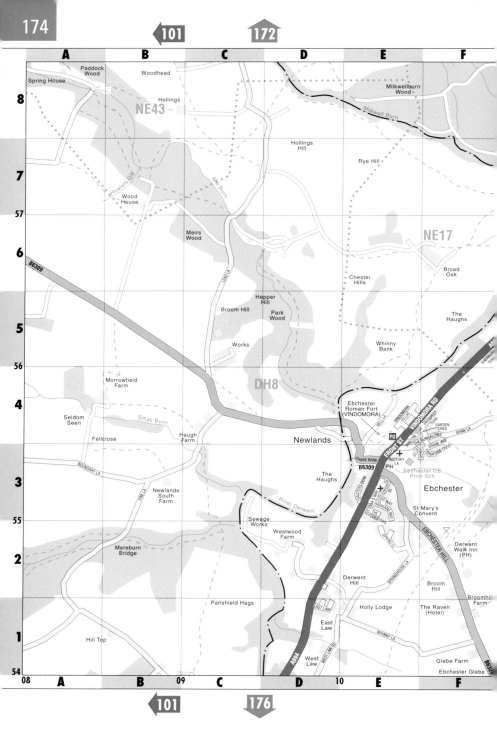

A   **B**   **C**   **D**   **E**   **F**

Chopwell Mill Farm

Chopwell Wood House

CAMPFIELD CRES
WOODSIDE TERR
MARX TERR
E. D MOREL
SOUTH VIEW
BALFOUR TERR 1
FREDERICK ST 3
LESBURY TERR 3
DALTON TERR 4
SYMON TERR 5
PENNINE VIEW 6
SOUTH TERR
LENIN TERR
MOORLAND VIEW

8

Chopwell

Carr House

Chopwell Wood

7

Blackhall Farm

Tongue Burns

EAST TERR

Galleyburn Wood

Blackhall Mill

PARK COTTS 1
RIVERSDALE 2
PEARTREE CT 3

Peartree Farm

CONNOLLY TERR

ARMONDSIDE RD

Armondside

57

A694 Newcastle upon Tyne (A1114)

Galley Burn

Haggdene Wood

NURSERY DENE

River Derwent

6

Derwentcote Steel Furnace

Derwentcote Farm

VICTORIA TERR

PH
PO

Derwent Valley Villas

ENNERDALE TERR

SUMMERFIELD

LANGDALE TERR

AXFORD TERR

COTTS

OAKWELL CT

EDGE LA

Hagg Farm

5

Low Westwood

Hamsterley

Cemy

White Byerside

NE17

A694

LINTZFORD RD

TOLLGATE RD

B6310

FENWICK GR

ONE CLOSE RD

PARKLANDS

56

BYERSIDE CVN SITE

Byerside Wood

Hamsterley Mill

NE39

Crabtree Hill

Tyne & Wear STREET ATLAS

SHAW LA

WEST LA

THE BUNGALOWS
LONSDALE CT

CUT THROAT LA

Make-me-Rich Plantation

4

High Westwood

Allendale Farm

ong Bank

Peel Flats

Peelflats Plantation

Black Byerside Wood

LONGCLOSE BANK

Southfield La

Hamsterley Burn

Hamsterleyhall Spring Wood

Southfield Farm

3

55

East Farm

North Wood

2

DENECREST

THE DENE

ADAMS TERR

CHESTER

Medomsley Grange Farm

Bishop Ian Ramsey CE Prim Sch

WEST FARM RD

THE GAP

WEST FARM

MANOR RD

DH8

Housing La

Cowclose Wood

The Dene

NORTH VIEW 1
GRANGE TERR 2
ROTHLEY TERR 3
CO-OPERATIVE TERR 4

PH
PO

FINES RD

B6308

B6308

NORTH MAGDALENE

SOUTH TERR

Medomsley

Hollin Hill

South Burn

Shipmaster's Hill

1

B6310

Medomsley Edge

South Burn

54

A   **B**   12   **C**   **D**   13   **E**   **F**

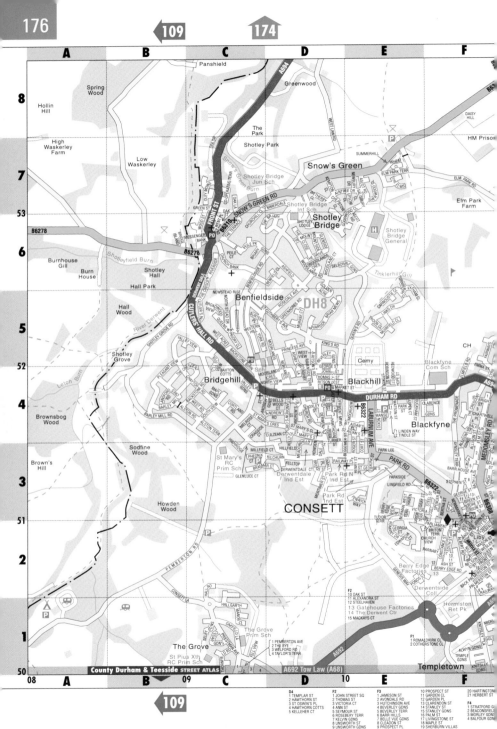

A692 Tow Law (A68)

County Durham & Teesside STREET ATLAS

BERWICK-UPON-TWEED

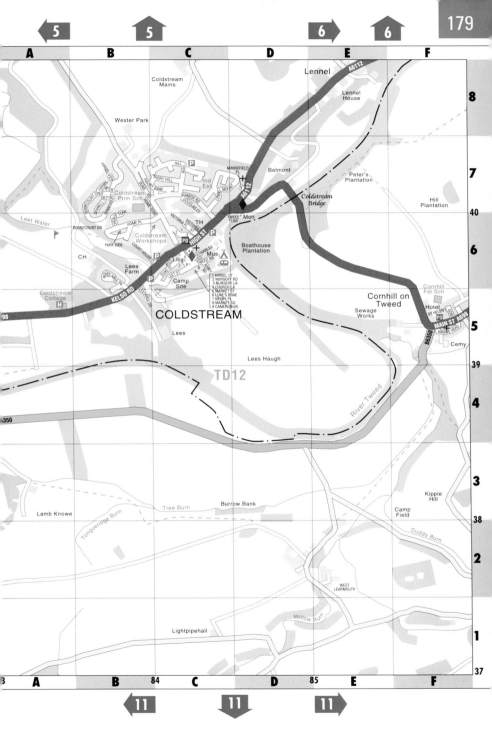

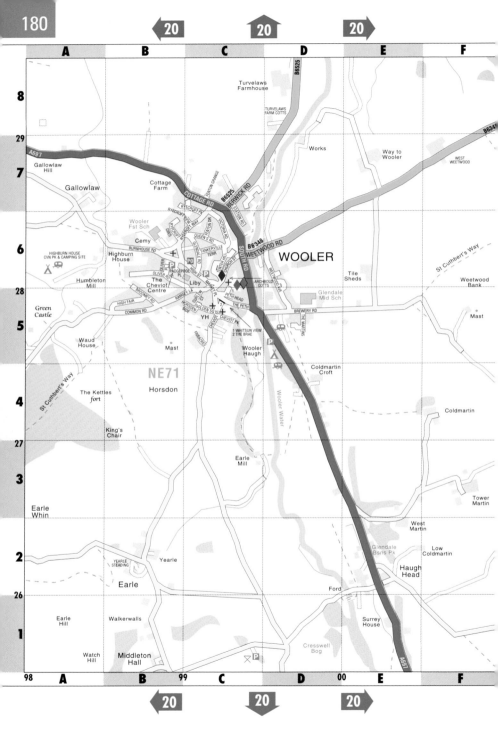

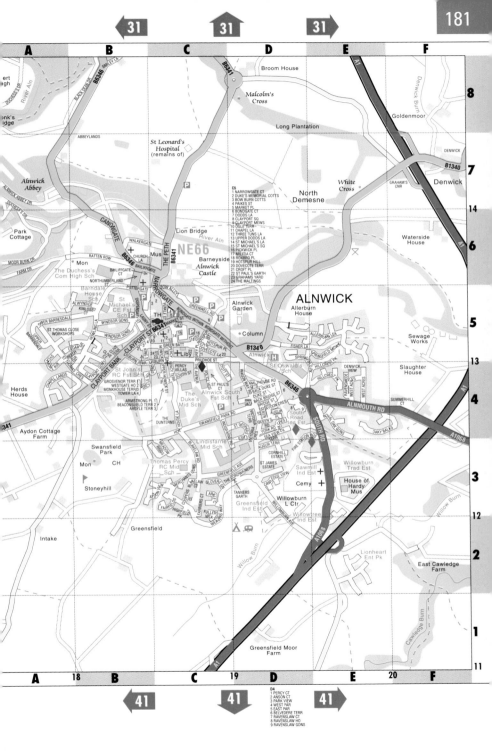

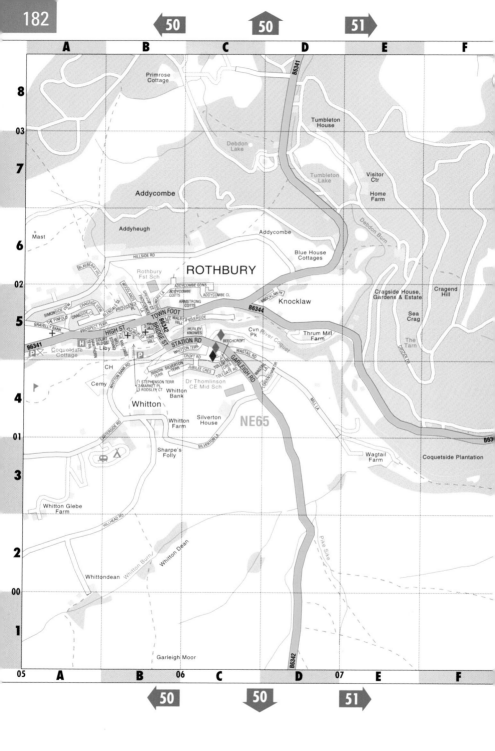

A B C D E F

8
7
05
6
05
5
04
4
3
03
2
1
02

Old Helsay
Castles Dike
Coquet View CVN PK

BEAL BANK
RIVERBANK
Beal Bank Farm
audlin

Guilders Burn

Warkworth Harbour

North Pier

North Jetty
South Jetty

The Braid
Marina
The Gut

LB Sta
OLD COASTGUARD HOS
BAY VIEW
Pan Point
GORDON VILLA
SEA VIEW
BLACKWOOD ST
ISLAND VIEW
Cemy

Gloster Hill

The Braid

Liby

Allot Gdns
MEADOWBURN

Schs
SANDY WAY

Amble Links
Wellhaugh Point

1 CHURCHILL AVE
2 STEPHENSON RD
3 COQUETDALE
4 GLENDALE CT
5 REDESDALE

Cemy
WEST DR
SCOTT ST
THE CLOSE
ACKLINGTON ST

New Hall

Mast
Amble Ind Est

NEW PARK CVN SITE

Coquet High Sch
ACKLINGTON RD

Amble Mid Sch
MARKS BRIDGE

NE65

DANDSFIELD SQ
CHEVIOTDALE

AMBLE

ETHEL'S CT
SYLVIA'S CT
SHEILA'S CT

Recn Gd

Coquet Ent Pk

High Hauxley

Hope House

Hauxley Moorhouse Farm

KIRKWELL COTTS
AIRWAY
HAUXLEY LA
Hauxley Farm

North Togston

A1068

Togston Hall

Radcliffe

C5
1 CROSS ST
2 GIBSON ST
3 BROWNS CT
4 EASTGARTH AVE
5 LAMB'S TERR
6 OSWALD ST
7 WEST CT
8 GREENFIELD TERR
9 WESTFIELD
10 WOODBINE ST
D5
1 DILSTON TERR
2 ST OSWALD'S CT
3 SECOND AVE
4 STRAFFEN CT
5 DOLPHIN CT
D6
1 CARTINGTON CT
2 HENDERSON ST
3 SMITH ST
4 OCEAN RD
5 WINDSOR TERR

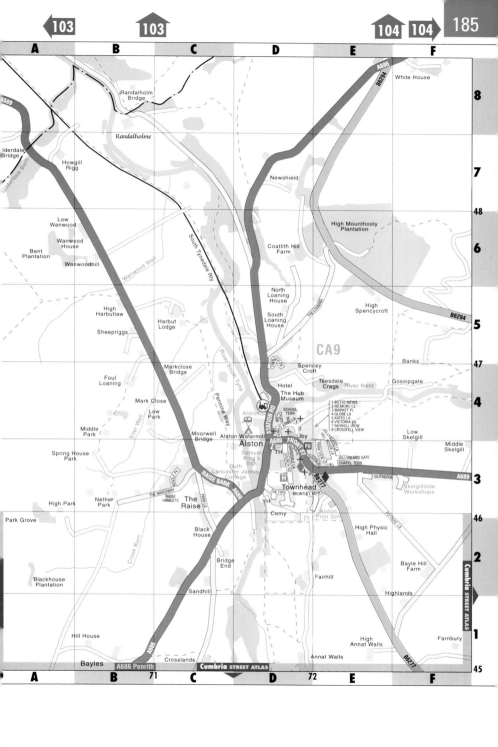

Index

Church Rd **6** Beckenham BR2......... **53** C6

Place name	**Location number**	**Locality, town or village**	**Postcode**	**Page and**
May be abbreviated on the map	Present when a number indicates the place's position in a crowded area of mapping	Shown when more than one place has the same name	**district** District for the indexed place	**grid square** Page number and grid reference for the standard mapping

Public and commercial buildings are highlighted in magenta   **Places of interest** are highlighted in blue with a star ★

Abbreviations used in the index

Acad	**Academy**	Comm	**Common**	Gd	**Ground**	L	**Leisure**	Prom	**Promenade**
App	**Approach**	Cott	**Cottage**	Gdn	**Garden**	La	**Lane**	Rd	**Road**
Arc	**Arcade**	Cres	**Crescent**	Gn	**Green**	Liby	**Library**	Recn	**Recreation**
Ave	**Avenue**	Cswy	**Causeway**	Gr	**Grove**	Mdw	**Meadow**	Ret	**Retail**
Bglw	**Bungalow**	Ct	**Court**	H	**Hall**	Meml	**Memorial**	Sh	**Shopping**
Bldg	**Building**	Ctr	**Centre**	Ho	**House**	Mkt	**Market**	Sq	**Square**
Bsns, Bus	**Business**	Ctry	**Country**	Hospl	**Hospital**	Mus	**Museum**	St	**Street**
Bvd	**Boulevard**	Cty	**County**	HQ	**Headquarters**	Orch	**Orchard**	Sta	**Station**
Cath	**Cathedral**	Dr	**Drive**	Hts	**Heights**	Pal	**Palace**	Terr	**Terrace**
Cir	**Circus**	Dro	**Drove**	Ind	**Industrial**	Par	**Parade**	TH	**Town Hall**
Cl	**Close**	Ed	**Education**	Inst	**Institute**	Pas	**Passage**	Univ	**University**
Cnr	**Corner**	Emb	**Embankment**	Int	**International**	Pk	**Park**	Wk, Wlk	**Walk**
Coll	**College**	Est	**Estate**	Intc	**Interchange**	Pl	**Place**	Wr	**Water**
Com	**Community**	Ex	**Exhibition**	Junc	**Junction**	Prec	**Precinct**	Yd	**Yard**

Index of localities, towns and villages

A

Acklington 53 C4
Acomb 91 D1
Acton 105 F6
Addison 168 F5
Akeld 19 F8
Allendale Town 97 F3
Allenheads 111 C8
Allensford 109 F5
Alnham 38 A6
Alnmouth 42 B5
Alnwick 181 E5
Alston 185 D3
Alwinton 36 F1
Amble 183 E4
Ancroft 8 D8
Anick 161 F8
Annitsford 133 B1
Ashington 117 B3
Axwell Park 169 E1
Aydon 92 E1
Ayle 103 F4

B

Backworth 143 C4
Bamburgh 17 A6
Bankfoot 152 A6
Bardon Mill 156 A6
Bar Moor Lowick 8 C1
Bar Moor Ryton 168 A5
Barrasford 91 C8
Baybridge 107 F5
Bayles 185 B1
Beaconhill Green 132 E6
Beadnell 24 C8
Bearsbridge 97 A4
Bebside 127 E7

Bedlington 122 A1
Bedlington Station ...122 B3
Belford 15 F4
Belford Station 16 B4
Bellingham 184 D4
Bell's Close 169 E6
Bellshiel 46 D2
Bellshill 16 B1
Belsay 84 F5
Beltingham 156 B4
Benfieldside 176 C5
Benton Square 143 B1
Berrington 8 D5
Berwick Hill 130 A3
Berwick-upon-Tweed ...3 D8
Biddlestone 37 D3
Bilton 41 F5
Bingfield 92 B7
Birgham 5 A2
Birtley 81 B5
Black Callerton 149 A8
Blackfyne 176 F4
Blackhall Mill 175 B7
Blackhill 176 E4
Blagdon Park 131 D6
Blagill 104 B2
Blanchland 108 A5
Blaydon 169 E3
Blaydon Burn 168 E1
Blaydon Haughs 169 D4
Bleach Green 169 C1
Blyth 128 C7
Bolam 75 E1
Bolton 39 F8
Boltshope Park 107 E2
Bomarsund 122 C6
Bothal 116 B2
Boulmer 32 D1
Bowsden 8 C4
Bradford 84 C6

Branch End 171 D7
Branton 28 F3
Branxton 12 C8
Brenkley 131 D3
Bridge End Hexham ..161 C6
Bridge End Stamfordham 136 A4
Bridge End Warden ...91 A1
Bridgehill 176 C4
Broomhaugh 100 F7
Broomhill 53 E4
Broomley 170 D5
Brownieside 23 C2
Brunswick Green 141 A5
Brunswick Village ...141 A6
Brunton 24 A3
Brunton Park 141 B1
Budle 16 E5
Burnfoot 95 A7
Burnmouth 1 A7
Burnstones 95 B1
Burradon 142 C6
Burtree Ford 111 B3
Byrness 45 E5
Bywell 170 F8

C

Callaly 39 A4
Callerton 149 B6
Callerton Lane End ...148 E7
Cambo 74 D4
Camboois 123 C5
Camperdown 142 C5
Capheaton 83 E7
Carham 5 B1
Carrshield 105 C2
Carterway Heads 109 C6
Castleside 109 F3
Catton 97 E4

Causey Park Bridge ...64 F5
Charlton 70 F4
Chathill 23 E5
Chatton 21 D7
Chesterhope 72 D4
Chesterwood 157 D7
Cheswick 4 D1
Chillingham 21 D5
Chollerford 91 B5
Chollerton 91 D6
Choppington 121 E5
Chopwell 173 B1
Christon Bank 24 A1
Clara Vale 167 E6
Clennell 36 F2
Clifton 120 B2
Coalburns 173 D7
Coalcleugh 110 C8
Coanwood 95 C5
Coldstream 179 C5
Collingwood 133 B4
Colwell 82 C2
Consett 176 D3
Copthill 111 B3
Corbridge 163 B5
Cornhill on Tweed ...179 F5
Cowpen 128 A7
Cowshill 111 B3
Cramlington 132 E5
Cramlington Village 133 B7
Craster 32 D6
Crawcrook 167 E4
Cresswell 113 A7
Crookhall 177 B2
Crookham 7 A1
Crookhill 168 D5
Cross Bank 153 B3
Cullercoats 145 D3

D

Dalton Eachwick 13
Dalton Whitley Chapel ...9
Darras Hall 13
Denton Burn 16
Denwick 18
Detchant ....
Dilston 16
Dinnington 14
Dipton Mill 9
Dirt Pot 10
Doddington ....
Donaldson's Lodge ...
Donkleywood 6
Duddo ....
Dudley 14
Dukesfield 9
Dunstan 3
Dunterley 7

E

Eachwick 13
Eals 9
Earle 18
Earsdon ....
East Cramlington 13
Eastfield 13
East Hartford 12
East Holywell 14
East Horton ....
East Lilburn ....
East Ord ....
East Sleekburn 12
East Woodburn 3
Ebchester 17
Edges Green ....
Edlingham ....

A

A J Cook Ct NE63 . . . . .117 C3
Abbey Cl NE25 . . . . .144 D4
Abbey Ct **5** NE46 . . . . .161 B5
Abbey Dr NE5 . . . . .149 B4
Abbey Gate NE61 . . . . .119 D7
Abbey Mdws NE61 . . . . .119 D7
Abbey Rd TD12 . . . . .179 C6
Abbey Terr
  7 Morpeth NE61 . . . . .114 F1
  Shiremoor NE27 . . . . .143 E3
Abbey View
  Hexham NE46 . . . . .161 C4
  18 Morpeth NE61 . . . . .114 F1
Abbeyfields Fst Sch
  NE61 . . . . .119 E8
Abbeylands NE61 . . . . .181 B7
Abbie Ct NE24 . . . . .128 D7
Abbot's Way NE25 . . . . .119 E8
Abbots Cl NE62 . . . . .122 B8
Abbots Way NE29 . . . . .144 D1
Abbotsford Ho NE24 . . . . .128 C6
Abbotsford Pk NE25 . . . . .144 F4
Abbotside Pl NE5 . . . . .149 D2
Aberford Cl NE5 . . . . .149 B3
Abingdon Ct NE21 . . . . .169 C3
Abingdon Sq NE23 . . . . .127 C1
Acacia Terr NE63 . . . . .117 D3
Acklington CE Fst Sch
  NE65 . . . . .53 C4
Acklington Dr NE63 . . . . .53 D4
Acklington Rd
  Amble NE65 . . . . .183 B4
  Togston NE65 . . . . .53 E4
Acklington St NE65 . . . . .183 C5
Acklington Sta NE65 . . . . .53 C4
Acomb Ave NE25 . . . . .134 D2
Acomb Cl NE61 . . . . .120 C5
Acomb Ct
  Bedlington NE22 . . . . .122 A1
  Killingworth NE12 . . . . .142 D3
Acomb Dr NE41 . . . . .167 A7
Acomb Fst Sch NE46 . . . . .91 D1
Acorn Ave NE22 . . . . .126 F8
Acorn Sq NE42 . . . . .166 D2
Acreford Ct NE62 . . . . .121 E6
Acton Cres NE65 . . . . .52 E4
Acton Rd NE5 . . . . .169 F8
Adams Dr TD15 . . . . .178 C1
Adams Terr DH8 . . . . .175 A2
Adamsez Ind Est NE15 . . . . .169 F4
Adderlane Fst Sch NE42 . . . . . . .166 E3
Adderlane Rd NE42 . . . . .166 E3
Adderstone Ave NE23 . . . . .133 B5
Adderstone Gdns NE29 . . . . .144 B1
Adderstone Mains Cotts
  NE70 . . . . .16 C2
Addington Dr NE24 . . . . .128 E1
Addison Ct NE40 . . . . .168 B5
Addison Ind Est NE21 . . . . .168 F5
Addison Rd NE15 . . . . .169 D7
Addycombe Ct NE65 . . . . .182 C5
Addycombe Cotts NE65 . . . . . . .182 B5
Addycombe Terr NE65 . . . . .182 C5
Adeline Ct NE49 . . . . .153 D5
Admington Ct NE63 . . . . .121 F7
Admiral Ave NE66 . . . . .28 C7
Admiral Collingwood Ct **5**
  NE61 . . . . .120 A8
Aesica Rd NE49 . . . . .153 D5
Aged Miner's Cotts
  NE43 . . . . .171 F8
Aged Miners Cotts
  NE42 . . . . .166 B1
Aged Miners Homes
  Blyth NE24 . . . . .128 B5
  Broomhill NE65 . . . . .53 F3
  Cambois NE24 . . . . .123 D4
  Newbiggin-by-t-S NE64 . . . . . . .118 D3
  1 Newsham NE24 . . . . .149 E3
Aged Miners' Homes
  Annitsford NE23 . . . . .133 B1
  Ashington NE63 . . . . .117 A4
  Ashington,Woodbridge
  NE63 . . . . .117 F5
  Brunswick Village NE13 . . . . . . .141 A6
  Cramlington NE23 . . . . .132 F7
  Dudley NE23 . . . . .134 E6
  New Hartley NE25 . . . . .134 C6
  Ryton NE40 . . . . .168 E4
  Shiremoor NE27 . . . . .143 F3
  Stakeford NE62 . . . . .122 C8
Aged Mineworkers Homes
  Longhirst NE61 . . . . .116 B7
  Throckley NE15 . . . . .148 B2
  6 Widdrington Sta NE61 . . . .65 E5
Agincourt NE12 . . . . .142 D4
Aidan Ave NE26 . . . . .135 B6
Aidan Cl
  Brunswick Village NE13 . . . . . . .141 A6
  Cramlington NE27 . . . . .143 C1
Aidan Gr NE61 . . . . .112 E4
Aidan Rd NE63 . . . . .183 C5
Ainderby Rd NE15 . . . . .148 B2
Ainsdale Gdns NE15 . . . . .149 C2
Aintree Cl NE63 . . . . .117 C2
Aintree Dr DH8 . . . . .176 D7
Airport Freightway
  NE13 . . . . .139 E2
Airport Sta NE13 . . . . .139 E2
Aisgill Cl NE23 . . . . .133 B6
Aisgill Dr NE15 . . . . .149 C1

Akeld Cl NE23 . . . . .133 B5
Akeld Cotts NE71 . . . . .19 F8
Albany Gdns **2** NE26 . . . . . . .145 B4
Albatross Way NE24 . . . . .128 E3
Albert Pl **8** TD15 . . . . .178 B5
Albert Rd
  Bedlington NE22 . . . . .122 E2
  Consett DH8 . . . . .176 F2
  Seaton Sluice NE26 . . . . .135 D6
  Spittal TD15 . . . . .178 D1
Albert St Amble NE65 . . . . .183 C5
  Blyth NE24 . . . . .128 E8
Albert Terr
  Longbenton NE12 . . . . .142 C1
  6 Whitley Bay NE26 . . . . . . .145 B4
Albion Cl NE65 . . . . .53 E8
Albion Ret Ctr NE24 . . . . .128 D8
Albion Terr
  Hexham NE46 . . . . .161 A5
  Lynemouth NE61 . . . . .113 A3
Albion Way Blyth NE24 . . . . .128 C7
  Cramlington NE23 . . . . .127 D1
Alcester Cl NE42 . . . . .121 F7
Alconbury Cl NE24 . . . . .128 E1
Alcroft Cl NE5 . . . . .149 B3
Aldborough St NE24 . . . . .128 E7
Aldeburgh Ave NE15 . . . . .169 C8
Aldenham Gdns NE30 . . . . .145 C1
Alder Cl NE61 . . . . .120 A8
Alder Ct NE25 . . . . .128 E4
Alder Gr Leadgate DH8 . . . . .177 D3
  Whitley Bay NE25 . . . . .144 E6
Alder Way NE12 . . . . .142 C4
Alderbush Ct **10** TD15 . . . . . .3 B6
Alderley Dr NE12 . . . . .142 F4
Alderley Way NE23 . . . . .127 D1
Alderney Gdns NE5 . . . . .149 C2
Alderton Ct NE62 . . . . .121 F7
Alderwood NE63 . . . . .117 C2
Aldwick Rd NE15 . . . . .169 F6
Alemouth Rd NE46 . . . . .161 B5
Alexander Pl **12** NE46 . . . . . . .161 A5
Alexander Terr NE13 . . . . .141 A5
Alexandra Cres NE46 . . . . .160 F5
Alexandra Gdns NE40 . . . . .168 F4
Alexandra Rd
  Ashington NE63 . . . . .117 F3
  Morpeth NE61 . . . . .120 A8
Alexandra St **11** DH8 . . . . . . .176 F2
Alexandra Terr
  Bedlington NE22 . . . . .122 B1
  Haydon Bridge NE47 . . . . .158 A6
  Hexham NE46 . . . . .160 F5
  Stocksfield NE43 . . . . .171 D7
  4 Whitley Bay NE26 . . . . . . .145 B4
Alexandra Way NE23 . . . . .133 B5
Alfred Ave NE22 . . . . .122 B1
Alfred St NE24 . . . . .128 E6
Algernon Cl NE66 . . . . .167 F5
Algernon Ind Est NE27 . . . . .143 F1
Algernon Pl NE26 . . . . .145 B4
Algernon Rd NE15 . . . . .169 C6
Algernon Terr NE41 . . . . .167 A6
Alice St NE21 . . . . .169 B1
All Saints Coll NE5 . . . . .149 E2
Allan Rd NE64 . . . . .118 D5
Allanville NE12 . . . . .142 C5
Allchurch Dr NE63 . . . . .118 A3
Allen Banks Nature Reserve*
  NE47 . . . . .156 D3
Allen Dr NE46 . . . . .161 B4
Allen Mill Cotts NE47 . . . . .97 F3
Allen Terr NE40 . . . . .167 F4
Allen View NE47 . . . . .97 F4
Allendale Cres
  Shiremoor NE27 . . . . .144 A3
  Stakeford NE62 . . . . .117 A1
Allendale Dr NE47 . . . . .98 A3
Allendale Mid Sch NE47 . . . . . . .98 A2
Allendale Rd Blyth NE24 . . . . . . .128 F2
  Hexham NE46 . . . . .160 F4
Allenfields NE47 . . . . .97 F2
Allenheads
  Newcastle u T NE5 . . . . .149 E1
  Seaton Delaval NE25 . . . . .149 E1
Allenheads Contemporary
  Arts NE47 . . . . .111 C8
Allenheads Heritage Ctr*
  NE47 . . . . .111 B8
Allensford Bank DH8 . . . . .109 F4
Allensgreen NE23 . . . . .133 B6
Allerburn Lea NE66 . . . . .181 E5
Allerdean Cl
  Newcastle u T NE15 . . . . .169 B7
  Seaton Delaval NE25 . . . . .149 E1
Allerhope NE23 . . . . .133 B5
Allerwash NE5 . . . . .149 E1
Allery Banks NE61 . . . . .120 A8
Allgood Terr NE22 . . . . .122 B1
Allison Gdns DH8 . . . . .176 F4
Allison St Amble NE65 . . . . .183 C5
  Consett DH8 . . . . .176 F4
Allonby Mews NE23 . . . . .127 D2
Alma Pl **8** Morpeth NE61 . . . .120 A8
  Whitley Bay NE25 . . . . .145 C4
Almond Ave NE40 . . . . .168 C2
Almond Cr NE24 . . . . .128 C4
Almshouses NE15 . . . . .168 F7
Aln Ct Ellington NE61 . . . . .65 C6
  Newcastle u T NE15 . . . . .169 C6
Aln Gr NE15 . . . . .169 C6
Aln St NE63 . . . . .117 F5
Alnham Ct NE3 . . . . .183 E5
Alnham Gr NE5 . . . . .149 C2
Alnmouth Rd NE66 . . . . .181 E4
Alnmouth Sta NE66 . . . . .42 A6
Alnmouth Terr NE66 . . . . .160 F8
Alnside NE66 . . . . .39 C7

Alnside Cl NE66 . . . . .42 A6
Alnwick Abbey* NE66 . . . . .181 A7
Alnwick Abbey Dr NE66 . . . . . . .181 A7
Alnwick Ave NE26 . . . . .145 A5
Alnwick Castle* NE66 . . . . .181 C6
Alnwick Ct NE22 . . . . .121 D2
Alnwick Fords
  Longframlington NE65 . . . . .51 F6
  Swarland NE65 . . . . .52 A7
Alnwick Gdn* NE66 . . . . .181 D5
Alnwick Infmy NE66 . . . . .181 D5
Alnwick South Fst Sch
  NE66 . . . . .181 C4
Alnwick St NE15 . . . . .168 F8
Alnwick Terr NE13 . . . . .141 C7
Alnwood **3** NE66 . . . . .42 B5
Alresford NE12 . . . . .142 A3
Alston Ave NE23 . . . . .133 D5
Alston Gdns NE15 . . . . .148 B2
Alston Gr NE26 . . . . .135 B7
Alston Prim Sch CA9 . . . . .185 E3
Alston Rd Consett DH8 . . . . .176 C4
  New Hartley NE25 . . . . .134 D6
Alston Sta CA9 . . . . .185 D4
Alston Terr DH8 . . . . .176 C4
Alston Watermill* CA9 . . . . .185 D4
Alstone Ct NE62 . . . . .121 F7
Alston Ct NE61 . . . . .120 E5
Alverston Cl NE62 . . . . .169 C8
Alveston Cl NE62 . . . . .121 F7
Alwinton Cl NE24 . . . . .128 C8
Alwinton Ct NE24 . . . . .144 A3
Alwinton Sq **5** NE63 . . . . . . .117 F2
Alwyn Gdns DH8 . . . . .176 E1
Alwynside NE61 . . . . .181 B5
Amber Ct NE24 . . . . .128 C6
Amberley Chase NE12 . . . . .142 E4
Amberley Prim Sch
  NE12 . . . . .142 E4
Amberley Way NE24 . . . . .128 E5
Amble Ave NE25 . . . . .145 B4
Amble Cl NE24 . . . . .128 C5
Amble Fst Sch NE65 . . . . .183 C5
Amble Ind Est NE65 . . . . .183 D4
Amble Links Fst Sch
  NE65 . . . . .183 C5
Amble Mid Sch NE65 . . . . .183 C4
Amble Pl NE12 . . . . .142 F1
Ambleside NE15 . . . . .148 E8
Ambleside Cl NE25 . . . . .134 D3
Ambleside Mews DH8 . . . . .177 D4
Ambridge Way NE25 . . . . .134 A4
Ambrose Ct NE21 . . . . .169 A1
Amersham Rd NE24 . . . . .128 E4
Amesbury Cl NE15 . . . . .149 B3
Ancroft Pl NE63 . . . . .117 F1
Ancroft Rd NE25 . . . . .134 B3
Ancroft Town Farm TD15 . . . . . . .8 C8
Anderson Cres NE65 . . . . .183 E5
Andrew Dr NE65 . . . . .183 E5
Angelica Cl DH8 . . . . .177 A2
Angerton Ave
  Shiremoor NE27 . . . . .143 F2
  Tynemouth NE30 . . . . .145 A1
Angerton Terr NE23 . . . . .141 F8
Anglesey Gdns NE5 . . . . .149 C1
Angram Wlk **1** NE5 . . . . .149 C1
Angus Cl NE12 . . . . .142 C2
Ann St Blaydon NE21 . . . . .169 A1
  2 Consett DH8 . . . . .176 F2
  Shiremoor NE27 . . . . .143 E4
Ann's Row NE24 . . . . .123 E1
Annaside Mews DH8 . . . . .177 D4
Anne Cres NE65 . . . . .183 E5
Annfield Rd NE23 . . . . .127 B2
Annitsford Dr NE23 . . . . .142 B8
Annitsford Rd NE23 . . . . .133 E1
Anson Ct **2** NE66 . . . . .181 D4
Anson Pl NE5 . . . . .149 F3
Anstead Cl NE23 . . . . .133 B6
Anton Pl NE23 . . . . .133 B5
Antonine Wlk NE15 . . . . .147 F2
Anvil Ct DH8 . . . . .176 B3
Apex Bsns Village NE23 . . . . . . .133 B1
Apperley NE5 . . . . .149 E1
Apperley Rd NE43 . . . . .171 C6
Appian Pl NE15 . . . . .148 E2
Apple Cl NE15 . . . . .134 C8
Appledore Cl NE40 . . . . .139 F4
Appledore Rd NE24 . . . . .128 E5
Appletree Bank NE47 . . . . .97 C4
Appletree Dr NE42 . . . . .166 D3
Appletree Gardens Fst Sch
  NE25 . . . . .144 E3
Appletree Gdns NE25 . . . . .144 E3
Appletree La NE45 . . . . .163 A5
Appletree Rise NE45 . . . . .163 A5
Applewood NE12 . . . . .142 F3
Aqua Terr NE64 . . . . .118 D4
Aquila Dr NE15 . . . . .147 E2
Arcade The NE20 . . . . .84 F5
Arcadia Terr NE24 . . . . .128 E6
Archbold Cotts NE71 . . . . .180 C6
Arcot Ave
  Cramlington NE23 . . . . .132 E8
  Whitley Bay NE25 . . . . .144 E3
Arcot Dr
  Newcastle u T NE5 . . . . .137 E1
  Whitley Bay NE25 . . . . .144 E3
Arcot Terr **5** NE24 . . . . .128 E8
Arden Ave NE3 . . . . .141 B1
Arden Rd NE24 . . . . .123 C1
Argyle St
  10 Alnmouth NE66 . . . . .42 B5
  Blyth NE24 . . . . .128 E8
Argyle Terr Alnwick NE66 . . . . . .181 C4
  Hexham NE46 . . . . .161 B4

Argyle Terr continued
  Newbiggin-by-t-S NE64 . . . . . . .118 D4
Ariel St NE63 . . . . .117 E3
Arkle Ct NE66 . . . . .181 C3
Arkle St NE13 . . . . .141 A4
Arkleside Pl NE5 . . . . .149 D1
Arlington Gr NE23 . . . . .127 B2
Armondside Rd NE17 . . . . .175 C6
Armstrong Cl NE46 . . . . .160 F3
Armstrong Cotts
  Bamburgh NE69 . . . . .17 B5
  Rothbury NE65 . . . . .182 C5
Armstrong Ct
  West Woodburn NE48 . . . . .72 D3
  Woolsington NE5 . . . . .149 B7
Armstrong Terr NE61 . . . . .120 A8
Arncliffe Gdns NE5 . . . . .149 C2
Arnison Cl NE47 . . . . .97 F2
Arnison Terr NE47 . . . . .97 F2
Arnside Wlk NE5 . . . . .149 C2
Arrow Cl NE12 . . . . .142 B2
Arthur St **1** NE62 . . . . .128 E8
Arundel Cl
  Bedlington NE22 . . . . .122 C3
  Brunswick Village NE13 . . . . . . .141 A5
Arundel Dr
  Newcastle u T NE15 . . . . .169 E7
  Whitley Bay NE25 . . . . .144 E3
Arundel Sq NE63 . . . . .117 C3
Ascot Gr NE63 . . . . .117 D2
Ascot Rd DH8 . . . . .176 F7
Ash Ave NE13 . . . . .140 C7
Ash Banks NE61 . . . . .120 A7
Ash Cl NE46 . . . . .160 E3
Ash Gr NE29 . . . . .145 A7
Ash Gr Morpeth NE61 . . . . .119 E7
  Ryton NE40 . . . . .168 C6
Ash St Blaydon NE21 . . . . .169 C1
  Consett DH8 . . . . .176 F2
  Mickley Square NE43 . . . . .171 F8
Ash Terr DH8 . . . . .177 D4
Ash Tree Dr NE22 . . . . .121 F2
Ashbourne Cl NE27 . . . . .143 C5
Ashbourne Cres NE23 . . . . .117 C3
Ashbrooke NE25 . . . . .144 E5
Ashbrooke Dr NE20 . . . . .128 E7
Ashbury NE25 . . . . .144 C6
Ashby Cres DH8 . . . . .176 D5
Ashby La DH8 . . . . .176 D4
Ashcroft Terr NE49 . . . . .153 E5
Ashdale NE20 . . . . .138 C3
Ashdale Cres NE5 . . . . .149 D1
Ashdale Rd DH8 . . . . .177 A3
Ashfield DH8 . . . . .176 D6
Ashfield Ct NE12 . . . . .142 E1
Ashfield Gr NE26 . . . . .145 A7
Ashfield Terr
  Ryton NE40 . . . . .168 C5
  Shilbottle NE66 . . . . .41 D3
Ashford Cl Blyth NE24 . . . . .128 E5
  1 Tynemouth NE29 . . . . .144 F1
Ashford Gr NE5 . . . . .149 B4
Ashington Alexandra Fst Sch
  NE63 . . . . .117 F3
Ashington Alexandra Mid Sch
  NE63 . . . . .117 F4
Ashington Central Fst Sch
  NE63 . . . . .117 E3
Ashington Com High Sch
  NE63 . . . . .117 E3
Ashington Dr NE62 . . . . .122 A8
Ashington Hirst Park Mid Sch
  NE63 . . . . .117 E3
Ashington Hospl NE63 . . . . .117 C3
Ashington Mews NE63 . . . . .121 F7
Ashington Rd NE61 . . . . .112 D4
Ashington Wansbeck Bsns Ctr
  NE63 . . . . .117 A4
Ashkirk NE23 . . . . .142 A8
Ashkirk Way NE25 . . . . .134 D2
Ashleigh Cl NE21 . . . . .169 E1
Ashleigh Rd NE15 . . . . .169 E8
Ashley Cl NE12 . . . . .142 F4
Ashley Gdns NE62 . . . . .122 A8
Ashmead Cl NE12 . . . . .142 B2
Asholme NE5 . . . . .149 E1
Ashton Cl NE15 . . . . .149 B4
Ashton Gr NE10 . . . . .168 D4
Ashton Way NE26 . . . . .144 E7
Ashtree Gdns NE25 . . . . .144 E5
Ashwood Cl NE23 . . . . .132 E8
Ashwood Gr NE13 . . . . .141 B5
Ashwood Rd NE40 . . . . .161 C4
Ashwood Terr NE40 . . . . .167 F1
Askew Cres TD15 . . . . .178 B2
Askrigg Wlk **2** NE5 . . . . .149 C1
Aspen Ct DH8 . . . . .176 E4
Aspen Way NE24 . . . . .128 D4
Astley Com High Sch
  NE25 . . . . .134 C3
Astley Ct NE12 . . . . .142 D3
Astley Dr NE26 . . . . .144 E8
Astley Gdns
  Seaton Delaval NE25 . . . . .134 C3
  Seaton Sluice NE26 . . . . .135 B7
Astley Gr NE26 . . . . .135 B7
Astley Rd NE25 . . . . .134 D3
Astley St NE65 . . . . .127 B3
Astley Villas NE26 . . . . .135 B7
Athlone Ct **11** NE24 . . . . .128 E8
Athol Gdns NE20 . . . . .144 D3
Athol Ho NE20 . . . . .138 F6

Atkin St NE12 142
Atkinson House Sch
  NE23 133
Atley Way NE23 126
Attlee Cl NE23 142
Attlee Terr NE64 118
Auburn Pl NE61 119
Audland Wlk **3** NE5 149
Augur Pl NE66 181
Augur Terr NE66 181
Augusta Cl NE13 181
Augustus Dr NE22 121
Austral Pl NE13 141
Austwick Wlk **4** NE5 149
Ava Lodge TD15 178
Avalon Dr NE15 169
Avebury Ave NE62 122
Avebury Pl NE23 127
Avenue Cres NE25 134
Avenue Rd Ellingham NE12 134
Avenue Terr NE61 . . . . .120 A8
Avenue St Meen NE49 153
Avenue Terr NE25 134
Avenue The
  Alnwick NE66 181
  Berwick-u-T TD15 178
  Blaydon NE21 169
  Callaly NE66 39
  Consett DH8 177
  Corbridge NE45 162
  Ellingham NE66,NE67 23
  Medburn NE20 119
  Morpeth NE61 119
  Rock NE66 31
  Seaton Delaval NE25,NE26 134
  Seaton Sluice NE26 135
  Swarland NE65 52
  Whitley Bay NE25 145
Avis Ave NE64 145
Avocet Cl NE24 128
Avon Ct NE25 134
Avondale Ave NE24 127
Avondale Cl **1** NE24 127
Avondale Gdns NE63 118
Avondale Rd
  2 Consett DH8 176
  Ponteland NE20 138
Axbridge Cl NE62 122
Axford Terr NE17 175
Axminster Cl NE23 127
Axwell Dr NE24 128
Axwell Park Cl NE12 142
Axwell Park Rd NE21 169
Axwell View NE21 169
Aydon Ave NE65 163
Aydon Castle* NE45 92
Aydon Cl NE30 145
Aydon Cres
  Alnwick NE66 181
  Corbridge NE45 163
Aydon Dr NE45 163
Aydon Gdns NE45 163
Aydon Gr NE45 163
Aydon Rd NE45 163
Aydon Rd Est NE45 163
Aydon View NE66 181
Aydon Way NE45 163
Aydon Wlk NE5 149
Aylesford Sq NE24 128
Aylsham Cl NE5 149
Aynsley Terr DH8 176
Ayton Cl
  Newcastle u T NE15 149
  Stocksfield NE43 171
Ayton Ct NE22 121
Azalea Way NE15 168

B

Back Bridge St NE66 181
Back Croft Rd NE22 128
Back Dr NE48 59
Back Duke St NE66 181
Back East Par DH8 177
Back Grangewood Terr
  NE61 65
Back La Blaydon NE21 169
  Leadgate DH8 177
  Whitley Bay NE25 144
Back Mowbray Terr
  NE62 122
Back Palmerston St
  DH8 176
Back Riggs **10** NE61 114
Back Row NE45 163
Back St NE21 169
Backstone Burn DH8 176
Backstone Rd DH8 176
Backworth Bsns Pk
  NE27 143
Backworth La NE23 142
Backworth Park Prim Sch
  NE27 143
Backworth Terr NE27 143
Bader Cres NE63 118
Bader Ct NE24 128
Badgers Gn NE61 114
Bailey Green Prim Sch
  NE12 142
Bailiffgate NE66 181
Bailiffgate Ct NE66 181
Bailiffgate Mus* NE66 181
Bainbridge La NE65 182
Baker Rd NE23 128
Baker St NE22 177
Bale Hill DH8 108

four Gdns [4] DH8 ....176 F4
four St [2] Blyth NE24 .128 D8
  nsett DH8 ....176 F4
four Terr NE17 .....173 B1
igonie Cotts NE40 ..168 C5
iol Rd NE43 ....171 D7
last Hill NE24 ....128 F8
lliol Ave NE24 ......142 C1
moral Ct NE22 .....122 C2
moral Gdns NE26 ..144 F6
moral Gr DH8 ....177 A4
moral Way NE24 ...128 C8
mborough St NE23 .142 A8
mburgh Castle* NE69 .17 B6
mburgh Ct NE28 ....128 C7
mburgh Cres NE27 ..143 F3
mburgh Ct NE47 ......23 E5
mburgh Dr NE61 ...115 F3
mburgh Ho NE5 ....149 E3
mburgh Rd
  mgbenton NE12 ....142 F1
  ewcastle u T NE5 .149 E3
mburgh Terr NE63 ..117 C3
mford Terr NE12 .....142 F1
nbury Way NE24 ...128 E5
nk Cotts NE61 ....85 C8
nk Ct NE21 ....169 F4
nk Head NE46 ......161 B5
nk Hill TD15 ....178 B4
nk House Cotts NE65 .53 B8
nk House Farm NE65 .53 B8
nk Top
  nillingham NE66 ....21 D5
  awcrook NE40 .....167 E3
  eenside NE40 .....168 B3
  nemouth NE30 ....145 C3
nk Top Flats NE61 ...53 F2
nk's Terr NE43 .....153 C5
nk's Terrace (Back)
  E49 ....153 C5
nkdale Gdns NE24 ..128 A7
nkfoot NE19 ....59 F3
nkhead Rd NE15 ...148 F1
nkside NE61 ....120 A8
nkside Rd NE15 ....169 F5
nkside Wlk NE62 ...122 B8
nnister Dr NE12 ....143 A1
nnockburn NE12 ...142 C4
rbondale Lonnen
  E5 ....149 C2
rdon Cl NE5 ....149 F4
rdon Cres NE34 ....134 F2
rdon Mill Sta NE47 ..155 F5
relees Farm Cotts TD12 .6 C1
rents Cl [2] NE5 ...149 F2
rley Mill Cres DH8 ..176 B4
rley Mill Rd DH8 ....176 B4
rlow La NE21 ......168 F1
rmoor Bank NE61 ..120 D5
rmoor Dr NE3 .....141 A2
rmoor La NE40 ....168 B5
rmoor Pl NE40 ....168 B5
rmoor Terr NE40 ..168 A5
rnard Cl NE22 .....121 E1
rnard St NE24 .....128 E7
rndale House Sch
  E66 ....181 B5
rney's Cut NE48 ....55 E1
rns Rd Felton NE65 ..52 E3
  Parkworth NE65 ...52 E3
rnstaple Rd NE29 ..144 D1
rnston NE63 ....118 B3
rr Hills [6] DH8 ....176 F3
rr House Ave DH8 ..176 F3
rras Ave
  nnitsford NE23 ....133 B1
rras Gdns NE23 ....133 B1
rras Ave W NE24 ..128 D5
rras Gdns NE23 ....133 B1
rrasford Cl NE23 ...117 A2
rrasford Dr NE13 ..141 C5
rrasford Rd NE23 ..133 B1
rrass Ave NE23 ....133 F1
rrington Ave NE30 .144 F2
rrington Ind Est
  E22 ....122 A4
rrington Pk NE22 ..122 F3
rrington Rd NE22 ..122 B3
rrowburn Pl NE23 ..134 A1
rton Cl NE30 ......145 B1
ssington Ave NE23 .132 E7
ssington Dr NE23 ..132 E8
ssington Ind Est
  E23 ....132 D8
ssington La NE23 ..132 D8
st House Rd NE43 .171 E6
tes La NE21 ....169 F2
teys Terr NE47 .....97 E4
th La Blyth NE24 ..128 F7
  onsett DH8 ....176 F3
th Terr NE24 ......128 F7
ttle Hill NE46 ......161 B4
vington Gdns NE30 .145 B1
vington Rd NE25 ..134 D2
xter Pl NE25 ......134 D3
xter's Bldgs NE25 .134 D3
xton Cotts DH8 ....176 C4
y Terr TD15 ....178 C4
y View NE65 ......183 E2
y View E NE64 .....118 E5
y View W NE64 ....118 E5
ybridge Rd NE5 ...149 E3
aytree Gdns NE25 .144 F3
each Ave NE26 ....145 A5
each Croft Ave NE30 .145 B1
each Rd NE30 ......145 B1

Beach Terr NE64 .....118 D3
Beach View NE66 .....42 D8
Beach Way NE30 ....145 A1
Beachborough Cl [6]
  NE29 ....144 F1
Beachway NE24 .....129 A4
Beacon Ct NE13 ....141 A5
Beacon Dr NE13 ....141 A5
Beacon Ho [4] NE26 .144 F8
Beacon La NE23 .....132 E6
Beacon Rd NE65 .....41 A2
Beaconsfield Cl NE25 .144 D7
Beaconsfield St
  Blyth NE24 ....128 F7
  [2] Consett DH8 ...176 F4
Beaconsfield Terr
  Alnwick NE66 .....181 C4
  Chopwell NE17 ....173 B1
Beadnell Gdns NE27 .143 F3
Beadnell Hall NE67 ...24 D8
Beadnell Rd NE24 ..128 B5
Beal Bank NE65 .....53 E8
Beal Cl NE24 ....128 C7
Beal Croft NE65 .....53 E8
Beal Dr NE12 ....142 F1
Beal Rd NE27 ....143 F3
Beamish Ct NE25 ...144 E3
Beamsley Terr NE63 .117 D3
Beanley NE66 ....29 D5
Beanley Ave NE15 .169 C6
Bearl Farm Cotts NE43 .165 B5
Bearl View NE43 ....171 E8
Beatrice Ave NE24 ..128 B4
Beatrice St NE63 ...117 E4
Beatty Rd NE22 .....72 B8
Beaufront Ave NE46 .161 D4
Beaufront Castle Flats
  NE46 ....162 A8
Beaufront Ho NE46 ..91 F1
Beaufront Wood Head Cotts
  NE46 ....91 F1
Beaumont Ct NE25 .144 D6
Beaumont Dr NE25 .144 D7
Beaumont Manor NE24 .127 F7
Beaumont St Blyth NE24 .128 D8
  Hexham NE46 .....161 B5
Beaumont Terr
  Brunswick Village NE13 .141 A6
  Newcastle u T NE3 .149 F3
  Prudhoe NE42 ....166 C2
Beaumont Way NE42 .166 B1
Bebdon Ct NE24 ....127 A2
Bebside Furnace Rd
  NE24 ....127 D8
Bebside Mid Sch NE24 .127 F8
Bebside Rd NE24 ...127 C7
Beckside Gdns NE24 .127 A3
Beda Hill NE61 .....169 C3
Bedale Dr NE25 ....144 F3
Bede Ave TD15 .....178 A7
Bede Cl NE30 ......145 C3
Bede St NE65 ......183 C5
Bedeburn Foot NE5 .149 F5
Bedeburn Rd NE5 ..149 F5
Bedford Pl NE5 .....149 C1
Bedlington Bank NE22,
  NE24 ....127 A2
Bedlington West End Fst Sch
  NE22 ....121 E1
Bedlingtonshire Com High
  Sch NE22 ....122 D2
Beech Ave
  Cramlington NE23 .133 D5
  Dinnington NE13 ..140 B7
  Hexham NE46 .....160 E5
  Morpeth NE61 ....120 C7
Beech Cl NE13 .....141 A6
Beech Croft [3] NE68 ..17 F2
Beech Ct Ponteland NE20 .138 A1
  [5] Widdrington NE61 ..65 E5
Beech Dr Alnwick NE66 ..30 C1
  Corbridge NE45 ...161 A6
  Ellington NE61 ....112 D5
Beech Est NE61 .....41 D3
Beech Gr Alnwick NE66 .181 B5
  Bedlington NE22 ..122 A1
  Blackhall Mill NE17 .175 B6
  Haltwhistle NE49 .153 C5
  Prudhoe NE42 ....166 B2
  Whitley Bay NE26 .144 F5
Beech Gr S NE42 ...166 B2
Beech Grove Est NE40 .167 F4
Beech Grove Terr NE40 .167 F4
Beech Grove Terr S
  NE40 ....167 F4
Beech Hill NE46 ...160 E5
Beech Hill Prim Sch
  NE5 ....149 F2
Beech St DH8 ......177 D3
Beech Terr
  Ashington NE63 ..117 E2
  Bedlington NE22 ..169 C2
Beech Tree Cl NE65 ..51 F3
Beech Way NE12 ..142 C4
Beechcroft
  Chollerford NE46 ...91 B5
  Rothbury NE65 ....182 C4
  Swarland NE65 .....52 C6
Beechdale Rd DH8 ..177 A3
Beecher St NE24 ..128 B8
Beeches The
  Ponteland NE20 ..138 D6
  Stannington NE61 .125 C4
Beechlea NE63 .....125 C3
Beechway NE63 ....118 A3

Beechwood Ave
  Ryton NE40 ....168 C5
  Stakeford NE62 ...122 A8
  Whitley Bay NE25 .144 D4
Beechwood Pl NE20 .138 E7
Belford Ave NE27 ...143 F3
Belford Mid Sch NE70 ..15 F4
Belford Inst Est NE70 ..16 A4
Belford Mid Sch NE70 ..15 F4
Belgrave Cres NE24 .128 F6
Belgrave Gdns NE63 .118 A2
Bell Cl NE23 ....117 A2
Bell Rd [4] Belford NE70 ..15 F4
  Wylam NE41 ....167 B6
Bell Tower Pk TD15 .178 B5
Bell Tower Pl [1] TD15 .178 B5
Bell View NE42 ....166 F3
Bell Villas NE20 ....138 F6
Bell's Cotts NE40 ..168 A1
Bell's Hill NE61 ....124 D3
Bell's Pl NE22 ......127 A8
Bellburn Ct NE23 ..133 D8
Belle Vue NE39 ....173 F5
Belle Vue Gdns
  Alnwick NE66 .....181 C4
  [2] Consett DH8 ..176 F3
Belle Vue St NE30 .145 C3
Belle Vue Terr NE40 .167 F4
Bellevue Cres NE23 .127 B2
Bellgreen Ave NE3 .141 D1
Belling Forest Wlk The*
  NE46 ....69 B7
Bellingham Com Mid Sch
  NE48 ....184 C4
Bellingham Ct NE22 .122 A1
Bellingham Fst Sch
  NE48 ....184 C4
Bellister Bank NE49 .153 B2
Bellister Rd NE49 ..153 C3
Bells Cl [2] Blyth NE24 .127 F8
  Newcastle u T NE15 .169 E5
Bells Close Ind Est
  NE15 ....169 E5
Bells Lonnen NE42 .166 D4
Bells Wood Ct DH8 .176 D4
Bellsburn Ct NE63 ..117 B2
Bellshiel Rd NE19 ...46 D4
Bellwood Terr DH8 .177 D3
Belmont Ave NE25 ..144 D4
Belmont Cotts [6] NE47 .149 F3
Belmont Gdns NE47 .158 A6
Belmont Ave NE47 .141 D1
Belsay Av
  Hazlerigg NE13 ...141 A4
  Whitley Bay NE25 .145 B4
Belsay Castle* NE20 ..84 D5
Belsay Cl NE24 ....128 C7
Belsay Ct NE24 ....128 C7
Belsay Fst Sch NE20 ..84 F5
Belsay Gr NE22 ....122 C3
Belsay Hall* NE20 ..84 D5
Beltingham NE5 ....149 E1
Belvedere Ave NE15 .144 F4
Belvedere Terr [2] NE66 .144 E1
Benbrake Ave NE70 .144 E1
Benfield Cl DH8 ....176 D6
Benfield Rd NE6 ...135 B7
Benfieldside Prim Sch
  DH8 ....176 C5
Benfieldside Rd DH8 .176 C6
Benjamin St [11] NE40 .167 A1
Benlaw Gr NE65 .....52 E4
Bennecourt Cres TD12 .179 B7
Bennecourt Dr TD12 .179 B7
Bennett Ct NE15 ...169 C6
Bennett's Wlk NE61 .120 A8
Benridge Pk NE24 ..128 C6
Benson Cl NE46 ....160 E4
Benthal NE67 ....24 D7
Bentinck Cres NE61 .115 E3
Benton La NE12 ....142 B1
Benton Rd NE27 ...143 E1
Benton Square Ind Est
  NE12 ....143 B1
Bents La DH3 ....111 B2
Berberis Way NE26 .168 E8
Beresford Ct NE26 .135 D6
Beresford Rd
  Seaton Sluice NE26 .135 D5
  Tynemouth NE30 ..145 A3
Berkeley Cl NE12 ..142 E4
Berkeley Sq NE3 ...141 B1
Berkley Ave NE21 .169 E2
Berkley St NE15 ...169 F8
Berkley Terr NE15 ..168 F8
Berkshire Cl NE15 ..149 F2
Berksyde DH8 ......177 A1
Berrington TD15 ....178 A7
Berrington law TD15 ..8 B6
Berrishill Gr NE25 ..144 C6
Berry Edge Factories
  DH8 ....176 E2
Berry Edge Rd DH8 .176 F2
Berry Edge View DH8 .176 F3
Berry Hill NE40 ...168 B1
Berryhill Cl NE21 ..169 D1
Berrymoor Rd NE21 .117 E4
Bertha St DH8 .....176 F3
Bertram Terr
  Ashington NE63 ..117 D3
  Pegswood NE61 ..115 E8
Berwick Cl NE15 ..169 A7
Berwick Ct NE20 ..138 F7
Berwick Hill Cotts NE20 .130 A4
Berwick Hill Rd NE20 .138 F8
Berwick Infmy TD15 .178 B5
Berwick Main Guard Mus*
  TD15 ....178 C4

Berwick Mid Sch TD15 .178 B6
Berwick Rd NE71 ...180 C2
Berwick St Mary's CE Fst Sch
  TD15 ....178 A8
Berwick-upon-Tweed
  Barracks (Mus)*
  TD15 ....178 C5
Berwick-upon-Tweed Com
  High Sch TD15 ....178 B1
Berwick-upon-Tweed
  Ramparts* TD15 ..178 C4
Berwick-upon-Tweed Sta
  TD15 ....178 B5
Bessemer St DH8 ..176 E3
Bessie Terr NE21 ..169 A2
Bet's La NE61 ......124 D8
Beverley Cl NE3 ....141 B2
Beverley Dr NE62 ..117 A1
Beverley Pk NE25 ..144 E4
Beverley Rd NE25 .144 F4
Beverley Terr
  [N] Consett DH8 ..176 F3
  Tynemouth NE30 ..145 C3
  Walbottle NE15 ...149 A2
Beverley Villas NE30 .145 C3
Beweshill Cres NE21 .169 A1
Beweshill La NE21 ..169 A3
Bewick Cres NE15 .169 D7
Bewick Garth NE43 .165 E1
Bewick La NE42 ...166 B4
Bexhill Sq NE24 ...128 E5
Bickerton Wlk [2] NE5 .149 E1
Bickerton's Field NE66 .24 C4
Biddlestone NE65 ...37 C3
Bideford Gdns NE26 .145 A6
Big Waters Cl NE13 .141 A6
Big Waters Ctry Pk*
  NE13 ....141 A7
Billendean Rd TD15 .178 C2
Billendean Terr TD15 .178 B2
Billy Mill La NE29 ..144 C1
Bilton Cotts NE66 ...41 F5
Bingfield Agricultural Hos
  NE46 ....92 A7
Birch Cl NE46 ......160 E3
Birch Ct NE42 .....166 D3
Birch Rd NE21 .....169 D3
Birch St DH8 ....176 F2
Bircham Dr NE21 ..169 D1
Birches Nook Cotts
  NE43 ....171 C7
Birches The NE61 ...74 E5
Birchfield Gdns NE15 .169 E7
Birchgate Cl NE21 ..169 A1
Birchtree Gdns NE25 .144 F3
Birchwood Ave NE13 .141 C5
Birchwood Cl NE23 .133 F1
Birdsworld Roman Fort
  (Mus)* CA8 ....86 B1
Birkdale NE25 ......144 D5
Birkdene NE43 .....171 D6
Birks Rd NE15 .....148 B5
Birkshaw Wlk [1] NE5 .149 E1
Birney Edge NE20 ..138 C1
Bishop Ian Ramsey CE Prim
  Sch DH8 ....175 C1
Bishopbourne Ct [5]
  NE29 ....144 F1
Bishopdale Ave NE24 .128 A6
Bishops Cl NE5 ....169 F8
Bishops Dr NE40 ..168 D4
Bishops Hill NE46 ..91 F5
Bishops Mdw NE22 .121 F1
Bishopton St NE24 .128 E6
Bishopton Way NE46 .160 E3
Bisley Rd NE25 ....183 C5
Biverfield Rd NE42 .166 E3
Black Bull La NE49 .153 D5
Black Carts Turret 29a*
  NE46 ....90 E6
Black La NE21 .....169 A4
Black Dean Dr NE66 ..31 A2
Black Watch Terr TD15 .178 C4
Black Way NE47 ...106 A6
Blackclose Bank NE63 .117 D1
Blackclose East NE63 .117 D1
Blackdene NE63 ...117 B2
Blackett Cotts
  Matfen NE20 ....93 B6
  Wylam NE41 ......167 A6
Blackett Cl NE41 ..167 A6
Blacktyne Com Sch
  DH8 ....176 F4
Blackhall Cl TD15 ...3 F5
Blackhouse La NE40 .168 B5
Blackrow La NE15 .148 A4
Blackstone Ct NE21 .169 A2
Blackthorn Dr NE63 .128 C4
Blackthorn Way NE61 .117 B2
Blackwood NE65 ...183 E6
Blaeberry Hill NE65 .182 A6
Blagdon Cl NE61 ..119 E8
Blagdon Cres NE23 .132 E8
Blagdon Ct NE22 ..122 C2
Blagdon Dr NE24 ..128 A6
Blagdon Terr
  Cramlington NE23 .133 B6
  Seaton Burn NE13 .141 B8
Blakelaw Ct NE66 ..181 C3
Blakelaw Rd NE66 ..181 C3

Blaketown NE23 .134 A1
Blakewell Gdns TD15 .178 A4
Blakewell Rd TD15 ..178 A4
Blanchland Ave
  Newcastle u T NE15 .169 C7
  Wideopen NE13 ..141 B6
Blanchland Dr NE25 .134 F2
Blandford Rd NE29 .144 D1
Blaydon Bank NE21 .169 C2
Blaydon Bsns Ctr NE21 .169 E3
Blaydon Bsns Pk NE21 .169 F4
Blaydon Haughs Ind Est
  NE21 ....169 E4
Blaydon Highway NE21 .169 C3
Blaydon Ind Pk NE21 .169 D3
Blaydon Trad Pk NE21 .169 F3
Blaydon West Prim Sch
  NE21 ....169 C3
Blayney Row NE15 .168 C8
Blencathra NE30 ...145 A2
Blenheim Cl NE22 ..142 D4
Blenheim Ct NE22 ..128 D3
Blenheim Gdns NE61 .115 E4
Blenheim Pl NE61 .178 D1
Blenkinsop Mews NE1 ..149 A1
Blenkinsopp Castle Home Pk
  CA8 ....152 A5
Blenkinsopp Terr CA8 .152 A6
Blezard Bsns Pk NE13 .132 B1
Blezard Ct NE21 ...169 E4
Bloody Bush Rd NE48 ..67 E8
Blucher Rd NE12 ...142 C2
Blucher Terr NE15 .149 B1
Blue Reef Aquarium*
  NE30 ....145 D1
Blue Row NE15 ....147 F2
Blue Top Cotts NE23 .133 D6
Bluebell Cl
  Leadgate DH8 .....177 C3
  Wylam NE41 ......167 B7
Blueburn Dr NE12 .142 F1
Blyth Cl NE21 .....141 F8
Blyth College Com Ed Ctr
  NE24 ....128 D5
Blyth Com Coll NE24 .127 F7
Blyth Community Hospl
  NE24 ....128 D8
Blyth Ct NE15 .....169 C7
Blyth Dr NE61 .....120 E1
Blyth Rd NE26 .....135 E2
Blyth St Chopwell NE17 .173 C1
  Seaton Delaval NE25 .134 C3
Blyth Terr NE63 ...117 E4
Boat Rd NE68 .....184 B4
Boatmans Pl NE24 ..24 D3
Bob Elliott Ho The [5]
  NE24 ....128 E8
Bog Houses NE23 ..127 C2
Bohemia Terr NE24 .128 E6
Bolam Ave Blyth NE24 .128 D7
  Tynemouth NE30 ..145 A1
Bolam Ct NE15 ....148 D1
Bolam Dr NE63 ....117 E2
Bolam Gr NE30 ....145 A1
Bolam Lake Ctry Pk*
  NE20 ....84 C8
Bolam Pl NE22 ....122 C2
Bolam Rd NE12 ...142 C3
Bolam Way NE25 ..134 C3
Bolam West Hos NE61 .75 B1
Boland Rd NE61 ...113 A3
Bolsover St NE63 ...117 D3
Bolsover Terr
  Ashington NE63 ..117 D3
  Pegswood NE61 ..115 F4
Bolton's Bglws NE17 .175 B8
Bomarsund Cvn Site
  NE22 ....122 B6
Bonchester Cl NE22 .121 F2
Bonchester Pl NE23 .133 D8
Bondene Way NE22 .127 B2
Bondgate Ct NE46 .161 B4
Bondgate Ct
  [6] Alnwick NE66 .181 C5
  Hexham NE46 ....161 B4
Bondgate Within NE66 .181 C5
Bondgate Without
  NE66 ....181 C5
Bondicar Rd NE65 ..53 F3
Bondicar Terr NE24 .128 E3
Bonnivard Gdns NE23 .134 A1
Booths NE63 ....117 A4
Border History Mus*
  NE46 ....161 B5
Borrowdale DH8 ...177 D4
Borrowdale Ave NE24 .128 A8
Bosworth NE12 ....142 D4
Bothal Ave NE62 ..121 E7
Bothal Bank NE61 ..116 C2
Bothal Cl Blyth NE24 .128 C7
  Pegswood NE61 ..115 E3
Bothal Cotts NE63 ..116 F4
Bothal Mid Sch NE63 .116 F4
Bothal Terr
  Ashington NE63 ..116 F4
  Stakeford NE62 ..122 B8
Boulmer Cl NE61 ...32 D1
Boulmer Gdns NE13 .141 B6
Boulmer Rd NE66 ...32 B1
Boulsworth Rd NE29 .144 E1
Boundary Dr NE61 .120 A7
Boundary La DH8 ..101 F2
Boundary Way NE35 .135 D6

Bournemouth Gdns
Newcastle u T NE5 ....149 F3
Whitley Bay NE26 ....145 A6
Bow Alley NE6 ....181 C5
Bow Burn Cotts 🟦
NE66 ....181 C5
Bow Well Cotts TD15 ....2 C2
Bower's Cres TD15 ....178 A4
Bowes Ct NE24 ....128 E7
Bowes St NE24 ....128 E8
Bowfell Gdns NE62 ....122 A8
Bowfield Ave NE3 ....141 C1
Bowler's Hill NE43 ....171 F7
Bowman Dr NE23 ....142 B8
Bowman Sq NE63 ....117 D2
Bowmere NE66 ....42 D8
Bowmont Rd NE23 ....13 C5
Bowmont Dr NE23 ....133 D8
Bowmonthill TD12 ....11 C2
Bowsden TD15 ....8 C4
Boyd St Consett DH8 ......177 A1
Newburn NE15 ....168 E8
Boyd Terr
Newcastle u T,Walbottle
NE15 ....149 B1
🟦 Newcastle u T,Westerhope
NE5 ....149 F3
Boyne Ct 🟦 NE24 ....128 E8
Boyne Gdns NE27 ....143 E3
Brabourne Gdns 🟦
NE29 ....141 C4
Bracken Cl NE13 ....140 B6
Bracken Ridge NE61 ....114 C1
Bracken Way NE40 ....168 A3
Brackenside NE3 ....141 C1
Bracknell Gdns NE5 ....149 C1
Bradbury Ct
New Hartley NE25 ....134 D6
Ponteland NE20 ....138 F6
Bradbury Pl NE25 ....134 D6
Bradford NE70 ....16 E3
Bradley Bglws DH8 ....177 C6
Bradley Cotts DH8 ....177 C6
Bradley Fell La NE41 ......167 C2
Bradley Fell Rd NE40,
NE42 ....173 C8
Bradley Rd NE42 ....166 F3
Bradley St DH8 ....177 C4
Bradley View 🟦 NE40 .....167 F3
Bradley Workshops Ind Est
DH8 ....177 C4
Bradshawgate Cotts
NE67 ....24 A7
Brady St 🟦 NE68 ....17 F2
Brae The NE71 ....180 C5
Braemar Ct NE24 ....178 C3
Braemar Gdns NE25 ....144 C2
Braeside Embleton NE66 ...24 D1
Falstone NE48 ....69 D6
St Johns Chapel DL13 ....111 E1
Tweedmouth TD15 ....178 A1
Braeside Cl NE30 ....145 A3
Braewell Cl NE48 ....72 C5
Bramble Cl NE24 ....128 D4
Brambling Lea NE22 ....122 C2
Bramley Ct 🟦 NE46 ....161 B4
Brampton Ct NE23 ....133 C8
Brampton Gdns NE15 ......148 E2
Bramwell Terr DH8 ....177 A4
Brancepeth Cl NE15 ....169 C7
Branch End Terr NE43 .....171 F7
Branch St NE21 ....169 B1
Branckenpeth Mews
NE3 ....141 B1
Brandling Dr NE3 ....141 D1
Brandling Mews NE3 ......141 D1
Brandon Ave NE27 ....143 E3
Brandon Cl NE24 ....128 B8
Brandon Farm Cotts
NE66 ....28 F4
Brandon White Ho NE66 ...29 A4
Brandon Way NE25 ....144 D4
Brantwood Cl NE21 ....169 D2
Breamish NE61 ....112 E5
Breamish Cotts NE66 ....29 B3
Breckon Cl NE63 ....117 E1
Bremenium Way NE19 ......46 F1
Brendale Ave NE5 ....149 E3
Brenkley Ave NE27 ....143 F2
Brenkley Ct NE13 ....140 B7
Brenkley Ct NE13 ....141 B8
Brenkley Way NE13 ....132 B1
Brennan Cl NE63 ....118 A3
Brentwood Ave NE46 ......118 D5
Brentwood Cl NE25 ....134 E2
Brettanby Gdns NE40 .....168 C6
Brettonby Ave NE43 ......171 D7
Brewery Bank TD15 ....178 A3
Brewery Cl NE18 ....136 A4
Brewery La
Ponteland NE20 ....138 E6
Rothbury NE65 ....182 B5
Tweedmouth TD15 ....178 A3
🟦 Warkworth NE65 ....42 B1
Brewery Rd NE71 ....180 D5
Brewery St 🟦 NE24 ....128 F8
Briar Ave NE25 ....145 A6
Briar Cl NE21 ....169 A2
Briar Ct NE26 ....145 A5
Briar Hill
Bellingham NE48 ....184 C4
Wearhead DL13 ....111 C1
Briar La NE15 ....148 E1
Briar Mews DH8 ....176 D5
Briar Vale NE25 ....144 D3

Briardale
Bedlington NE22 ....121 E1
Dinnington NE13 ....140 B7
Briardale Rd NE24 ....128 A8
Briardene NE43 ....117 B2
Briarlea NE61 ....120 E4
Briarside DH8 ....176 D5
Briarwood NE23 ....142 B8
Briarwood Rd NE42 ....128 F6
Briary Gdns DH8 ....148 C2
Briary The Consett DH8 ...176 D6
Throckley NE15 ....148 C2
Brickfield Lodge TD15 ....178 B1
Bride's Brae TD15 ....8 D7
Bridge Cotts NE23 ....142 B8
Bridge Ct TD15 ....178 A4
Bridge End
Berwick-u-T TD15 ....178 B4
Felton NE65 ....52 E3
Lesbury NE66 ....42 A6
Bridge End Cotts NE18 ...136 A4
Bridge End Ind Est
NE46 ....161 C6
Bridge Island DH8 ....176 B6
Bridge Rd NE61 ....113 A2
Bridge St Alnwick NE66 ...183 D2
Amble NE65 ....183 D6
Berwick-u-T TD15 ....178 B4
Blaydon NE21 ....169 C4
Blyth NE24 ....128 F7
Consett DH8 ....176 D3
Newbiggin-by-t-S NE64 ....118 E4
Rothbury NE65 ....182 B5
Seaton Burn NE13 ....141 B8
🟦 Warkworth NE65 ....42 B1
Bridge Terr
Bedlington NE22 ....122 C3
🟦 Berwick-u-T TD15 ......178 B4
Shiremoor NE27 ....143 F4
Stakeford NE62 ....122 B8
Bridge View 🟦 NE65 ......42 B1
Bridle The NE27 ....144 B2
Bridport Rd NE29 ....144 D1
Brier Dene Cres NE26 .....144 F8
Brierdene Cl NE26 ....144 F8
Brierdene Ct NE26 ....144 F8
Brierdene Rd NE26 ....135 F1
Brierdene View NE26 .....144 E8
Brierley Cl NE24 ....128 B7
Brierley Gdns NE19 ....59 E4
Brierley Rd NE24 ....128 B7
Briery Hill La NE61 ....125 C3
Brigantium (Mus)*
NE19 ....46 E1
Bright St DH8 ....129 A1
Brigside Cotts NE13 ......141 C8
Brinkburn Ave
Blyth NE24 ....128 F6
Cramlington NE23 ....133 C6
Brinkburn Cres NE61 .....117 E4
Brinkburn Gdns NE62 ....122 A8
Brinkburn Pl
Amble NE65 ....183 D5
Stamfordham NE18 ....93 F6
Brinkburn Priory* NE65 ..51 D1
Bristol St NE25 ....134 D6
Bristol Wlk NE25 ....134 D6
Briton Terr DH8 ....176 F3
Broad Oak Terr NE17 .....173 B1
Broad Rd NE48 ....17 E3
Broadacres
Fourstones NE47 ....90 F2
Henshaw NE47 ....155 D5
Broadgates NE46 ....161 B4
Broadmead Way NE15 ....169 F5
Broadstone Gr NE5 ....149 C1
Broadway Blyth NE24 .....128 C6
Fourstones NE47 ....90 F2
Guide Post NE62 ....121 F7
Tynemouth NE30 ....169 D7
Ponteland NE20 ....138 C3
Broadway Circ NE28 ....128 E7
Broadway Cl NE30 ....145 B3
Broadway Cres NE24 .....128 C6
Broadway Gdns NE46 .....160 F5
Broadway The
Tynemouth NE30 ....145 B2
Tynemouth NE30 ....145 C1
Broadway Prim Sch
NE15 ....149 F7
Broadwood Rd NE15 ......169 F7
Broadwood View DH8 .....176 C5
Brock La NE22,NE62 ....122 F5
Brockdam Farm NE67 ....23 B3
Brockwell Cl NE21 ....169 A1
Brockwell Ct NE24 ....128 C5
Brockwell Ctr The NE23 ..133 B8
Brockwell Mid Sch
NE23 ....133 D8
Brockwell St 🟦 NE40 ....136 D3
Brockwood Cl DL13 ......117 B1
Broken Way DL13 ....111 E1
Brokenheugh NE5 ....149 F1
Bromley Ave NE25 ....144 E4
Bromley Gdns NE24 ......128 E5
Brook Cl Bedlington NE22 .122 A4
Bedlington NE22 ....127 A8
Brook St NE26 ....84 B6
Brookfield Cres NE5 ......149 C1
Brookland Dr NE12 ....142 E3
Brookland Terr NE12 ......145 A1
Brooklands NE20 ....138 A3
Brookside NE23 ....142 A7

Brookside Ave
Blyth NE24 ....128 B7
Brunswick Village NE13 ....141 A6
Broom Cl NE61 ....120 C7
Broom House Farm NE61 ..31 C2
Broom Wood Ct NE42 .....166 B1
Broomdykes TD11 ....2 A8
Broomey Rd NE71 ....180 B5
Broomfield Cres NE17 ....175 B8
Broomhaugh CE Fst Sch
NE44 ....100 F8
Broomhaugh Cl NE46 .....161 C4
Broomhill Fst Sch NE65 ...53 E4
Broomhill Rd NE42 ....166 E3
Broomhill St NE65 ....183 D6
Broomhill Terr DH8 ....177 A8
Broomhouse La NE42 .....166 D3
Broomhouse Rd NE42 .....166 D3
Broomlea NE29 ....144 B1
Broomlea Ct NE21 ....169 C3
Broomlee NE15 ....117 E2
Broomlee Rd NE12 ....142 B1
Broomley Fst Sch NE43 ...171 B8
Brooms La DH8 ....177 F4
Broomy Hill Rd NE15 .....148 D2
Broomylinn Pl NE23 ......133 C8
Brown Rigg Cvn & Camping
Pk NE48 ....184 A3
Brownrigg Dr NE23 ....133 C5
Browns Ct 🟦 NE65 ....183 C5
Brownsman Ct NE68 ......17 E2
Bruce Cl NE5 ....149 F2
Brucegate TD15 ....178 B5
Brumell Dr NE61 ....114 D1
Brumwell Ct NE43 ....171 B7
Brundon Ave NE26 ....144 F7
Brunswick Gr NE13 ....141 A6
Brunswick Ind Est NE13 ..140 F6
Brunswick Park Ind Est
NE13 ....141 A6
Brunswick Rd NE27 ......143 F2
Brunswick Sq NE27 ......143 F2
Bruntley Mdws CA9 ......185 E3
Brunton Bank NE6 ....91 C4
Brunton La
Hazlerigg NE13 ....140 E2
Newcastle u T,Brunton Park
NE3,NE13 ....141 B2
Newcastle u T,Melton Park
NE3 ....141 C1
Brunton Mews NE13 ......140 F2
Brunton Turret 26b*
NE46 ....91 C4
Brunton Way NE23 ....127 B2
Buck's Nook La NE40 .....173 C7
Buckham St DH8 ....176 E4
Buckton TD15 ....9 F1
Buddle St DH8 ....177 A1
Buddle Terr 🟦 NE27 .....143 E1
Bude Ct NE23 ....144 D1
Bude Sands NE69 ....16 E6
Budworth Ave NE26 ......135 D5
Buller's Gn NE61 ....114 E1
Bungalows The
Ebchester DH8 ....174 F4
Medomsley NE17 ....175 B4
Burdon Ave NE23 ....132 F7
Burdon Terr NE22 ....121 F1
Burgham Pk NE65 ....64 D7
Burghley Gdns NE61 .....115 F4
Burgoyne Terr NE41 ......167 A6
Burn Ave NE3 ....141 D1
Burn Foot DL13 ....111 E1
Burn Hos NE66 ....31 D7
Burn La Hexham NE46 ....161 A6
Humshaugh NE46 ....91 B6
Burn Rd NE21 ....169 A1
Burn View NE23 ....142 B8
Burnaby Dr NE40 ....168 C6
Burnbank Ave NE25 ......144 B5
Burnbridge NE13 ....141 B8
Burncroft 🟦 NE46 ....161 A4
Burnet Ct NE63 ....117 E1
Burnfoot Rural Workshops
DL13 ....111 E1
Burnfoot Terr NE26 ......145 C4
Burnham Ave NE15 ......169 B7
Burnham Cl NE24 ....128 B7
Burnhills Gdns NE40 .....168 A1
Burnhills La NE40 ....168 C1
Burnhouse Rd NE71 .....180 B6
Burnland Terr NE46 ......160 F5
Burnlea Gdns NE23 ......133 D6
Burnley St NE21 ....169 C2
Burnmill Bank DH8 ......109 D7
Burns Ave NE24 ....128 C5
Burnside Amble NE65 ....183 D5
Ashington NE63 ....118 A3
Bardon Mill NE47 ....155 E7
Bedlington NE22 ....121 F4
🟦 Belford NE70 ....15 F4
Holywell NE25 ....145 A3
Longhoughton NE66 ....32 B2
Morpeth NE61 ....115 A1
Ovington NE42 ....165 D4
Ponteland NE20 ....138 B3
Burnside Ave NE23 ......128 B8
Burnside Cl Blyth NE24 ..128 B8
Ovington NE42 ....165 D4
Seghill NE23 ....133 E1

Burnside Cotts
Annitsford NE23 ....142 C8
Mickley Square NE43 ....165 E1
Burnside Ct DH8 ....108 A5
Burnside Rd NE30 ....145 B3
Burnside Villas NE46 .....160 F5
Burnside View NE23 ......133 E1
Burnstones NE5 ....149 E1
Burnt House Rd NE25 ....144 E3
Burnt Houses NE40 ......168 B1
Burnwood Cl NE17 ....173 B1
Burradon Farm Cotts
NE23 ....142 D7
Burradon Prim Sch
NE23 ....142 C5
Burradon Rd NE23 ....142 C7
Burswood Ave NE46 ......160 F5
Burswood Villas NE46 ....160 F5
Burt Cres NE23 ....142 B8
Burt Meml Homes NE62 ..121 E5
Burt Rd NE22 ....122 E3
Burt St NE24 ....128 E8
Burt Terr Morpeth NE61 ..120 A8
Walbottle NE15 ....149 A2
Burton Rd NE65 ....183 E5
Burwell Ave NE5 ....169 F8
Bushman's Rd NE19 ......46 E4
Buston Barns Cotts NE65 ..42 A2
Butcher's La NE61 ....115 F5
Bute Dr NE39 ....173 F4
Bute N Rd NE39 ....173 F4
Bute Rd S NE39 ....173 F3
Buteland Rd NE15 ....169 F7
Buteland Terr NE64 ......118 D4
Butterfield Cl NE40 ......167 F4
Buttermere Cl NE12 ......142 C3
Buttermere Rd NE30 .....145 A2
Buttermere Way NE24 ....123 E3
Butterwell Dr NE61 ......115 E3
Butts Mews CA9 ....185 D4
Butts The 🟦 NE65 ....42 B1
Buxton Gdns NE5 ....149 F3
Buxton Gn 🟦 NE5 ....149 F3
By-Way The NE15 ....168 E4
Bye The DH8 ....176 C1
Byerside Cvn Site NE17 ..175 C5
Byewell Terr NE26 ....135 D6
Bygate Rd NE25 ....144 E4
Byres Cl 🟦 NE70 ....15 F4
Byrness NE5 ....149 E5
Byrness Fst Sch NE19 ....45 E5
Byrness Row NE23 ....133 C6
Byron Ave NE24 ....128 C6
Byron Cl NE62 ....121 E7
Byron Ct NE5 ....149 C2
Byron Pl NE63 ....117 F2
Byron St NE65 ....183 C5
Byron Terr CA8 ....152 A6
Bywell Ave Hexham NE46 .161 D4
Newcastle u T,Denton Burn
NE15 ....169 E7
Bywell Cl NE40 ....167 E3
Bywell Dr NE40 ....144 A3
Bywell Home Farm
NE43 ....164 F3
Bywell Rd NE22 ....117 D2
Bywell View NE43 ....171 D7

C

Cadehill Rd NE43 ....171 C6
Cadlestone Cl NE23 ......133 D8
Cairn Pk NE65 ....51 E4
Cairn View NE65 ....51 E4
Cairnglass Gr NE23 ......133 D8
Cairns Rd NE48 ....184 B5
Cairnsmore Cl NE23 .....133 B4
California NE21 ....169 B1
California Gdns 🟦
NE61 ....120 A8
Callaly Ave NE23 ....133 C6
Callaly Cl NE61 ....115 F3
Callaly Way NE6 ....39 B6
Callerdale Rd NE24 ......128 A7
Caliers Ct 🟦 TD15 ....3 E6
Callerton NE12 ....142 D5
Callerton Cl
🟦 Ashington NE63 ....117 F2
Cramlington NE23 ....133 C6
Callerton Ct NE20 ....138 E4
Callerton La NE5,NE15,
NE20 ....138 E3
Callerton Lane End Cotts
NE5 ....148 E7
Callerton Parkway Sta
NE13 ....139 E1
Callerton Rd NE15 ....169 E7
Callerton View NE5 ....149 B4
Calvus Dr NE15 ....147 F2
Cambo Ave
Bedlington NE22 ....122 C2
Whitley Bay NE25 ....123 D3
Cambo Cl NE24 ....128 C7
Cambo Dr NE23 ....133 C6
Cambo Fst Sch NE61 .....74 A2
Cambois Fst Sch NE24 ...123 C4
Cambridge Ave NE26 .....145 A5
Cambridge Rd NE22 ......128 C7
Cambridge St NE6 ....169 C8
Cameron Ho TD12 ....179 C6
Cameron Rd NE12 ....142 C3
Camilla Rd NE15 ....147 F2
Camp Dr NE65 ....30 D1
Camperdown NE5 ....149 F1
Camperdown Ave NE12 ..142 B4

Camperdown Ind Est
NE12 ....142 B🔲
Campion Way NE63 ....117 C🔲
Campsie Cres NE30 ......145 A🔲
Campus Martius NE15 ....147 F🔲
Canberra Ave NE63 ......117 C🔲
Candlish St NE33 ....142 C🔲
Canon Savage Dr NE46 ..160 F🔲
Canonbie Sq NE23 ....133 D🔲
Canonsfield Cl NE15 .....149 E🔲
Canterbury Cl NE63 ......117 C🔲
Canterbury Way NE13 ...141 E🔲
Canty's Terr TD15 ....3 E🔲
Capel Ave NE49 ....153 C🔲
Capercaillie Lodge
NE23 ....133 A🔲
Capheaton NE19 ....83 E🔲
Cardigan Gr NE30 ....145 A🔲
Cardinal Cl NE15 ....149 E🔲
Carew Cl NE23 ....133 C🔲
Carey Cl NE66 ....32 E🔲
Carey Pl NE24 ....142 C🔲
Carham Ave NE23 ....133 C🔲
Carham Cl NE45 ....163 D🔲
Carisbrooke NE22 ....121 F🔲
Carisbrooke NE22 ....122 A🔲
Carlcroft Pl NE23 ....133 C🔲
Carlisle Cl NE27 ....143 C🔲
Carlisle Terr 🟦 NE27 ....143 E🔲
Carlisle View NE15 ....119 F🔲
Carlisle Way NE27 ....143 C🔲
Carlow Dr NE62 ....122 C🔲
Carlton Ave NE24 ....128 C🔲
Carlton Gdns NE15 ....169 E🔲
Carlton Gr NE63 ....117 D🔲
Carlton Ho NE64 ....118 E🔲
Carlton St NE24 ....128 E🔲
Carlton Terr NE24 ....128 C🔲
Carnaby Cl NE42 ....127 A🔲
Carnaby Ct NE42 ....166 C🔲
Carnoustie Cl DH8 ....176 E🔲
Carnoustie Ct NE25 ......144 E🔲
Caroline Terr NE21 ....169 E🔲
Carolyn Cres NE26 ....145 C🔲
Carolyn Way NE26 ....145 C🔲
Carr Field NE20 ....138 F🔲
Carr House Mews DH8 ...177 B🔲
Carr St NE24 ....128 E🔲
Carrick Cl TD15 ....178 A🔲
Carrick Dr NE24 ....128 C🔲
Carrier's La NE46 ....82 C🔲
Carrington Cl NE23 ......133 C🔲
Carrs Cl NE42 ....166 C🔲
Carrsfield NE45 ....163 A🔲
Carterside Rd NE65 ....50 C🔲
Cartington Ave NE27 .....143 E🔲
Cartington Ct 🟦 NE65 ...183 C🔲
Carvoran Roman Army Mus*
CA8 ....152 B🔲
Carway Bank DL13 ....111 C🔲
Caseton Cl NE25 ....144 C🔲
Casterton Gr NE5 ....149 F🔲
Castle Bank NE61 ....120 A🔲
Castle Cl NE48 ....90 C🔲
Castle Lea NE42 ....166 B🔲
Castle Mdw NE26 ....119 C🔲
Castle Rd NE42 ....166 B🔲
Castle Sq
Backworth NE27 ....143 B🔲
Morpeth NE61 ....120 A🔲
Castle St Hazlerigg NE13 .141 A🔲
Morpeth NE61 ....120 A🔲
Norham TD15 ....2 C🔲
🟦 Warkworth NE65 ....42 B🔲
Castle Terr
Ashington NE63 ....117 E🔲
Berwick-u-T TD15 ....3 E🔲
Morpeth NE61 ....3 E🔲
Castle View Amble NE65 ..183 B🔲
Horsley NE15 ....116 E🔲
Ovington NE42 ....166 E🔲
Prudhoe NE42 ....166 E🔲
Castle Way NE13 ....140 F🔲
Castle Wlk NE61 ....120 A🔲
Castle Wynd NE69 ....16 C🔲
Castledale Ave NE24 .....128 A🔲
Castledene Rd DH8 ....177 E🔲
Castlefields Dr NE42 .....166 B🔲
Castlegate TD15 ....178 B🔲
Castlegate Ct 🟦 TD15 ...178 B🔲
Castlenook Pl NE15 ......169 E🔲
Castleside Cl NE23 ....142 E🔲
Castleside Prim Sch
DH8 ....109 F🔲
Castleton Cl NE23 ....127 A🔲
Castleway NE13 ....140 F🔲
Castlewood Cl NE5 ....149 D🔲
Catcleugh NE48 ....43 B🔲
Catherine St CA8 ....152 A🔲
Catherine View 🟦 NE40 .167 F🔲
Catheugh Dr NE66 ....30 D🔲
Catholic Row NE26 ....126 E🔲
Catkin Wlk NE40 ....167 A🔲
Catrail Pl NE23 ....133 C🔲
Cattle Market NE46 ......161 C🔲

auldwell Ave NE25 .....144 D3
auldwell Cl NE25 ......144 E4
auldwell La NE25 ......144 E4
auseway Rd DL13 .....111 B1
auseway The
🅱 Glanton NE66 ....29 C1
ongframlington NE65 ....51 E3
hrockley NE15 ....148 D1
ausey Brae NE46 .....160 F3
ausey Hill Rd
Hexham NE46 ....160 F3
Hexham NE46 ....161 B1
ausey Hill Way NE46 ..160 E3
ausey Pk NE46 ....160 F4
ausey Way NE46 ......160 F3
ave Ct NE61 ....30 E1
avendish Gdns NE63 ..117 D3
avendish Sq NE63 ....115 E3
avendish Terr NE63 ...117 D3
aversham Rd NE5 .....149 B3
awledge View NE66 ...181 D3
ayton Gr NE5 ....149 B2
ecil Ct NE20 ....138 E6
ecil Terr NE46 ....161 B5
edar Cl Bedlington NE22 .121 F2
Whitley Bay NE25 .....144 F3
edar Ct
ynemouth NE29 ......144 E1
🅱 Widdrington Sta NE61 ..65 E5
edar Gdns DH8 ....176 C1
edar Gr Alnwick NE66 ..181 B5
Blyth NE24 ....128 C4
Ryton NE40 ....168 C6
edar Rd NE21 ....169 C2
edar Way NE12 ....142 E1
edartree Gdns NE25 ..144 E3
eladon Cl NE15 ......169 C8
elandine Ct NE46 .....117 B1
emetery La TD15 .....178 A1
entenary Cotts NE22 ..126 F8
entral Ave Amble NE65 .163 C6
uide Post NE62 ....121 E7
entral Dr NE44 ......153 C4
enturian Way NE22 ...121 E2
enturion Rd NE15 ....169 F8
enturion Way NE15 ...147 E2
hadderton Dr NE5 ....169 B3
haffinch Cl NE63 .....117 B2
haffinch Way NE12 ...142 C4
hainbridge Honey Farm*
TD15 ....2 F5
hainbridge Ind Est
NE21 ....169 F4
hainbridge Rd
Blaydon NE21 ....169 D3
Blaydon,Derwenthaugh
NE21 ....169 F4
hainbridge Road Ind Est
NE21 ....169 F4
hainlo Dr NE25 ......162 F6
halloner's Gdns NE46 .114 E1
haloner Pl NE61 .....119 F8
hamberlain St
Blyth NE24 ....128 C6
Crawcrook NE40 ......167 F4
hancery La NE24 .....128 D7
handlery The TD15 ...178 B4
hantry Dr NE13 ......141 B6
hantry Est NE45 .....162 F6
hantry Mews 🄝 NE61 .120 A8
hantry Pl 🄟 NE61 ....120 A8
hapel Bank NE47 .....105 A7
hapel Cl Acomb NE46 ..91 C1
Newcastle u T NE3 ....141 D1
hapel Ct Newburn NE15 .168 E8
Seaton Burn NE13 .....141 B8
handlery The TD15 ...178 B4
hapel House Dr NE15 .149 C1
hapel House Mid Sch
NE15 ....149 B2
hapel House Rd NE15 .149 C1
hapel La
🄝 Alnwick NE66 .....181 C5
Wall NE46 ....91 B3
Whitley Bay NE26 .....145 B5
Wylam NE41 ....167 A6
hapel Lands NE66 ....181 A4
hapel Park Mid Sch
NE5 ....149 C3
hapel Rd NE13 ....141 B8
hapel Row Craster NE66 ..32 C7
Mickley Square NE43 ..150 B5
Seahouses NE68 ....17 F3
Togston NE65 ....53 E4
hapel St TD15 ....178 B5
hapel Terr CA9 ......185 E3
hapel View NE13 ....141 A6
hare Bank DH8 ....174 E3
hare Ends TD15 ......10 D5
hare The NE46 ....91 B3
hareway NE46 ....161 A6
hareway La NE46 ....161 A6
harles Ave
Shiremoor NE27 ......143 F4
Whitley Bay NE26 .....145 B5
harles Dr NE23 ......142 B8
harles Rd NE65 ......183 E5
harles St
Hebburn NE13 ....141 A5
Pegswood NE61 ....115 F3
harlie St NE40 ....167 F1
harlotte St NE40 ....167 F4
harlton Ct NE45 .....160 F2
harlton Ct NE15 .....144 E3
harlton Mews NE15 ..169 D6

Charlton St
Ashington NE63 ......117 C4
Blyth NE24 ....128 D7
Newcastle u T NE15 ...169 D6
Charlton View NE48 ...184 B5
Charlton Villas NE40 ..168 B1
Chartwell Pl DH8 .....176 F4
Chase Farm Dr NE24 ..127 F7
Chase Mdws NE24 ....127 F6
Chase Mews NE24 ....127 F7
Chase The Hexham NE46 .160 F3
Longbenton NE12 ......142 A2
Chasedale Cres NE24 .128 A7
Chat's La NE47 ....98 B3
Chatham Cl NE25 .....134 D1
Chathill Cl Morpeth NE61 .120 B6
Whitley Bay NE25 .....144 F3
Chathill Sta 🄝 NE66 ...23 E6
Chatsworth Dr NE22 ..122 C3
Chatsworth Gdns
🄝 Newcastle u T NE5 .149 F3
Backworth NE25 ......144 E3
Chatton Av NE23 .....133 C6
Chatton CE Fst Sch NE66 .23 E1
Chatton Cl NE61 .....120 C5
Chatton Park Cotts 21 E7
Chaytor Rd DH8 ......176 C4
Cheadle Ave NE23 ...127 A1
Cheldon Cl NE23 .....144 C6
Cheltenham Ct NE63 ..117 C2
Chelton Cl NE13 .....141 B4
Chepstow Cl DH8 .....176 D7
Chepstow Rd NE15 ...169 F6
Cherry Gr
Killingworth NE12 ....142 C4
Prudhoe NE42 ....166 B3
Cherry Tree Dr NE22 .121 F1
Cherry Tree Gdns NE15 .166 C8
Cherry Tree La NE41 .167 A6
Cherry Trees NE24 ...128 D6
Cherry Trees The NE19 ..59 E4
Cherry Way NE12 ....142 C4
Cherryburn (Mus)*
NE43 ....165 F2
Cherryburn Cotts NE43 .165 E2
Cherryhope NE65 .....51 E4
Cherrytree Cl NE12 ..142 F2
Cherrytree Ct NE22 ..122 D2
Cherrytree Gdns NE25 .144 F3
Cherrywell NE65 .....37 F2
Cherwell Sq NE12 ....142 C1
Chesham Gdns NE23 .149 B2
Cheshire Cl NE63 ....117 A4
Chesmond Dr NE21 ..169 C3
Chester Cl NE20 .....138 B4
Chester Gr Blyth NE24 .128 C6
Seghill NE23 ....133 E1
Chester Hill Cotts NE70 .16 C5
Chester Sq NE61 .....113 A3
Chester Well NE65 ...52 C6
Chesterhill NE23 ......149 B2
Chesters Dene DH8 ..174 E3
Chesters Gdns NE40 .167 E4
Chesters Mus* NE46 ..91 B3
Chesters Roman Fort
(Cilvrnvm)* NE46 ....91 B5
Chesters The
Ebchester DH8 ....174 E3
Newcastle u T NE5 ....149 C1
Whitley Bay NE25 .....144 E6
Chesters Walled Gdn*
NE46 ....91 A5
Chestnut Ave Blyth NE24 .123 D1
Newcastle u T NE5 ....144 F4
Chestnut Cl NE12 ....142 B4
Chestnut St NE63 ....117 D3
Chestnut Way 🄝 NE61 ..65 E5
Cheswick Bldgs TD15 ..8 F8
Cheswick Rd NE25 ...134 E2
Chevington Ave NE65 ..53 D2
Chevington Cl NE61 ..115 E3
Chevington Gn NE65 ..53 F2
Chevington Gr NE25 ..144 D7
Cheviot Centre The*
NE71 ....180 B6
Cheviot Cl Ellington NE61 .112 D4
Tynemouth NE29 ......144 F2
Cheviot Cres NE65 ...53 F2
Cheviot Ct Blaydon NE21 .169 C3
Morpeth NE61 ....120 A6
Whitley Bay NE26 .....145 A6
Cheviot Gr NE61 .....115 E3
Cheviot Grange NE23 .142 C6
Cheviot Lodge NE65 ..51 E3
Cheviot Pk NE71 .....180 C5
Cheviot Rd Blaydon NE21 .169 C1
Shilbottle NE66 ......41 C3
Sunderland SR7 NE71 .180 C5
Cheviot Terr
Coldstream TD12 .....179 B6
Scremerston TD15 ....4 A4
Cheviot View
Ashington NE63 ......117 E5
Brunswick Village NE13 .141 A6
Longframlington NE65 ..5 D1
Lowick TD15 ....9 B7
Ponteland NE20 ......139 A5
Prudhoe NE42 ....166 E2
Seghill NE23 ....133 F1
Whitley Bay NE26 .....145 B5
Cheviot Way
Hexham NE46 ....161 A4
Stakeford NE62 ....122 B8
Cheviotdale NE65 ....183 E4
Cheyne Rd NE42 .....166 C2
Chibburn Ave NE65 ..53 F3
Chibburn Dr NE61 ....65 E5

Chichester Ave NE23 .132 F8
Chichester Cl NE63 ..118 A2
Chichester Gr NE22 ..121 F2
Chillingham Castle & Gdns*
NE66 ....21 E4
Chillingham Cl NE24 ..128 B5
Chillingham Cres NE23 .117 C3
Chillingham Newtown Cotts
NE66 ....21 C4
Chillingham Wild Cattle Pk*
NE66 ....21 D5
Chillingham Woods Walks*
NE66 ....21 E5
Chiltern Cl
Ashington NE63 ......117 F1
🄝 East Ord TD15 .....3 E6
Chiltern Rd NE29 ....144 F2
Chip The NE61 ....119 F5
Chipchase Ave NE23 ..133 B6
Chipchase Castle* NE48 ..81 B2
Chipchase Cl
Bedlington NE22 .....121 D1
Pegswood NE61 ......115 F3
Chipchase Cres NE5 ..149 E3
Chipchase Ct NE25 ...134 D6
Chipchase Mews NE3 ..141 A1
Chirdon Cres NE46 ...161 C4
Chirnside NE23 ......133 B4
Chirton Gn NE24 ....128 B5
Chishill Way NE48 ...81 F1
Chishill Ways NE48 ..91 B8
Chisholm Pl 🄖 NE46 .161 B5
Chollerford Ave NE25 .145 B4
Chollerford Mews NE25 .134 F2
Chollerton CE Fst Sch
NE48 ....91 D7
Chollerton Dr NE22 ..122 A1
Chollerton Farm Cotts
NE48 ....91 D7
Choppington Fst Sch
NE62 ....121 E5
Choppington Rd
Bedlington NE22,NE62 .121 F2
Morpeth NE61 ....120 B6
Chopwell Prim Sch
NE17 ....173 B1
Chopwell Rd NE17 ....175 C6
Chopwell Wood Wlks*
NE39 ....173 F2
Christon Bank Farm Cotts
NE66 ....24 B1
Christon Bank Mews ..24 B1
Chudleigh Gdns NE5 ..149 B2
Church Ave
Choppington NE62 ...121 E5
West Sleekburn NE62 .122 D7
Church Bank
Consett DH8 ....176 C6
Newburn NE15 ....168 F7
Church Chare NE22 ..138 F7
Church Cl
Bedlington NE22 .....126 F8
Broomhill NE65 ......53 F2
Dinnington NE13 .....140 B7
Ebchester DH8 ....174 E3
Riding Mill NE44 .....149 C4
Whitley Bay NE25 ....144 C4
Church Cotts NE67 ...24 D8
Church Ct NE22 .....126 F8
Church Fields NE65 ..50 A5
Church Flatt NE66 ....138 F7
Church Hill Rd NE66 ..21 D7
Church La Alnwick NE66 .181 B6
Bedlington NE22 .....127 A7
Coldstream TD12 .....179 C6
Edmondbyers DH8 ...108 F5
Holy Island TD15 ....10 D4
Leitholm TD12 ....5 A7
Lowick TD15 ....9 C7
Nenthead CA9 ....110 A6
Newbrough NE47 ....90 C2
Riding Mill NE44 .....100 F8
Thropton NE65 ......50 B5
Wark NE48 ....80 E4
Church Mews
Ashington NE63 ......117 B4
Backworth NE27 .....143 C5
Consett DH8 ....176 C6
Newburn NE15 ....168 F7
Rennington NE66 .....31 E5
Stannington NE61 ....125 C3
Tweedmouth TD15 ....178 B3
Wylam NE41 ....167 A6
Church Row NE48 ...168 E5
Church Row 🄝 NE46 .161 B5
Church Sq NE61 .....113 B3
Church St Amble NE65 .183 D5
Bamburgh NE69 .....17 A5
Belford NE70 ....15 F4
Berwick-u-T TD15 ....178 B5
Blyth NE24 ....128 E8
Castleside DH8 ......109 F3
Consett DH8 ....176 F2
Cramlington NE23 ...133 B6
Craster NE66 ....32 C6
Leadgate DH8 ....107 B4
Longframlington NE65 ..51 E4
Rothbury NE65 ......182 B5
Wooler NE71 ....180 C6
Church Terr Birtley NE48 .81 A5
Church View 176 E2

Church View continued
Earsdon NE25 ....144 A5
Longhorsley NE65 ....64 A5
Newbiggin-by-t-S NE64 .118 C5
Whittingham NE66 ...39 B6
Church Way NE25 ....144 A6
Church Wlk NE61 ....119 E8
Church Wlk Dr NE61 ..119 F6
Churchill Ave
Amble NE65 ....183 E5
Whitley Bay NE25 ....144 E5
Churchill Ct DH8 ....176 C6
Churchill Way NE65 ..53 D4
Churchlands NE46 ...161 D4
Circle Pl NE46 ......161 A5
Citadel E NE12 .....142 D3
Citadel W NE12 .....142 D3
Clap Shaw DH8 .....108 A5
Clara Ave NE27 .....144 B3
Clara St NE21 ....169 B1
Clarabad Terr NE12 ..143 A1
Clare Lea NE43 .....172 A3
Claremont Ave NE15 .169 C2
Claremont Cres NE26 .144 E5
Claremont Ct NE26 ..144 E8
Claremont Gdns NE26 .144 E6
Claremont Rd NE26 ..144 F7
Claremont Terr NE24 .128 C7
Clarence Cres 🄚 NE26 .145 B4
Clarence Gdns DH8 ..176 F4
Clarence St NE2 ....141 C6
Clarendon Mews NE3 .141 C2
Clarendon St 🄞 DH8 ..176 F3
Clark Pl NE70 ....15 F5
Clark Terr DH8 ......177 B6
Clarke's Terr NE23 ..142 A6
Clarke's Yard NE23 ..142 A6
Clarks Hill Wlk NE15 .168 F7
Claude St 🄝 NE40 ...167 F3
Claverdon St NE5 ...149 B4
Clavering Rd NE21 ..169 C1
Clavering Way NE21 .169 E2
Clarerley Dr NE27 ...143 C5
Clayport Bank NE61 ..181 B4
Clayport Gdns NE61 ..181 B4
Clayport Mews 🄥 NE66 .181 C5
Clayport Sq 🄞 NE61 ..181 C5
Clayport St NE66 ....181 B5
Clayton St
Bedlington NE22 .....122 D3
Dudley NE23 ....141 F8
Clayton Terr NE15 ...147 F2
Clayton Terrace Rd
Chopwell NE17 ......173 C2
🄝 High Spen NE13,NE39 .178 D4
Clayworth Rd NE3 ...141 B1
Cleadon St 🄝 DH8 ...176 F3
Cleaswell Terr NE22 ..122 A7
Cleaswell Hill NE62 ..121 F7
Cleaswell Hill Special Sch
NE62 ....121 F7
Cleehill Dr NE29 ....144 F1
Cleet Ct TD15 ....178 C4
Clement Ave NE22 ..122 C1
Cleveland Ave NE64 ..118 D4
Cleveland Terr NE64 .118 D4
Clickemin NE20 .....139 A6
Cliff Ave NE26 ......30 E1
Cliff Row NE26 .....145 C6
Cliff Top Cvn Pk 🄝 NE68 .17 F2
Clifford Gdns 🄚 NE40 .167 F3
Clifford St NE6 .....169 C3
Clifford Terr NE40 ..168 E4
Stakeford NE62 ....122 A8
Clifton Ct NE46 ....144 E7
Clifton Gdns NE24 ..128 D4
Clifton Gr NE25 ....144 E6
Clifton Rd NE23 ....133 C5
Clifton La NE61 .....120 B2
Clifton Rd NE23 ....133 C5
Clifton Terr NE5 ....149 B2
Cliftonville Gdns NE26 .145 A6
Climbing Tree Wlk
NE61 ....115 C3
Clintburn Ct NE23 ...133 C8
Clinton Pl NE3 ......141 D2
Clipstone Cl NE15 ..148 C2
Clipstone Gn NE5 ...149 A3
Clipstone Gn NE5 ...149 A3
Clitheroe Gdns NE23 .121 D2
Clive Ct NE66 ....181 B5
Clive Terr NE66 ....181 B5
Clock Hos NE70 .....15 F4
Cloggs The NE20 ....138 F7
Close Hos NE61 .....74 D4
Close The Amble NE65 .183 B5
Blaydon NE21 ......169 A1
Blyth NE24 ....123 C1
Consett DH8 ....176 D6
Newcastle u T NE5 ...148 A1
Ponteland NE20 ......138 E5
Seghill NE23 ....133 F1
Stannington NE61 ...125 C3
Closefield Gr NE25 ..144 E5
Closes The DH8 .....108 F5
Cloudy Crags Dr NE46 ..30 E1
Clousden Dr NE12 ..142 E1
Clousden Grange NE12 .142 E1
Clove Ct 🄖 TD15 ...178 C4
Clovelly
Bedlington NE22 .....126 F8
Whitley Bay NE25 ...144 D4
Clovelly Gdns NE24 ..128 D1
Clovelly Pl NE20 ....138 C2
Cloverdale NE22 ....122 B4
Cloverhill Cl NE23 ..133 A4
Cloverhill Dr NE40 ..167 A4
Clyde St NE17 ......173 C1

Co-operative Bldgs
NE25 ....134 D3
Co-Operative Terr
Backworth NE27 .....143 E3
Brunswick Village NE13 .141 A6
Consett DH8 ....176 C7
High Spen NE39 .....173 F5
Longbenton NE12 ....143 A1
Medomsley DH8 .....81 B5
Pegswood NE61 .....115 F3
🄝 Shiremoor NE27 ...143 E1
Coach La
Brunswick Village NE13 .140 E4
Hazlerigg NE13 ......141 B4
Coach Rd NE15 .....148 C1
Coal La NE42 ....165 D4
Coal Rd Gunnerton NE48 ..81 C3
Slaley NE47 ....100 D2
Coalburn Terr NE61 ..120 D4
Coalway La NE40,NE41 .167 D1
Coanwood Rd NE22 ..123 C5
Coast View NE65 ....52 C6
Coastguard Cotts
Berwick-u-T TD15 ....178 C4
Low Newton-by-t-S NE66 .24 D3
Cobalt Cl NE15 .....169 D1
Cobbler's La NE15,NE43 .93 D1
Cobden Rd NE23 ....133 C6
Cobden St DH8 .....177 A3
Coburg St NE24 ....128 F7
Coburn Cl NE23 ....142 C5
Cochran St NE21 ...169 C4
Cochrane Terr NE13 .140 B7
Cock Pit Dr NE61 ...31 A1
Cock Pit La NE46 ...127 D4
Cockle Park New Cotts
..................65 A2
Cockshaw NE46 .....161 A5
Cockshaw Ct 🄏 NE46 .161 A5
Cockshaw Dean NE42 .166 A5
Cockshott Dean NE42 .166 C3
Cohort Cl DH8 .....174 E3
Colbourne Ave NE23 .126 E1
Colbourne Cres NE23 .126 E1
Colbury Ct NE23 ....127 A2
Coldbeck Ct NE23 ..133 C5
Coldside Gdns NE5 ..149 B3
Coldside Cottage Hospl
TD12 ....179 A5
Coldstream Mus* TD12 .179 C6
Coldstream Prim Sch
TD12 ....179 B7
Coldstream Workshops
TD12 ....179 C6
Coldwell Rd NE42 ..166 F3
Coldwell Rd NE5 ...149 B4
Coley Hill Cl NE5 ...149 C4
College Pl
Ashington NE63 .....117 C2
🄝 Berwick-u-T TD15 .178 B5
College Rd NE63 ...117 C2
Collier Cl NE15 .....148 D1
Colliers Cl NE66 ....41 C5
Colliery La NE42 ...97 D5
Collingwood Ct NE23 .132 F8
Collingwood Cotts
NE20 ....138 B7
Collingwood Cres NE20 .138 D4
Collingwood Dr NE29 .144 F1
Collingwood Dr NE46 .160 F2
Collingwood Pl NE22 .122 A7
Collingwood Rd
Earsdon NE25 ....144 A5
Newbiggin-by-t-S NE64 .118 D5
Collingwood Terr
Blyth NE24 ....128 E2
Whitley Bay NE26 ...145 C4
🄝 Collywell Bay Rd NE26 .135 D5
Collywell Ct NE26 ..135 D5
Colston Way NE25 ..144 F7
Colt Pk NE17 ....175 B5
Coltparts NE15 .....149 F1
Coltpark Pl NE23 ...133 B5
Columbia Terr NE24 .128 E6
Colwell Rd
Ashington NE63 .....117 F1
Shiremoor NE27 .....143 F2
🄝 Tynemouth NE29 ..144 F1
Comb Hill Rd NE49 ..153 C5
Combe Dr NE15 ....169 B7
Combhill Terr NE49 .153 D5
Comet Row NE12 ...142 C4
Commercial Pl 🄘 NE46 .161 B4
Commercial Rd
🄖 Blyth NE24 ....128 E8
Consett DH8 ....176 C2
Newcastle u T NE5 ...149 F2
Commercial St 🄪 NE61 .169 B1
Common Bank NE71 ..97 A3
Common Rd NE71 ...180 B5
Concorde Ho NE5 ...134 C1
Coniscliffe Ave NE64 ..118 C3
Coniston Cl
Killingworth NE12 ...142 C3
Newcastle u T NE5 ...168 E7
Coniston Rd Blyth NE21 .123 A1
Tynemouth NE30 ....145 A2
Coniston Way DH8 ..177 D4
Connisby Cl NE40 ..166 F3
Conniscliffe Rd NE46 .160 F3
Connolly Terr NE17 ..175 C6
Connolly Terr NE17 ..175 C6
Consett Bsns Pk DH8 .177 A3
Consett Inf Sch DH8 .177 A3
Consett Jun Sch DH8 .177 A3
Consett La DH8 .....176 B2

enton Park Sh Ctr
E5 .....149 E2
enton Rd NE15 ....169 F6
enton View NE21 ....169 B2
enway Gr NE26 ....135 B7
enwick NE66 ....181 F7
enwick Ave NE15 ....169 C6
enwick View NE66 ....181 E4
eputy Row TD15 ....4 A4
ere Pk DH8 ....177 C4
ere Rd DH8 ....177 B1
ere St Barrasford NE46 ....91 F8
olwell NE46 ....82 C1
reat Whittington NE19,
E46 ....92 B7
Vest Woodburn NE48 ....72 F6
exham CI NE26 ....135 D5
ereham Rd NE26 ....135 D5
ereham Terr NE62 ....122 C8
erwent Ave NE15 ....168 E2
erwent Cote NE17 ....175 B5
erwent Cres
amsterley NE17 ....175 B5
oadgate DH8 ....177 D5
erwent Ctr The 14
H8 ....176 F2
erwent Dale DH8 ....176 C6
erwent Haven NE17 ....175 B5
erwent Mews DH8 ....176 D4
erwent PI DH8 ....176 C6
erwent Rd
exham NE46 ....161 C4
eaton Sluice NE26 ....135 C6
ynemouth NE30 ....145 B2
erwent St
lackhall Mill NE17 ....175 C6
hopwell NE17 ....173 B1
onsett DH8 ....176 D4
erwent Valley Villas
E17 ....175 A6
erwent View
laydon NE21 ....169 B1
hopwell NE17 ....173 C2
erwent Water Terr TD15 ..4 A4
erwent Way
laydon NE21 ....169 E1
illingworth NE12 ....142 C3
erwentcote Steel Furnace*
E17 ....175 E6
erwentdale Ct DH8 ....176 D3
H8 ....176 D3
erwentdale Ind Est
E16 ....169 F3
erwenthaugh Rd NE21 ....169 F2
erwentside Bsns Ctr
H8 ....177 B4
erwentside Coll DH8 ....176 F2
erwentwater Rd NE64 ..118 C3
evil's Cswy TD15,NE71 ..116 F4
evon Rd NE29 ....144 D1
evon St NE15 ....178 C4
evonshire Dr NE27 ....143 C1
evonshire Terr 7
E26 ....145 B4
exworth PI NE24 ....128 A7
iwar's La 7 NE15 ....178 B4
ewberry CI NE24 ....128 C4
ewley CI NE23 ....133 B5
ewley Ct NE23 ....133 B5
ewley PI NE5 ....149 E4
ewsgreen NE23 ....133 B6
eyncourt NE20 ....138 D2
eyncourt CE NE12 ....138 D1
al Cottage Mus*
E12 ....142 C1
amond Sq 6 NE46 ....161 B4
ck St 9 NE46 ....161 B4
ckens Wlk NE5 ....149 C3
ckson Dr NE46 ....160 E3
Iston Ave
exham NE46 ....161 D4
Whitley Bay NE25 ....145 B4
Iston CI
egswood NE61 ....116 A3
hiremoor NE27 ....143 F2
Iston Dr
ashington NE63 ....117 D2
Newcastle u T NE12 ....149 E3
Iston Haugh Cotts
E45 ....162 D4
Iston Terr 5 NE15 ....183 D5
Iston West Cotts
E45 ....162 C2
nmont PI NE23 ....133 B5
nningside 9 NE70 ....15 F4
nnington Fst Sch
E13 ....140 C7
pton CI NE46 ....161 E4
pton Gr NE23 ....133 B6
pton Rd NE23 ....144 D2
spensary St NE66 ....181 B5
sraeli St Blyth NE24 ....128 E6
lyth NE24 ....128 E6
sraeli Terr NE17 ....173 B1
xburn Rd NE66 ....30 F7
xon Ave NE24 ....174 F4
xon St DH8 ....176 E4
octor's La NE46 ....99 C7
oddington CI NE15 ....169 B7
oddington Dr NE23 ....133 B6
oddington Mill NE71 ..14 A3
odds La 7 NE66 ....181 C5
odsworth N NE40 ....168 B1
odsworth Terr NE40 ....168 B1

Dodsworth Villas NE40 ..168 B1
Dogger Bank NE61 ....114 E1
Dolphin Ct 5 NE65 ....183 D5
Dolphin Villas NE13 ....141 B4
Donkin Terr NE30 ....167 E3
Dorchester CI NE5 ....149 B3
Dorchester Ct NE25 ....134 C6
Dorking CI NE24 ....128 E4
Dorset CI NE63 ....116 F4
Dorset Gr NE29 ....144 D1
Dorset Rd NE15 ....169 F6
Dotland CI NE46 ....161 E4
Double Row NE25 ....134 B5
Douglas Bader Ho NE24 ..128 F6
Douglas CI TD15 ....178 A7
Douglas Cres NE65 ....52 C5
Douglas Ct TD12 ....179 C7
Douglas Gdns NE47 ....158 A5
Douglas Smiths Bglws
NE49 ....153 B4
Douglas Terr NE46 ....91 B6
Dove CI NE12 ....142 C4
Dove CI NE35 ....145 C3
Dove Ho NE30 ....145 C3
Dove Row NE30 ....145 C3
Dovecote CI NE25 ....144 C6
Dovecote La NE66 ....181 C5
Dovecote St NE65 ....183 D5
Dovedale Ave NE24 ....128 A8
Dover CI Bedlington NE22 ..121 D1
Newcastle u T NE5 ....149 C3
Dovespoint NE47 ....106 B1
Dowling Ave NE25 ....144 F4
Downe CI NE24 ....128 E4
Downend Rd NE5 ....149 F3
Downham NE5 ....149 F1
Downing Dr NE12 ....119 E7
Downswood NE12 ....142 F3
Doxford Farm NE67 ....23 E2
Doxford PI NE23 ....121 F1
Dr Pit Cotts NE22 ....121 F1
Dr Thomlinson CE Mid Sch
NE65 ....182 C4
Drakestone View NE65 ..48 D7
Drawback NE42 ....166 D2
Drawback CI NE42 ....166 D2
Drey The NE20 ....138 A3
Drey The Consett DH8 ..176 D6
Newcastle u T NE15 ....169 F8
Stannington NE61 ....125 D6
Tranwell NE61 ....119 D1
Tynemouth NE30 ....145 D1
Drivers La TD15 ....178 B4
Drove Rd NE15 ....169 A3
Drummonds CI NE65 ....64 A5
Drumoyne Gdns NE25 ..144 D3
Druridge Ave NE65 ....52 F3
Druridge Bay Ctry Pk*
NE65 ....54 A3
Druridge Bay Nature
Reserve* NE61 ....66 B7
Druridge Cres NE24 ....128 B5
Druridge Dr NE24 ....128 B5
Dryburn Wlk TD15 ....8 E2
Drysdale Cres NE13 ....141 A6
Drysdale Ct NE13 ....141 B6
Duchess St NE46 ....145 A5
Duchess Trail* NE48 ....55 C4
Duchess's Com High Sch
The NE65 ....181 B6
Duchess's Dr NE66 ....31 A1
Duckets Dean NE42 ....166 D3
Duddo TD15 ....7 C5
Dudlees Rd NE19 ....47 D3
Dudley Bsns Ctr NE23 ..133 A2
Dudley Dr NE23 ....142 A8
Dudley La
Annitsford NE23 ....133 A2
Cramlington,Collingwood
NE23 ....133 A4
Cramlington,Hall Close
NE23 ....133 A6
Seaton Burn NE13 ....141 D8
Dudley Lane Cotts
NE13 ....141 C8
Dudley PI NE47 ....111 C8
Duke Ct Alnwick NE66 ....181 D6
Ashington NE63 ....117 C4
Coldstream TD12 ....179 C6
Whitley Bay NE26 ....145 A5
Duke's Gdns NE24 ....128 C8
Duke's Meml Ct 2
NE66 ....181 C5
Duke's Mid Sch The
NE66 ....181 C5
Dukes Cott NE5 ....168 F7
Dukes Ct NE42 ....166 E4
Dukes Dr NE3 ....141 B1
Dukes Mdw NE13 ....149 E8
Dukes Rd NE46 ....160 E5
Dukes Trail* NE48 ....55 D4
Dukes Way NE42 ....166 E4
Dukesfield CI NE23 ....133 B6
Dulverton CI NE5 ....149 C3
Dumas Wlk NE5 ....149 C3
Dunbar CI NE5 ....149 A3
Dunblane Cres NE5 ....149 F1
Dunblane Dr NE24 ....128 E4
Duncan Gdns NE61 ....119 F7
Dunces Hos NE5 ....120 D7
Dundee CI NE5 ....149 C3
Dunelm CI DH8 ....177 D3
Dunelm Way NE40 ....177 D3

Dunelm Wlk DH8 ....177 D3
Dunes Ct NE67 ....24 D7
Dunford Gdns NE5 ....149 D4
Dunkeld CI NE24 ....128 E4
Dunlin CI NE24 ....168 E4
Dunlin CI NE61 ....113 A3
Dunlin Dr NE24 ....128 E4
Dunne Rd NE21 ....169 E4
Dunnock Lodge NE15 ..169 D6
Duns Rd Berwick-u-T TD15 ..1 A1
Coldstream TD12 ....1 D1
Dunsdale Dr NE23 ....133 D8
Dunsdale Rd NE25 ....134 E2
Dunsgreen NE20 ....138 E5
Dunsgreen Ct NE20 ....138 E5
Dunsley Gdns NE13 ....140 B7
Dunslow Croft NE15 ....146 C1
Dunstable PI NE5 ....149 B3
Dunstan Sq NE66 ....32 B7
Dunstan View 1 NE68 ..17 F2
Dunstan Sq NE5 ....149 F1
Dunstanburgh Castle*
NE66 ....32 C8
Dunstanburgh CI NE22 ..121 D1
Dunstanburgh Rd NE66 ..32 C7
Dunston PI NE24 ....128 B8
Dunston Steads NE24 ....24 E1
Dunterns The NE66 ....181 C4
Dunwoodie Terr 6
NE46 ....161 A5
Durban St NE41 ....128 D8
Durham CI NE22 ....121 D2
Durham Rd Consett DH8 ..176 E4
Cramlington NE23 ....127 C1
Leadgate DH8 ....177 D3
Durken Bsns Pk NE23 ..133 F2
Dutton CI NE21 ....169 E4
Dyke Heads La NE40 ....168 B1

E

E D Morel Terr NE17 ....175 C8
Eagle Dr TD15 ....3 B5
Ealing Dr NE30 ....145 C1
Ealing Sq NE23 ....132 D6
Eals Bank NE49 ....95 C2
Earl's Gdns NE12 ....142 E1
Earlington Ct NE12 ....142 E1
Earls CI NE42 ....166 E4
Earlston Way NE23 ....127 C2
Earlswood Gr NE24 ....128 D3
Earnshaw Way NE25 ....144 D7
Earsdon Ct NE25 ....144 D4
Earsdon Rd
Shiremoor NE27 ....143 E4
Whitley Bay NE25 ....144 C4
Earsdon Terr 9 NE27 ....143 E1
Earsdon View NE27 ....143 F4
Earth Balance* NE22 ....122 C5
Easedale Ave NE3 ....141 C1
Easedale Ct NE24 ....128 C3
Easington Ave NE23 ....127 C2
Easington Demesne
NE70 ....16 B6
East Acres
Barrasford NE48 ....91 B8
Blaydon NE21 ....169 D1
Dinnington NE13 ....140 C8
Widdrington Sta NE61 ....65 E4
East Allerdean TD15 ....3 D1
East Allerdean Cotts TD15 ..3 D1
East Ancroft TD15 ....8 E8
East Bailey NE12 ....142 F3
East Blackdene DL13 ....111 E1
East Brizlee Dr NE66 ....30 E2
East Burton NE69 ....17 A3
East CI NE20 ....93 B6
East Cres NE22 ....122 D2
East End NE26 ....135 E4
East Farm NE46 ....91 C6
East Farm Terr NE23 ....133 B6
East Field NE66 ....32 B2
East Flodden NE71 ....12 F6
East Ford Rd NE62 ....122 C7
East Gate NE61 ....120 A6
East Grange NE25 ....134 F2
East Hartford Sch NE22 ..127 B3
East Horton NE71 ....14 D1
East Kirknewton Farm
NE71 ....12 E1
East Law DH8 ....159 B2
East Lea Humshaugh NE46 ..91 C6
Newbiggin-by-t-S NE64 ..118 E5
East Lilburn Cotts NE71 ..21 C2
East Loan NE61 ....115 A2
East Ord Cvn Pk TD15 ....6 A1
East Ord Cvn Pk 17 TD15 ..6 A1
East Ord Ind Est TD15 ....3 E6
East Par 5 Alnwick NE66 ..181 D4
Consett DH8 ....177 A2
Whitley Bay NE26 ....145 B5
East Park Gdns NE21 ....169 C1
East Park View NE24 ....129 A7
East Pastures NE63 ....117 B3
East Riggs NE22 ....126 F8
East Sea View NE64 ....118 F5
East St Chopwell NE17 ....173 D1
Consett,Crookhall DH8 ..177 B2
High Spen NE39 ....173 F4
Mickley Square NE43 ....165 F1
Spittal TD15 ....178 C2
East Terr Chopwell NE17 ..175 C7
Stakeford NE62 ....122 C7

East Thorp NE5 ....149 F5
East View
8 Bedlington NE22 ....122 D3
Blaydon NE21 ....169 D3
Consett DH8 ....176 F4
Crawcrook NE40 ....167 E6
Greenhead CA8 ....152 A6
Haltwhistle NE49 ....153 C4
Morpeth NE61 ....120 A8
New Hartley NE25 ....134 C5
Seghill NE23 ....133 F1
Stakeford NE62 ....122 C7
Togston NE65 ....53 E4
Wideopen NE13 ....141 B7
East View Ave NE23 ....133 B6
East View La TD15 ....178 A3
East View Terr NE23 ....142 A8
East Woodlands NE46 ..161 D4
Eastbourne Gdns
Cramlington NE23 ....132 D6
Whitley Bay NE26 ....145 A6
Eastcliffe TD15 ....178 C1
Easter Wynd 6 TD15 ....178 B4
Easterfield Ct NE61 ....115 A1
Easterfield La TD15 ....178 B4
Eastern Way NE20 ....138 D3
Eastfield Ave NE25 ....144 D4
Eastfield Hall NE65 ....41 F1
Eastfields NE46 ....161 D4
Eastgarth Ave 4 NE65 ..183 C5
Eastgate
Choppington NE62 ....121 F5
Hexham NE46 ....161 B4
Eastgate Bank NE43 ....171 F8
Eastgreen NE62 ....121 F5
Eastlands Blaydon NE21 ..169 B1
Kirkwhelpington NE19 ....74 A3
Easton Holmes NE22 ....122 C5
Eastward Gn NE25 ....144 D4
Eastwood Ave NE24 ....128 D3
Eastwood CI NE23 ....142 C5
Eastwood Grange Ct
NE46 ....161 E4
Eastwood Grange Rd
NE46 ....161 E4
Eastwood Mid Sch
NE42 ....166 F3
Eastwood PI NE23 ....127 C2
Eastwood Villas NE42 ..166 F4
Eastwoods Rd NE42 ....166 F3
Ebchester CE Prim Sch
DH8 ....174 E3
Ebchester Hill DH8 ....174 F2
Eccles Ct NE27 ....143 C5
Eccles Terr 2 NE27 ....143 E1
Eccleston CI NE27 ....143 C4
Eddrington Gr NE5 ....149 C2
Eden Ave DH8 ....177 D5
Eden CI NE5 ....149 C2
Eden Cotts DH8 ....177 C5
Eden Dale NE40 ....167 F4
Eden PI NE30 ....145 A1
Eden Terr NE61 ....113 A3
Eden's Lawn NE49 ....153 D5
Edendale Ave NE24 ....128 B8
Edendale Ct NE24 ....128 B8
Edenhill Rd NE64 ....118 D5
Edengarth NE30 ....145 A2
Edge Hill NE20 ....138 C1
Edge Mount NE12 ....142 E4
Edgefield Ct NE3 ....141 A1
Edgefield Dr NE23 ....127 C2
Edgehill NE61 ....120 B6
Edgehill CI NE20 ....138 C1
Edgewell Ave NE42 ....166 B1
Edgewell Grange NE42 ..166 C2
Edgewell House Rd
NE42,NE43 ....172 B8
Edgewell Rd NE42 ....166 B1
Edgewood Hexham NE46 ..161 D4
Prudhoe NE42 ....166 D2
Edgeworth CI NE38 ....101 E6
Edinburgh Dr NE22 ....121 E2
Edington Gdns NE40 ....167 E6
Edington Gr NE30 ....145 A1
Edington Rd NE30 ....145 A1
Edith Ave NE21 ....169 C2
Edith St Consett DH8 ....176 F2
11 Widdrington Sta NE61 ..65 E5
Edlingham Castle* NE66 ..30 A4
Edmund Rd NE27 ....143 D1
Edward Rd NE22 ....121 E3
Edward St Blyth NE24 ....128 D7
Crawcrook NE40 ....167 E3
Morpeth NE61 ....115 F3
Pegswood NE61 ....115 F3
Edwardia Ct DH8 ....176 E2
Edwards Rd NE26 ....145 B4
Edwin St Amble NE65 ....183 C5
Brunswick Village NE13 ..141 A6
Edwin Terr NE40 ....168 C2
Edwins Ave NE12 ....142 E1
Eggleston Dr DH8 ....176 F1
Egglestone Dr DH8 ....177 A1
Egham Rd NE5 ....149 C2
Eglingham Ave NE30 ....145 C1
Eglingham CE Fst Sch
NE66 ....29 F6
Eglingham Way NE61 ....120 B6
Egmont PI NE40 ....145 B4
Egremont Way NE23 ....132 D6
Eider CI NE24 ....128 E3
Eider Wlk NE12 ....141 B1
Eighteenth Ave NE24 ....128 D5

Eighth Ave
Ashington NE63 ....117 E2
Blyth NE24 ....128 D6
Morpeth NE61 ....120 B7
Eighth Row NE63 ....117 B4
Eilansgate NE46 ....161 A5
Eilansgate Ho NE46 ....160 F5
Eilansgate Terr NE46 ....161 A5
Eilanville NE46 ....161 A5
Eildon View TD15 ....3 F5
Eland Edge NE20 ....138 F6
Eland La NE20 ....138 F7
Eland View NE20 ....138 F6
Elder Sq NE63 ....117 E2
Eldon PI NE15 ....169 D7
Eldon Rd Hexham NE46 ..161 D4
Newcastle u T NE15 ....169 D7
Eldon Sq NE48 ....80 F4
Eleanor St NE30 ....145 C3
Eleanor Terr NE40 ....168 A4
Elenbel Ave NE22 ....122 C1
Eleventh Ave Blyth NE24 ..128 D5
Morpeth NE61 ....120 B7
Eleventh Row NE63 ....117 B4
Elford CI NE25 ....144 D5
Elford Farm Cotts NE68 ..17 B1
Elgar Ave 3 NE5 ....149 C2
Elgin CI Bedlington NE22 ..122 D2
Cramlington NE23 ....132 D6
Elizabeth Cres NE23 ....142 A8
Elizabeth Ct NE12 ....143 A1
Elizabeth Dr NE12 ....143 A1
Elizabeth St
Chopwell NE17 ....173 B1
East Cramlington NE23 ..133 F5
Widdrington Sta NE61 ....65 E4
Ellersmere Gdns NE30 ..145 B2
Ellerton Way NE23 ....127 C2
Ellesmere Gdns NE62 ..122 C8
Ellingham CE Fst Sch
NE67 ....23 D4
Ellingham Glebe NE67 ....23 D4
Ellingham CI NE15 ....169 B7
Ellington Cvn Pk NE61 ..112 B7
Ellington Fst Sch NE61 ..112 E5
Ellington Terr NE46 ....116 F4
Ellington Way NE61 ....112 C4
Elliot Bldgs NE47 ....158 A5
Elliot CI NE12 ....120 B7
Elliott St NE24 ....128 C4
Elliott Terr NE48 ....80 C4
Ellis Sq NE61 ....115 F3
Ellison Terr NE40 ....167 F1
Elm Ave NE13 ....140 B7
Elm Bank Rd NE41 ....167 B5
Elm CI Cramlington NE23 ..127 C2
Hexham NE46 ....160 E3
Elm Ct NE46 ....53 E4
Elm Gr NE12 ....142 D1
Elm Park Rd DH8 ....176 F7
Elm Park Terr DH8 ....176 F7
Elm Rd Blaydon NE21 ....169 D2
Ponteland NE20 ....139 A5
Elm St Consett DH8 ....176 F4
Mickley Square NE43 ....171 E8
Seaton Burn NE13 ....141 C8
Elm Terr DH8 ....177 D4
Elm Trees NE24 ....128 D6
Elmbank Cvn Pk
Berwick-u-T TD15 ....4 A5
Spittal TD15 ....178 D1
Elmdale Rd DH8 ....177 A3
Elmfield Gdns NE15 ....169 E1
Elmfield Rd Consett DH8 ..176 F4
Throckley NE15 ....148 E2
Elmfield Terr NE65 ....41 A1
Elms The Consett DH8 ..176 F7
Ellington NE61 ....112 D4
Elmtree Dr NE46 ....168 B1
Elmtree Gdns NE25 ....144 E3
Elmwood NE15 ....169 C6
Elmwood Ave NE13 ....141 C5
Elmwood Dr NE20 ....138 E7
Elmwood Gr NE26 ....145 A5
Elmwood Mews NE13 ....141 B4
Elmwood Rd NE25 ....144 E4
Elrick CI NE5 ....149 C2
Elsdon Cres NE25 ....134 D3
Elsdon CI NE24 ....128 C7
Elsdon Dr NE12 ....142 A2
Elsdon Gdns NE23 ....128 D3
Elsdon PI NE15 ....176 F5
Elston CI NE5 ....149 C2
Elstree Gdns NE24 ....128 D3
Eltringham Cotts NE43 ..165 F1
Eltringham Rd NE42 ....166 A2
Elvaston Gr NE46 ....161 B3
Elvaston Park Rd NE46 ..161 A3
Elvaston Rd
Hexham NE46 ....161 B4
Ryton NE40 ....168 C6
Elveit CI NE13 ....141 A6
Elwick Dr NE16 ....16 A7
Elwin CI NE26 ....135 D5
Elwin PI NE26 ....135 D5
Elworthy Rd NE65 ....32 B2
Ember Gdns NE65 ....53 E8
Embleton CI NE65 ....51 E4
Embleton Ct NE24 ....128 C5
Embleton Dr NE63 ....117 B3
Embleton Terr NE65 ....53 E8
Embleton Vincent Edwards
CE First Sch NE66 ....24 D1
Emily Davison Ave
NE61 ....119 E8

Emma St DH8 .... 176 F4
Emma View **7** NE40 ..167 F3
Emmaville NE40 .... 168 A4
Emmaville Prim Sch
NE40 .... 167 F3
Emmerson Ct NE23 ....143 E3
Emmerson Pl NE27 ....143 E3
Emmerson Rd NE64 ....118 D5
Ena St NE61 .... 65 E5
Enderby Dr NE46 ....160 E3
Engine Rd
Hedley on t H NE17 ....172 E4
Prudhoe NE42 ....172 F5
Enid St NE13 .... 141 A1
Ennerdale Rd Blyth NE24 .127 F8
Tynemouth NE30 ....145 C2
Ennerdale Terr NE17 ..175 A5
Ennis Cl NE32 ....122 D8
Enterprise Ct NE23 ....126 F1
Epping Ct NE23 ....132 D6
Epsom Cl DH8 ....176 E7
Epsom Dr NE63 ....117 C2
Epsom Way NE24 ....128 D3
Epwell Gr NE23 ....127 C2
Eric Tolhurst Ctr **12**
NE24 .... 128 F8
Errington Cl NE20 ......138 C2
Errington Pl NE42 ......166 C2
Errington Rd NE20 ......138 B2
Errington St NE24 ......127 E7
Errington Terr NE12 ..142 E1
Errol Hut Smithy* TD12 ...7 C2
Esher Gdns NE24 ....128 D3
Esher Pl NE23 ....132 D6
Eshmere Cres NE5 ......149 C3
Eskdale Ave NE24 ......128 D3
Eskdale Terr NE26 ......145 C4
Eslington Mews NE61 ..117 F4
Esmeralda Gdns NE23 .133 F1
Esplanade NE26 ....145 B5
Esplanade Ave NE26 ..145 B5
Esplanade Pl NE26 ....145 B5
Espley Ct NE61 .... 64 D1
Essex Cl NE63 ....117 A4
Eston Ct NE24 ....128 B8
Estuary The TD15 ......178 B3
Etal TD12 .... 7 B2
Etal Ave NE25 ....145 B4
Etal Castle* TD12 .... 7 B2
Etal Cl NE27 ....143 F3
Etal Cres NE27 ....143 F3
Etal Ho NE63 ....117 F4
Etal Rd Berwick-u-T TD15 ...3 E6
Blyth NE24 ....128 B3
Tweedmouth TD15 ......178 A1
Etal Way TD15 ....178 A1
Ethel Ave NE21 ....169 C2
Ethel St NE23 ....142 A6
Ethel Terr
2 Hexham NE46 ......161 A4
High Spen NE39 ....173 F3
Ethel's Cl NE65 ....183 B4
Eton Cl NE23 ....127 C2
Ettrick Cl NE12 ....142 C4
Eva St NE15 ....169 C6
Evelyn Terr NE15 ......169 C3
Everard St NE23 ....127 B3
Eversleigh Pl NE15 ....148 E2
Evesham Ave NE26 ....144 F6
Evesham Pl NE23 ......132 D7
Ewesley Gdns NE11 ..141 B6
Exchange Bldgs NE26 ..145 B5
Exeter Cl Ashington NE63 .118 A2
Cramlington NE23 ......132 E6
Exeter Ct NE29 ....144 C1

F

Factory Rd NE21 ....169 D4
Fair Gn NE25 ....144 C4
Fair Hill NE49 ....153 D5
Fair View NE42 ....166 C2
Fairfield Consett DH8 ..177 B1
Hexham NE46 ....160 F4
Fairfield Ave NE24 ....128 D4
Fairfield Cres NE46 ..161 E8
Fairfield Dr
Ashington NE63 ....118 A2
Tynemouth NE30 ....145 B2
Whitley Bay NE25 ......144 D4
Fairfield Gn NE40 ......149 C4
Fairfield Pk NE40 ......153 D5
Fairfield Rd NE49 .... 41 D3
Fairfields Alnwick NE66 .181 C3
Ryton NE40 ....168 B5
Fairhill View CA9 ......185 E3
Fairholme Ave NE49 ..153 C6
Fairlands Cl NE65 .... 52 C6
Fairney Cl NE20 ....138 F6
Fairney Edge NE20 ....138 F6
Fairshaw Cres NE48 ..184 B5
Fairspring **8** NE5 ....149 F2
Fairview Dr DH8 ....177 C2
Fairville Cl NE23 ....127 B2
Fairway Morpeth NE61 ..119 F5
Stakeford NE62 ....122 A8
Fairway The
High Hauxley NE65 ....183 F3
Ryton NE21 ....169 A4
Fairways Consett DH8 ..176 F5
Whitley Bay NE25 ......144 D5
Fairwood Rd NE46 ....161 D4
Falcon Ct NE63 ....117 B1

Falcon Grange NE47 ..155 E6
Falcon Hill NE61 ....119 D7
Falcon Terr NE41 ......167 B6
Falkirk NE12 ....142 D4
Falloden Terr TD15 ....178 B2
Falloden Ave NE66 ...... 41 D3
Fallow Park Ave NE28 .128 C6
Fallowfield Way NE63 .117 F2
Falmouth Rd NE29 ....144 D1
Falmouth Wlk NE23 ..128 B3
Falston Rd NE24 ....128 C5
Falstone **3** NE5 ......169 E8
Falstone Burn Forest Wlk*
NE48 .... 69 D6
Falstone Cres NE63 ..117 E1
Falstone Way NE46 ..160 F3
Farbridge Cres DH8 ..174 F3
Fareham Way NE23 ..133 B2
Farlam Ave NE30 ......145 A1
Farm Cotts
Ellingham NE67 .... 23 C4
Holywell NE25 ....134 F2
Farm Ct NE61 .... 66 B6
Farm Dr Alnwick NE66 .. 30 F1
Alnwick NE66 .... 30 F2
Farm View Ho NE23 ..133 C5
Farm Well Pl NE42 ....166 D3
Farnborough Cl NE23 .133 B8
Farndale Ave NE62 ....122 A8
Farndale Cl NE13 ......140 B7
Farndale Ct NE24 ......128 D4
Farne Ave NE63 ....117 D2
Farne Cres NE68 .... 17 E3
Farne Rd Shilbottle NE66 ..41 C3
Shiremoor NE27 ....143 F3
Tweedmouth TD15 ......178 A2
Longbenton NE12 ......142 E1
Farnham Cl NE15 ......169 D6
Farnham Gr NE24 ......128 A6
Farnham St NE15 ......169 D6
Farriers Ct Alnwick NE66 .181 C3
Stakeford NE62 ....122 A8
Farriers Rise NE66 ...... 41 C3
Farringdon Rd NE30 ..145 A2
Faversham Pl NE23 ..133 B8
Fawdon Gr NE61 ....115 D3
Fawdon House Farm
NE61 .... 115 D5
Featherstone Gr
Bedlington NE22 ....121 E2
Newcastle u T NE3 ....143 A1
Feetham Ave NE12 ....143 A1
Feetham Ct NE12 ......143 A1
Felkington TD15 .... 7 D7
Fell View Consett DH8 ..176 C1
10 Crawcrook NE40 ..167 C1
Haltwhistle NE49 ....153 C5
Spartylea NE47 ....167 B2
Fell View W **15** NE40 ..167 C1
Fell Way The NE5 ......149 D1
Fellside NE20 ....138 B1
Fellside Cl NE40 ....138 B1
Felltop NE25 ....176 D3
Felstead Pl NE24 ......128 D4
Felton Ave NE25 ....145 B4
Felton Cl Morpeth NE61 ..120 B6
Shiremoor NE27 ....143 F3
Felton Dr NE12 ....142 B2
Felton Terr NE61 ......117 D2
Fenham Rd NE61 ......112 F3
Fenharnhill TD15 .... 9 D4
Fenkle St Alnwick NE66 .181 C5
Holy Island TD15 ....10 C5
Fennybeds Est **9** NE65 ...65 E5
Fenrother La NE61 ...... 64 D3
Fenton Dr NE71 ....180 C6
Fenton Grange NE71 .180 C7
Fenton Hill NE71 .... 13 E6
Fenton Wlk **3** NE5 ..149 F2
Fenwick TD15 .... 9 D3
Fenwick Ave NE24 ....128 D5
Fenwick Gr
4 Hexham NE46 ......161 A5
Morpeth NE61 ....115 A1
Fenwick Stead TD15 .... 9 F2
Fenwick Way DH8 ....176 E3
Ferguson Cres NE13 ..141 A4
Fern Ave NE23 ....127 B2
Fern Ct NE62 ....121 E7
Fern Dr NE23 ....142 B8
Fern St DH8 ....176 F3
Ferndale NE66 ....135 C6
Ferndale Ave NE3 ....141 D1
Ferndale Cl NE28 ......128 A8
Ferndene Gr NE40 ....168 D6
Ferndown Ct NE40 ....168 A4
Fernlea NE23 ....142 B8
Fernlea Gdns NE40 ..168 A4
Fernley Villas NE13 ..133 D6
Fernway NE61 ....120 B8
Fernwood Gr NE39 ....175 F5
Fernwood Rd NE15 ..169 D6
Ferny Bank NE65 .... 52 C6
Ferry Landing NE47 ..165 F3
Ferry Rd NE46 ....161 C6
Festival Cotts NE12 ..142 B5
Field House Cl NE65 .. 53 D4
Field Terr **4** NE61 ..115 A1
Fieldfare Ho **9** NE42 ..128 E8
Fieldhouse La NE61 ..120 C6
Fieldhouse La NE61 ..120 E5
Fife Terr NE17 ....175 B6
Fifteenth Ave NE24 ..128 D6
Fifth Ave Ashington NE63 .117 C3
Blyth NE24 ....128 B6

Fifth Ave continued
Morpeth NE61 ....120 B7
Fifth Row NE61 ....112 A3
Fifth St DH8 ....177 B2
Filey Cl NE23 ....132 D3
Filton Cl NE23 ....133 B8
Finchale Gdns NE15 ..148 D3
Fine La DH8 ....174 B3
Fines Rd DH8 ....175 B1
Fir Gr NE11 ....112 D4
Firbank Ave NE30 ....145 B2
Fire Station Hos NE16 ..154 A1
Firs The CA9 ....185 D3
First Ave Ashington NE63 .117 E4
Blyth NE24 ....128 B6
Morpeth NE61 ....120 B7
First Row
Ashington NE63 ....117 A4
Ellington NE61 ....112 A2
Linton NE61 ....112 A3
First St Consett DH8 ..177 B2
Leadgate DH8 ....177 C6
Leadgate DH8 ....177 C6
Firtree Ave NE12 ......142 D1
Firtree Cres NE12 ....142 C1
Firtree Gdns NE25 ....144 F3
Fisher La Alnwick NE66 .181 D5
Cramlington NE13,NE23 .132 B5
Fisher Rd NE27 ....143 B6
Fishers' Back Rd TD15 ..9 E4
Fishwick TD15 .... 2 D6
Fiveacres NE71 ....180 C5
Fleming Ct NE49 ......153 C5
Flexbury Gdns NE15 ..169 E7
Flodden NE12 ....142 D4
Flodden Cres NE23 ....12 C8
Flodden Field* TD12 ..12 B8
Florence St NE21 ......165 F1
Flotterton NE65 .... 49 D5
Fold The NE25 ....144 E5
Folly La Catton NE47 .. 97 E5
Greenside NE40 ....168 B2
Folly Yd NE40 ....168 C2
Font Side NE61 ....114 A1
Fontburn amble NE65 .183 D5
Fontburn Cres NE63 ..117 F3
Fontburn Gdns NE61 ..119 E7
Fontburn Rd
Bedlington NE22 ....122 C1
Seaton Delaval NE25 ..134 D3
Fonteyn Pl NE23 ......127 B2
Ford TD15 .... 13 B8
Ford Ave NE13 ....141 C2
Ford Cres NE27 ....143 E3
Ford Ct **10** TD15 ....178 B4
Ford Dr NE24 ....128 C4
Ford Pk NE62 ....122 C8
Ford Rise NE43 ....171 C7
Ford Terr
Guide Post NE62 ....121 F7
Riding Mill NE44 ....170 A8
Ford The NE42 ....166 C3
Ford View NE23 ....133 A1
Ford Westfield TD15 ...13 A7
Fordley Com Prim Sch
NE23 .... 142 A8
Fordmoss Wlk **7** NE5 .149 F2
Fore St NE46 ....161 B5
Forest Dr Byrness NE19 ..45 E3
Byrness NE48 .... 44 F1
* Kielder NE48 ....55 D5
Forest Gate NE12 ....143 A1
Forest Hall Prim Sch
NE12 .... 142 D1
Forest Hall Rd NE12 ..142 E1
Forest Way NE23 ......133 F1
Forestborn Ct **5** NE5 .149 F2
Forge Cl NE17 ....175 B6
Forge St NE61 .... 65 D3
Forge La NE17 ....175 E5
Forge The NE46 .... 91 C1
Forge Wlk NE15 ......148 F1
Forres Pl NE23 ....133 B8
Forster Ave NE22 ....121 E1
Forster St Blyth NE24 ..128 F7
Consett DH8 ....177 A2
Forsterstead NE47 ..... 98 A3
Forsyth St NE29 ......144 B1
Forth St NE17 ....173 C1
Forum Ct NE62 ....121 F1
Forum The NE15 ......169 F7
Forum Way NE23 ......133 A6
Foss Way NE15 ....174 E3
Fosse Law NE15 ......148 E1
Foul Ford **0** TD15 ....178 B4
Fountain Cl NE15 ......148 F1
Fountain Head Bank
NE26 .... 135 C6
Fountain La NE21 ......168 A4
Four Lane Ends DL13 .111 E1
Fourstones **6** NE5 ..149 F2
Fourteenth Ave NE24 .128 D6
Fourth Ave
Ashington NE63 ....117 D3
Blyth NE24 ....128 B6
Fourth Row NE61 ......112 A3
Fourth St Consett DH8 ..177 C5
Leadgate DH8 ....177 C5
Leadgate DH8 ....177 C5
Fowberry Cotts NE71 ..21 B8
Fowberry Rd NE15 ....169 F4
Fox Covert La NE20 ..138 D6
Fox Lea Wlk NE23 ....133 C1
Foxcover NE61 ....117 F1

Foxglove Cl NE24 ......128 C4
Foxhill Cl NE63 ....117 B1
Foxhunters Light Ind Site
NE25 .... 144 F3
Foxhunters Rd NE25 ..144 F3
Foxley Cl NE12 ....142 F4
Foxton Ave NE30 ......145 B3
Foxton Dr NE62 .... 42 C6
Frances St NE21 ......169 A2
Frances Ville NE62 ....121 E4
Francis Way NE21 ....143 D1
Frank St NE40 ....168 D6
Frankham St **1** NE5 .149 F2
Frankland Dr NE25 ..144 E3
Franklin Pk NE21 ......169 E4
Franklyn Ave NE26 ..135 B7
Frederick St NE17 ....175 B8
Freehold Ave NE62 ..121 F7
Freehold St **5** NE24 .128 F8
Freeman Way
Ashington NE63 ....117 F1
Whitley Bay NE26 ......144 E7
Freemens Ct **2** TD15 .178 B5
French St NE24 ....128 B1
Frenchman's Row NE15 .148 B2
Frenton Cl NE5 ....149 C2
Friars Ct NE69 .... 17 A5
Friars Gate NE61 ......119 D7
Friars Well Dr NE46 ...30 F3
Friary Farm NE66 ...... 17 A5
Friary Gdns **2** NE66 .142 B5
Frome Pl NE48 ....133 B8
Front Dr NE48 .... 81 F3
Front Row NE61 .... 74 D4
Front St Alston CA9 ..185 D3
Annitsford NE23 ....133 B1
Bamburgh NE69 .... 17 B5
Bellingham NE48 ......184 B8
Blaydon NE21 ....169 B1
Blyth NE24 ....127 E7
Castleside DH8 ....109 F3
Consett DH8 ....176 C6
Consett,Templetown DH8 .176 F2
Corbridge NE45 ....166 F5
Cramlington NE23 ......133 B6
Earsdon NE25 ....144 A5
Ebchester DH8 ....176 F7
Ellington NE61 ....112 C5
Embleton NE66 .... 24 D1
4 Glanton NE66 ...... 29 C1
Guide Post NE62 ......121 F7
Killingworth NE12,NE23 .142 B5
Leadgate DH8 ....177 C4
Longframlington NE65 ..51 F4
Newbiggin-by-t-S NE64 .118 E4
Prudhoe NE42 ....166 D2
Prudhoe,Eltringham NE42 .166 F5
Seghill NE23 ....133 F2
Tynemouth,Cullercoats
NE30 .... 145 C3
Wall NE46 .... 91 B3
Wearhead DL13 ....111 B2
Whitley Bay NE25,NE26 .144 E4
Front St E NE22 ....127 A8
Front St W NE22 ......126 F8
Fulbrook Cl NE3 ....127 B2
Fullers Wlk NE66 ......181 C3
Fulmar Dr NE24 ....128 E2
Furnace Bank NE22 ..122 D1

G

Gables End NE61 .... 65 E4
Gables The
3 Blyth NE24 ....128 D8
Widdrington Sta NE61 ..65 E4
Gainsborough Cl NE25 .144 C7
Gainsborough Pl NE23 .133 B3
Gainslaw Hill Farm Cotts
NE13 .... 3 B7
Gairloch Cl NE23 ......127 B1
Gallowhill La NE15,NE42 .166 E7
Gallows Bank NE46 ..161 B3
Ganton Ave NE23 ......133 B4
Gaprigg Ct NE46 ......161 B4
Gaprigg La NE46 ......161 A4
Gaps The NE46 .... 91 D1
Garasdale Cl NE24 ....128 D4
Garden City Villas NE63 .117 D3
Garden Cl
11 Consett DH8 ......176 F3
Seaton Burn NE13 ......141 A8
Garden Cres DH8 ......174 F8
Garden House Dr NE40 ..91 C1
Garden House Est NE40 .167 E4
Garden Pl
12 Consett DH8 ......176 F3
Leadgate DH8 ....177 C4
Garden Terr
13 Alnmouth NE66 ...42 B5
16 Blaydon NE21 ....169 B1
Crawcrook NE40 ....167 E2
Crawcrook,Ryton Woodside
NE40 .... 168 A3
Earsdon NE25 ....144 A5
8 Glanton NE66 ...... 29 C1
Hexham NE46 ....161 C4
Leadgate DH8 ....177 C4
Lesbury NE66 .... 42 A6
Shilbottle NE66 .... 41 D3
Stanley NE25 ....144 F4
Garden Villas NE12 ..143 A5
Gareston Cl NE24 ....128 B7
Garforth Cl NE23 ......133 A4
Garleigh Cl NE12 ......142 F3
Garleigh Rd NE65 ....182 C3

Garmondsway Bank NE66 .39
Garner Cl NE5 149
Garret's Hill Bank NE47 .106
Garsdale Rd NE26 135
Garth Cotts NE46 161
Garth Cres NE11 169
Garth Farm Rd NE21 .169
Garth La NE61 65
Garth Sixteen NE12 ..142
Garth The
7 Blaydon NE21 169
Medomsley DH8 169
Newcastle u T NE5 149
Garth Thirty Three
NE12 142
Garth Thirty Two NE12 .142
Garth Twenty NE12 ..142
Garth Twenty Five NE12 .142
Garth Twenty Four
NE12 142
Garth Twenty One NE12 .142
Garth Twenty Seven
NE12 142
Garth Twenty Two NE12 .142
Gas House La NE61 ..115
Gas La NE21 169
Gatacre St NE24 128
Gatehouse Factories **13**
DH8 176
Gateley Ave NE24 128
Genesis Way DH8 176
George Rd NE22 122
George St Amble NE65 .183
Ashington NE63 117
Blaydon NE21 169
Blyth NE24 128
Brunswick Village NE13 .141
Consett DH8 176
Consett,Blackhill DH8 ..176
5 Crawcrook NE40 ..167
4 Seahouses NE68 ...17
Walbottle NE15 148
George Stephenson Com
High Sch NE12 142
George Stephenson's
Cottage* NE41 167
Georgia Ct DH8 176
Georgian Ct NE12 142
Gerrard Cl
Cramlington NE23 133
Whitley Bay NE26 135
Gerrard Rd NE16 154
Ghyll Edge NE61 114
Gibside View NE21 ..169
Gibson Fields NE46 ..161
Gibson Ho **8** NE46 ..161
Gibson Pl **8** NE46 ..161
Gibson St **2** Amble NE65 .183
Consett DH8 176
Newbiggin-by-t-S NE64 .118
Gibson Terr NE40 168
Gilderdale Way NE23 .133
Giles Pl **10** NE46 161
Gilesgate NE46 161
Gilesgate Ct **10** NE46 .161
Gilhespy Green Cvn Pk
NE29 128
Gill St DH8 141
Gill Side View DH8 ..176
Gill St DH8 176
Gilmore Cl Alston CA9 .185
Newcastle u T NE5 149
Gilsland CE Prim Sch
CA8 86
Gisland Gr DH8 127
Gilwell Way NE23 132
Gingler La NE40 168
Gisburn Ct NE23 132
Glade The NE15 149
Gladewell Cl NE62 121
Gladstone Ave NE26 ..144
Gladstone Gdns DH8 .177
Gladstone St Blyth NE24 .128
Consett DH8 177
Morpeth NE61 169
Newcastle u T NE15 ..169
Gladstone Terr
Bedlington NE22 145
8 Whitley Bay NE26 .145
Glamis Ave NE11 169
Glamis Hill TD15 178
Glanton Ave NE25 144
Glanton Cl NE61 120
Glanton Cl NE28 120
Glanton Ho NE22 128
Glanton Rd NE46 122
Glassey Terr NE22 ..122
Glazebury Way NE23 .127
Glebe Cl
Newcastle u T NE5 149
Ponteland NE20 138
Glebe Cres NE12 142
Glebe Ct NE22 121
Glebe Farm NE22 121
Glebe Mews NE22 121
Glebe Rd
Bedlington NE22 121
Longbenton NE12 142
Glebe Terr
Choppington NE62 121
Longbenton NE12 142
Glebe The
Stannington NE61 125
Ward NE48 107
Glebe Villas NE12 142
Glebelands NE45 163
Glen Ave NE43 170
Glen Terr NE46 160

enallen Gdns NE30 ...145 C1
encoe NE12 ....142 D4
encoe Ave NE23 .....133 B3
endale NE65 ....183 E4
endale Ave Blyth NE24 127 E8
akeford NE22 ....122 A8
hitley Bay NE26 ....145 A7
endale Bsns Pk NE71 .180 E2
endale Cl
ewcastle u T NE5 .....149 D3
hitley NE65 ....182 B5
endale Ct NE65 ....183 E5
endale Gdns NE62 ....122 A8
endale Mid NE71 .....180 D5
endale Pl
shington NE63 ....118 A2
hiremoor NE27 ....144 A3
ooler NE71 ....180 C6
endford Pl NE24 ......128 D4
eneagle Cl NE5 ....149 D3
eneagles NE25 ....144 D6
eneagles Ct NE25 .....144 D6
enfield Ave NE23 .....127 E1
enhurst Dr NE5 ....149 D3
enluce Cl Consett DH8 .176 C3
ramlington NE23 ......133 B4
enluce Dr NE23 ....133 B3
enmuir Ave NE23 .....133 A3
enside Consett DH8 ...176 D6
Jington NE61 ....127 E5
enside Pk TD15 ....3 D6
enwhelt Bank CA8 .....152 B8
enwood NE63 ....117 C2
enwood Wlk NE5 .....149 D3
obe La CA9 ....185 D3
oria Ave NE25 ....134 D6
ossop St NE39 ....173 F4
oster Pk NE65 ....183 B4
oucester Rd DH8 .....177 B1
oucester St NE25 .....134 D6
overs Gn NE66 ....181 C3
overs Pl ☒ NE46 .....161 A5
ynwood Cl NE23 .....127 B1
lden Acre DH8 ....176 D5
lden Cl NE67 ....23 C4
lden Sq
erwick-u-T TD15 ......178 B4
altwhistle NE49 ....153 D8
ooler NE71 ....180 C5
ldhill La DH8 ....109 D2
ldstone Cl NE12 ......142 E4
ldthorpe Cl NE23 .....127 B1
och Ave NE22 ....122 A4
odwood Cl NE12 .....142 E3
odwood Cl
onsett DH8 ....176 E6
ewcastle u T NE5 .....149 D3
odwood Ct NE63 .....117 D2
ose Hill NE61 ....120 A8
rdon Ho NE26 ....145 C4
rdon Rd NE25 ....145 C4
rdon Sq NE26 ....145 C4
rdon St NE65 ....183 E6
rdon Terr
rdington NE23 ....127 A8
rudhoe NE42 ....166 D2
akeford NE62 ....122 C7
gston NE65 ....53 E4
hitley Bay NE26 ......145 C5
rdon Terrace W
E62 ....122 C7
rdon Villas NE65 .....133 E6
rsedene Ave NE15 ...135 D6
rsedene Rd NE26 ....135 F1
rseway NE61 ....119 D7
schen St NE24 ....128 D8
sforth Park Villas
E13 ....141 C4
sport Way NE24 .....128 D8
wanburn NE23 ......133 A3
wanlea TD12 ....179 C6
wk La NE20 ....85 A5
acefield Cl NE5 ......149 D3
adys Yd NE15 ....148 D3
afton Rd NE26 ....145 A4
aham's Cnr NE66 ....131 F7
ahams Yd ☑ NE66 ...181 C5
ampian Cl ☑ NE29 ..144 F1
ampian Pl NE21 ......142 B1
anaries The NE39 ....173 F4
anary Cotts NE66 .....24 C1
anary Ct DH8 ....177 D7
anary The ☑ TD15 ...178 B4
and Loaning TD15 .....1 D1
and Par NE30 ....145 D1
andstand The NE61 ...119 D6
ange Ave
edlington NE22 ......122 E3
iremoor NE27 ....143 F4
amfordham NE18 .....93 F6
ange Cl Blyth NE24 ..128 D4
nemouth NE30 ....145 B2
hitley Bay NE25 .....144 D4
ange Cres NE40 .....168 C4
ange Pk
ange NE66 ....31 E5
hitley Bay NE25 .....144 D4

Grange Rd
Haltwhistle NE49 ....153 D4
Morpeth NE61 ....120 A6
Newburn NE15 ....168 E8
Ponteland NE20 ....138 F7
Ryton NE40 ....168 C5
Shilbottle NE66 ....41 D3
Stamfordham NE18 ...136 A4
Widdrington Sta NE61 ...65 E4
Grange Terr
Medomsley DH8 ....175 B1
Prudhoe NE42 ....166 D2
Grange The NE12 ......121 A1
Grange View Ryton NE40 168 C4
Widdrington Sta NE61 ...65 E4
Grange View Fst Sch
NE61 ....65 E4
Grangeburn Cl 🆃 TD15 ...3 E6
Grangemoor Rd NE61 ...65 E5
Grangeside Ct 🆃 NE24 .144 F1
Grangewood Ho NE61 ...65 D5
Grangewood Terr NE61 ...65 D5
Grantham Pl NE23 .....133 A4
Grantham St NE24 ....128 F6
Granville Ave
Longbenton NE12 .....142 E1
Seaton Sluice NE26 ...135 D5
Granville Dr NE5 ......149 D3
Granville Gdns NE22 ..122 A8
Grasmere Ave NE15 ..168 E7
Grasmere Cres NE26 ..144 F7
Grasmere Ct
Killingworth NE12 .....142 C3
Newburn NE15 ....168 E7
Grasmere Terr NE64 ..118 D4
Grasmere Way NE24 ..128 A8
Grasmoor Pl NE15 ....169 E7
Grassholme Cl DH8 ...177 A1
Grassington Dr NE23 .133 A4
Grassmere Mews DH8 ...177 D4
Gravelly Bank NE65 ..182 A5
Gray Ave NE13 ....141 C7
Gray St Cambois NE24 ...123 E1
Consett DH8 ....176 E3
Great Lime Rd
Dudley NE12,NE13,NE23 ..142 A5
Longbenton NE12 .....142 D1
Great North Rd
Stannington NE61 .....120 A4
Newcastle u T NE1 ...141 C2
Great Park Way
Hazlerigg NE13 ....140 F2
Newcastle u T NE13 ..141 A3
Grebe Cl Ashington NE63 ..117 E1
Blyth NE24 ....128 E5
Greely Rd NE5 ....149 F2
Green Acres
Morpeth NE61 ....119 E7
Ponteland NE20 ......138 C1
Green Bank NE46 ....161 C4
Green Batt NE66 .....181 C5
Green Cl Lowick TD15 ...3 E2
Stannington NE61 ....125 C4
Tynemouth NE30 .....145 B1
Whitley Bay NE25 ....144 D4
Green Cres NE23 .....141 F8
Green Gr NE40 ....168 B3
Green La Acklington NE65 ..53 D6
Ashington NE63 ......153 D6
Cornhill on T TD12 ....6 B2
Dudley NE23 ....141 F8
Harbottle NE65 ....48 E8
Holy Island TD15 ......10 D5
Killingworth NE12 ....142 E2
Morpeth NE61 ....115 B1
Stannington NE61 ....124 D2
Stannington,Duddo Hill
NE61 ....124 D5
Woolsington NE13 ...149 F8
Morpeth,Stobhillgate NE61 120 B7
Green Sq NE25 ....144 D4
Green St Consett,Shotley Bridge
DH8 ....176 C2
Leadgate DH8 ....176 F4
Green The Acomb NE46 ...91 D1
Chopwell NE17 ....175 B8
Ovington NE42 ....158 F7
Ponteland NE20 ....138 F7
Walbottle NE15 ......148 F1
Whitley Bay NE25 ....144 E6
Widdrington Sta NE61 ...65 E4
Green-Fields NE40 ...168 B3
Greenacres NE68 ......17 E2
Greenacres Cl NE40 ..168 A3
Greenacres Rd DH8 ..176 D5
Greenbank NE21 .....169 C2
Greenchester-Potts Durtrees
NE67 ....59 D6
Greencroft
Ashington NE63 ......117 C2
Haltwhistle NE49 .....153 C5
Greencroft Ave
Corbridge NE45 ......163 A6
Haltwhistle NE49 .....153 C5
Greener Cl NE42 .....166 B1
Greenfield Ave NE66 .181 C3
Greenfield Dr NE62 ..121 E6
Greenfield Pl NE40 ..168 D5
Greenfield Rd NE13 .141 B1
Greenfield Terr 🆃
NE65 ....183 C5
Greenfields Com Prim Sch
NE13 ....141 C6
Greengate La NE49 ..154 C4
Greenhaugh NE12 ...142 B1

Greenhaugh Fst Sch
NE48 ....70 E6
Greenhaugh Rd NE25 ..144 B5
Greenhead Bank CA8 .151 F7
Greenhead CE Fst Sch
CA8 ....152 A7
Greenhead Rd NE17 ..173 B3
Greenhead Terr NE17 .173 B2
Greenhill Cotts NE69 ...17 C5
Greenhills NE12 ......142 D5
Greenholme Cl NE23 .127 B1
Greenholme Rd NE49 .153 C5
Greenlands Ct NE25 .134 D4
Greenlaw NE5 ....169 E8
Greenlaw Rd NE23 ...133 A3
Greenlea NE29 ....144 B1
Greenlea Rd NE65 .....52 D6
Greenlee NE63 ....117 E2
Greenlee Lough Nature
Reserve* NE47 ....88 E4
Greenrigg Blaydon NE21 .169 D1
Seaton Sluice NE26 ...135 C6
Greenriggs Ave NE3 .141 D1
Greenrising NE42 .....165 D4
Greensfield Cl NE65 ...53 D8
Greensfield Ind Est
NE66 ....181 D3
Greenside NE63 ......117 C4
Greenside Ave
🆃 Berwick-u-T TD15 ...178 B5
Brunswick Village NE13 .141 A6
Greenside Bank NE65 ...49 D5
Greenside Ho NE24 ..128 B8
Greenside Prim Sch
NE40 ....167 F1
Greenside Rd
Crawcrook NE40 .....167 F3
Greenside NE40 ......167 F2
Greenway East Ord TD15 ...3 E6
Newcastle u T NE5 ...149 D4
Whitley Bay NE26 ....144 D4
Greenwell Cl NE21 ...169 A1
Greenwell Dr NE42 ..166 D3
Greenwell Rd NE46 ..161 B5
Greenwell Terr NE40 .167 E4
Greenwich Gdns NE47 .157 F5
Greenwood East Ord TD15 ...3 E6
Killingworth NE12 ....142 F3
Greenwood Ave NE22 .122 D3
Gregory Ct NE65 .....182 B5
Grenada Cl NE26 .....144 F8
Grenada Pl NE26 .....144 F8
Grenville Ct
Cramlington NE23 ....133 A5
Ponteland NE20 ......138 A4
Grenville Dr NE3 .....144 F1
Grenville Way NE42 ..144 E7
Gresham Cl NE23 ....133 B4
Grey Ave NE23 ....133 A3
Grey Lady Wlk NE42 .166 D3
Grey Pl Alnwick NE66 .181 C5
🆃 Morpeth NE61 .....120 A8
Grey St NE1 ....141 A6
Greyfield Est NE66 ....24 C1
Greystead Cl NE5 ....149 D3
Greystead Rd NE25 ..144 B5
Greystoke Gdns 🆃
NE61 ....114 F1
Greystoke Pl NE23 ...133 A3
Grieve St NE24 ....123 D1
Grieves' Row NE23 ...133 A1
Griffith Terr 🆃 NE27 .143 E1
Grimsby St NE24 .....128 E6
Grindon TD15 ....7 A7
Grindon Cl
Cramlington NE23 ....133 A3
Whitley Bay NE25 ....144 E2
Grisedale La CA9 .....185 D3
Grosvenor Cl NE23 ..133 A3
Grosvenor Ct NE5 ....149 D3
Grosvenor Gdns NE26 145 A4
Grosvenor Pl NE24 ..127 F6
Grosvenor Terr
🆃 Alnmouth NE66 .....42 B5
Alnwick NE66 ....181 B5
Consett DH8 ....177 A3
Grosvenor Way NE5 .149 D3
Grousemoor Dr NE63 .117 C1
Grove Gdns NE13 ....178 A2
Grove Gdns S TD15 .178 A1
Grove Prim Sch The
DH8 ....176 C1
Grove Rd NE15 ....148 F2
Grove Specl Sch The
TD15 ....178 A2
Grove The
Newcastle u T NE5 ...149 D1
Ponteland NE20 ......138 D5
Stocksfield NE43 .....150 A3
Whitley Bay NE25 ....144 E4
Guardian Ct NE26 ...145 C4
Guardians Ct NE20 ..138 F7
Guards La NE46 ....99 D7
Guards Rd TD12 ......179 C7
Gubeon Wood NE61 .119 C2
Guessburn NE43 .....171 B6
Guide Post Mid Sch
NE62 ....121 F7
Guide Post Ringway Fst Sch
NE62 ....121 F8
Guildens The NE65 ....53 E8
Guilford Sq NE61 ....113 A3
Guillemot Cl NE24 ...128 E5
Guillemot Row NE12 .142 C4
Gunnerton Cl NE23 ..133 B4
Guyzance Ave NE65 ...53 E4

H
Hackwood Pk NE46 ..161 B3
Hackworth Gdns NE41 .167 B6
Haddington Rd NE25 ..144 D7
Haddon Cl NE25 .....144 B5
Haddon Gn NE25 ....144 B5
Hadrian Cres NE15 ....93 F4
Hadrian Ct
Chollerford NE46 ......91 B5
Killingworth NE12 ....142 E3
Ponteland NE20 ......138 C6
Hadrian Gdns NE21 ..169 D1
Hadrian Ho 🆃 NE15 ..148 D2
Hadrian Pl NE15 .....148 E2
Hadrian Rd NE24 ....128 C3
Hadrian's Cres CA8 ...86 D1
Hadrian's Wall*
Greenhead CA8,NE49 ...87 D1
* Halton NE65 ....92 D3
Hadrian's Wall* NE15 .147 D3
Hadstone Ind Est NE65 ...53 E3
Hagg Bank Cotts NE41 .166 F5
Haggerston Barns TD15 ...9 B6
Haggerston Castle Holiday
Pk TD15 ....9 B6
Haig Ave NE25 ....144 F3
Haig Rd NE22 ....127 B8
Haldane St NE63 .....117 F4
Half Fields Rd NE21 .169 B1
Half Moon St NE62 ..122 B8
Halidon Terr TD15 ....1 E1
Halkirk Way NE23 ...127 A1
Hall Bank NE49 ....95 B7
Hall Ct NE12 ....142 C5
Hall Farm Cl NE43 ..171 B8
Hall Gdns NE26 ......135 A6
Hall Gn NE24 ....128 B7
Hall Pk NE21 ....169 A4
Hall Rd Chopwell NE17 ..173 C2
Consett DH8 ....176 C2
Hall Road Bglws NE17 .173 B2
Hall Terr NE24 ......128 E8
Hallbank La NE65 ...183 C5
Hallgarth DH8 ....176 C1
Hallgarth Rd NE21 ..169 B2
Hallgate NE46 ....161 B5
Hallington Dr NE25 .134 D6
Hallington Mews NE12 ..142 C3
Hallorchard Rd NE46 .161 B5
Hallow Dr NE15 .....148 D1
Hallowstell View TD15 .178 C2
Hallside Rd NE24 ...128 B6
Hallside Bank NE46 .161 B5
Hallwood Cl NE22 ...126 A8
Halton Cl NE43 .....171 D6
Halton Dr
Backworth NE27 .....143 D3
Wideopen NE13 .....141 B6
Halton Way NE3 .....141 A1
Haltwhistle Fst Sch
NE49 ....153 C5
Haltwhistle Sta NE49 .153 C4
Haltwhistle War Meml Hospl
NE49 ....153 C5
Hambledon Ave NE30 .145 A3
Hambledon St NE24 .128 D8
Hambleton Cl NE63 .117 F1
Hamilton Dr NE26 ...144 F8
Hamilton Terr 🆃 NE61 120 A8
Hammermill La DH8 .109 E8
Hampstead Cl NE24 ..128 C2
Hampton Cl NE23 ...133 D7
Hampton Dr NE25 ...144 C4
Hampton Rd NE30 ..145 A2
Hamsterley Cres NE15 .169 B7
Hamsterley Dr NE12 .142 C4
Handley Cross DH8 ..175 C2
Hanover Cl NE5 .....149 C2
Hanover Ct NE23 ...133 B1
Hanover Dr NE21 ...169 A1
Hanover Pl NE23 ....127 A2
Hanover Wlk 🆃 NE5 .149 C2
Harbottle Ave NE27 .144 A2
Harbottle CE Fst Sch
NE65 ....48 D7
Harbour Rd Amble NE65 .183 D6
Beadnell NE67 ....24 D8
Seahouses NE68 ......17 F3
Harbour View NE22 ..143 F1
Harcar Ct 🆃 East Ord TD15 ..3 E6
Seahouses NE68 ......17 E2
Harden View NE66 ....37 F2
Hardhaugh NE46 .....91 A1
Hardman Gdns NE40 .168 D5
Hardy Cl NE61 ......113 A3
Harecross Pk NE65 ...53 E3
Harelaw Dr NE63 ...117 B1
Harelaw Gr NE5 .....149 D1
Haresby Rd NE47 .....89 D1
Hareshaw Rd NE23 ..144 B5
Hareside NE23 ....133 A4
Hareside Cl NE15 ...168 F8
Hareside Ct NE15 ...168 F8
Hareside Wlk NE15 ..168 F8
Harewood Cl NE25 ..144 B4
Harewood Cres NE25 .144 B4
Harewood Dr NE22 ..122 E4
Harewood Gdns NE61 .115 E4
Hareydene NE5 ......149 F5
Hargrave Ct NE24 ...128 C6
Harle Cl NE5 ....149 E1

Harle Rd NE27 ....143 D3
Harlebury NE27 ......143 C1
Harlow Ave NE27 ...143 D3
Harlow Cl NE23 .....127 A1
Harnham Gr NE23 ...133 A5
Harper St NE24 ......128 D7
Harriet St NE21 .....169 C2
Harrington Gdns NE62 .122 C8
Harriot Dr NE12 .....142 B2
Harrison Ct NE23 ...142 B8
Harrow Gdns NE13 ..141 C5
Harrow St NE27 .....143 E4
Hartburn Dr NE5 ....149 D3
Hartburn Rd NE30 ..145 A1
Hartburn Terr NE25 .134 D3
Hartford NE12 ....142 D5
Hartford Bank NE23 .126 C4
Hartford Bridge Farm
NE22 ....126 C5
Hartford Cres
Ashington NE63 ......117 D2
Bedlington NE22 ....126 E8
Hartford Ct NE22 ...126 E8
Hartford Cvn Pk NE22 .126 B5
Hartford Dr NE22 ...126 D6
Hartford Rd NE22 ...126 D6
Hartford Rd E NE22 .126 F8
Hartford Rd W NE22 .126 F8
Hartford Rd NE11 ....112 E5
Hartington Rd NE30 .145 B2
Hartington St DH8 ...177 A3
Hartlands NE61 ......126 E8
Hartleigh Pl NE24 ...128 B7
Hartley Ave NE26 ...144 E5
Hartley Ct
Brunswick Village NE13 140 F5
New Hartley NE25 ...134 D6
Hartley Gdns NE25 .134 C3
Hartley Ho NE26 ....144 F5
Hartley La Holywell NE25 144 B7
Whitley Bay NE25,NE26 135 C2
Hartley St NE26 .....135 D4
Hartley St W NE25 .134 C3
Hartley Terr NE24 ...128 C4
Hartside NE15 ....169 C7
Hartside Cres
Backworth NE27 .....143 D4
Broomhill NE65 ......53 F3
Cramlington NE23 ...127 A2
Hartside Pl NE3 .....141 C1
Harvey Cl NE63 ......118 A3
Harvey Combe NE12 .142 B3
Harvey Ct NE63 ......177 A3
Harwood Cl NE23 ...133 A1
Harwood Dr NE12 ...143 A3
Hascombe Cl NE25 ..144 D6
Hassop Way NE22 ...121 F2
Hastings Ave
Seaton Sluice NE26 ..135 C7
Whitley Bay NE26 ...135 F1
Hastings Ct
Bedlington NE22 ....122 C2
New Hartley NE25 ...134 D6
Hastings St NE23 ...133 C5
Hastings Terr
Cramlington NE23 ...127 D1
New Hartley NE25 ...134 D7
Hatfield Dr NE23 ....134 A2
Hatfield Gdns NE25 .144 B5
Hatherton Ave NE30 .145 B3
Hattery La NE24 .....127 D5
Hatters La TD15 .....178 B5
Haugh La Hexham NE46 .161 B5
Ryton NE5,NE40 .....168 E6
Ryton,Ryton Haugh NE21 169 A5
Haugh Lane Ind Est
NE46 ....161 A6
Haughs The NE42 ...166 A6
Haughton Cres NE5 .149 E1
Haughton Terr NE24 .128 E2
Hauxley Cl NE12 ....142 D5
Hauxley Dr NE23 ...133 A1
Hauxley La NE65 ....183 F3
Hauxley Links NE65 ...54 C5
Hauxley Nature Reserve*
NE65 ....54 C5
Hauxley Way NE25 ..183 D5
Havanna NE12 ......142 D5
Havannah Cres NE13 .140 B6
Havant Gdns NE13 ..141 B7
Havelock Cres NE22 .122 F3
Havelock Mews NE22 .122 F3
Havelock Rd NE27 ...143 D3
Havelock St NE24 ...128 E8
Havelock Terr NE17 .173 B1
Havelock Villas NE22 .122 F3
Haven Cl NE32 ......128 C6
Haven Ct NE26 ....32 C6
Haven Ho DH8 ......177 C4
Haven The Beadnell NE67 .24 D8
Leadgate DH8 ....177 C4
Hawburn Rd NE22 ..166 D2
Shilbottle NE66 ......166 F6
Haw View NE64 .....118 E4
Haw Hill NE65 ....182 B5
Haweswater Cres NE64 .118 C4
Hawkhope Hill NE48 ...69 D6
Hawkhope Rd NE48 ...69 C6
Hawksmoor Cl NE23 .117 C1
Hawkwell NE18 ....93 F6
Hawkwell Rise NE15 .148 D1
Hawthorn Ave NE13 .141 A6

Hawthorn CE Fst Sch NE63 ....117 D1
Hawthorn Cotts 4 DH8 .176 D4
Hawthorn Ct NE61 ....119 E8
Hawthorn Gdns
Ryton NE40 ....168 E4
Whitley Bay NE26 ....144 F5
Hawthorn Pl NE12 ....142 C4
Hawthorn Rd
Ashington NE63 ......117 E3
Blaydon NE21 ....169 C5
4 Widdrington Sta NE61 ...65 E5
Hawthorn St
2 Consett DH8 ......176 D4
Walbottle NE15 ......148 F2
Hawthorn Terr
Bellingham NE48 .....184 B4
Consett DH8 ....176 D4
Crawcrook NE40 ......167 E3
Gunnerton NE48 ....81 D2
Redburn NE47 ....155 E6
Rothbury NE65 ....182 A5
Shilbottle NE66 ......41 D3
Hawthorn Villas NE23 .133 D6
Hawthorn Way NE40 ...138 D3
Hawthorne Cres TD15 .178 A1
Hawthorne Rd NE24 ...128 F7
Haydon Bridge Com Mid Sch & Sports Coll NE47 .157 F6
Haydon Bridge Sta NE47 ....158 A6
Haydon Dr NE25 ......144 F3
Haydon Gdns NE27 ...143 D4
Haydon Rd NE63 .....117 D2
Hayes Wlk NE13 .....141 B6
Hayleazes Rd NE15 ...169 F7
Hayton Cl NE23 ....133 C7
Hayton Rd NE30 .....145 A2
Hayward Ave NE25 ...134 D3
Hazel Gr Ellington NE61 .112 E5
Killingworth NE12 .....142 B2
Hazel Rd NE21 ....169 D2
Hazeldene NE25 ......144 E5
Hazelmere Ave
Bedlington NE22 ......121 E1
Newcastle u T NE3 ...141 D1
Hazelmere Cres NE23 .133 C8
Hazelmere Dene NE23 .133 C1
Hazelwood Ave NE2 ..142 F3
Hazelwood Ave NE46 .118 D5
Hazelwood Com Prim Sch NE13 ....141 B5
Hazlitt Pl NE23 ......134 A1
Healeyfield La DH8 ...109 E2
Heather Gr NE65 ......53 D8
Heather Lea La NE42 .166 D3
Heather Pl NE40 .....168 A4
Heatherlands NE49 ...153 D5
Heatherlea Gdns NE62 .122 A8
Heatherslaw Light Rlwy* TD12 ....7 B1
Heatherslaw Mill* TD12 .7 C1
Heatheryhill NE46 ....160 A4
Heathfield NE61 .....120 B6
Heathfield Farm NE40 .167 E3
Heathfield Gdns NE40 .168 A1
Heathfield Pl NE3 ....141 D1
Heathwell Rd NE15 ..169 F7
Hebron Ave NE61 ....115 E4
Hebron Pl NE63 ......117 F3
Hebron Way NE23 ...133 F4
Hector St NE27 ......143 F4
Heddon Ave NE13 ....141 A4
Heddon Banks NE15 .147 E1
Heddon Cl NE40 .....168 D5
Heddon View
Blaydon NE21 ....169 B2
Ryton NE40 ....169 B2
Hedgefield Ave NE21 .168 F5
Hedgefield Cotts NE21 .168 F5
Hedgefield Ct NE21 ..168 F5
Hedgefield Gr NE21 ..128 C3
Hedgefield View NE23 .133 A1
Hedgehope Cres NE65 ..53 F2
Hedgelea NE40 ....168 A4
Hedgeley Rd NE5 ....169 E8
Hedgely West Cotts NE66 ....29 A4
Hedgerow Mews NE63 .117 B2
Hedley Ave NE24 ....128 F6
Hedley Ct NE24 ......128 F6
Hedley Rd
Seaton Delaval NE25 .134 C2
Wylam NE41 ....167 B6
Heely Dod Rd
Elsdon NE19 ....60 D8
Holystone NE19 ....48 D1
Heighley St NE15 ....169 F5
Helen St Blaydon NE21 .168 A4
East Cramlington NE23 .133 F5
Helena Ave NE25 ....145 B5
Hellpool La NE46 ....160 F5
Helston Ct NE15 .....169 B7
Hencotes NE46 ......161 A4
Hencotes Ct 7 NE46 .161 A4
Hencotes Mews 4 NE46 ....161 A4
Henderson Cl NE46 ..160 F3
Henderson Ct TD15 ..178 B3
Henderson St 2 NE65 .183 D6
Henderson's Bldgs NE46 ....118 E5
Hendon Ho NE63 ....117 A4
Henley Cl NE23 ......133 D7
Henley Gdns DH8 ....177 A2

Henley Rd NE30 .....145 C1
Henley Sq NE61 .....113 A3
Henlow Rd NE15 ....169 C7
Henry St DH8 ....176 E3
Henshaw CE Fst Sch NE47 ....155 C5
Henshaw St NE63 ...117 B2
Henshaw Gr NE25 ...134 F2
Hepburn Forest Walks* NE66 ....21 F3
Hepple Ct NE24 .....128 C6
Hepple Rd NE64 ....118 C3
Hepscott Dr NE25 ...144 D6
Hepscott Manor Cotts NE61 ....120 D3
Hepscott Wlk NE15 .115 E3
Herbert St 2 DH8 ...176 F3
Herd Cl NE21 ....169 A1
Herd House La NE21 .168 F2
Herdlaw NE23 ....133 A6
Herdley Bank Fst Sch NE48 ....95 C6
Heritage Ctr (Mus)* NE48 ....184 C4
Hermiston NE25 .....144 E5
Hermiston Ret Pk DH8 .176 F1
Hermitage Dr NE65 ...42 B1
Heron Cl Ashington NE63 .117 E1
Blyth NE24 ....128 E4
Netherton NE65 ......37 F2
Herring Gull Cl NE24 .128 E3
Herring Ho TD15 ......10 D4
Herterton House Gdns* NE61 ....74 D7
Hertford Cl TD15 ....144 D7
Hertford Gr NE23 ...133 C7
Hesleyside 4 NE63 .117 F2
Hesleyside Rd NE25 .144 A5
Hester Ave NE25 ....134 D6
Hester Bglws NE25 ..134 D6
Hester Gdns NE25 ..134 E6
Heswall Rd NE23 ....127 A2
Hetton Steads TD15 ..14 E6
Heugh House La NE47 .157 E6
Heugh Rd NE66 ......32 C6
Heugh Wynd NE66 ...32 C6
Hewley Cres NE15 ..148 D1
Hexham Abbey* NE46 .161 B5
Hexham Ave NE23 ..133 D7
Hexham Bsns Pk NE46 .161 A6
Hexham East Fst Sch NE46 ....161 C4
Hexham General Hospl NE46 ....161 C4
Hexham Mid Sch NE46 .161 B4
Hexham Old Rd NE21, NE40 ....168 E5
Hexham Priory Sch NE46 ....161 C4
Hexham Race Course NE46 ....160 D1
Hexham Rd
Heddon-on-t-W NE15 .147 E2
Throckley NE15 ......148 C2
Wark NE48 ....80 F3
Blaydon NE16 ....169 F1
Hexham Sta NE46 ...161 C4
Hextol Cres NE46 ...161 A4
Hextol Ct NE46 .....160 F4
Hextol Gdns NE15 ..169 F7
Hextol Terr NE46 ...160 F4
Hickstead Gr NE23 ..133 D7
Hide Hill TD15 ......178 B4
High Angerton NE61 ..75 E4
High Axwell NE21 ...169 D2
High Bowling Green Dr NE66 ....30 D1
High Burswell NE46 .160 F5
High Buston NE66 ....42 A3
High Castle Terr CA8 .86 F1
High Cl NE42 ....166 B4
High Dale Cotts NE66 .24 D1
High Dewley Burn NE15 .148 D3
High Fair NE21 ......180 B5
High Gables 8 NE46 .161 B4
High Gosforth Park (Newcastle Race Course) NE3 ....141 D2
High Gr NE40 ....168 D4
High Greens TD15 ...178 B5
High Hedgefield Terr NE21 ....168 E5
High House Cl NE61 .119 D8
High Market NE63 ...117 A4
High Moor Dr NE66 ...30 D1
High Newton Farm Cotts NE66 ....24 D4
High Palmstrother Dr NE66 ....30 E2
High Pk NE61 ....120 A7
High Powburn NE66 ...29 B3
High Quay NE24 ....128 F8
High Reins NE46 ....160 E5
High Ridge
Bedlington NE22 .....121 E1
Hazlerigg NE13 ......141 B4
High Riding NE49 ....95 C6
High Row
Newcastle u T NE15 .169 C6
Ryton NE40 ....168 E4
High Shaw NE42 ....166 B1
High Spen Ind Est NE39 .173 F5
High Spen Prim Sch NE39 ....173 F3
High St Amble NE65 .183 C5
Belford NE70 ....15 F4
Bellingham NE48 ....184 B4

High St continued
Blyth NE24 ....128 D7
Blyth NE24 ....128 E7
Choppington NE62 ..121 E6
Coldstream TD12 ....179 C6
Guide Post NE62 ....121 E7
Prudhoe NE42 ......118 F5
Newburn NE15 ......168 F7
Rothbury NE65 .....182 B5
Wooler NE71 ....180 C6
High Stanners NE61 .114 F1
High Stobhill NE61 ..120 A6
High View
Hebburn H NE43 ....171 F3
Ponteland NE20 .....138 D2
High Weetslade Farm Cotts NE23 ....142 A6
Higham Dykes NE20 ..85 C2
Highburn NE23 ......133 A5
Highburn House Cvn Pk & Camping Site NE71 .180 A6
Highbury NE25 ......144 E5
Highcliffe TD15 .....178 C1
Highcrofts NE15 ....166 C8
Highcross Rd NE30 .145 A3
Highfield Birtley NE64 .127 F7
Highfield Rd NE42 ..166 D2
Swarland NE65 ....52 C6
Highfield Cl NE63 ..149 F3
Highfield La NE42 ..166 C1
Highfield Pk NE66 ..181 D3
Highfield Pl NE13 ..141 A5
Highfield Rd NE5 ...149 F3
Highfield Terr NE42 .166 B2
Highfields Mid Sch NE42 ....166 C2
Highford Gdns NE61 .119 E7
Highford La NE46 ...160 E4
Highgrove NE5 .....149 D2
Highmoor NE61 .....119 D7
Highridge DH8 ......176 C3
Highstead Ave NE23 .127 A1
Highsteads NE21 ...175 B1
Highwell La 4 NE5 .149 F4
Highwood Rd NE15 .169 F7
Hilda Terr 7 NE25 ..148 D2
Hill Ave NE23 ....134 A2
Hill Croft NE15 .....146 C1
Hill Gate NE61 ......120 A8
Hill Head Dr NE5 ...149 F4
Hill House La CA9 ..185 A3
Hill House Rd NE15 .148 C2
Hill Pk NE20 ....138 D2
Hill Rise NE40 ......169 D7
Hill St NE43 ....166 B4
Hill The NE42 ......166 B4
Hill Top Blaydon NE21 .169 B1
Langley NE47 ....97 F8
Lucker NE70 ....16 E1
Hill Top Cl NE62 ...121 F8
Hill View TD12 ......179 C7
Hillary Cl NE66 .....32 B2
Hillcrest Ashington NE63 .118 A2
Castleside DH8 ......109 F3
East Ord TD15 ....3 D6
Prudhoe NE42 ......166 D2
Whitley Bay NE25 ...144 E5
Hillcrest Ave NE62 .121 F8
Hillcrest Ct NE42 ...166 D2
Hillcrest Dr NE46 ..161 C4
Hillcrest Pk NE66 ..181 E4
Hillersdon Terr CA9 .110 A6
Hillfield Consett DH8 .176 D3
Whitley Bay NE25 ..144 E5
Hillford Terr NE17 ..173 B1
Hillhead Parkway NE5 .149 C2
Hillhead Rd NE5 ...149 D2
Hillhead Way NE5 ..149 C2
Hillheads Ct NE25 ..145 A4
Hillheads Rd NE25,NE26 .145 A4
Hills Ct NE21 ......169 E4
Hillsden Rd NE25 ..144 D7
Hillside Ashington NE63 .117 C4
Bellingham NE48 ....184 C4
Blaydon NE21 ......184 B2
Hipsburn NE66 ......42 A6
Killingworth NE12 ..141 F7
Ponteland NE20 .....138 C1
Tweedmouth TD15 ..178 A1
Hillside Ave NE15 ..169 F8
Hillside Rd Belford NE70 .15 F5
Hexham NE46 ......161 D4
Rothbury NE65 .....182 B6
Hillside Rd W NE65 ..50 C4
Hilltop Cotts CA9 ..110 A6
Hilton Cl NE23 .....127 A2
Hilton Pl NE49 .....153 A3
Hindhope Linn Forest Wlk* NE19 ....46 A3
Hinding La NE46 .....31 A3
Hindley Cl NE40 ....167 E3
Hippingstones La NE45 .162 F6
Hipsburn NE66 ......42 A5
Hipsburn Fst Sch NE66 .42 A6
Hirsel Cl TD15 .....179 C6
Hirsel Ctry Pk & Mus The* TD12 ....5 D3
Hirsel Pl TD12 .....179 B7
Hirsel View TD12 ...179 B7
Hirst Ave TD15 .....122 A1
Hirst Head NE46 ...117 F2
Hirst High Sch NE63 .117 F2
Hirst Terr N NE22 ..122 A1
Hirst Villas NE22 ..122 B1
Hiveacres Rd TD15 ...3 E5

Hobart NE26 ....144 F7
Hodgson's Rd NE24 .123 D1
Hogarth Cotts NE22 .127 A8
Holborn Pl NE5 .....149 E1
Holborn TD15 ....14 F7
Holburn Cl NE40 ...168 D5
Holburn Cres NE40 .168 E5
Holburn Gdns NE40 .168 E5
Holburn La NE40 ...168 D6
Holburn Lane Ct NE40 .168 D6
Holburn Terr NE40 .168 E5
Holburn Way NE40 .168 E5
Holburn Wlk NE40 .168 E5
Holeyn Hall Rd NE41 .167 A7
Holeyn Rd NE15 ....148 C1
Holinghill Rd NE25 .134 E2
Hollings Terr NE17 .173 A1
Hollinhill Terr NE44 .100 F8
Hollis La NE45 .....162 C6
Hollow The NE63 ...118 B2
Holly Ave Earsdon NE25 .144 B5
Longbenton NE12 ...142 D1
Morpeth NE61 ......119 E7
Ryton NE40 ....168 C4
Whitley Bay NE26 ..145 A5
Holly Bush Gdns NE40 .168 C4
Holly Cl Hexham NE46 .160 E3
Killingworth NE12 ..142 C4
Holly Ct NE62 ......144 F5
Holly Gdns NE9 ....145 A5
Holly Mews NE26 ..145 A5
Holly St NE63 ......117 D3
Hollymount Ave NE22 .127 A8
Hollymount Sq NE22 .127 A8
Hollymount Terr NE22 .127 A8
Hollyoak Ho NE24 .128 B5
Hollywell Gr NE13 .149 F8
Holly Gdns NE25 ...144 D4
Holmcourt NE48 ....184 B4
Holmcroft NE64 ....118 E5
Holmdale
Ashington NE63 .....117 C3
Hexham NE46 ......161 C4
Holme Terr NE49 ...161 A4
Holmeside Cres NE49 .153 C5
Holmlands NE25 ...144 E5
Holmlands Cl NE25 .144 E5
Holmwood Ave
Newbiggin-by-t-S NE64 .118 D5
Whitley Bay NE25 ..144 D4
Holwick Cl DH8 ....177 A1
Holy Island 8 NE46 .161 A5
Holy Island CE Fst Sch TD15 ....10 D5
Holy Island Her Ctr* TD15 ....10 D4
Holy Trinity CE Fst Sch TD15 ....178 B5
Holyfields NE27 ....143 E2
Holyoake St NE32 ..166 D3
Holystone Ave
Blyth NE24 ....128 C5
Whitley Bay NE26 ..128 B5
Holystone Cl NE24 .128 B5
Holystone Dr NE27 .143 C2
Holystone Forest Walks* NE65 ....48 E5
Holystone Grange NE27 .143 C1
Holystone Prim Sch NE27 ....143 C2
Holystone Way NE27 .143 C1
Holywell Ave
Holywell NE25 ......134 F2
Whitley Bay NE26 ..144 F6
Holywell Cl
Blaydon NE21 ......169 D1
Holywell NE25 ......134 F2
Holywell Cres NE65 .183 D5
Holywell Dene Rd NE25 .134 F2
Holywell Mews NE26 .144 F6
Holywell Terr NE27 .143 D1
Holywell Village Fst Sch NE25 ....134 F2
Home Farm Birgham TD12 .5 A1
Newbrough NE47 .....90 D2
Home Farm Cl NE63 .116 F4
Home Farm Cotts NE65 .52 C6
Home Pl TD12 ......179 B6
Home Terr TD12 ....179 B7
Homebank 8 TD15 ...3 E6
Homedale NE42 ....166 E2
Homedale Pl NE42 .166 E1
Homedale Terr NE42 .166 D2
Homeprior Ho NE25 .144 E4
Homer's La NE46 ...92 E5
Homes The NE49 ...153 E3
Honister Cl NE15 ...169 D7
Honister Pl NE15 ...169 D7
Honister Rd NE30 ..145 B2
Honister Way NE24 .128 C3
Hood Sq NE21 ......169 A1
Hood St Morpeth NE61 .114 F1
St Johns Chapel DL13 .111 E1
Hookergate La NE39 .173 F4
Hope House La NE66 .181 C4
Hope La NE20 ....93 B5
Hope St DH8 ....176 E4
Hopefoot Cotts NE65 .59 E5
Hopefoot Rd NE19 ..59 E7
Hordley Acres NE47 .157 F5
Horncliffe Fst Sch TD15 .2 F5
Horncliffe Mains TD15 ..2 F4
Horncliffe Pl NE15 .148 B2
Horncliffe Wlk NE15 .169 A7
Hornsea Cl NE13 ..141 B5
Horsden Side NE71 .180 C5
Horse Crofts NE15 .169 C3

Horsegate Bank NE17, NE40 173
Horsley Ave
Crawcrook NE40 167
Shiremoor NE27 143
Horsley Cl NE62 121
Horsley Gdns NE5 ..134
Horsley Rd NE42 ...166
Horsley View NE23 .166
Horsley Wood Cotts NE15 166
Horsleys Bldgs 3 NE61 .120
Horton Ave
Bedlington NE22 127
Shiremoor NE27 143
Horton Cres NE13 ..140
Horton Dr NE23 127
Horton Grange Fst Sch NE24 127
Horton Manor NE24 .127
Horton Pl NE24 127
Horton Rd NE22,NE24 .127
Horton St 3 NE24 ..128
Hortondale Gr NE24 .128
Horwood Ave NE5 ..149
Hospital La NE15 ...169
Hotch Pudding Pl NE5 .149
Hotspur Ave
Bedlington NE22 126
Whitley Bay NE25 ..145
Hotspur Ct 10 NE65 .42
Hotspur Hill 10 NE66 .181
Hotspur Pl NE66 ...181
Hotspur St NE66 ...181
Hotterel Dr NE66 30
Hotts La DL13 111
Houghton Ave NE30 .145
Houndslow Dr NE63 .117
House of Hardy Mus NE66 181
Houssteads Vercovicivm Roman Fort* NE47 ...89
Housing La DH8 175
Houxty Rd NE25 144
Howard Cl NE27 ...143
Howard Gr NE61 ...115
Howard Rd NE61 ...115
Howard Terr
High Spen NE39 173
6 Morpeth NE61 ..114
Howden Cres NE61 .115
Howden DH8 176
Howdene Rd NE15 .169
Howford La NE46 91
Howick Hall Gdns* NE66 32
Howick Terr TD15 ..178
Howlett Hall Rd NE15 .169
Howling La NE66 ...181
Howtel TD12 182
Hub Mus The* CA9 .185
Huddleston NE26 ..145
Hudshaw Gdns NE46 .161
Hudson Ave
Bedlington NE22 122
Dudley NE23 142
Hugar Rd NE39 173
Huggin Rd NE47 143
Hugh Joicey CE Fst Sch TD15 13
Hulne Priory* NE66 ..30
Hulne Terr NE17 173
Humber St NE17 ...173
Humford Dr NE24 ..128
Humford Ho NE24 ..128
Humford Way NE22 .127
Humsford Gr NE23 .133
Humshaugh CE Fst Sch NE46 91
Hunn's Bldgs NE62 .121
Hunter Ave NE24 ...128
Hunters Cl DH8 176
Huntingdon Dr NE23 .133
Huntley Cres NE23 .133
Huntly Rd NE25 144
Hurley Knowes NE65 .182
Hutchinson Ave 3 DH8 .176
Hutchison Prim Sch TD15 .2
Hylton Cl NE21 169
Hysehope Terr DH8 .177

I

Ilderton Pl NE5 169
Ilford Ave NE23 169
Ilfracombe Gdns NE26 .144
Infirmary Sq 7 TD15 .178
Ingham Gr NE23 ...144
Ingham Terr NE41 ..167
Ingleby Terr NE11 ..169
Ingleby Way NE24 ..128
Ingleton Dr NE15 ..128
Ingleton Gdns NE24 .128
Inglewood Cl NE24 .128
Inglewood Pl NE3 ..127
Ingoe Cl NE40 128
Ingoe St NE15 128
Ingram Dr Blyth NE24 .128
Newcastle u T NE5 7
Ingram La NE69 7
Inlandpasture TD15 ...1
Ingleborough Dr NE40 .168
Innerhaugh Mews NE47 .157
Institute Rd NE46 ..100
Intake Way NE46 ...160
Irestone La DL13 ...111

..s Cl NE21 ....169 A2
.s Terr NE40 ....167 F3
n Bridge Dr NE66 ....30 F1
ning NE61 ....112 E5
ning Pk CA8 ....86 D1
bella Rd NE24 ....128 C6
bella Wlk NE15 ....148 D1
and View Amble NE65 ..183 E6
enwick TD15 ....9 D3
estone Ct
mburgh NE69 ....17 A5
◻ East Ord TD15 ....3 E6
estone Dr NE68 ....17 D2
nhoe NE25 ....144 E5
son Rd NE46 ....160 E3
ston Rd DH8 ....177 B1
nson Rd TD15 ....3 E6
Ave
ewbiggin-by-t-S NE64 ..118 C5
ton NE40 ....168 C6
Cl NE40 ....168 C6
Pl ◻ TD15 ....178 B5
St Amble NE65 ....183 D6
Terr NE40 ....167 E3

ckson Ave NE20 ....138 F7
ckson Pl NE68 ....17 E2
ckson Terr ◻ NE61 .....120 A8
ckson Dr NE15 ....169 C8
nes Ave NE27 ....143 F4
mes St
ewcastle u T NE5 ......149 F2
eahouses NE68 ....17 E2
meson Dr NE45 ....163 B7
meson St ◻ DH8 ....176 F3
nus Cl NE5 ....149 C4
smin Ave NE5 ....149 C4
smine Ct NE63 ....117 C1
sper Ave NE40 ....168 B1
dburgh Cl NE5 ....149 C4
rsey Sq NE61 ....113 A3
smond Terr NE26 ......145 B4
oling Ave NE21 ....169 B2
oling Cres NE61 ....120 B6
ck's Knowe Rd NE19 ...47 B6
hn & Margaret Common
omes for Aged Miners ◻
E24 ....127 F8
hn Ave NE40 ....168 B1
hn Brown Ct NE22 .....121 F1
hn Martin St NE47 ....158 A5
hn St Amble NE65 .....183 D6
hnshington NE63 ......117 C4
llyth NE24 ....128 B8
onsett DH8 ....176 F3
onsett,Blackhill DH8 ...176 D4
arsdon NE25 ....144 A5
eggswood NE61 ....115 F3
ruolhoe NE42 ....166 E3
nemouth NE30 ....145 C3
hn Street Sq ◻ NE4 ..176 F2
hn Wesley Ct NE42 ...166 D2
hnson St NE15 ....169 C6
hnson Terr NE39 ....173 F4
hnson's Bldgs DH8 ....177 E1
hnson's Villas NE62 ...121 B7
llybeard Gate CA9 ....185 E3
llybeard La CA9 ....185 E3
nquil Cl NE5 ....149 C4
seph Terr NE17 ....173 B1
bilee Bldgs ◻ NE46 ..161 B4
bilee Cotts
reenside NE40 ....173 D7
nemouth NE11 ....113 A3
bilee Cres NE65 ....182 C4
bilee Ct
nitsford NE23 ....133 B1
bilee Dr NE24 ....128 D6
bilee Est NE63 ....117 D1
bilee Lodge NE23 .....133 B4
bilee Rd NE68 ....17 F2
bilee Rd Blyth NE24 ..128 E6
bilee Terr NE24 ....165 C4
bilee Terr
edlington NE22 ....122 D2
rawcrook NE40 ....167 E3
ewbiggin-by-t-S NE64 ..118 E4
aton Burn NE13 ....141 B8
liet St NE63 ....117 D3
niper Cl NE47 ....128 C4
ewcastle u T NE3 ....141 D1
niper Ct NE21 ....169 C3
niper Wlk NE15 ......149 D4
ries The NE66 ....29 C1

nes Cl TD15 ....2 F7
rieth Dr NE66 ....24 D4
tes La CA9 ....185 D3
therine St NE63 ......117 E4
arsley Cl NE25 ....134 D3
arton Ave NE5 ....149 C3
ats Ave NE24 ....128 C5
ats Gr NE63 ....117 F3
eble Cl NE63 ....118 B3
el Row ◻ NE66 ....128 E8
eble Dr NE23 ....132 D6
elmans Ho ◻ NE24 ...128 E8
elmans Terr NE24 .....128 E8

Keir Hardie Ct NE64 ....118 E5
Kelfield Gr NE23 ....127 B2
Kelleher Ct ◻ DH8 ....176 D4
Kelly Cl DH8 ....176 D4
Kelsey Way NE23 ......127 B2
Kelso Cl NE5 ....149 C4
Kelso Gdns NE22 ......122 C1
Kelso Rd TD12 ....179 B5
Kelson Way NE5 ....149 C4
Kelvin Gdns ◻ DH8 ...176 F2
Kelvin Pl NE12 ....143 A1
Kemble Cl NE23 ....127 B2
Kempton Cl DH8 ......176 D7
Kendal Ave Blyth NE24 ..128 B7
Tynemouth NE30 ....145 B2
Kendal Dr NE23 ....133 C8
Kendal Rise NE22 .....121 D2
Kendale Wlk NE5 .....149 E3
Kendor Gr NE61 ....119 F6
Kenilworth NE12 ......142 D4
Kenilworth Rd
Ashington NE63 ....117 C3
Whitley Bay NE25 .....144 F4
Kenmoor Way NE5 ....149 C3
Kenmore NE65 ....52 C6
Kenmore Cres NE40 ..168 B2
Kenmore Croft NE65 ..52 C6
Kenmore Dr NE65 .....52 C6
Kenmore Rd NE65 .....52 C6
Kennedy Rd NE65 .....183 E5
Kennersdene NE30 ....145 C1
Kensington Cl NE25 ...144 F5
Kensington Cotts NE61 ..120 B8
Kensington Gdns NE25 ..144 F5
Kensington Villas ◻
NE5 ....149 E3
Kent Cl NE63 ....117 A4
Kentmere Cl NE23 ....134 A2
Kepier Chare Com Prim Sch
NE40 ....167 F3
Kepwell Bank Top NE42 ..166 C3
Kepwell Ct NE42 ......166 D3
Kepwell Rd NE42 .....166 C2
Kern Gn NE48 ....79 E3
Kerry Cl NE24 ....128 E8
Keston Dr NE23 ....127 B2
Kestrel Dr NE63 ....117 B1
Keswick Dr NE30 ......145 B2
Kettering Pl NE23 ....133 C8
Kew Gdns NE26 ....144 B6
Kidderminster Dr NE5 ..149 C3
Kidland Cl NE63 ....117 F4
Kielder Ave NE23 .....132 D6
Kielder Castle* NE48 ..55 D4
Kielder Castle Forest Park
Ctr* NE48 ....55 D4
Kielder Cl Blyth NE24 ..128 B5
Killingworth NE12 .....142 C4
Kielder Com Fst Sch
NE48 ....55 D4
Kielder Dr NE63 ....117 C3
Kielder Gdns NE62 ....117 A1
Kielder Pl NE25 ....144 E5
Kielder Rd Earsdon NE25 ..144 B5
Newcastle u T NE15 ...169 C7
Kilchurn DH8 ....176 D3
Kilham TD12 ....112 B3
Killhope Lead Mining Ctr*
DH13 ....110 E5
Killiebrigs NE15 ....147 E2
Killin Cl NE5 ....149 C4
Killingworth Ave NE27 ..143 B4
Killingworth Cthr The
NE12 ....142 D4
Killingworth Dr NE12 ..142 B2
Killingworth Hall NE12 ..142 C2
Killingworth La NE27 ..143 A5
Killingworth Rd NE12 ..142 E2
Killingworth Way NE12,
NE27 ....142 D4
Kiln Cotts NE47 ....90 E2
Kiln Hill TD15 ....148 B6
Kiln Lonnen NE46 .....41 D3
Kilnshaw Pl NE3 ......141 D1
Kilsyth Ave NE29 .....144 E2
Kimberley Gdns NE43 ..171 C7
Kimberley St NE24 ....128 D8
Kimberley Terr ◻ NE24 ..128 E8
Kincham Ave TD12 .....5 D4
King Edward Rd NE40 ..168 E4
King Edward St NE65 ..183 C5
King Edward VI Sch The
NE61 ....114 F2
King George's Rd NE64 ..118 D5
King James Ct ◻ TD15 ..178 B4
King John's St NE30 ..138 A4
King St Alnwick NE66 ..181 B5
Blyth NE24 ....128 E8
Newbiggin-t-S NE64 ..118 E5
Seahouses NE68 ....17 F2
King's Arms La CA9 ..185 D4
King's Ave NE61 ......114 F1
King's Dr Greenside NE40 ..168 B1
Whitley Bay NE26 .....145 A4
King's Gdns NE24 .....128 C8

Kingsgate ◻ NE46 .....161 A5
Kingsgate Terr NE46 ..161 A5
Kingsley Ave
Newcastle u T NE3 ....141 D1
Whitley Bay NE25 .....145 A4
Kingsley Rd NE61 .....113 A2
Kingsley Terr NE40 ...167 E4
Kingston Cl NE26 .....144 F8
Kingston Ct ◻ NE26 ..144 F8
Kingston Dr NE26 .....144 F8
Kingston Way ◻ NE26 ..144 F8
Kingsway Blyth NE24 ..128 E6
Ponteland NE20 ....138 E6
Kingswell NE61 ....120 B7
Kingswood Dr NE61 ..120 A7
Kingswood Rd NE23 ..133 C8
Kinloss Cl NE46 ....181 B5
Kinloss Sq NE23 ......133 C8
Kinver Dr NE5 ....149 C3
Kippy Law NE68 ....17 E2
Kirk St DH8 ....176 E3
Kirkbride Pl NE23 .....133 C8
Kirkdale Ct NE46 .....181 D5
Kirkharle Cotts NE19 ..74 C1
Kirkharle Dr NE61 ....115 E4
Kirkhaugh Sta CA9 ...103 D4
Kirkland Wlk NE27 ...143 E3
Kirklands NE23 ....142 C5
Kirkley Dr
Ashington NE63 ....117 E2
Ponteland NE20 ....138 E7
Kirkley Hall Gdns* NE20 ..85 D4
Kirkley Rd NE23 ......143 F2
Kirklinton Rd NE30 ...145 A2
Kirkston Ave NE15 ...169 D7
Kirkstone Ave NE30 ..145 A2
Kirkwell Cotts NE15 ..183 E3
Kirkwood NE23 ....142 C5
Kirkwood Pl NE3 .....141 B1
Kirton Way NE23 .....133 C8
Kittiwake Cl NE24 ....128 E3
Kittiwake Ho NE26 ...145 B5
Kitty Brewster Ind Est
NE24 ....123 F1
Kitty Brewster Rd NE24 ..123 F8
Knaresborough Cl NE22 ..121 D2
Knarsdale Pl ◻ NE5 ..149 E1
Knightside Wlk NE5 ..149 C3
Knitsley Gdns DH8 ...176 F1
Knitsley La DH8 ......176 F1
Knivestone Ct
◻ East Ord TD15 ....3 E6
Killingworth NE12 .....142 E4
Knocklaw Pk NE65 ...182 D5
Knogley Way NE65 ....51 E4
Knoll The NE61 ....112 C5
Knop Law Fst Sch NE5 ..149 C3
Know House
Cornhill on T TD12 ...179 F5
Tweedmouth TD15 .....178 A3
Knowehead ◻ NE23 ..133 A4
Knowes Cl TD15 ....2 C8
Knowledge Hill NE61 ..169 B1
Knox Cl NE22 ....122 D2
Knox Rd NE22 ....127 B8
Knutsford Wlk NE23 ..133 C8
Kyle Gdns TD15 ....10 D4
Kylins The NE61 ......120 A6
Kyloe Ave NE25 ......134 D2
Kyloe Pl NE22 ....121 E2
Kyloe Rd NE19 ....46 E7
Kyloe View TD15 ......8 E2
Kyo Bog La NE41,NE42 ..167 B1
Kyo La NE40 ....173 D7

L

Laburnum Ave
Blyth NE24 ....128 D8
Consett DH8 ....176 E4
Whitley Bay NE26 .....145 A5
Laburnum Cl NE12 ....142 C4
Laburnum Rd NE21 ...169 C2
Laburnum Terr
Ashington NE63 ....117 D3
Wylam NE41 ....167 A6
Laburnum Ct NE42 ...121 E7
Lacey St NE66 ....132 B2
Ladbroke St NE65 ....183 E6
Lady Hamilton Dr NE65 ..52 C6
Lady Waterford Hall*
TD15 ....13 B8
Lady's Well Dr NE65 ..31 A2
Lady's Wlk NE61 .....114 E1
Ladybank NE5 ....149 B4
Ladyburn Ho NE65 ....53 F3
Ladycutters La NE45 ..162 F3
Ladykirk Way NE23 ..132 E6
Ladyrigg NE20 ....138 D4
Ladywell NE42 ....171 D6
Ladywell Rd TD15 ....178 A3
Ladywell Rd
Blaydon NE21 ....169 C2
Tweedmouth TD15 .....178 A3
Ladywell Way NE20 ..138 D7
Lagny St NE66 ....181 B5
Laing St DH8 ....176 F3
Lake App NE21 ....169 F1
Lake View NE65 ......53 F3
Lakeside NE21 ....169 F1
Lamb Cl TD15 ....3 F5
Lamb St NE63 ....117 D4
Lamb herr St ◻ NE22 ..143 E1
Lamb's Terr ◻ NE25 ..183 C5
Lambert Terr NE61 ...65 E4
Lamberts's La NE66 ..24 C2

Lambley Ave NE30 ...145 B2
Lambrook Ho NE24 ..128 A7
Lambton Ave TD15 .....8 E2
Lambton Cl NE40 ....167 F4
Lamonby Way NE23 ..133 A4
Lampton Ct NE22 ....122 C2
Lancaster Ho NE23 ..133 D5
Lancaster Terr NE61 ..115 A1
Lancastrian Rd NE23 ..133 A5
Lanchester Gn NE22 ..121 F2
Land Ends Rd
Haydon Bridge NE47 ..157 D3
Haydon Bridge NE47 ..158 A5
Landscape Terr NE40 ..168 B1
Landsdowne Gdns NE62 ..122 A8
Lane Head
Coanwood NE49 ....95 C6
Ryton NE40 ....168 C5
Lanehill DL13 ....111 C1
Lanercost Ave NE21 ..169 B2
Lanercost Dr NE5 ....149 B1
Lanercost Gdns NE15 ..148 D2
Lanercost Pk NE23 ...133 D5
Langdale NE25 ....144 E5
Langdale Cl DH8 .....177 D8
Langdale Dr NE23 ...132 E6
Langdale Terr NE17 ..175 A5
Langdon Cl NE29 ....144 F1
Langdon Rd NE5 .....149 E2
Langley Ave Blyth NE24 ..128 B8
Hexham NE46 ....144 A3
Shiremoor NE27 ......144 A3
Whitley Bay NE25 .....144 D3
Langley Fst Sch NE25 ..144 D3
Langley Gdns NE47 ..157 F5
Langley Rd
Ashington NE63 ....117 C3
Newcastle u T,West Denton
NE5 ....169 F8
Langton Cl NE20 .....138 B4
Langton Dr NE23 .....133 C2
Langwell Cres NE63 ..117 C4
Langwell Terr NE46 ..115 F4
Lansdowne Ct NE46 ..160 F2
Lanton Cl NE65 ....52 C6
Lanty's Lonnen NE49 ..153 D5
Lapford Dr NE23 .....127 C1
Lapwing Cl NE24 .....128 E4
Larch Gr NE24 ....128 C4
Larch Rd NE21 ....169 B2
Larch St DH8 ....176 F3
Larchlea NE20 ....138 C2
Larchlea S NE20 .....138 C2
Larchwood Ave NE13 ..141 C5
Larchwood Dr NE13 ..117 C1
Larriston NE42 ....166 A4
Larriston Pl NE23 ....133 C8
Lassells Rigg NE42 ..166 D4
Latton Cl NE23 ....133 A4
Laurel Ave NE12 .....143 A1
Laurel Dr Ashington NE63 ..117 C1
Leadgate DH8 ....177 D3
Laurel Rd NE21 ......169 C2
Laurel Rd NE21 ......169 D2
Laurel St NE15 ....148 D3
Laurel Terr NE12 ....134 E2
Laurel Way NE40 ....168 A3
Lavender Cl NE63 ....117 C1
Lavendon Cl NE23 ...133 C8
Laverock Hall Rd NE24 ..128 B3
Laverock Pl NE24 ....128 B3
Lawn Cl NE63 ....117 B3
Lawn The NE40 ......168 C6
Lawrence Ave NE21 ..169 C3
Lawrence Ct NE21 ...169 C3
Lawson St NE65 .....183 D6
Layburn Gdns NE15 ..169 E8
Laycock Gdns NE23 ..133 F1
Layfield Rd NE3 .....141 C1
Lea Terr NE47 ....141 C1
Lea The NE65 ....52 C6
Leabank NE15 ....169 D8
Leaburn Terr NE42 ..166 B2
Lead La Horsley NE15 ..146 C1
Newlands DH8 ....174 C6
Lead Rd Greenside NE40 ..168 B1
High Spen NE17,NE40 ..173 D6
Slaley NE43,NE47 ....160 B8
Stocksfield NE43 .....171 B2
Whittonstall NE43,NE44,
DH8 ....101 C4
Leadgate Bank NE47 ..97 A1
Leadgate Com Jun Sch
DH8 ....177 D3
Leadgate Cotts NE47 ..173 A4
Leadgate Inf Est DH8 ..177 C3
Leadgate Inf Sch NE47 ..177 C3
Leadgate Rd
Consett DH8 ....177 B4
Leadgate DH8 ....177 B4
Leadgate Terr NE47 ..97 F2
Leadside Bank NE47 ..98 A3
Leaholme Cres NE24 ..128 A6
Lealands NE46 ....42 A6
Leamington La NE65 ..52 C6
Leander Ave NE65 ...122 B8
Leander Dr NE62 ....122 B8
Leaplish Waterside Pk*
.........................68 D6
Leas The NE65 ....144 D4
Leaside CA8 ....94 F5
Leatherland Rd NE46 ..161 B5
Leazes NE45 ....161 F6
Leazes Cres NE46 ...160 F5
Leazes La Corbridge NE45 ..92 D1
Hexham NE46 ....160 E5

Leazes La continued
Whitley Chapel NE46,NE47 ..99 C4
Leazes Parkway NE15 ..148 D1
Leazes Pk NE46 ......160 E5
Leazes St NE65 ....183 D6
Leazes Terr
Corbridge NE45 ....162 F6
Hexham NE46 ....160 F5
Leazes The NE15 ....148 C1
Leazes View NE42 ...165 D4
Lee Ave NE66 ....41 D3
Lee Cl NE65 ....182 B5
Lees La TD15 ....178 B3
Lees Mill Dr TD12 ....179 B5
Leet St TD12 ....179 C6
Legg Ave NE22 ......122 E3
Legges Dr NE13 .....141 B8
Legion Gr NE15 .....169 F7
Legion Rd NE15 .....169 F7
Leland Pl NE61 ......119 D7
Lemington Rd NE15 ..169 B6
Lemington Riverside Prim
Sch NE15 ....169 C6
Lemmington Bank NE66 ..40 C6
Lena Ave NE25 ......144 E4
Lenin Terr NE17 .....175 C8
Lennel Mount TD12 ..179 C7
Lenore Terr NE40 ....168 B2
Lesbury Ave
Ashington NE63 ......117 D2
Shiremoor NE27 .....143 E3
Stakeford NE62 ......117 A1
Lesbury Gdns NE13 ..141 C6
Lesbury Rd NE66 .....42 A6
Lesbury St NE15 .....169 C6
Lesbury Terr NE17 ...175 B8
Leslie Cl NE40 ....168 E4
Leslie Dr NE65 ....183 D5
Leslies View NE13 ...114 E2
Letch Way NE15 .....169 C7
Letchwell Villas NE12 ..142 E1
Leucar Villas NE12 ...142 E1
Lewin's La TD15 ......10 D5
Lewisburn Trail* NE48 ..68 A8
Leybourne Ave NE12 ..142 D1
Leybourne Dene NE12 ..142 D2
Leyburn Ct NE23 .....133 A4
Lichfield Cl NE63 ....117 A4
Liddell Terr NE61 ....65 E4
Liddles St ◻ NE22 ..122 D3
Lieven St NE13 ......141 A4
Lilac Ave NE24 ......128 D8
Lilac Cl NE5 ....149 B4
Lilac Cl NE5 ....149 B4
Lilac Ct Ashington NE63 ..117 E1
Ellington NE61 ....112 C6
Lilac Pl DH8 ....177 D3
Lilburn Rd NE27 .....144 A4
Lilburn Terr TD15 ....10 D5
Lilliput La NE70 .....22 F7
Lily Ave NE22 ....127 B8
Lily Ave NE22 ....169 A2
Lily Est NE63 ....148 D3
Lime Gr Prudhoe NE42 ..166 B3
Ryton NE40 ....168 C5
Lime St Amble NE65 ..183 D6
Blaydon NE21 ....
Threckley NE15 ......148 E4
Limes Ave NE24 .....123 D1
Limes Rd NE61 ......125 C3
Limestone La NE20 ..138 B7
Limetree Dr NE71 ....13 A4
Limewood Gr NE13 ..141 B5
Linbridge Dr NE5 ....149 E1
Lincoln Gn NE3 ......141 D3
Lincoln Rd NE23 .....127 C1
Lincrest Ct NE5 .....149 F2
Lindean Pl NE13 ....132 F6
Linden Acres NE62 ...64 A7
Linden Cl NE62 .....122 A8
Linden Cres NE65 ....64 A7
Linden Dr DH8 ......177 D3
Linden Rd Blaydon NE21 ..169 D2
Seaton Delaval NE25 ..134 B3
Linden Terr NE25 ...145 B5
Linden Way Consett DH8 ..176 E4
Ellington NE61 ....112 D5
Ponteland NE20 ......138 C3
Lindisfarne Ave NE69 ..17 B5
Lindisfarne Castle*
.........................10 E4
Lindisfarne Cl
Morpeth NE61 ....120 A6
Newcastle u T NE5 ..149 F1
Pegswood NE61 .....116 A4
Lindisfarne Cswy TD15 ..10 A5
Lindisfarne Gdns ◻ TD15 ..3 E6
Lindisfarne La NE61 ..120 A6
Lindisfarne Mid Sch
TD15 ....181 C3
Lindisfarne Priory*
.........................10 D4
Lindisfarne Rd
Alnwick NE66 ....181 C4
Amble NE65 ....183 C5
Lindisfarne Wlk NE62 ..121 E7
Lindsay Ave NE24 ...128 C6
Linfield Cl NE23 ......53 D8
Lingfield DH8 ....176 E3
Lingholme NE23 .....176 E3
Lingholme PRU NE5 ..149 F7
Linhope Ave NE3 ....141 A4
Linhope Cres NE65 ..53 F2
Linhope PRU NE5 ....149 F7
Link Ave NE22 ....121 D1
Link House Farm NE66 ..24 D5
Link Rd NE15 ....141 A4

Link The NE46 . . . . .160 F5
Linkham La NE65 . . . . .63 F2
Links Ave Amble NE65 . . .183 E5
Tynemouth NE30 . . . . . . .145 C2
Whitley Bay NE26 . . . . . .144 F7
Links Ct NE26 . . . . .145 A7
Links Dr DH8 . . . . .176 E5
Links Rd Amble NE65 . . . .183 E5
Bamburgh NE69 . . . . .17 B5
Blyth NE24 . . . . .128 F4
Seaton Sluice NE24 . . . . .129 A2
Tynemouth NE30 . . . . . . .145 C2
Links The NE26 . . . . .145 A7
Links View
Ashington NE63 . . . . .123 A8
Blyth NE24 . . . . .128 C4
Links Wlk NE5 . . . . .149 F2
Linnel Dr NE15 . . . . .169 E7
Linnels Bank NE46 . . . . . .99 F8
Linnet Ct NE63 . . . . .117 B2
Linnheads NE42 . . . . .166 B1
Linshiels Gdns **1** NE63 .117 F2
Linslade Wlk NE23 . . . . . .132 F6
Linthorpe Rd NE30 . . . . . .145 B1
Linton NE12 . . . . .142 D5
Linton Fst Sch NE61 . . . .112 A3
Linton La NE61 . . . . .65 F3
Linton Rd NE26 . . . . .135 E1
Lintonburn Pk NE61 . . . . .65 F4
Lintonville Ent Pk NE63 .117 D5
Lintonville Parkway
NE63 . . . . .117 D5
Lintonville Rd NE63 . . . . .117 C4
Lintzford Gdns NE15 . . . .169 E7
Lintzford Rd NE39 . . . . . .175 F5
Linwood Pl NE3 . . . . .141 C1
Lionheart Ent Pk NE66 . .181 C2
Lisburn St NE65 . . . . .181 C5
Lisburn Terr NE66 . . . . . .181 B5
Lish Ave NE26 . . . . .145 C4
Lishman Terr NE40 . . . . . .168 A4
Lister Ave NE40 . . . . .173 F8
Lister St NE15 . . . . .169 F5
Litchfield Cres **2** NE21 .169 B1
Litchfield La NE21 . . . . . .169 B1
Litchfield St **1** NE21 . . .169 B1
Litchfield Terr **3** NE21 .169 B1
Little Bldgs NE42 . . . . . . .165 D4
Livingstone St **17** DH8 .176 F3
Lloyd St **3** NE40 . . . . . .167 F3
Loaning Mdws TD15 . . . . .178 A3
Loaning The CA9 . . . . . . .185 E5
Lobelia Cl NE5 . . . . .149 B3
Locarno Pl NE40 . . . . .118 E4
Lochcraig Pl NE23 . . . . . .132 E6
Lockerbie Gdns NE15 . . . .169 E7
Lockerbie Rd NE23 . . . . . .132 F6
Locksley Cl NE29 . . . . . . .144 B1
Locomotion Way NE12 . . .142 B5
Locomotive Ct NE42 . . . . .166 C2
Lodsworth Dr NE23 . . . . .133 A4
Lola St NE13 . . . . .140 F4
Long Close Rd NE39 . . . . .175 F5
Long Dr NE61 . . . . .119 F5
Long Drag
Sinderhope NE47 . . . . . . .106 C7
Whitley Chapel NE47 . . . . .98 F2
Long Meadow Cl NE40 . . .168 A3
Long Pk NE64 . . . . .118 D4
Long Ridge Rd NE21,
NE40 . . . . .168 D2
Long Row Embleton NE66 . .31 F8
Longhoughton NE66 . . . . . .32 C4
Rennington NE66 . . . . .31 F6
Long Row Cl NE40 . . . . . .173 F8
Longbeach Dr NE47 . . . . . .24 D7
Longclose Bank DH8,
NE39 . . . . .175 E3
Longdale Gr DL13 . . . . . .111 E1
Longframlington Gdns*
NE65 . . . . .52 A3
Longhirst
Killingworth NE12 . . . . . .142 D5
Newcastle u T NE5 . . . . . .149 F2
Longhirst Ct NE61 . . . . . .115 F4
Longhirst Dr
Cramlington NE23 . . . . . .133 A4
Widdigen NE13 . . . . .141 B5
Longhirst Rd NE61 . . . . . .115 F4
Longhirst Village NE61 . .115 F7
Longhorn Ends DL13 . . . .111 B3
Longhoughton CE Fst Sch
NE66 . . . . .32 B2
Longhoughton Rd NE66 . .42 A6
Longlands **11** NE46 . . . .161 A4
Longleat Gdns NE61 . . . . .115 E4
Longmeadows NE20 . . . . .138 B3
Longridge NE21 . . . . .169 A2
Longridge Ct NE22 . . . . . .122 A4
Longridge Dr NE22 . . . . . .114 E7
Longridge Pk TD15 . . . . . . .3 B4
Longridge Towers Sch
TD15 . . . . .3 B4
Longridge Way
Bedlington NE22 . . . . . . .122 A4
Cramlington NE23 . . . . . .132 F6
Longriggs The NE44 . . . . .100 F8
Longrow Ave NE30 . . . . . .145 B3
Longstone Cl NE67 . . . . . .24 D8
Longstone Cres NE67 . . . .24 D8
Longstone Ct NE12 . . . . . .142 E4
Longstone Pk NE67 . . . . . .24 D8
Longstone Sq NE5 . . . . . .149 D1
Lonkley Terr NE61 . . . . . . .97 F2
Lonnen The NE40 . . . . . . .168 E5

Lonsdale Ave NE24 . . . . . .127 E8
Lonsdale Ct NE17 . . . . . . .175 B4
Loraine Terr NE15 . . . . . .169 C6
Lord's Mount TD15 . . . . . .178 B5
Lordenshaw NE5 . . . . .149 F2
Lordenshaw Dr NE65 . . . .182 D5
Lorne St NE49 . . . . .153 B4
Lorton Ave NE30 . . . . . . .145 A2
Lotus Cl NE5 . . . . .149 B3
Loughborough Ave
NE30 . . . . .145 C1
Loughbrow Pk NE46 . . . . .161 B2
Loughrigg Ave NE23 . . . . .132 F6
Louisville NE20 . . . . .138 F7
Loup St NE21 . . . . .169 C3
Louvain Terr NE62 . . . . . .121 F7
Lovaine Ave NE25 . . . . . . .145 A4
Lovaine St NE15 . . . . .168 E8
Lovaine Terr
8 Alnmouth NE66 . . . . . .42 B5
Berwick-u-T TD15 . . . . . .178 B6
Love Ave NE23 . . . . .142 B7
Love Avenue Cotts
NE23 . . . . .142 B8
Love La **3** TD15 . . . . . .178 B4
Low Angerton NE61 . . . . . .75 E3
Low Bowling Green Dr
NE66 . . . . .30 D1
Low Burswell NE46 . . . . . .160 F5
Low Castle Terr CA8 . . . . .86 F1
Low Chesters NE65 . . . . . .52 C6
Low Cl NE42 . . . . .166 E3
Low Cotts NE66 . . . . .28 C8
Low Farm NE61 . . . . .112 D4
Low Gate Fst Sch NE46 . .160 A4
Low Gosforth Ct NE3 . . . .141 D1
Low Greens TD15 . . . . . . .178 B5
Low Haber Cvn Pk NE47 . .97 A2
Low Haugh NE20 . . . . . . .138 F7
Low Hedgeley NE66 . . . . . .29 B4
Low Hos NE45 . . . . .92 C2
Low Humbleton NE71 . . . . .20 B7
Low Main Pl NE23 . . . . . .133 B6
Low Middleton NE70 . . . . .15 F7
Low Pastures NE65 . . . . . .52 C6
Low Pk NE48 . . . . .72 C5
Low Prudhoe Ind Est
NE42 . . . . .166 D4
Low Quay NE24 . . . . .128 F8
Low Row NE40 . . . . .168 E3
Low Stobhill NE61 . . . . . .120 A7
Low Stobhill NE61 . . . . . . .66 C2
Low Walker NE6 . . . . .149 E5
Lowbiggin NE5 . . . . .149 E5
Lowbyer Pk CA9 . . . . .185 D5
Lower Barresdale NE66 . .181 A5
Lower Crone St NE27 . . . .143 F4
Loweswater Cl NE24 . . . . .122 F1
Lowfield NE47 . . . . .90 D2
Lowgate NE15 . . . . .148 D1
Lowick Fst Sch TD15 . . . . . .8 E2
Lowlean Ct NE5 . . . . .149 F1
Lowther Cl NE63 . . . . .117 F1
Lowther Sq NE23 . . . . . . .132 E6
Loxton Sq NE23 . . . . .133 A3
Lucker Hall Steading
NE70 . . . . .16 E1
Lucker Rd NE69 . . . . .17 A5
Lucy St NE21 . . . . .169 D3
Ludlow Dr NE25 . . . . .144 B5
Luke's Brae TD12 . . . . . . .179 C6
Lumley Ct NE22 . . . . .122 C2
Lumley's La NE43 . . . . . . .172 B6
Lumsden's La NE61 . . . . . .114 F1
Lupin Cl NE5 . . . . .149 C4
Lydbury Cl NE23 . . . . .127 C1
Lydney Cl NE15 . . . . .148 C1
Lyncroft NE63 . . . . .117 C2
Lyndale NE23 . . . . .127 C1
Lyndhurst Lodge NE25 . . .144 E5
Lyndhurst Rd
Ashington NE63 . . . . .117 F1
Whitley Bay NE25 . . . . . .144 E5
Lyndon Wlk NE24 . . . . . . .127 F8
Lyne Terr NE61 . . . . .112 F3
Lyneburn Grange NE61 . .112 D5
Lynemouth Fst Sch
NE61 . . . . .113 B3
Lynemouth Rd NE61 . . . .112 D4
Lynfield NE20 . . . . .144 E7
Lynfield Ct NE5 . . . . .149 C4
Lynnbrae Ave NE24 . . . . .128 A7
Lynwood Ave
Blaydon NE21 . . . . .169 C3
Newbiggin-by-t-S NE64 . .118 D5
Lynwood Cl NE20 . . . . . . .138 C2
Lysander Ct NE65 . . . . . . .118 F3
Lysdon Ave NE25 . . . . . . .134 D6
Lytham Cl Consett DH8 . . .176 E5
Cramlington NE23 . . . . . .132 E6
Lytham Dr NE25 . . . . .144 D5

M

Mabel St NE21 . . . . .169 C3
Mackays Ct **15** DH8 . . . .176 F2
Maddison Gdns NE23 . . . .133 E1
Maddison St NE24 . . . . . .128 E8
Madeira Ave NE26 . . . . . .144 F7
Madeira Cl NE5 . . . . .149 C4
Mafeking Pl NE29 . . . . . . .144 B1
Mafeking St NE26 . . . . . . .145 B5
Magdalene Dr TD15 . . . . .178 A7
Magdalene Fields NE65 . . .53 E8
Magenta Cres NE5 . . . . . .149 C4
Magnolia Dr NE23 . . . . . .117 C1
Magpie Cl NE63 . . . . .117 B2
Maiden La NE40 . . . . .168 A2

Maiden Way NE49 . . . . . . .95 A7
Maiden's Wlk NE46 . . . . .161 C4
Maidens Croft NE46 . . . . .160 F4
Main Rd Dinnington NE13 .140 C6
Ryton NE40 . . . . .168 B5
Wylam NE41 . . . . .167 B6
Main St Acomb NE46 . . . . .91 D1
Consett DH8 . . . . .177 B2
Corbridge NE45 . . . . .163 A5
Cornhill on T TD12 . . . . . .179 F5
Crawcrook NE40 . . . . . . .167 F4
Felton NE65 . . . . .52 E3
Haltwhistle NE49 . . . . . . .153 D5
Horncliffe TD15 . . . . .2 E4
Leitholm TD12 . . . . .5 A7
Lowick TD15 . . . . .8 E2
Ponteland NE20 . . . . .138 E6
Seahouses NE68 . . . . .17 E2
Spittal TD15 . . . . .178 C3
Tweedmouth TD15 . . . . . .178 A3
Tweedmouth TD15 . . . . . .178 A4
Wark NE48 . . . . .80 F4
Main St N NE23 . . . . .133 F1
Main St S NE23 . . . . .133 F1
Mains Pl NE61 . . . . .114 F1
Mainstone Cl NE23 . . . . . .133 A6
Maitland Terr NE64 . . . . . .118 D4
Malaga Cl NE5 . . . . .149 B4
Malcolm St NE25 . . . . . . .144 D4
Malden Cl NE23 . . . . .132 F6
Mallard Cl
Ashington NE63 . . . . .122 D8
Broomhill NE65 . . . . .53 F3
Mallard Ct NE12 . . . . .142 C4
Mallard Way NE23 . . . . . .128 F3
Malthouse Rd NE66 . . . . .181 D4
Malting Cl NE48 . . . . .184 B4
Maltings The
24 Alnwick NE66 . . . . . .181 C5
Rothbury NE65 . . . . .182 B5
Maltkiln NE46 . . . . .161 A4
Malton Cl Blyth NE24 . . . .128 B7
Newcastle u T NE15 . . . . .169 E6
Malvern Cl NE63 . . . . .117 F1
Malvern Ct NE15 . . . . . . .169 B7
Malvern Rd
Seaton Sluice NE26 . . . . .135 D5
Tynemouth NE29 . . . . . . .144 F1
Malvin's Close Fst Sch
NE24 . . . . .128 C7
Malvins Close Rd NE24 . .128 C7
Malvins Rd NE24 . . . . . . .128 B8
Manchester Sq NE48 . . . .184 B4
Manchester St NE61 . . . . .114 F1
Mandale Cres NE30 . . . . .145 A3
Mandarin Cl NE5 . . . . . . .149 C5
Mangrove Cl NE5 . . . . . . .149 C4
Manley View NE63 . . . . . .118 A3
Manners Gdns NE25 . . . . .134 C4
Manningford Cl NE23 . . . .133 A5
Manor Ave NE15 . . . . . . .168 F8
Manor Cl Consett DH8 . . .176 C1
Riding Mill NE44 . . . . . . .100 F8
Whalton NE61 . . . . .77 A5
Manor Cotts NE45 . . . . . .162 F6
Manor Ct NE61 . . . . .65 D3
Manor Dr NE64 . . . . .118 E5
Manor Gr NE15 . . . . .168 F7
Manor Grange NE65 . . . . . .53 E3
Manor House Farm NE65 D3
Manor Pk NE20 . . . . .138 D6
Manor Rd DH8 . . . . .175 C1
Manor Terr NE61 . . . . . . .169 A1
Manor View NE42 . . . . . . .118 E5
Manor Walks Sh Ctr
NE23 . . . . .133 A6
Manors The NE42 . . . . . . .166 E3
Manse St DH8 . . . . .176 E4
Mansefield Pl TD12 . . . . . .179 D7
Mansefield Rd TD15 . . . . . .3 E6
Mansel Terr NE23 . . . . . . .127 E7
Maple Ave NE25 . . . . .144 F4
Maple Cl Bedlington NE22 .121 F1
Newcastle u T NE15 . . . . .169 E6
Maple Cres NE24 . . . . . . .127 C8
Maple Ct
Killingworth NE12 . . . . . .142 C4
New Hartley NE25 . . . . . .134 D6
Maple Dr **2** NE61 . . . . . .65 F5
Maple Gdns DH8 . . . . . . .176 C4
Maple Gr NE42 . . . . .166 B2
Maple Rd NE21 . . . . .169 C2
Maple St Ashington NE63 .117 D3
18 Consett DH8 . . . . . . .176 F3
Mapperley Dr NE15 . . . . .149 B4
March Rd NE23 . . . . .132 C4
March Terr NE13 . . . . . . .140 A7
Marchburn La NE44 . . . . .100 F8
Marcross Cl NE15 . . . . . . .149 B2
Marden Ave NE30 . . . . . . .145 A4
Marden Bridge Mid Sch
NE25 . . . . .145 A4
Marden Cl NE61 . . . . .119 D7
Marden Cres NE26 . . . . . .145 C4
Marden Ct NE26 . . . . .145 C4
Marden Farm Dr NE30 . . .145 B3
Marden High Sch NE30 . .145 B1
Marden Rd NE26 . . . . .145 A4
Marden Rd S NE25 . . . . . .145 B4
Marden Terr NE30 . . . . . . .145 C3
Marc Cl NE23 . . . . .134 A3
Margaret Cotts NE25 . . . .144 F2
Margaret Rd NE26 . . . . . .145 C4
Margaret St NE61 . . . . .65 E4
Maria Way NE61 . . . . .112 B8
Marina Dr NE25 . . . . .144 C4
Marine Ave NE26 . . . . . . .144 F5
Marine Ct E NE26 . . . . . . .145 A6

Marine Ct W NE26 . . . . . .145 A6
Marine Gdns NE26 . . . . . .145 A6
Marine Park Fst Sch
NE26 . . . . .145 A6
Marine Rd
14 Alnmouth NE66 . . . . .42 B5
Amble NE65 . . . . .183 E6
Marine St NE64 . . . . .118 E5
Marine Terr NE24 . . . . . . .128 E2
Marine View NE26 . . . . . .135 C2
Mariners Ct NE65 . . . . . . .183 B5
Mariners View NE65 . . . . .183 B5
Marine Pl **4** NE61 . . . . .114 F1
Marius Ave NE15 . . . . . . .147 F2
Marjorie St NE23 . . . . . . .133 F5
Market Pl
Allendale Town NE47 . . . . .97 F2
5 Alnwick NE66 . . . . . .181 C5
Alston CA9 . . . . .185 D3
Bedlington NE22 . . . . . . .126 F8
Belford NE70 . . . . .15 F4
Blyth NE24 . . . . .128 E8
Broomhill NE61 . . . . .53 F2
Corbridge NE45 . . . . .162 F5
Haltwhistle NE49 . . . . . . .153 D6
2 Hexham NE46 . . . . . .161 B5
Morpeth NE61 . . . . .119 F8
Rothbury NE65 . . . . .182 B5
Wooler NE71 . . . . .180 C5
Market Sq
Coldstream TD12 . . . . . . .179 C6
Lynemouth NE61 . . . . . . .113 B2
Market St Alnwick NE66 . .181 C5
Blyth NE24 . . . . .128 E8
Broomhill NE61 . . . . .53 F2
Coldstream TD12 . . . . . . .179 C6
Consett DH8 . . . . .176 D4
Dudley NE23 . . . . .142 A8
Hexham NE46 . . . . .161 B5
Marks Bridge NE65 . . . . .183 C4
Marlborough Ho NE26 . . .144 F6
Marlborough Terr NE62 . .121 F4
Marlish Farm Visitor Ctr*
NE61 . . . . .75 C4
Marlow St NE24 . . . . .128 D7
Marmion Terr NE25 . . . . .144 F4
Marmion View TD15 . . . . . .2 C2
Marquis Ave NE5 . . . . . . .149 C4
Marquis Ct NE42 . . . . . . .166 E4
Marsham Cl NE15 . . . . . . .169 E7
Marsham Rd NE5 . . . . . . .149 A3
Marshes' Houses NE62 . .122 D7
Marshmont Ave NE30 . . . .145 C1
Marston NE12 . . . . .142 D4
Mart The NE49 . . . . .153 D5
Martin Way NE13 . . . . . . .141 A6
Martindale Pl NE25 . . . . .134 C3
Martindale Wlk NE12 . . . .142 C3
Martins Cl NE47 . . . . .158 B5
Martins The NE71 . . . . . . .180 D5
Marwood Ct NE25 . . . . . .144 D6
Marx Terr NE17 . . . . .175 C8
Mary St Blaydon NE21 . . .169 C3
Blaydon,Winlaton NE21 . .169 A2
8 Widdrington Sta NE61 . .65 E5
Marygate
Berwick-u-T TD15 . . . . . .178 B5
Holy Island TD15 . . . . . . .10 D4
Maryside Pl NE40 . . . . . . .167 F7
Mason Ave NE26 . . . . . . .145 B5
Mason St
Brunswick Village NE13 . .141 A6
Consett DH8 . . . . .176 F2
Mason View NE13 . . . . . . .141 B8
Mast La NE30 . . . . .145 B3
Master's Cres NE42 . . . . .166 B2
Matfen Ave
Hazlerigg NE13 . . . . .141 A4
Shiremoor NE27 . . . . .144 A2
Matfen Cl Blyth NE24 . . . .128 C7
Newcastle u T NE15 . . . . .169 E6
Matfen Terr NE64 . . . . . . .118 D3
Mathesons Gdns NE61 . . .119 F8
Matlock Gdns NE5 . . . . . .149 F3
Matlock Sq NE61 . . . . . . .113 A2
Matthew Rd NE24 . . . . . . .128 F5
Maud St NE15 . . . . .169 C6
Maud Terr **5** NE27 . . . .143 E1
Maud's Terr NE64 . . . . . . .118 E5
Maughan St NE24 . . . . . . .128 F7
May Ave NE40 . . . . .168 C6
May St NE21 . . . . .169 B1
Mayfair Gdns NE20 . . . . .138 F6
Mayfield Morpeth NE61 . .119 E7
Seahouses NE68 . . . . .17 E2
Mayfield Ave
Cramlington NE23 . . . . . .133 C6
Throckley NE15 . . . . .148 E1
Mayfield Gdns NE15 . . . . .148 E1
Mayfield Pl NE13 . . . . . . .141 A5
McCracken Dr NE13 . . . . .141 C7
Mclaren Way NE70 . . . . . .15 F4
Mcnulty Ct NE23 . . . . . . .141 F8
Meadow Bank Dr NE12 . .142 B2
Meadow Brook Dr NE17 .173 C2
Meadow Cl Blaydon NE21 .168 F1
Haltwhistle NE49 . . . . . . .153 D5
Ryton NE40 . . . . .168 D5
Seghill NE23 . . . . .133 F2
Meadow Ct
Bedlington NE22 . . . . . . .121 E1
Ponteland NE20 . . . . .138 E5
Meadow Dale **22** TD15 . . .3 E6
Meadow Dr NE13 . . . . . . .141 C8
Meadow Gdns **10** TD15 . .3 E6
Meadow Grange
Berwick-u-T TD15 . . . . . .178 A7

Meadow Grange continued
Haltwhistle NE49 153
Meadow Hill TD15 1
Meadow La Beadnell NE67 . .24
Crawcrook NE40 168
Meadow Lands TD15 3
Meadow Pk
Haltwhistle NE49 153
Riding Mill NE44 100
Meadow Rd
Newcastle u T NE15 169
Seaton Sluice NE26 135
Whitley Bay NE25 144
Meadow Rigg **18** TD15 3
Meadow Riggs NE65 181
Meadow Rise DH8 177
Meadow Terr NE49 153
Meadow View
Haltwhistle NE49 153
New Hartley NE25 134
Meadow Wlk NE40 168
Meadowbank NE23 142
Meadowburn NE65 183
Meadowcroft Pk NE65 . . .50
Meadowdale Cres NE22 .121
Meadowdale Mid Sch
NE22 121
Meadowfield
Ashington NE63 118
Consett DH8 176
Ponteland NE20 138
Whitley Bay NE25 144
Meadowfield Cres NE40 .168
Ponteland NE20 138
Meadowfield Ind Est
NE20 138
Meadowfield Pk NE20 . . .138
Meadowfield Pk S NE43 .171
Meadowfield Rd NE43 . . .171
Meadowfield Terr
Longbenton NE12 142
Stocksfield NE43 171
Meadowgarth NE70 16
Meadowlands
Kirkwhelpington NE19 74
Lesbury NE66 42
Meadows Crest NE43 172
Meadows The
Belford NE70 16
Berwick-u-T TD15 178
Ryton NE40 168
Thropton NE65 50
Meadowsweet Cl
3 Blyth NE24 128
Consett DH8 177
Meadowvale
Backworth NE27 143
Ponteland NE20 138
Meal Mkt **7** NE46 161
Means Cl NE23 142
Means Dr NE23 142
Medburn Ave NE30 145
Medburn Rd
Newcastle u T NE15 169
Seaton Delaval NE25 134
Medomsley Cross Rds
DH8 177
Medomsley Rd DH8 176
Medway Pl NE23 127
Medwyn Cl NE24 128
Megstone Ave NE23 133
Megstone Ct **10** NE68 17
Megstone Ct
24 East Ord TD15 3
Killingworth NE12 142
Melbourne Cres NE25 . . .144
Melbury NE25 144
Meldon Cl NE40 169
Meldon Gdns NE61 121
Meldon Ho NE24 128
Meldon Pk* NE61 75
Meldon Terr
Greenside NE40 167
Newbiggin-by-t-S NE64 . . .118
Melkridge Pl NE61 113
Melling Rd NE23 133
Melness Rd NE13 141
Melock Ct NE13 141
Melrose Ave
Backworth NE27 143
Bebside NE22 122
Seaton Delaval NE25 134
Tynemouth NE30 145
Whitley Bay NE25 144
Melrose Cl
Newcastle u T NE3 144
Newcastle u T,Bell's Close
NE15 169
Melrose Ct
Bedlington NE22 122
Consett DH8 176
Melrose Gdns NE65 183
Melrose Terr
Bedlington NE22 122
Newbiggin-by-t-S NE64 . .118
Melrose Villas NE22 122
Meltham Ct NE15 149
Melton Cres NE15 135
Melton Dr NE25 134
Melville Ave NE24 128
Melville Gdns NE25 144
Memorial Sq NE64 118
Mendip Cl
Ashington NE63 117
Tynemouth NE29 144
Merchants Gdns NE66 . . .181
Mercia Way NE15 169
Merley Dr NE13 141

rle Gdns NE61 ......114 D2
rley Gate NE61 ......120 A6
lin Brae Forest Wlks*
48 ......68 E5
lin Way NE27 ......144 A1
rrington Cl NE25 ......134 D7
rryshields Terr NE43 ......171 C8
rse View TD15 ......2 F8
rsey St Chopwell NE17 ......173 C1
adgate DH8 ......177 D5
ton Cotts NE46 ......24 C1
ton Rd NE20 ......138 E6
ton Sq NE24 ......128 E8
ton Way NE27 ......138 E6
ssenger Bank DH8 ......176 C6
calfe Rd DH8 ......177 B1
chven Way NE23 ......127 C2
ws The NE21 ......169 E2
kleton Cl DH8 ......176 C1
kleton Cl CL DH8 ......176 C1
klewood Cl NE61 ......115 E6
le Fst Sch NE43 ......165 E1
dle Cowden NE48 ......81 D5
dle Dr ......
nteland NE20 ......138 C3
olsington NE13 ......139 F1
dle Farm Cotts NE23 ......139 F1
dle Gate ......
rpeth NE61 ......119 F6
le u T NE5 ......149 D1
dle Gn NE25 ......144 C4
dle Pk CA9 ......185 C3
dle Rd NE66 ......41 C3
dle Row Cambo NE61 ......74 D4
on NE40 ......168 E3
dle St Blyth NE24 ......128 B4
nsett DH8 ......179 E7
bridge NE45 ......162 F5
ttal TD15 ......178 C2
dlebrook NE20 ......138 B3
dleburn End NE48 ......79 E3
dleton Cl DH8 ......177 A1
dleton Cotts NE70 ......15 F6
dleton St ......
ble NE65 ......183 D5
th NE24 ......128 E7
burn Cl NE46 ......160 F2
burn Rd NE63 ......117 D2
burn Terr NE22 ......122 C6
ce Rd NE61 ......65 F4
ecastle Ct NE5 ......149 C2
castle Fst Sch NE5 ......149 C2
ield Com Prim Sch ......
71 ......13 A4
ield Hill NE71 ......12 F5
ord Gdns NE13 ......141 B1
tary Rd NE15 ......147 C3
tia Ct NE66 ......181 C5
khope Ctr NE13 ......131 D5
kwell NE45 ......163 A6
kwell La NE45 ......163 A7
Cl NE44 ......100 F8
Cotts NE47 ......106 B1
Ct Ellington NE61 ......112 C4
msterley NE17 ......175 B6
Dyke Cl NE25 ......144 C6
Farm NE61 ......112 C4
Grange NE44 ......170 A8
Hill Farm NE66 ......21 D7
Hill Rd NE5 ......169 F8
La Ebchester DH8 ......174 E4
ttwhistle NE49 ......153 E5
ddon-on-t-W NE15 ......147 F3
nbury NE63 ......122 A2
ghill NE23 ......133 D1
ley NE44 ......100 D5
amfordham NE18 ......136 B5
' Race Cl NE17 ......175 B6
' Rd NE17 ......175 B8
Strand TD15 ......178 A3
' The DH8 ......107 F2
View Rise NE15,NE42 ......166 D4
Way NE15,NE42 ......166 D7
bank Cres NE22 ......122 A1
bank Pl NE22 ......127 B8
bank Rd NE22 ......122 B1
bank Terr NE22 ......122 A1
brook Rd NE23 ......127 C1
burn Terr CA8 ......151 F8
dale Ave NE24 ......128 A2
er's Cl NE65 ......53 E8
er's La ......
at Whittington NE19 ......92 F5
tfen NE19,NE20 ......93 A5
ersfield NE46 ......91 C1
field Bedlington NE22 ......127 C4
aton Sluice NE26 ......135 D5
field Cl NE15 ......168 F7
field Ct ......
don Mill NE47 ......155 F6
lington NE22 ......127 A8
nsett DH8 ......176 C3
le NE46 ......160 F5
aton Sluice NE26 ......135 D5
field E NE22 ......127 A7
field Gdns ......
th NE24 ......123 D1
le NE46 ......160 F5
field La NE15 ......168 E8
field N NE22 ......127 A8
field Pl TD15 ......3 D6
field Rd NE24 ......128 A4
field S NE22 ......127 A7
field Terr ......
ttwhistle NE49 ......153 C4
le NE46 ......160 F5
field W NE22 ......127 A8

Millne Ct NE22 ......121 F1
Millside NE61 ......119 F8
Millview Dr NE30 ......145 B1
Millway NE26 ......135 D5
Millway Gr NE26 ......135 D5
Millway Loaning NE61 ......31 E4
Milne Graden West Mains ......
TD12 ......6 B7
Milner Cres NE21 ......169 A1
Milsted Ct NE15 ......149 B2
Milton Gr Ashington NE63 ......117 F3
Prudhoe NE42 ......166 B2
Milton St NE40 ......167 E1
Mindrum Farm Cotts ......
TD12 ......11 D4
Mindrum Way NE25 ......134 D3
Mindrummill Cotts TD12 ......11 D4
Minerva Cl NE15 ......149 C4
Minster Ct NE15 ......149 B3
Minting Pl NE23 ......133 A5
Mirlaw Rd NE23 ......132 F5
Mitchell Ave ......
Seahouses NE68 ......17 F2
Whitley Bay NE25 ......144 D4
Mitchell Dr NE13 ......118 B3
Mitchell St NE40 ......167 E3
Mitford Ave Blyth NE24 ......128 C6
Pegswood NE61 ......115 E4
Seaton Delaval NE25 ......134 E2
Mitford Dr ......
Ashington NE63 ......117 D2
Newcastle u T NE5 ......149 E3
Mitford Gdns ......
Stakeford NE62 ......121 F8
Wideopen NE13 ......141 C6
Mitford Rd NE61 ......114 E1
Mitford Way NE13 ......140 B7
Mithras Ct NE46 ......91 B4
Mithras Gdns NE15 ......147 E2
Mobray First Sch NE62 ......121 F7
Modigars La NE43 ......171 F4
Molesdon Cl NE30 ......145 A1
Mollfair Cl NE40 ......168 A4
Monarch Terr NE21 ......169 C2
Monk's Terr NE46 ......161 D4
Monkdale Ave NE24 ......128 A6
Monkhouse Ave NE30 ......145 A1
Monkhouse Prim Sch ......
NE30 ......145 B1
Monkhouse Terr NE66 ......181 B5
Monkridge ......
Newcastle u T NE15 ......149 B2
Whitley Bay NE25 ......144 E7
Monks Ave NE25 ......144 D3
Monks Ho NE68 ......17 D4
Monks Mdws NE46 ......161 D4
Monks Rd NE25 ......144 C3
Monks Ridge NE61 ......119 D7
Monks Way NE30 ......145 C1
Monkseaton Com High Sch ......
NE25 ......144 E2
Monkseaton Dr NE25, ...
NE26 ......144 E6
Monkseaton Mid Sch ......
NE25 ......144 E4
Monkseaton Rd NE25 ......144 B5
Monkseaton Sta NE25 ......144 F5
Monkseaton Terr NE63 ......117 E1
Monkside NE23 ......132 F5
Monkstone Cres NE30 ......145 C1
Monkstone Grange ......
NE30 ......145 B1
Monmouth Ct NE15 ......65 E5
Monmouth Gr NE12 ......5 D4
Montague St NE15 ......169 D6
Montrose Cl NE25 ......134 D6
Montrose Gdns NE61 ......119 F7
Moonfield NE46 ......161 B4
Moor Burn Dr NE66 ......181 A6
Moor Croft NE64 ......118 E5
Moor Edge Prim Sch ......
NE12 ......142 C3
Moor Edge Rd NE27 ......143 E8
Moor Grange NE42 ......166 D1
Moor La Ponteland NE20 ......138 C4
Stannington NE61 ......125 C6
Moor Rd NE42 ......172 E7
Moor View ......
Crawcrook NE40 ......168 A4
Haltwhistle NE49 ......153 C4
Killingworth NE12 ......142 C4
Melkridge NE49 ......154 E4
Newbiggin-by-t-S NE64 ......118 E5
Moor View NE13 ......115 E3
Moor View Wlk NE12 ......142 C4
Moorcroft Cl NE15 ......169 F7
Moorcroft Rd NE15 ......169 E6
Moordale Ave NE24 ......128 A6
Moor Ct NE15 ......168 B7
Moorfields NE61 ......120 A6
Moorhouse Est NE63 ......117 F3
Moorhouse La NE63 ......117 F3
Moorland Ave ......
Bedlington NE22 ......122 A3
Haltwhistle NE49 ......153 D5
Moorland Cotts ......
NE22 ......122 D3
Moorland Cres ......
Bedlington NE22 ......122 A3
Castleside DH8 ......176 F3
Moorland Ct NE22 ......122 A3
Moorland View ......
Castleside DH8 ......109 F3
Chopwell NE17 ......175 B8
Moorland Villas NE22 ......122 A3
Moorland Way NE23 ......126 E1
Moorlands Consett DH8 ......176 D5

Moorlands continued
Prudhoe NE42 ......166 E1
Moorlands Cres DH8 ......176 D4
Moorlaw Dr NE66 ......30 C1
Moorside NE12 ......142 B2
Moorview DH8 ......176 E4
Moorway Dr NE15 ......169 E7
Moraine Cres NE17 ......175 B6
Mordington Ave TD15 ......3 E6
Moresby Rd NE23 ......127 C2
Morgan Bsns Ctr NE12 ......142 B5
Morley Ct NE23 ......127 A2
Morpeth Way NE12 ......5 D4
Morgy Hill E NE40 ......167 F3
Morgy Hill W NE40 ......167 F3
Morgy Hill W NE40 ......167 F3
Morley Gdns NE13 ......176 F4
Morley Hill Rd NE5 ......169 F8
Morley Pl NE27 ......143 F4
Morpeth All Saints CE Fst ......
Sch NE61 ......114 D2
Morpeth Ave ......
Pegswood NE61 ......115 E4
Wideopen NE13 ......141 C7
Morpeth Chantry Bagpipe ......
Mus* NE61 ......120 A8
Morpeth Chantry Mid Sch ......
NE61 ......120 A8
Morpeth Cl NE62 ......121 E7
Morpeth Clock Twr* ......
NE61 ......119 F8
Morpeth Collingwood ......
NE61 ......120 B7
Morpeth Cottage Hospl ......
NE61 ......119 F6
Morpeth Fst Sch NE61 ......120 A8
Morpeth Fst Sch NE61 ......120 A8
Morpeth Newminster Mid ......
NE61 ......114 E1
Morpeth Rd ......
Ashington NE63 ......116 C1
Guide Post NE62 ......121 E7
Morpeth Road Fst Sch ......
NE24 ......128 D8
Morpeth Sta NE61 ......119 F8
Morpeth Stobhillgate Fst Sch ......
NE61 ......120 B7
Morris Ct NE23 ......142 B8
Morrison Rd NE61 ......115 A1
Morston Dr NE5 ......149 F3
Mortimer Ave NE5 ......149 F3
Mortimer Chase NE27 ......143 E4
Mortimer St DH8 ......176 D3
Mortimer Terr ......
Pegswood NE61 ......115 C4
Seaton Delaval NE25 ......134 E2
Morton Cres NE5 ......149 B6
Morven Lea NE21 ......169 B2
Morven Pl NE63 ......117 B4
Morven Terr NE63 ......117 B4
Morwick Cl NE23 ......133 A5
Morwick Rd NE65 ......53 D7
Moss Cl NE15 ......169 C8
Moss Side NE40 ......168 A4
Mosspool NE21 ......169 A2
Mosswood Cotts DH8 ......109 E5
Motcombe Way NE23 ......127 D2
Mouldshaugh La NE65 ......52 F3
Mount Cl ......
Killingworth NE12 ......142 D4
NE15 ......148 D2
Mount Pleasant ......
NE21 ......169 B1
Mount Pleasant Ct ......
NE15 ......148 D2
Mount Rd TD15 ......178 B3
Mount The Consett DH8 ......176 D6
Ryton NE40 ......168 A4
Throckley NE15 ......148 C2
Mount View ......
Crawcrook NE40 ......167 F3
Embleton NE66 ......24 B1
Glanton NE66 ......29 C1
Mount View Terr NE43 ......171 A7
Mountford Rd NE30 ......134 D7
Mountside DH8 ......176 D5
Mouseyhaugh NE48 ......69 D6
Mowbray Terr NE43 ......171 A7
Mowden Hall (Prep Sch) ......
NE43 ......164 E7
Muirfield Rd NE23 ......144 D5
Muirfield DH8 ......176 D5
Mulberry Cl NE24 ......128 A2
Mullen Dr NE40 ......168 D4
Murray Ct DH8 ......176 D5
Murray St NE21 ......169 C3
Murrayfield NE23 ......133 F2
Murrayfields NE27 ......143 D1
Murston Ave NE23 ......127 C2
Murton Farm Cotts TD15 ......3 C3
Murton La NE27,NE29 ......144 B2
Mylord Cres NE12 ......142 B5
Myrtle Cres NE12 ......142 D1
Myrtle Rd NE23 ......169 C1
Myrtle Rd NE63 ......117 D4

Naylor Ct NE21 ......169 E4
Naylor Pl NE26 ......135 B7
Neale St NE42 ......166 D3
Nearlane Cl NE13 ......141 C8
Neasdon Cres NE30 ......145 B1
Nedderton Cl NE15 ......149 B4
Needham Pl NE23 ......133 C8
Needless Hall Farm Cotts ......
NE61 ......76 A5
Nellie Gormley Ho ......
NE12 ......142 B2
Nelson Ave NE23 ......132 F8
Nelson Cl NE63 ......117 C2
Nelson Dr ......
Cramlington NE23 ......126 F1
Swarland NE65 ......52 C6
Nelson Ind Est NE23 ......126 E2
Nelson Park Ind Est ......
NE23 ......126 E1
Nelson Park Networkctr ......
NE23 ......126 E1
Nelson Park W NE23 ......126 D1
Nelson Rd ......
Cramlington NE23 ......126 D1
Earsdon NE25 ......144 B5
Stakeford NE62 ......122 A7
Nelson St Consett DH8 ......176 F2
Greenside NE40 ......167 F1
Leadgate DH8 ......177 C4
Nelson Terr NE17 ......173 B1
Nelson Way NE23 ......132 F8
Nelson Wy NE46 ......161 C4
Nenthead Mines Heritage ......
Ctr* CA9 ......110 A6
Neptune Rd ......
Newcastle u T,Denton Burn ......
NE15 ......169 E7
Newcastle u T,Lemington ......
NE15 ......169 D6
Nesbit NE71 ......13 F4
Nesby Pl TD12 ......179 C6
Ness Ct NE21 ......169 A2
Ness St TD15 ......178 C2
Nether Riggs NE22 ......126 F8
Netherby Dr NE5 ......149 D1
Netherton NE12 ......142 C4
Netherton Gdns NE13 ......141 B6
Netherton La NE22 ......121 C1
Netherton Northside Fst Sch ......
NE61 ......37 F2
Netherton Southside ......
NE65 ......37 F2
Netherwitton Way NE3 ......141 B1
Neuk The NE70 ......15 F4
Nevill Rd NE43 ......171 D7
Neville Rd NE15 ......169 E7
Neville Sq NE61 ......113 A2
Nevis Cl NE25 ......144 E8
Nevis Ct NE25 ......144 E8
Nevis Way NE46 ......161 C4
New Alston NE47 ......90 A1
New Barns Cl NE65 ......53 E8
New Barns Way NE65 ......53 E8
New Bewick NE66 ......29 B7
New Cotts Ilderton NE66 ......28 C8
Mitford NE61 ......114 A1
New Delaval Fst Sch ......
NE24 ......128 B4
New Haggerston TD15 ......8 F6
New Hartley Fst Sch ......
NE25 ......134 D6
New Horton Grange Cotts ......
NE13 ......130 F4
New Kennels NE48 ......90 E8
New King St NE64 ......118 F5
New Ladykirk Farm Cotts ......
TD15 ......2 B3
New Moor Cl NE23 ......116 F4
New Park Cvn Site ......
NE65 ......183 E5
New Phoenix Yd ......
NE15 ......120 A8
New Queen St NE64 ......118 E5
New Rd Berwick-u-T TD15 ......178 A5
Chatton NE66 ......21 D7
New Ridley Rd NE43 ......171 D5
New Sandridge NE64 ......118 F5
New Shoreston Cotts ......
NE69 ......17 C3
New Watling St DH8 ......177 D4
New York Rd ......
Shiremoor NE27 ......143 E2
Tynemouth NE29 ......144 B2
Newark Cl NE23 ......121 D2
Newarth Cl NE15 ......169 E6
Newbank Wlk NE21 ......169 A1
Newbiggin La NE5 ......149 F4
Newbiggin Mid Sch ......
NE64 ......118 C4
Newbiggin Rd NE63 ......117 E1
Newbiggin-by-the-Sea ......
Moorside Fst Sch ......
NE64 ......118 D5
Newbrough CE Fst Sch ......
NE47 ......90 E2
Newburgh Ave NE25 ......134 D2
Newburgh St NE25 ......183 D6
Newburn Bridge Rd ......
NE15,NE21 ......168 E6
Newburn Hall Motor Mus* ......
NE15 ......
Newburn Haugh Ind Est ......
NE15 ......169 C6
Newburn Ind Est NE15 ......169 D6
Newburn Lane End ......
NE15 ......148 D2
Newburn Manor Fst Sch ......
NE15 ......168 F8

Mer – Nor 199

Newburn Rd ......
Newburn NE15 ......168 F8
Throckley NE15 ......148 E1
Newbury NE12 ......142 D4
Newbury Cl NE15 ......169 D7
Newbury Dr DH8 ......176 E7
Newby Cl NE22 ......122 C3
Newcastle International ......
Airport NE13 ......139 D3
Newcastle Rd ......
Blyth NE24 ......128 C4
Corbridge NE45 ......163 B5
Newdene Wlk NE15 ......169 D7
Newfields TD15 ......178 A8
Newgate St NE61 ......114 F1
Newham Ave NE13 ......141 A4
Newham Hall NE67 ......23 D8
Newham Howeway NE67 ......23 D7
Newholme Ave NE24 ......153 D5
Newington Dr NE29 ......144 F1
Newlands Consett DH8 ......176 D4
Tynemouth NE30 ......145 A2
Newlands Ave ......
Blyth NE24 ......128 C5
Newcastle u T NE3 ......141 D1
Whitley Bay NE25 ......144 D3
Newlands Farm Cotts ......
NE70 ......16 A3
Newlands Pl NE24 ......128 D5
Newlands Rd NE24 ......128 D5
Newlyn Dr NE23 ......133 B8
Newman's Way ......
NE46 ......161 B4
Newmarket St DH8 ......176 F3
Newmoor Cl NE65 ......183 D4
Newsham Cl NE5 ......149 B4
Newsham Fst Sch NE24 ......128 C5
Newsham Rd NE24 ......128 C6
Newstead Rise DH8 ......176 C5
Newsteads Cl NE25 ......144 D5
Newsteads Dr NE25 ......144 D5
Newton Cl NE15 ......169 E7
Newton On The Moor ......
NE65 ......52 C8
Newton Pool Nature Reserve ......
& Bird Sanctuary* ......
NE66 ......24 E3
Newton Sq NE15 ......169 E4
Newton St NE49 ......153 C4
Newton Terr NE43 ......165 E1
Nicholson Terr NE12 ......142 E1
Nidderdale Cl NE24 ......128 A8
Nile Cl NE15 ......169 C8
Nile Dr NE65 ......52 C6
Nile St DH8 ......176 F2
Ninth Ave Blyth NE24 ......128 D6
Morpeth NE61 ......120 B7
Ninth Row NE63 ......117 B4
Nixon Terr NE24 ......128 F6
Noble St NE48 ......62 F3
Noble Terr NE61 ......120 A8
Nook The NE25 ......144 F4
Nordale Ho NE24 ......128 A8
Nordale Way NE24 ......128 A8
Norfolk Cl NE63 ......117 A4
Norfolk Way NE15 ......169 C8
Norman Castle* TD15 ......2 C2
Norham Cl Blyth NE24 ......128 C7
Brunswick Village NE13 ......141 A5
Norham Dr ......
Morpeth NE61 ......120 B5
Newcastle u T NE5 ......149 E3
Norham Fst Sch TD15 ......2 C2
Norham Gdns NE62 ......121 A1
Norham Gn TD15 ......4 A4
Norham Railway Sta* ......
TD15 ......2 C1
Norham Rd ......
Ashington NE63 ......117 D2
Whitley Bay NE25,NE26 ......144 F5
Norham Rd N NE27 ......144 A1
Norland Rd NE15 ......169 F6
Norma Cres NE26 ......145 C4
Normacot NE46 ......80 E4
Norman Terr ......
Consett DH8 ......176 E3
Morpeth NE61 ......120 A8
North Ave ......
Guide Post NE62 ......121 E7
Newcastle u T NE5 ......149 F2
North Bank Belford NE70 ......15 E5
Haydon Bridge NE47 ......157 F6
Haydon Bridge NE47 ......158 A5
North Burnside NE47 ......155 E7
North Charlton NE67 ......23 C1
North Cl NE40 ......167 F3
North Cross St DH8 ......177 C4
North Doddington NE71 ......14 A3
North End NE66 ......32 B2
North Farm NE22 ......126 A8
North Gr NE40 ......168 D5
North Grange NE20 ......138 E8
North Greenwich Rd ......
TD15 ......178 D2
North Haul Rd ......
Falstone NE48 ......69 B7
Kielder NE48 ......55 F2
Kielder NE48 ......56 A1
Kielder NE48 ......68 F8
North Holm NE46 ......77 D6
North La Norham TD15 ......2 C2
Seahouses NE68 ......17 E2
North Leech NE61 ......114 D2

North Lodge Apartments 🅚
NE21 ....169 B1
North Lyham Farm Cotts
NE66 ....15 B2
North Magdalene DH8 .175 B1
North Mason Lodge
NE13 ....140 B8
North Mdws NE42 ......166 B5
North Par
Choppington NE61 ....121 E6
Whitley Bay NE26 ....145 B5
North Pl NE61 ....114 E1
North Rd
Berwick-u-T TD15 ....178 A7
Haydon Bridge NE47 ......89 E3
Longhorsley NE65 ....64 A5
Ponteland NE20 ....138 E8
Slaley NE46,NE47 ....100 B6
North Ridge
Bedlington NE22 ....121 D1
Bedlington NE61 ....121 E1
Whitley Bay NE25 ....144 C6
North Road Ind Est TD15 ...1 F2
North Row Cambo NE61 ...74 D4
Prudhoe NE42 ....166 A2
North Seaton Ind Est
NE63 ....117 F1
North Seaton Rd
Ashington NE63 ....117 D2
Newbiggin-by-t-S NE64 ..118 D3
North Shore Kielder
Viaduct* NE48 ....55 D3
North Side Shilbottle NE66 .41 C3
Stamfordham NE18 ....93 F7
North Side Cotts NE61 ..76 A4
North St Amble NE65 ...183 C6
Blaydon NE21 ....169 A2
Consett DH8 ....177 B2
🔢 Seahouses NE68 ....17 F2
North Stead Dr DH8 ...176 C5
North Terr Chatton NE66 ..21 D7
Chopwell NE17 ....173 B2
Hexham NE46 ....161 B4
🔢 Shiremoor NE27 ....143 E1
Wark NE48 ....80 F4
North Tyneside General
Hospl NE29 ....144 E1
North View Amble NE65 .183 C5
Ashington NE63 ....117 C4
🔢 Bedlington NE22 ....122 D3
Cambois NE24 ....123 C6
Consett DH8 ....176 D4
Crawcrook NE40 ....167 E7
Dinnington NE13 ....140 B7
Hazlerigg NE13 ....141 A4
High Spen NE39 ....173 F3
Medomsley DH8 ....175 B1
Mickley Square NE43 ....165 E1
Newbiggin-by-t-S NE64 ..118 D3
Ryton NE40 ....168 A5
Stakeford NE62 ....122 C8
Whitley Bay NE30 ....145 C4
Widdrington NE66 ....39 B6
North View Terr
Prudhoe NE42 ....166 B2
Stocksfield NE43 ....171 C7
North Villas NE23 ....133 A1
North Walbottle Rd
Newcastle u T NE5 ......149 B4
Walbottle NE15 ....149 A2
North Wylam View
NE42 ....166 E4
Northbourne Ave NE61 .114 F2
Northburn Fst Sch
NE23 ....127 A1
Northcote Ave
Newcastle u T NE5 ......149 C1
Whitley Bay NE25 ....144 D4
Northcott Gdns NE23 ..133 E1
Northern Terr NE23 ...133 A1
Northfield Dr NE12 ...123 B4
Northfield Gr NE61 ...142 B2
Northfield View DH8 ..177 E2
Northgate NE12 ....142 D4
Northgate & Prudhoe NHS
Trust Northgate Hospl
NE61 ....114 D4
Northlands Blaydon NE21 .169 B1
Tynemouth NE30 ....145 B1
Northlands Rd NE61 ...114 E2
Northlea NE15 ....169 E8
Northolt Ave NE23 ....133 B7
Northside NE20 ....93 B6
Northside Pl NE25 ....134 E2
Northumberland Aged
Mineworkers Homes
NE23 ....133 D5
Northumberland Ave
Bedlington NE22 ....121 E1
Berwick-u-T TD15 ....178 B6
Newbiggin-by-t-S NE64 ..118 D4
Northumberland Cl
NE63 ....117 A4
Northumberland Coll
NE63 ....117 E2
Northumberland Coll
(Berwick Campus)
TD15 ....178 B1
Northumberland Ct
NE42 ....166 E4
Northumberland Gdns
NE5 ....149 B3

Northumberland Nat Pk
Visitor Ctr* NE66 ......28 D3
Northumberland National
Park Information Ctr &
Visitor Ctr* NE47 ......88 D1
Northumberland Rd
Newcastle u T,Lemington
NE15 ....169 C6
Ryton NE40 ....168 C6
Tweedmouth TD15 ....178 B2
Northumberland Sq
NE26 ....145 A5
Northumberland St
🔟 Alnmouth NE66 ....42 B5
Alnwick NE66 ....181 B6
Northumbria Ctr For Ent
NE63 ....117 D5
Northumbria Police HQ
NE20 ....85 E1
Northumbria Terr NE65 .183 C5
Northumbria Wlk NE5 ..149 F1
Northumbrian Rd NE23 .133 B6
Northumbrian Way
NE12 ....142 C2
Northway
Guide Post NE62 ....121 F7
Throckley NE15 ....148 D3
Norton Way NE15 ......169 E6
Norwell Brow NE66 ....32 C6
Norwich Ave NE13 .....141 B5
Norwich Cl NE63 ......118 A2
Norwich Way NE23 .....133 A7
Norwood Ave NE3 ......141 C1
Norwood Rd NE15 ......169 D8
Nottingham Ct NE22 ...121 D7
Number One Ind Est
DH8 ....177 A4
Nuneaton Way NE5 .....149 B4
Nunnykirk Cl NE42 ....166 A4
Nursery Ct NE17 ......175 B6
Nursery Grange NE46 ..160 F3
Nursery La
🔢 Belford NE70 ....15 F4
Coldstream TD12 ....179 C6
Nursery Pk NE63 ......117 E1
Nursery Rd TD12 ......179 C6
Nursery The NE20 .....137 E1
Nye Bevan Ho NE24 ....128 F6

O

Oak Ave NE13 ....140 C7
Oak Cl NE46 ....160 E3
Oak La DH8 ....176 C7
Oak St 🔟 Consett DH8 .176 F2
Mickley Square NE43 ....171 E8
Seaton Burn NE13 ....141 C8
🔢 Throckley NE15 ....148 D5
Oak Terr Blaydon NE21 .169 C1
Leadgate DH8 ....177 D4
Oakapple Cl NE22 .....121 F1
Oakdale NE22 ....126 B8
Oakdale Cl NE15 ......169 D6
Oakdale Rd DH8 ....177 A3
Oakenshaw NE15 ....169 E6
Oakfield Dr NE12 .....142 F3
Oakfield Grange NE13 .140 B7
Oakfield La DH8 ......176 C1
Oakfield N NE40 ......168 B5
Oakfield Pk NE42 .....166 B2
Oakfield Terr NE12 ...142 E1
Oakfield Way NE23 ....133 F1
Oakford NE61 ....74 E5
Oakland Rd NE25 ......144 D4
Oakland Terr
Ashington NE63 ....117 C3
Lynemouth NE61 ....113 A2
Oaklands Ponteland NE20 .138 D4
Riding Mill NE44 ....100 F8
Oaklands Ct NE20 .....138 D4
Oaklands Pl NE42 .....166 E2
Oaklands Rise NE44 ...100 F8
Oaklea Cl NE23 ....142 B8
Oakley Dr NE23 ....133 D7
Oaks The Greenside NE40 .168 B1
Hexham NE46 ....160 F3
Matfen NE20 ....93 B7
Oaktree Gdns NE25 ....144 E3
Oaktree Terr NE42 ....166 D2
Oakville NE63 ....118 A2
Oakwell Ct NE17 ......175 C5
Oakwell Terr
Haltwhistle NE49 ....153 E5
Prudhoe NE42 ....166 A2
Oakwood Ave
Newbiggin-by-t-S NE64 ..118 D5
Widdopen NE13 ....141 C5
Oakwood Bank NE46 ....161 C7
Oaky Balks NE66 ......181 E4
Oatens Bank
Harlow Hill NE15 ....93 F2
Horsley NE15 ....146 A2
Oatfield Cl NE63 .....117 B2
Ocean Rd 🔢 NE63 .....183 D6
Ocean View
Newbiggin-by-t-S NE64 ..118 E4
Whitley Bay NE26 ......145 B5
Ochiltree Cres NE25 ..135 D6
Octavia Cl NE22 ......121 E2
Odinel Ct NE42 ....166 D3
Ogle Ave Hazlerigg NE13 .141 A4
Morpeth NE61 ....119 E8
Ogle Dr NE24 ....129 A6
Ogle Terr 🔟 NE66 ....181 C5
Oil Mill La TD15 .....178 B4
Old Bakehouse Yd 🔟
NE61 ....114 F1

Old Barns Cl NE65 ....53 E8
Old Bewick NE66 ......29 B8
Old Brewery Sq NE42 ..165 C4
Old Coastguard Hos
NE65 ....183 E6
Old Ferneybeds Rd NE61 .65 E4
Old Forge The NE43 ...164 C5
Old Hall Rd DH8 ......177 B1
Old Heathershaw TD12 ..12 F8
Old Main St NE40 .....167 E3
Old Orchard The NE44 .170 A7
Old Rd NE66 ....21 D7
Old Row NE64 ....152 A6
Old Sawmill NE61 .....119 A8
Old School Rd NE61 ...53 F2
Old Station Ct NE20 ..138 C3
Old Tweedmill The NE55 .52 C6
Old Well Ave 🛇 NE21 .169 B1
Old Well La NE21 .....169 B1
Oldgate NE61 ....119 F8
Oldgate Ct NE61 ......119 F8
Oley Mdws DH8 ....176 C7
Oliver Pl NE71 ....180 B6
Oliver Rd NE71 ....180 B6
Olivers Mill NE61 ....119 F8
Ollerton Dr NE61 .....143 D2
Olney Cl NE23 ....133 D7
Olympia Ave NE62 .....121 F7
Olympia Gdns NE61 ....115 A1
Olympia Hill NE61 ....114 F2
Oram Cl NE61 ....120 B8
Orange Gr NE23 ....133 B1
Orchard Ave NE46 .....91 C1
Orchard Cl
Killingworth NE12 ......142 F2
Morpeth NE61 ....120 B8
Prudhoe NE42 ....166 D1
Ulgham NE61 ....65 D3
Orchard Cres NE45 ....163 A5
Orchard Ct
Greenside NE40 ....167 F1
Ryton NE40 ....168 C5
Orchard Hill NE42 ....166 D3
Orchard Loaning NE66 ..31 E5
Orchard Mews NE61 ....114 F1
Orchard Rd NE15 ......169 B7
Orchard Terr
🔢 Hexham NE46 ....161 B5
Lesbury NE66 ....42 A6
🔢 Throckley NE15 ......148 D2
Orchard The Acomb NE46 ..91 C2
Hepscott NE61 ....120 E5
Newcastle u T NE15 ....169 D6
Paxton TD15 ....2 F7
Swarland NE65 ....52 C6
Wylam NE41 ....167 A6
Orchard View
Corbridge NE45 ....162 F6
Humshaugh NE46 ....91 B6
Orchard-Leigh NE15 ...169 E6
Orchards The NE24 ....128 B8
Orchid Cl NE63 ....117 C2
Ord Dr TD15 ....3 E7
Ord Terr NE62 ....122 B8
Ordley Cl NE15 ....169 E6
Ormiscraig NE15 ......169 E6
Ormiston NE15 ....169 E6
Ormskirk Cl NE15 .....169 E6
Ormskirk Gr NE23 .....133 C7
Ormston St NE23 ......127 B3
Orpine Ct NE63 ....117 C2
Orpington Rd NE23 ....133 C7
Osborne Ave NE46 .....160 F5
Osborne Ct NE22 ......122 C2
Osborne Cotts 🔢 NE61 ..3 C5
Osborne Cres TD15 ....178 A4
Osborne Gdns
Seahouses NE68 ....17 E2
Whitley Bay NE26 ......144 F5
Osborne Pl
Longbenton NE12 ....142 F1
Tweedmouth TD15 ....178 A3
Osborne Rd TD15 ......178 A3
Osborne Terr
Cramlington NE23 ......133 A7
Seahouses NE68 ....17 E2
Osier Ct NE62 ....122 C7
Osprey Dr NE24 ....128 F5
Oswain Ave NE12 ......142 E1
Oswald Rd Morpeth NE61 .115 A2
Newbiggin-by-t-S NE64 ..118 D5
Oswald St 🛇 NE65 ....183 C5
Oswestry Pl NE23 .....133 C7
Oswin Ct NE12 ....142 E1
Oswin Rd NE12 ....142 E1
Otley Cl NE23 ....133 D7
Otter Burn Way NE42 ..166 B1
Otterburn Ave NE25 ...144 B4
Otterburn Ct NE25 ....144 B4
Otterburn Dr NE63 ....117 B1
Otterburn Fst Sch NE19 .39 D4
Otterburn Gn NE19 ....45 E5
Otterburn Gr NE24 ....128 B5
Otterburn Hall NE19 ..59 E5
Ottercap Cl NE15 .....169 D6
Ottercops NE42 ....166 B1
Ottershaw NE15 ....169 A1
Ottringham Cl NE15 ...169 D6
Oulton Cl NE23 ....133 C7
Our Lady & St Joseph's RC
Prim Sch DH8 ....177 D4
Ouston St NE15 ....169 A3
Oval The Bedlington NE22 .122 C1
Blyth NE24 ....128 B3
Felton NE65 ....52 E3
Stamfordham NE18 ......136 A4

Oval The continued
Tweedmouth TD15 ....178 A2
Woolsington NE13 ......149 F8
Overburn CA9 ....185 E3
Overdale Ct NE62 .....121 E6
Overdene NE15 ....169 F7
Overhill NE15 ....147 E2
Overstone Ave NE40 ...167 F2
Overstone Gdns NE46 ..161 A3
Overton Cl NE15 ......169 D6
Ovingham CE Fst Sch
NE42 ....166 A3
Ovingham Gdns NE13 ..141 B6
Ovingham Mid Sch
NE42 ....166 A3
Ovingham Rd NE41 ....167 A6
Ovington View NE42 ...166 B1
Owen Brannigan Dr
NE23 ....142 B7
Owen Terr NE17 ....175 C8
Owlet Cl NE21 ....169 A1
Owlet Grange NE39 ....175 E5
Oxford Ave NE23 ......133 C7
Oxford Rd NE62 ....122 A7
Oxford St Blyth NE24 .128 F7
Whitley Bay NE26 ......145 B5
Oxley St DH8 ....176 D4
Oxted Cl NE23 ....133 D7
Ozanan Cl NE23 ....142 B7

P

Paddock Cl Matfen NE20 ..93 B6
Prudhoe NE42 ....166 E2
Paddock Hill NE20 ....138 F7
Paddock La NE18 ......137 B5
Paddock Rise NE63 ....117 B2
Paddock The
Ashington NE63 ....118 B2
Blyth NE24 ....128 C7
East Cramlington NE23 .133 D5
Seaton Delaval NE25 ...134 E3
Stocksfield NE43 ......171 C5
Walbottle NE15 ....148 B3
Woolsington NE13 ......149 F8
Paddock Wood NE42 ....166 E2
Paddocks The NE24 ....123 C7
Pader Cl NE13 ....141 B5
Padgepool Pl NE71 ....180 B6
Paignton Ave NE25 ....144 B4
Paikes St 🛇 NE66 ....181 C5
Painshawfield Rd NE43 .171 C6
Palace Gn 🔢 TD15 ....178 B4
Palace Rd NE22 ....122 D2
Palace St TD15 ....178 B4
Palace St E TD15 .....178 B4
Palm La NE61 ....142 F1
Palm St 🔢 DH8 ....176 F3
Palmer Terr NE61 .....65 E4
Palmers Gn NE12 ......142 F1
Palmerston St DH8 ....176 F2
Palmersville NE12 ....142 F1
Palmersville Sta NE12 .143 A1
Palmstrother Dr NE66 .30 E2
Pangbourne Cl NE15 ...169 C8
Panhaven Rd NE65 .....183 E6
Parade TD15 ....178 C5
Parade School Mews 🔢
TD15 ....178 C5
Paradise Row NE23 ....133 B6
Park Ave Bedlington NE22 .122 E3
Blaydon NE21 ....169 C2
Blaydon,Bleach Green
NE21 ....169 B2
Consett DH8 ....177 A3
Haltwhistle NE49 ......153 C6
Hexham NE46 ....160 F5
Prudhoe NE42 ....166 E1
Shiremoor NE27 ....144 A3
Whitley Bay NE26 ......145 A5
Park Bank DH8 ....108 B5
Park Cotts NE17 ......175 B6
Park Cres NE27 ....143 F3
Park Dr Blyth NE24 ...128 B4
Morpeth NE61 ....119 F7
Newcastle u T NE3 .....141 C1
Stannington NE61 ......120 E1
Park Farm Villas NE24 .128 C7
Park Gate NE61 ....168 C5
Park Field Terr NE26 .135 C6
Park Gdns NE25 ....145 A5
Park Gr NE27 ....143 F3
Park La Alston CA9 ...185 C3
Prudhoe NE42 ....166 E1
Redburn NE47 ....155 D7
Shiremoor NE27 ....143 F3
Park Lea DH8 ....176 E3
Park Par NE26 ....145 A5
Park Rd Ashington NE63 .117 B3
Bedlington NE22 ....122 A8
Blyth NE24 ....128 F5
Consett DH8 ....176 E3
Haltwhistle NE49 ......153 B4
Longhoughton NE66 .....32 B2
Lynemouth NE61,NE63 ...113 A2
Newburn NE15 ....168 F8
Seaton Delaval NE25 ...134 F3
Shiremoor NE27 ....143 F3
Swarland NE65 ....52 C5
Whitley Bay NE26 ......145 A6
Park Rd Ind Est DH8 ...176 E3
Park Rd N Ind Est DH8 .176 D3
Park Rise NE15 ....169 C7
Park Road E NE63 .....117 C4
Park Side
Coldstream TD12 ....179 B6
Hepscott NE61 ....120 F5

Park Side continued
Slaley NE47 ....100 .
Park St DH8 ....176 .
Park Terr
Bedlington NE22 ....122 .
Blaydon NE21 ....169 .
Killingworth NE12 .....142 .
Leadgate DH8 ....177 .
Whitley Bay NE26 .....145 .
Park View
🛇 Alnwick NE66 ....181 .
Ashington NE63 ....117 .
Blaydon NE21 ....128 .
Blyth NE24 ....128 .
Consett DH8 ....176 .
Felton NE65 ....52 .
Longbenton NE12 ....142 .
Lynemouth NE61 ....113 .
Seaton Delaval NE25 ...134 .
Whitley Bay NE26 .....145 .
Widdopen NE13 ....141 .
Park View Cl NE40 ....168 .
Park View Ct NE26 ....145 .
Park View Gdns NE40 ..168 .
Park View La CA9 .....185 .
Park View Sh Ctr NE26 .145 .
Park Villas
Ashington NE63 ....117 .
Leadgate DH8 ....177 .
Parker's Bldgs DH8 ...177 .
Parkham Cl NE23 ......127 .
Parkhead Gdns NE21 ...169 .
Parkhead Sq NE21 .....169 .
Parkinson's Cotts NE40 .168 .
Parkland NE21 ....169 .
Parkland Ave NE21 ....169 .
Parklands
Haltwhistle NE49 ......153 .
Hamsterley Mill NE39 ..175 .
Ponteland NE20 ....138 .
Parklea NE26 ....135 .
Parks The NE65 ....53 .
Parkside Bedlington NE22 .122 .
Consett DH8 ....177 .
Throckley NE15 ....148 .
Tweedmouth TD15 ....178 .
Tynemouth NE30 ....169 .
Parkside Ave NE21 ....169 .
Parkside Cres NE30 ...145 .
Parkside Ct
Ashington NE63 ....117 .
Whitley Bay NE26 .....144 .
Widdopen NE13 ....141 .
Parkside Pl NE48 .....184 .
Parkway NE62 ....121 .
Parkwood Ave NE42 ....166 .
Parliament St DH8 ....176 .
Parmontley St NE15 ...169 .
Parnaby St DH8 ....176 .
Parson Rd NE41 ....167 .
Parsons St 🔟 NE24 ...128 .
Partanhall TD15 ......1 .
Paston Rd NE25 ....134 .
Pastures The Blyth NE24 .128 .
East Ord TD15 ....1 .
Morpeth NE61 ....119 .
Stocksfield NE43 ......171 .
Patience Ave NE13 ....141 .
Patina Cl NE15 ....169 .
Patrick Terr NE23 ....128 .
Patterdale Ho NE24 ...128 .
Patterdale Mews DH8 ..177 .
Patterdale Rd NE24 ...128 .
Patterson Cl NE46 ....160 .
Patterson St NE21 ....169 .
Patton Way NE61 ......115 .
Pavilion The NE16 ....169 .
Paxton Ho* TD15 ....2 .
Paxton Rd TD15 ....3 .
Pear Tree Terr NE17 ..175 .
Pearson's Terr 🔟 NE46 .161 .
Peartree Bglws NE17 ..175 .
Peary Cl NE5 ....149 .
Pease's Gdns 🔢 NE66 ..42 .
Pease's La 🔟 NE66 ....42 .
Pecket Cl NE24 ....128 .
Pedwell Way TD15 .....2 .
Peel Ct NE13 ....141 .
Peel Dr NE66 ....32 .
Peepy Cotts NE43 .....164 .
Pegswood Fst Sch NE61 .115 .
Pegswood Ind Est NE61 .115 .
Pegswood Prec NE61 ...115 .
Pegswood Sta NE61 .....115 .
Pegswood Village NE61 .115 .
Peile Ct DH8 ....176 .
Peile Pk DH8 ....176 .
Pelaw Ave NE64 ....118 .
Peltondale Ave NE24 ..128 .
Pemberton Ave DH8 ....176 .
Pemberton Rd
Castleside DH8 ....109 .
Consett DH8 ....108 .
Pembroke Ct
🔟 Blyth NE24 ....128 .
Newbiggin-by-t-S NE64 ..118 .
Pembroke Dr NE20 .....138 .
Pembroke Gdns NE15 ...169 .
Pemdamor Ct NE61 .....116 .
Pendleton Dr NE23 ....116 .
Pennine Dr NE63 ......117 .
Pennine Rd CA8 ....94 .
Pennine View NE17 ....175 .
Pennine Way
Green Humbleton TD5 ...179 .
Wark NE48 ....80 .
Penrith Ave NE30 .....145 .

Pen – Riv 201

arith Ct NE22 121 D2
at Ct NE40 168 A1
atland Cl
ington NE63 117 E1
amlington NE23 127 B1
emouth NE29 144 F1
atland Gr NE12 142 B1
atridge Cl NE23 133 C7
cy Ave
emouth NE30 145 C3
itley Bay NE26 145 A5
cy Cl NE46 160 F3
cy Cotts NE25 134 E2
cy Ct 1 NE66 181 D4
cy Dr Amble NE65 183 D4
arland NE65 52 C6
cy Gdns
rrasford NE48 91 B8
nsett DH8 177 B1
akeford NE62 122 A8
itley Bay NE25 145 A4
cy Hedley Senior Sch The
12 142 D2
cy Lonnen NE42 166 D3
cy Rd Shilbottle NE66 41 C3
itley Bay NE26 145 B5
cy St Alnwick NE66 181 C5
ble NE65 183 D6
ington NE63 117 E4
th NE24 128 F8
amlington NE23 133 C5
gbenton NE12 142 F1
wcastle u T,Lemington
15 169 C6
cy St S NE24 128 F7
cy Terr Alnwick NE66 181 C4
llingham NE48 184 C4
rwick-u-T TD15 178 B6
nsett DH8 177 B1
wburn NE15 168 F7
itley Bay NE25 144 E5
cy View NE48 81 A5
cy Villas NE66 181 C4
cy Way NE15 149 A1
cy's Cross* NE19 59 D4
ry Stone Mews
22 127 A8
cott Ct 7 NE46 161 B4
h Head Hexham NE46 161 C5
oler NE71 180 C5
h La NE40 168 D6
h The
endale Town NE47 97 F2
wick NE66 181 C6
ton NE65 52 E3
oler NE71 180 C5
hgate Ct 10 NE61 120 A8
rel Way NE24 128 F4
worth Gdns NE61 115 E4
ensey Cl NE29 144 F1
eonix Ct DH8 176 C3
lip Dr NE65 183 D5
llips Pl TD15 8 E2
obe Grange Cotts
42 166 D2
oenix Ct NE61 119 F8
oenix St NE24 128 B4
kwick Pl 16 NE66 181 C5
r Rd TD15 178 C4
e Hill DH8 109 F8
grims Way NE61 119 D7
on Rd NE5 149 F3
on Wlk 4 NE5 149 F3
e Ave
nington NE13 140 C7
ide Post NE62 121 D7
e Rd NE21 169 C2
e St Greenside NE40 168 B1
aton Burn NE13 141 C8
rockley NE15 148 D3
egarth NE20 138 C2
es The Broomhill NE65 53 F3
eenside NE40 168 B1
etree Gdns NE25 144 E3
ewood Ave
amlington NE23 127 B1
deopen NE13 141 C5
ewood Dr NE61 114 D2
fold The
Alnmouth NE66 42 B5
thbury NE65 182 A5
neer Terr NE22 122 C2
er Gate NE48 81 B5
er La NE48 80 F5
er Rd NE42 166 B5
erdean La TD12 11 D6
istrelles The NE65 65 A8
house La DH8 177 B8
St DH8 176 F2
istow Way NE23 127 B1
ne St DH8 177 A2
net Pl NE12 142 C2
ntation Ct NE40 173 E8
ntation St DH8 177 D4
shetts Forest Wlk*
48 68 E8
ywell Ct 3 NE66 29 C1
ywell Rd NE66 29 C2
asant View
nsett DH8 176 B4
adgate DH8 177 B6
nmeller Colliery Rd
49 153 D2
nmeller Rd NE49 153 E3
ssey Ave NE24 128 F6
ssey Cres NE25 145 B4
ssey Ct NE24 128 B4
ssey Rd NE24 128 D5

Plessey Road Fst Sch
NE24 128 F7
Plessey Road Workshops
NE24 128 B4
Plessey St NE23 127 B3
Plessey Woods Ctry Pk*
NE22 126 B4
Plover Cl NE24 128 E4
Ploverfield Cl NE63 117 C2
Polden Cres NE29 144 F1
Police Hos Alnwick NE66 181 C4
Haltwhistle NE49 153 D5
Polmaise St NE21 169 C2
Polwarth Dr NE3 141 C1
Polwarth Rd NE3 141 C1
Ponds Ct DH8 176 E2
Pont Bglws DH8 177 B6
Pont Haugh NE20 138 F7
Pont La DH8 177 C6
Pont Pk NE20 130 A2
Pont Rd DH8 177 D5
Pont St NE63 117 D3
Pont Terr DH8 177 C4
Pont View Consett DH8 177 B5
Ponteland NE20 138 F7
Ponteland Com High Sch
NE20 138 F5
Ponteland Fst Sch NE20 138 F7
Ponteland Mid Sch
NE20 138 F5
Ponteland Rd
Ponteland NE20 139 A5
Throckley NE15 148 D5
Ponthead Mews DH8 177 D4
Pontop View DH8 177 B1
Poole Cl NE23 133 C7
Poplar Ave Blyth NE24 123 D1
Dinnington NE13 140 C7
Poplar Gr NE22 122 C1
Poplar Rd NE21 169 C1
Poplar St Ashington NE63 117 D4
Throckley NE15 148 D3
Porchester Dr NE23 133 C7
Porlock Ct NE23 127 A1
Portal Ct NE66 32 B2
Portal Pl NE66 32 B2
Portia St NE63 117 E4
Portland Gdns NE23 133 C7
Portland Ind Pk NE63 116 F5
Portland Rd NE15 148 E2
Portland St 1 NE24 128 D8
Portland Terr
Ashington NE63 116 F5
Hexham NE46 160 F5
Post Office St 4 NE24 128 F8
Post Office Terr CA8 94 B6
Postern Cres NE61 119 F7
Potland View NE61 112 A3
Pottergate NE66 181 B5
Potters' La CA9 185 E2
Pottery Bank NE61 114 E2
Pottery Bank Ct NE61 114 E2
Pow Hill Ctry Pk* DH8 108 F6
Precinct The
Blaydon NE21 169 D3
Broomhill NE65 53 F3
Prestbury Ave NE23 127 A1
Prestdale Ave NE24 128 A7
Preston Gate NE29 144 F1
Preston Grange Prim Sch
NE29 144 E1
Preston North Rd NE29 144 F1
Preston Terr 12 NE27 143 E1
Preston Twr* NE67 23 E4
Preston Wood NE30 145 A1
Prestwick Carr Rd NE13 140 A8
Prestwick Terr NE20 139 C3
Pretoria Ave NE61 119 F8
Price St NE61 114 E1
Priestclose Cotts NE42 166 F2
Priestclose Rd NE42 166 D2
Priestlands Ave 12
NE46 161 A4
Priestlands Cl NE46 161 A3
Priestlands Cres NE46 161 A4
Priestlands Dr NE46 161 A4
Priestlands Gr NE46 161 A3
Priestlands La NE46 161 A4
Priestlands Rd NE46 161 A4
Priestman Ave DH8 176 C1
Priestpopple NE46 161 B4
Primrose Cl NE23 142 A8
Primrose Ct NE63 117 B1
Prince Charles Cres TD15 4 A3
Prince Charles Pl TD15 4 A4
Prince Charles Rd TD15 4 A4
Prince Charles St TD15 4 A4
Prince Edward Rd TD15 178 A3
Prince St NE17 173 B1
Prince's Gdns NE24 128 C8
Princes Gdns NE25 144 E5
Princes Rd NE3 141 B1
Princes St
Corbridge NE45 163 A5
Spittal TD15 178 C2
Princess Ave DH8 176 D5
Princess Ct NE42 166 D4
Princess Louise Fst Sch
NE24 128 D7
Princess Louise Rd
NE24 128 E7
Princess Way NE42 166 C4
Prior La TD15 10 D4
Prior Rd TD15 178 A1
Prior Terr
Corbridge NE45 162 F6
Hexham NE46 161 A6
Prior View TD15 178 A1

Priors Wlk NE61 119 E7
Priory Ave NE25 144 F4
Priory Bank TD12 179 B7
Priory Cl DH8 176 C5
Priory Gdns NE45 162 F7
Priory Grange NE24 128 C8
Priory Hill TD12 179 C7
Priory Pk NE65 183 E4
Priory Pl
Brunswick Village NE13 141 A5
Stakeford NE62 122 A8
Priory View NE61 65 F6
Priory Way NE5 149 F4
Promenade
Newbiggin-by-t-S NE64 118 E4
Spittal TD15 178 D2
Whitley Bay NE26 145 B5
Promenade The DH8 176 F4
Promontory Terr NE26 145 C4
Prospect Ave NE25 134 C3
Prospect Bsns Pk DH8 177 C3
Prospect Cotts NE22 122 C5
Prospect Pl
12 Alnmouth NE66 42 B5
9 Consett DH8 176 F3
Newbiggin-by-t-S NE64 118 F5
Prospect St 10 DH8 176 F3
Prospect Terr
Ebchester DH8 174 F4
Prudhoe NE42 166 B2
Rothbury NE65 182 A5
Providence La NE65 182 B5
Providence Pl NE65 182 B5
Prudhoe Castle* NE42 166 C3
Prudhoe Castle Fst Sch
NE42 166 B2
Prudhoe Com High Sch
NE42 166 D1
Prudhoe Hospl NE42 166 F1
Prudhoe St NE66 181 C5
Prudhoe Sta NE42 166 B4
Prudhoe West Fst Sch
NE42 166 C2
Pudding La TD15 178 A4
Pudding Mews 3 NE46 161 B5
Puffin Cl NE24 128 F3
Purbeck Cl NE29 144 F2
Purbeck Gdns NE23 133 C7
Purdy's Ho NE61 114 E1
Pykerley Mews NE25 144 E4
Pykerley Rd NE25 144 E5

Q

Quakers Row NE66 24 D1
Quantock Cl NE29 144 F2
Quarry Ave NE65 53 D4
Quarry Cotts NE63 118 B6
Quarry Edge NE46 161 C3
Quarry Hos NE23 142 C6
Quarry Rd NE15 169 C6
Quarryfields NE68 17 F2
Quatre Bras NE46 160 F5
Quay Rd NE24 129 A7
Quay Walls TD15 178 B4
Quayside NE24 128 F8
Quayside Ct 7 NE24 128 F8
Queen Elizabeth High Sch
NE46 160 E4
Queen Elizabeth II Ctry Pk*
NE63 117 F6
Queen St Alnwick NE66 181 D4
Amble NE65 183 C5
Ashington NE63 117 E4
Consett DH8 176 F2
Lynemouth NE61 113 A2
Morpeth NE61 120 A8
Newbiggin-by-t-S NE64 118 E5
Togston NE65 53 E4
Queen's Dr NE26 145 A5
Queen's Gdns
Blyth NE24 128 C8
Morpeth NE61 119 E7
Queen's Rd Alnwick NE66 181 D4
Bedlington NE22 122 D2
Consett DH8 176 E5
Whitley Bay NE26 144 F6
Wooler NE71 180 C6
Queens Cl NE46 91 D1
Queens Ct
Newcastle u T,Brunton Park
NE3 141 C2
Walbottle NE15 149 A1
Queens Gdns NE23 133 B1
Queens Pl NE64 118 E5
Queens Rd
Annitsford NE23 133 B1
Seaton Sluice NE26 135 D6
Walbottle NE15 149 A1
Queens Way
Consett DH8 176 C5
Hexham NE46 160 E5
Queensbury Dr NE15 149 B2
Queensway
Morpeth NE61 119 D7
Newcastle u T,Brunton Park
NE3 141 B1
Ponteland NE20 138 D2
Quick Silver Way NE27 143 E1

R

Raby Cl NE22 121 D1
Radcliffe Cotts 5 NE15 148 D2
Radcliffe Pk NE69 17 A5
Radcliffe Rd
Bamburgh NE69 17 A5
Hexham NE46 161 C4
Raglan St DH8 176 F2
Railway Cotts
Blyth,Bebside NE24 127 E8
Blyth,South Newsham
NE24 128 C2
Riding Mill NE44 170 A8
10 Widdrington Sta NE61 65 E5
Wylam NE41 166 F5
Railway Mus* NE41 167 B6
Railway Pl DH8 176 D3
Railway St
Berwick-u-T TD15 178 A5
Consett DH8 177 A2
Leadgate DH8 177 D4
Railway Terr Blyth NE24 128 D7
Haltwhistle NE49 153 C4
Raise Bank CA9 185 C3
Raise Hamlets CA9 185 C3
Rake La Acklington NE65 53 C5
Tynemouth NE29 144 E1
Ramparts The NE15 169 F8
Ramsay Rd NE17 173 B2
Ramsay St NE21 169 B1
Ramsey Cres TD12 5 A7
Ramsey La NE71 180 B5
Ranmore Cl NE23 133 B7
Rapperton Ct 7 NE5 149 F3
Ratcliffe Rd NE47 158 A5
Ratten Row NE66 181 B6
Ravenburn Gdns NE15 169 F6
Ravens Hill Dr NE63 117 A2
Ravensburn Wlk 6
NE15 148 D2
Ravensdale Gr NE24 128 A7
Ravensdowne TD15 178 C4
Ravenshill Rd NE5 149 E1
Ravenside Terr
Chopwell NE17 173 A1
Consett DH8 176 D4
Ravenslaw Ct 7 NE66 181 D4
Ravenslaw Gdns 9
NE66 181 D4
Ravenslaw Ho 8 NE66 181 D4
Ravensmede NE66 181 E4
Ravensworth Ct NE22 122 D3
Ravensworth Gdns
NE61 112 D4
Ravensworth St 2
NE22 122 D3
Ravensworth Terr 3
NE22 122 D3
Rayleigh Dr NE13 141 B7
Raynes Cl NE61 119 D7
Raynham Cl
6 Belford NE70 15 F4
Cramlington NE23 132 F3
Reasby Gdns NE40 168 B5
Reasby Villas NE40 168 B5
Reavley Ave NE22 122 E3
Recreation La NE65 52 E3
Rectory Dene NE61 119 F7
Rectory La
Ebchester DH8 174 E3
Blaydon NE21 169 B1
Rectory Pk NE61 119 F7
Red Barns Cres NE69 17 C5
Red Hos NE47 90 D2
Red House Dr NE25 144 C6
Red House Farm NE22 126 D8
Red Peth NE49 152 E3
Red Row Ct NE22 122 C4
Red Row Dr NE22 122 C3
Red Row Fst Sch NE61 53 F2
Red Stead NE66 32 C3
Redburn Cres NE46 91 C1
Redburn Rd NE5 149 F4
Rede Ave NE46 161 C4
Rede Ct NE61 112 E5
Rede Terr NE46 161 C4
Redesdale NE65 183 E5
Redesdale Cl NE15 169 E7
Redesdale Pl NE24 128 B7
Redesmouth NE48 71 F1
Redesmouth Ct NE48 184 C4
Redesmouth Rd NE48 184 C4
Redewater View NE19 59 E4
Redford Pl NE23 142 C5
Redheugh Rd NE25 144 B5
Redhill Wlk NE23 133 B7
Redshank Dr NE24 128 E4
Redstead Cotts NE66 24 B1
Redwell Ct NE42 166 D2
Redwell Rd NE42 166 E2
Redwood Cl NE12 142 C4
Redwood Ct
Ashington NE63 117 E2
Consett DH8 176 E4
Reed Ave NE12 142 C4
Reedside NE40 168 D5
Reedswood Cres NE23 133 E5
Reenes Way NE48 184 B5
Reeth Way NE15 148 C1
Regal Cl NE68 17 D2
Regency Cl NE61 65 F6
Regency Way NE20 138 A5
Regent Ct Blyth NE24 128 D7
Longbenton NE12 142 B2
Regent St NE24 128 E8
Regents Dr
Prudhoe NE42 166 E4
Tynemouth NE30 145 C1
Reid St NE61 120 A8
Reid's La NE23 133 E1
Reigate Sq NE23 133 B7
Reins Ct NE46 160 E5

Reiverdale Rd NE63 117 D4
Reivers & Tarset Trails*
NE48 70 C8
Reivers Gate NE65 64 A5
Relton Ct NE25 144 E5
Relton PL NE25 144 E5
Relton Terr NE25 144 E5
Remscheid Way NE63 117 C1
Remus Ave NE15 147 D2
Remus Cl NE13 141 B5
Rennington Ave NE30 145 C1
Rennington Cl
Morpeth NE61 120 B5
Tynemouth NE30 145 C1
Renwick Ho NE61 119 E7
Renwick Rd NE24 128 D7
Renwick Wlk NE61 119 E8
Resida Cl NE15 169 C8
Restoration Cotts TD15 4 A4
Retreat The NE15 168 F7
Reynolds Ave NE12 142 B2
Ribblesdale Ave NE24 128 A8
Richard Browell Rd
NE15 148 E1
Richard Coates CE Mid Sch
NE20 138 E7
Richard St NE24 128 E7
Richard Stannard Ho 11
NE24 128 F8
Richardson La NE65 48 D7
Richardson St NE63 117 E1
Richardson Terr NE17 173 B1
Richardson's Bldgs
NE62 121 E5
Richley Terr NE20 83 E1
Richmond Cl NE22 121 E2
Richmond Fields NE20 138 A5
Richmond Terr
Walbottle NE15 148 F1
Whitley Bay NE26 144 F7
Richmond Way
Cramlington NE23 133 A3
Ponteland NE20 138 A5
Riddell Cl NE65 52 E3
Ridge Ct NE13 141 B4
Ridge Terr NE22 121 E1
Ridge The NE40 168 C4
Ridge Villas NE22 121 E1
Ridgely Cl NE20 139 A6
Ridgely Dr NE20 139 A6
Ridgeway
Ashington NE63 118 A2
Seaton Delaval NE25 134 E1
Stakeford NE62 122 A8
Riding Cl NE40 167 E3
Riding Cotts NE46 161 A8
Riding Dene NE43 165 F1
Riding Grange NE44 100 F8
Riding Lea NE21 169 A1
Riding Mill Sta NE44 100 F8
Riding Terr NE43 165 F1
Ridings Ct NE40 167 E3
Ridings The NE25 144 C6
Ridley Ave NE24 128 F7
Ridley Cl Hexham NE46 160 F3
Morpeth NE61 119 E8
Ridley Mill Cotts NE43 171 B6
Ridley Mill Rd NE43 171 B5
Ridley St Blyth NE24 128 F8
Cramlington NE23 133 C5
Ridley Terr
Cambois NE24 123 D4
Hexham NE46 161 A6
Leadgate DH8 177 D3
Ridsdale NE42 166 B1
Ridsdale Ave NE5 149 E1
Ridsdale Cl NE25 134 C3
Ridsdale Sq NE63 117 C3
Riggs The NE45 162 F7
Rimside Gdns NE65 51 E4
Rimside View NE65 51 E4
Ringway NE62 117 A1
Ringwood Dr NE23 133 B7
Rink St NE24 128 F8
Ripley Cl NE22 121 D2
Ripley Dr NE23 133 A3
Ripon Cl NE23 132 F3
Rise The Ponteland NE20 138 B2
Ryton NE21 169 A4
Seaton Sluice NE26 135 E4
Ritson St DH8 176 D4
Ritson's Rd DH8 176 D4
Ritton Bank NE61 63 A4
River Bank NE62 122 C8
River Bank E NE62 122 C8
River Bank Rd 9 NE66 42 B5
River Dene TD15 178 A4
River La NE40 168 C6
River Terr NE49 153 C4
River View Bebside NE22 122 D1
Blackhall Mill NE17 175 B6
Blaydon NE21 169 B2
Lynemouth NE61 113 A3
Ovingham NE42 166 A4
Prudhoe NE42 166 C2
Ryton NE40 168 E5
River View Cl NE22 122 D1
Riverbank NE65 53 E8
Riverdale Cl NE48 184 A4
Rivermead NE48 55 D4
Rivermede NE20 138 F7
Riversdale
Blackhall Mill NE17 175 B6
Gilsland CA8 86 D1
Riversdale Ave NE62 122 A8

Riversdale Ct
Newcastle u T NE15 ....169 C6
Stakeford NE62 ....122 A7
Riversdale Ho NE62 .....122 A7
Riversdale Way NE15 ...169 C6
Riversway Consett DH8 ...176 C6
  Felton NE65 ....52 E3
  Lesbury NE66 ....42 A6
  Morpeth NE61 ....119 F8
  Ponteland NE20 ....138 E6
  Rothbury NE65 ....182 C5
Riverside Ave NE62 .....121 D7
Riverside Lodge NE15 ...168 E7
Riverside Pk NE65 ....183 C5
Riverside Rd
  Alnmouth NE66 ....42 B5
  Tweedmouth TD15 ......178 A4
Riverview Pk TD15 ......178 C2
RNLI Grace Darling Mus
  The* NE69 ....17 A5
Roachburn Cotts CA8 ...94 B6
Roachburn Rd NE5 ......149 E2
Roadside Cotts TD15 ......9 A6
Robert Allan Ct NE13 ...141 A6
Robert St NE24 ....128 E7
Robert Terr NE39 ....173 F4
Robert Terr Cotts NE39 ...173 F4
Roberts Lodge TD15 ......3 F5
Robertson St NE48 ....72 D3
Robinson Sq NE64 ....118 E5
Robinson St DH8 ....176 E4
Robson Ave NE65 ....160 F3
Robson St DH8 ....177 A3
Robson's Way NE65 .....183 B4
Rochester Cl NE63 ....118 A2
Rochford Gr NE23 ....133 A3
Rock NE66 ....31 D7
Rock Hall Sch NE66 ....31 D7
Rock Moor New Cotts
  NE66 ....31 B7
Rock South Farm NE66 ...31 C5
Rockcliffe NE26 ....145 C5
Rockcliffe Ave NE26 .....145 C4
Rockcliffe Fst Sch NE26 .145 C4
Rockcliffe Gdns
  Newcastle u T NE15 ....169 F7
  Whitley Bay NE26 ......145 C4
Rockcliffe St NE26 ....145 C4
Rockmore Rd NE21 ......169 C1
Rocksprings Cres NE47 ...158 A5
Rockwood Gdns NE40 ...167 E1
Rockwood Hill Est NE40 ...173 E8
Rockwood Hill Rd NE40 ...167 F1
Rockwood Terr NE40 .....167 F1
Roddam Ct 23 TD15 ....3 E6
Rodney Ct NE26 ....144 D7
Rodney Way NE26 ....144 D7
Rodsley Ct NE65 ....182 B5
Roger St DH8 ....176 E3
Rogerson Rd 12 NE70 ...15 F4
Rogerson Terr NE5 ....149 E3
Rokeby Ave NE15 ....169 D6
Rokeby St NE15 ....169 D6
Roker Ave NE25 ....144 F3
Rolley Way NE42 ....166 E3
Romaldkirk Cl 1 DH8 ...176 C1
Roman Way NE45 ....162 F6
Roman Way The NE5 ....169 B8
Romford Dr NE23 ....176 E2
Romford Ct NE23 ....133 A3
Romney Cl NE26 ....145 C4
Romney Cl NE23 ....133 B7
Romsey Gr NE15 ....169 C8
Rookery Cl NE24 ....128 B7
Rooksleigh 6 NE21 .....169 B1
Rookswood NE61 ....120 A6
Rookwood Dr NE13 ......141 C8
Ropehaugh Cotts NE47 ...106 B1
Rosalind Ave NE22 ......122 B1
Rosalind St
  Ashington NE63 ....117 E4
  Ashington,Hirst NE63 ...117 E3
Rosamond Pl NE24 ....128 F7
Rose Ave NE23 ....132 F8
Rose Cotts NE41 ....167 A6
Rose Hill CA8 ....86 D1
Rose Terr NE40 ....168 C2
Roseberry Grange NE12 ...143 A1
Roseberry Ave NE24 ....128 D7
Roseberry Terr 1 DH8 ...176 F2
Rosedale NE22 ....121 E1
Rosedale Ave DH8 ....176 D5
Rosedale Ct NE5 ....149 D2
Rosedale Rd NE40 ....167 F3
Roseden Farm Cotts
  NE66 ....28 D8
Rosedene Villas NE23 ...133 D6
Rosehill CA8 ....86 D1
Rosemary Terr NE24 ....128 F6
Rosemount
  Morpeth NE61 ....120 A7
  Newcastle u T NE5 .....149 C4
Rosemount Way NE25 ...144 C5
Roseneath Ct NE63 ......117 F3
Rosewood NE12 ....142 F3
Rosewood Cres NE26 ...135 D4
Roslin Pk NE22 ....122 C1
Roslin Way NE23 ....133 A3
Ross Gr NE23 ....132 F7
Ross Way NE26 ....144 E7
Rossdale 1 NE40 ....167 E1
Rotary Parkway NE63 ...117 B4
Rotary Way Blyth NE24 ...128 F5
  East Ord TD15 ....3 D6
  Hexham NE46 ....161 C6

Rotary Way continued
  Ponteland NE20 ....139 A4
Rothbury Ave NE24 ......128 B6
Rothbury Cl NE12 ....142 C4
Rothbury Fst Sch NE65 ...182 B6
Rothbury Gdns NE13 ....141 C6
Rothbury Rd NE65 ....51 E3
Rotherfield Cl NE23 ......133 B7
Rothley Cl NE26 ....176 C2
Rothill Farm Cotts NE66 ...39 C7
Rothlea Gdns NE63 ......122 A8
Rothley Ave NE63 ....117 D2
Rothley Cl NE20 ....138 D7
Rothley Cross Rds NE61 ...74 F8
Rothley Ct NE12 ....142 D3
Rothley Gdns NE30 ......145 B1
Rothley Gr NE25 ....134 C3
Rothley Hall NE61 ....75 A8
Rothley Terr NE18 ....175 B1
Rothley Way NE14 ....147 E4
Rothsay Terr NE64 ....118 D3
Row The CA9 ....110 A6
Rowan Cl NE22 ....121 F2
Rowan Ct NE24 ....128 D6
Rowan Dr NE20 ....138 E7
Rowan Gr
  Cramlington NE23 ....133 D5
  Prudhoe NE42 ....166 A1
Rowley Bank DH8 ....109 F3
Rowley St NE24 ....128 E7
Rowlington Terr NE63 ...117 D2
Rowntree Ave TD15 .....178 B2
Roxbro Ho 1 NE66 ......181 C5
Roxburgh Ho NE26 ......145 A5
Roxburgh Terr NE26 ....145 A5
Royal Oak Gdns NE66 ...181 E4
Ruabon Cl NE23 ....133 A3
Ruffside DH8 ....108 D6
Ruislip Pl NE23 ....132 F3
Runciman Way NE65 ....183 D6
Runhead Est NE40 ....168 B4
Runhead Gdns NE40 ....168 D5
Runhead Terr NE40 .....168 E5
Runnymede Gdns NE17 ...175 B7
Runnymede Rd NE20 ...138 C5
Rupert Terr NE15 ....168 F8
Rushbury Ct NE27 ....143 C5
Rushley Cres NE21 ......169 C3
Ruskin Ave
  Ashington NE63 ....117 F2
  Longbenton NE12 ......142 D1
Ruskin Ct NE42 ....166 B1
Russell Cl DH8 ....177 A3
Russell Sq NE13 ....141 B8
Russell Terr NE22 ....126 F8
Rustic Terr NE64 ....118 D3
Ruth Ave NE21 ....169 C2
Ruth Lancaster James
  Cottage Hospl CA9 .....185 D3
Rutherford Cl NE62 ......121 E7
Rutherford Pl NE61 ......119 F7
Rutherford St NE24 .....128 D7
Rutland St NE63 ....117 C3
Ryal Cl Blyth NE24 ....128 F7
  Seaton Delaval NE25 ...134 E3
Rydal Ave NE30 ....143 A4
Rydal Cl NE12 ....142 F3
Rydal Mews DH8 ....177 D4
Rydal Mount NE64 ......118 C4
Rydal Rd NE15 ....169 D8
Rydal Terr NE13 ....141 B4
Ryde Pl NE23 ....133 B7
Rye Cl NE15 ....148 E1
Rye Terr NE46 ....160 F5
Ryecroft Cres NE71 .....180 B6
Ryecroft Pk NE71 ....180 C7
Ryecroft View NE71 .....180 C6
Ryecroft Way NE71 .....180 C6
Ryedale Cl NE63 ....117 B2
Ryedale Ho NE24 ....127 F8
Ryehaugh NE20 ....138 F6
Ryelea NE21 ....169 C2
Ryton Com Inf Sch
  NE40 ....168 A5
Ryton Comp Sch NE40 ...168 B5
Ryton Hall Dr NE40 ......168 C6
Ryton Ind Est NE21 .....168 A5
Ryton Jun Sch NE40 .....168 A5
Ryton Terr NE27 ....143 D1

S

Sage Cl NE15 ....169 C8
St Acca's Ct NE46 ....160 F5
St Agnes RC Prim Sch
  NE40 ....167 E4
St Agnes' Gdns NE40 ...167 E4
St Agnes' Gdns N NE40 ...167 E4
St Agnes' Gdns W NE40 ...167 E4
St Agnes' Terr NE40 ....167 E4
St Aidan's
  Fourstones NE47 ....90 E2
  Seahouses NE68 ....17 E3
St Aidan's Ave NE12 ....143 C1
St Aidan's Cres NE61 ...120 A6
St Aidan's Pl DH8 ....176 D1
St Aidan's RC Fst Sch
  NE40 ....167 D1
St Aidan's Rd TD15 .....178 A8
St Aidan's Sq NE12 .....143 C1
St Aidan's St DH8 ....176 E4
St Aidans Pk NE47 ....90 E2
St Alban's Cl NE25 ......144 A5
St Albans Cl NE23 ....118 A2
St Albans View NE27 ....143 F2
St Andrew's CE Fst Sch
  NE15 ....147 E2
St Andrew's Cl DH8 .....176 D4
St Andrew's Cres DH8 ...176 D4
St Andrew's Gdns DH8 ...176 D4
St Andrew's La NE42 ...165 D4
St Andrew's RC Fst Sch
  NE24 ....128 C7
St Andrew's Rd
  Berwick-u-T TD15 ......178 A7
  Consett DH8 ....176 D4
  Hexham NE46 ....161 A4
St Andrew's Terr NE63 ...117 E3
St Andrews Cl NE25 ....144 D5
St Anne's Ct NE25 ....144 E3
St Bartholomew's Cres
  TD15 ....178 C2
St Bartholomews Cl
  NE61 ....113 A7
St Bede's RC Fst Sch
  NE22 ....126 E8
St Bedes Pl NE24 ....128 B4
St Bedes Rd NE24 ....128 B4
St Bedes Wlk NE27 .....143 C1
St Benedict's RC Mid Sch
  NE63 ....117 F3
St Benet Biscop RC High Sch
  NE22 ....126 E8
St Christopher's Ho
  NE61 ....119 E8
St Christophers Cl NE63 ...117 F5
St Clements Ct NE63 ....118 A2
St Cuthbert Ave NE65 ...183 D5
St Cuthbert's Ave DH8 ...176 D5
St Cuthbert's La NE46 ...161 A4
St Cuthbert's RC Fst Sch
  Amble NE65 ....183 E5
  Tweedmouth TD15 ......178 A4
St Cuthbert's RC Prim Sch
  NE15 ....148 F2
St Cuthbert's Rd
  Berwick-u-T TD15 ......178 A7
  Longbenton NE27 ......143 C1
St Cuthbert's Sq TD15 ...2 B2
St Cuthbert's Terr
  NE22 ....122 B1
St Cuthbert's Terr NE16 ...161 A4
St Cuthberts Way
  Blaydon NE21 ....169 D3
  Longbenton NE27 ......143 C1
St David's Cl NE26 ......144 F8
St David's Way NE26 ...144 F8
St Ebba's Way DH8 .....174 E3
St George's Hospl NE61 ...115 A2
St George's Pl
  Consett DH8 ....176 E3
  Newcastle u T NE15 ...169 E5
St George's RC Prim Sch
  NE15 ....169 D5
St George's Rd
  Berwick-u-T TD15 ......178 A7
  Hexham NE46 ....161 A4
  Newcastle u T NE15 ...169 E5
  Tynemouth NE30 ....145 C3
St George's Terr NE15 ...169 E5
St Georges Cres
  Alnwick NE66 ....181 D4
  Whitley Bay NE25 ......144 F4
St Helen's Gate NE47 ....99 C4
St Helen's Gdns TD12 ...179 F5
St Helen's La NE45 .....163 A6
St Helen's St NE45 ......162 F6
St Helen's Terr TD15 ...178 D2
St Helens CE Fst Sch
  NE65 ....64 A5
St Hilda's Rd NE46 ......161 A4
St Ives' Rd DH8 ....177 D4
St James Cl NE44 ....100 F8
St James Est NE66 ......181 D3
St James Rd NE46 ....161 A4
St James Terr
  7 Morpeth NE61 ....114 F1
  Riding Mill NE44 ....170 A7
St James' La NE49 ......153 D5
St John Vianney RC Prim Sch
  NE5 ....149 D1
St John Chapel Prim Sch
  DL13 ....111 A1
St John's Cl NE26 ....144 F8
St John's Cres NE22 ....122 D3
St John's Ct NE27 ....143 C5
St John's Pl
  Bedlington NE22 ....122 D3
  Whitley Bay NE26 ......144 F8
St John's RC Fst Sch
  NE66 ....181 B4
St John's Rd NE22 ......122 D2
St John W NE22 ....122 D3
St Johns Ct NE12 ....142 D1
St Johns Est NE65 ....53 F3
St Johns Rd NE46 ....161 A4
St Joseph's RC Mid Sch
  NE46 ....160 F4
St Joseph's RC Prim Sch
  NE21 ....169 B3
St Katherine's Pl TD15 ....3 D6
St Kitt's Cl NE26 ....144 F8
St Lawrence Ave NE65 ...183 D5
St Lawrence Terr 1
  NE65 ....42 B1
St Leonard's La NE61 ...114 B2

St Leonard's Wlk NE61 ...114 C2
St Lucia Cl NE26 ....144 E8
St Lukes Rd NE46 ....161 A4
St Margarets Ct NE26 ...145 C4
St Mark's RC Prim Sch
  NE5 ....149 F4
St Mark's St NE61 ....114 E1
St Marks Ct
  Backworth NE27 ....143 E3
  Newcastle u T NE5 .....149 F4
St Marks Rd NE61 ....161 A3
St Martin's Cl NE26 .....144 E7
St Martin's Ct NE26 .....144 E8
St Martin's Way NE26 ...144 E7
St Mary's 8 TD15 ....178 B5
St Mary's & St Thomas
  Aquinas RC Prim Sch
  NE21 ....169 A4
St Mary's Ave NE26 ....144 F7
St Mary's Chare 9
  NE46 ....161 B5
St Mary's Church (Mus)*
  NE63 ....118 C6
St Mary's Cl DH8 ....176 D4
St Mary's Cres DH8 .....176 D4
St Mary's Dr NE24 ......128 B6
St Mary's Field NE61 ...119 F7
St Mary's Lodge NE26 ...144 F5
St Mary's Pl NE15 ....148 E2
St Mary's RC Fst Sch
  NE46 ....161 A4
St Mary's RC Prim Sch
  Consett DH8 ....176 C3
  Longbenton NE12 ......143 A2
  Tynemouth NE30 ....145 A2
St Mary's St DH8 ....176 D4
St Mary's Terr NE40 ....168 B5
St Mary's Wynd
  8 Hexham NE46 ....161 B5
  Seaton Sluice NE26 ....135 E4
St Mathews La NE42 ....166 D2
St Matthew's RC Fst Sch
  NE42 ....166 C2
St Matthews Rd NE46 ...160 F3
St Michael's Ave NE25 ...134 D6
St Michael's CE Fst Sch
  NE66 ....181 B5
St Michael's La 14 NE66 ...181 C5
St Michael's Mount NE48 ...80 F4
St Michael's Sq 15
  NE66 ....181 C5
St Nicholas Cl NE63 .....117 F5
St Nicholas Rd NE46 ....161 A4
St Omer Rd NE65 ....53 D4
St Oswald's Ct 2 NE65 ...183 D5
St Oswald's Rd 10 NE26 ...161 A4
St Oswald's Sch NE66 ...181 D4
St Oswalds Ct NE42 .....166 E3
St Oswin's Ave NE30 ...145 C3
St Oswin's Pl 8 DH8 ...176 D4
St Patrick's RC Prim Sch
  DH8 ....176 F3
St Paul's Ct NE66 ....181 C4
St Paul's Garth 22
  NE66 ....181 C5
St Paul's Gdns NE24 ....145 A4
St Paul's RC Prim Sch
  NE23 ....133 B5
St Pauls Cl NE63 ....117 F5
St Pauls Rd NE46 ....160 F4
St Peter's RC Mid Sch
  NE26 ....133 B4
St Peters Terr TD15 ......3 A4
St Pius Xth RC Prim Sch
  NE46 ....176 C1
St Robert's RC Fst Sch
  NE61 ....119 F8
St Ronan's Dr NE26 .....135 B7
St Ronan's Rd NE25 ....144 F4
St Stephen's Cl NE25 ...134 B3
St Thomas Cl NE42 .....166 D3
St Thomas Close Workshops
  NE66 ....181 A5
St Thomas Mews NE42 ...166 D2
St Thomas More RC Sch
  NE21 ....169 B3
St Thomas' Cres NE66 ...181 B4
St Vincent's Pl NE26 ....144 F8
St Vincent's Way 1
  NE26 ....144 F8
St Vincents Cl NE15 .....169 E8
St Wilfred's RC Mid Sch
  NE24 ....128 C7
St Wilfred's Rd NE46 ...163 A6
St Wilfrid's Ct 9 NE46 ...161 A4
St Wilfrid's Rd NE46 ....161 A4
Salem Ave DH8 ....177 B1
Salisbury Cl
  1 Ashington NE63 ....117 F2
  Consett DH8 ....176 E7
  Cramlington NE23 ......132 E6
Salisbury St Blyth NE24 ...128 D8
  Consett DH8 ....177 A3
Sally Port TD15 ....178 B4
Salter's Rd NE66 ....37 D8
Salter's Rd NE66 ....37 F6
Salters Rd NE66 ....26 F2
Salters' La N,NE12 ......142 A1
Sam's Ct NE23 ....141 F8
Samuel King's Sch
  CA9 ....185 D3
Sanderling Cl NE40 .....168 D4
Sanderson Rd NE26 ....144 F5
Sanderson Terr NE61 ....65 C4
Sandfield Rd
  Cambois NE22 ....123 B4

Sandfield Rd continued
  Tynemouth NE30 145
Sandford Ave NE61 127
Sandford Mews NE13 ...141
Sandford Rd DH8 176
Sandgate 8 TD15 178
Sandham La TD15 10
Sandhurst Ave NE30 145
Sandison Ct NE13 140
Sandmartin Cl NE63 122
Sandon Cl NE27 143
Sandown NE25 144
Sandown Cl NE25 144
Sandpiper Cl Blyth NE24 ...128
  Ryton NE40 168
Sandpiper Way NE63 ...117
Sandridge NE64 118
Sandringham Cl NE25 ...144
Sandringham Dr
  Blyth NE24 128
  Whitley Bay NE25 144
Sandringham Rd NE5 ...169
Sandringham Way
  NE20 138
Sandstell Rd TD15 178
Sandwich Rd NE29 144
Sandy Bank NE44 100
Sandy Bay Cvn Pk NE63 ...123
Sandy Cl NE65 52
Sandy La Ashington NE63 ...118
  Brunswick Village NE13 ...140
  Riding Mill NE44 100
  Wideopen NE3,NE12 ...141
Sandy Lane Cl NE67 24
Sandy Lane Ind Area
  NE3 141
Sandy Way NE63 141
Sandyford Ave NE42 166
Sandysykes NE42 166
Sanson Cl 12 TD15 3
Sarabel Ave NE62 121
Sawmill Ind Est NE66 ...181
Saxon Dr NE30 145
Saxon Terr DH8 176
Scales Cres NE44 166
Scarborough Ct NE23 ...133
Schalksmuhle Rd NE22 ...121
School Ave NE62 123
School Cl DL13 111
School Hill DL13 111
School Rd NE22 122
School Row
  Hedley on t H NE43 ...171
  Prudhoe NE42 166
  Togston NE65 53
  Widdrington NE61 65
School Terr CA9 155
School Wynd TD12 5
Scot Terr NE17 173
Scotland Ct NE21 153
Scotsfield Terr NE49 153
Scott Ave NE23 133
Scott Cl NE46 160
Scott Ct Amble NE65 ...183
  East Hartford NE23 127
Scott's Ave 16 NE40 167
Scott's Pl TD15 118
Scoular Dr NE63 118
Scremerston Fst Sch
  TD15 4
Scremerston Hill Farm
  TD15 4
Scremerston Town Farm
  TD15 4
Scrogg Wood NE47 155
Sea Bank 15 NE66 42
Sea Crest Rd NE64 118
Sea La NE66 24
Sea Rd TD15 178
Sea View Amble NE65 ...183
  Ashington NE63 178
  Berwick-u-T TD15 178
  Longframlington NE65 ...51
  Longhoughton NE66 32
  Lynemouth NE61 113
Sea View La NE64 133
Sea View Pk NE23 133
Sea View Terr NE61 181
Sea View Villas NE23 ...133
Seaburn Ave NE25 135
Seaburn Gr NE26 135
Seaburn View NE25 134
Seacombe Ave NE30 ...145
Seacrest Apartments
  NE30 145
Seacrest Ave NE30 145
Seafield Rd Blyth NE24 ...128
  Seahouses NE68 17
Seaforth St NE24 128
Seahouses Fst Sch NE68 ...17
Seahouses Marine Life Ctr*
  NE68 17
Seahouses Mid Sch NE68 ...17
Seal Terr 13 NE64 161
Seaton Ave
  Annitsford NE23 133
  Bedlington NE22 122
  Blyth NE24 128
Seaton Burn Coll NE13 ...141
Seaton Cres
  Holywell NE25 145
  Whitley Bay NE25 144
Seaton Croft NE23 142
Seaton Delaval Fst Sch
  NE25 134

...ton Delaval Hall*
E26 ....135 A6
aton Hirst CE Mid Sch
E63 ....118 A2
aton Pl NE13 ....141 A6
aton Rd NE27 ....144 A4
aton Sluice Fst Sch
E26 ....135 D5
aton Sluice Mid Sch
E26 ....135 B7
atonville Cres NE25 ...144 E3
atonville Gr NE25 ...144 E3
atonville Rd NE25 ...144 E3
aview Cvn Pk TD15 ...178 C2
cond Ave
 Amble NE65 ....183 D5
llington NE63 ....117 D4
yth NE24 ....128 D6
orpeth NE61 ....120 B7
cond Row
llington NE61 ....112 E4
cond St Consett DH8 ...177 B2
adgate DH8 ....177 C5
adgate DH8 ....177 C6
dbergh Rd NE30 ....145 B2
dgefield Ct NE12 ....142 D3
dgemoor NE12 ....142 D4
eingsike Rd DL13 ....111 F3
fton Cl NE23 ....127 C1
...ghill Fst Sch NE23 ...133 F1
...ah Cl NE47 ....97 F2
...borne Gdns DH8 ....176 E6
...bourne Cl NE23 ....132 E6
...bourne Terr NE24 ....123 E5
...by Cl NE23 ....127 B1
...by Gdns DH8 ....176 C1
...by Rd NE66 ....41 C3
...le Ct [5] NE46 ....161 A4
...le Fst Sch The NE46 ...161 A5
...kirk Gr NE23 ....127 D3
...wyn Ave NE25 ....144 D3
...net Enterprise Workshops
E63 ....117 D2
...venth Ave
yth NE24 ....128 D6
orpeth NE61 ....120 B7
...venth Row NE63 ....117 B4
...vers St NE17 ....173 C1
...vers Terr NE15 ....149 B6
...xtant Ho [6] NE24 ....128 F8
...ymour Ct NE63 ....118 B3
...ymour St DH8 ....177 A2
...ymour Terr NE40 ....168 A5
...ze Bldg [5] NE46 ....161 B4
...adfen Cres NE61 ....115 E3
...adfen Park Rd NE30 ...145 A3
...aftesbury Ave NE26 ...144 F6
...aftesbury Cres NE30 ...145 A3
...aftoe Cl NE40 ....167 F3
...aftoe Cres NE46 ....161 A4
...aftoe Ct NE12 ....142 D3
...aftoe Leazes NE46 ....160 F4
...aftoe St NE15 ....158 A5
...aftoe Terr NE47 ....158 A5
...aftoe Trust Fst Sch
E47 ....158 A5
...aftoe Way NE13 ....140 B7
...alloin Cl NE63 ....117 C2
...amrock Cl NE15 ....169 C8
...anklin Pl NE23 ....132 E6
...ap Rd NE30 ....145 A2
...arnford Cl NE47 ....143 D5
...aron Cl NE12 ....142 B2
...arperton Dr NE3 ....141 A1
...aw La DH8,NE17 ....174 F4
...aws La Hexham NE46 ...160 D4
...exham NE46 ....160 D5
...aws Pk NE46 ....160 E6
...earwater Way NE24 ...128 F4
...eepwash Ave NE62 ...121 E7
...eepwash Bank NE62 ...121 E7
...eepwash Rd NE61,
E62 ....116 E3
...eila's Cl NE65 ....183 B4
...eldon Cl NE12 ....142 C1
...eldon Gr NE23 ....127 B1
...elford Gdns NE15 ...169 E7
...ellacres TD12 ....6 E6
...elley Cres NE24 ...128 C5
...elley Rd NE15 ...169 A7
...epheards Hill [1] NE46 ...42 B5
...epherd Terr NE49 ...153 E5
...erburn Terr
onsett DH8 ....177 A2
...amsterley NE17 ....174 F5
...erburn Villas [15] DH8 ...176 F3
...eringham Dr NE3 ....132 E6
...eringham Gdns NE15 ...148 B2
...erwood NE27 ....144 B2
...erwood Cl
onsett DH8 ....176 E7
...emmouth NE62 ....144 B2
...erwood Pl NE3 ....141 C2
...ibdon Bank NE21 ....169 D2
...ibdon Bsns Pk NE21 ...169 E3
...ibdon Cres NE21 ....169 D2
...ibdon Ct NE21 ....169 D3
...ibdon Park View
E21 ....169 D2
...ibdon Pond Nature
eserve* NE21 ....169 E2
...ibdon Rd
laydon NE21 ....169 D3
...ibdon Way NE21 ....169 E2
...idlaw TD12 ....5 B1

Shidlaw La Birgham TD12 ...5 B1
Coldstream TD12 ....11 A8
Shiel Gdns NE23 ....132 E6
Shield Ct NE46 ....161 B3
Shield Hill NE49 ....153 E7
Shield St NE47 ....97 F2
Shields Rd Morpeth NE61 ...120 B7
Nedderton NE22 ....126 C5
Whitley Bay NE25 ....144 F3
Shielfield Pk (Berwick
 Rangers FC) TD15 ....178 A2
Shielfield Terr TD15 ....178 A2
Shilbottle Fst Sch NE66 ...41 D3
Shilburn Rd NE47 ....98 A2
Shillaw Pl NE23 ....142 B5
Shilling Pot NE48 ....69 C6
Shiney Row NE26 ....93 A6
Shiningpool Bank NE20 ...85 A5
Shipley St NE15 ....169 C6
Shipleyburn Dr NE66 ....30 E3
Shire Farm Gr NE63 ....117 A2
Shiremoor Prim Sch
NE27 ....143 E3
Shiremoor Sta NE27 ...143 F4
Shirlaw Cl NE15 ....149 F4
Shop Spouts NE21 ....169 C3
Shopping Ctr The NE5 ...149 C2
Shoresdean TD15 ....3 B1
Shorestone Ave NE30 ...145 B3
Shoreswood Loan TD15 ...3 A2
Short Row NE15 ....149 B6
Shotley Bridge General Hospl
DH8 ....176 E6
Shotley Bridge Inf Sch
DH8 ....176 D6
Shotley Bridge Jun Sch
DH8 ....176 C7
Shotley Ct NE63 ....117 B2
Shotley Grove Rd DH8 ...176 B5
Shotley Lodge DH8 ....176 D6
Shotton Ave NE24 ....128 E6
Shotton Farm TD12 ....11 D1
Shotton La
 Cramlington NE23 ....126 C2
Shotton NE61,NE13 ....131 F8
Shotton St NE23 ....127 B3
Showfield The NE47 ....158 A4
Shrewsbury Dr NE27 ...143 C5
Sidgate NE47 ....90 D2
Sidgate La NE47 ....90 D2
Sidings The
 Cornhill on T TD12 ....6 B2
Embleton NE66 ....24 B1
Sidlaw Ave NE29 ....144 F1
Sidlaw Ct NE63 ....117 C2
Sidney St NE24 ....128 D7
Silkwood Cl NE23 ....127 B1
Silloth Pl NE30 ....145 B2
Silvas Ct NE61 ....115 A1
Silver Fox Way NE27 ...144 A1
Silver Hill NE19 ....83 E8
Silver St
 Berwick-u-T TD15 ....178 B4
Consett DH8 ....176 D4
NE12 ....142 B4
Silverbirch Ind Est
NE12 ....142 B4
Silverdale Dr NE21 ...169 A1
Silverdale Rd NE23 ...127 B1
Silverlink N The NE27 ...143 E1
Silvermere Dr NE40 ...168 D4
Silverstone NE12 ....142 E3
Silverton La NE65 ....182 C3
Silverton Terr NE65 ...182 B4
Silvertop Gdns NE40 ...168 A1
Simon Pl NE13 ....141 A5
Simonburn La [2] NE63 ...117 F2
Simonside Prudhoe NE42 ...166 B1
Seaton Sluice NE26 ....135 D4
Simonside Ave NE62 ...122 B8
Simonside Cl
 Morpeth NE61 ....119 D7
Seaton Sluice NE26 ...135 D4
Simonside Cres NE15 ...53 F3
Simonside Forest Wlk*
NE65 ....50 B2
Simonside Prim Sch
NE5 ....149 F5
Simonside Terr NE21 ...169 C1
Simonside Terr NE64 ...118 E4
Simonside View
 Ponteland NE20 ....138 D7
Rothbury NE65 ....182 A5
Simonside Way NE12 ...142 F4
Simprim Mains TD12 ....6 A8
Simpson Cl NE63 ....133 B1
Simpson St NE40 ....128 E8
Ryton NE40 ....168 A4
Tynemouth NE30 ....145 C4
Simpson Terr NE15 ...169 C1
Simpsons Meml Homes
NE40 ....168 A4
Sinclair Gdns NE23 ...134 D3
Sipton Terr NE47 ....106 A4
Sixth Ave Ashington NE63 ...117 E2
Blyth NE24 ....128 C6
Morpeth NE61 ....120 B7
Sixth St DH8 ....177 B2
Skelgillside Workshops
CA9 ....185 F3
Skerne Gr DH8 ....177 D5
Skipton Cl
 Bedlington NE22 ....121 D2
Cramlington NE23 ....127 C1
Slaley Ct NE22 ....122 A1
Slaley Fst Sch NE47 ...100 B4
Slaley Pk NE47 ....100 D2
Sled La NE40,NE41 ...167 D3

Sleekburn Ave NE22 ....122 E3
Sleekburn Bsns Ctr
NE22,NE24 ....123 A6
Sleekburn Ho NE22 ...122 D2
Smallburn NE22 ....85 E1
Smallburn Rd NE65 ....64 A5
Smallholdings NE64 ....118 C6
Smiley La NE66 ....31 B2
Smith St [3] NE65 ....183 D6
Smiths Terr NE47 ....158 B5
Smithy Ct NE66 ....32 C6
Smithy Sq NE63 ....133 B6
Snow's Green Rd DH8 ...176 C7
Snowdon Terr NE39 ....173 F5
Snowdrop Cl NE21 ...169 A2
Softley Pl NE15 ....169 F7
Solingen Est NE24 ....128 E6
Solway Ave NE30 ....145 B2
Somerset Cl NE23 ....117 A4
Sorrel Cl NE63 ....117 C2
South Acres NE66 ....32 C6
South Ave Amble NE65 ...183 C5
Ryton NE40 ....168 C5
South Beach Fst Sch
NE24 ....128 E4
South Bend NE3 ....141 B1
South Charlton NE66 ....30 F7
South Cl NE40 ....168 C4
South Cross St DH8 ...177 A4
South Doddington NE71 ...14 A3
South Dr Washington NE13 ...131 E6
Woolsington NE13 ....149 F8
South East Farm NE15 ...166 D8
South End Kielder NE48 ....55 D4
Longhoughton NE66 ....32 B1
South Farm Esholt NE65 ...65 B8
[9] Glanton NE66 ....29 C1
Nedderton NE22 ....126 B8
South Gr NE40 ....168 D4
South Greens NE19 ....45 E5
South Greenwich Rd
NE23 ....178 D1
South Hazelrigg Farm Cotts
NE66 ....15 A3
South La Felton NE65 ....52 E3
Norham TD15 ....2 C1
Seahouses NE68 ....17 E2
Horsley NE15 ....169 C1
South Lea Blaydon NE21 ...169 C1
South Lodge Wood
NE61 ....120 E4
South Magdalene DH8 ...175 B1
South Nelson Ind Est
NE23 ....132 E8
South Nelson Rd NE23 ...132 E8
South Newsham Rd
NE24 ....128 D3
South Par
 Choppington NE62 ....121 E6
Stocksfield NE43 ....171 A7
Whitley Bay NE26 ....145 B5
South Pk Hexham NE46 ...161 C4
Slaley NE47 ....100 B4
South Rd Alnwick NE66 ...181 E4
Belford NE70 ....16 A4
Chopwell NE17 ....173 C1
Longhorsley NE65 ....64 A5
Lowick TD15 ....8 E2
Prudhoe NE42 ....166 F2
Wooler NE71 ....180 C6
South Ridge NE63 ....118 B2
South Riggs NE22 ....126 F8
South Road Ind Est
NE66 ....181 D4
South Side
 Cresswell NE61 ....113 B7
Stamfordham NE18 ....93 F7
Ashington NE63 ....118 B2
South St Alnwick NE66 ...181 C4
Consett DH8 ....177 B2
High Spen NE39 ....173 F4
Seahouses NE68 ....17 F3
Shiremoor NE27 ....143 F4
South Terr
 Chopwell NE17 ....175 B8
Morpeth NE61 ....114 F1
Rothbury NE65 ....182 B4
South Tynedale Mid Sch
NE46 ....153 C5
South Tynedale Rly*
CA9 ....185 C6
South Victoria Terr ...17 A5
South View
 Annitsford NE23 ....133 B1
Ashington NE63 ....117 C4
Blyth NE24 ....128 C6
Cambois NE24 ....123 C6
Chopwell NE17 ....175 A8
Consett,Bridgehill DH8 ...176 C4
Crawcrook NE40 ....167 F4
Crawcrook,Clara Vale
NE40 ....167 F7
East Sleekburn NE22 ...122 F3
Felton NE65 ....52 E3
[7] Glanton NE66 ....29 C1
Guide Post NE62 ....121 E7
Hazlerigg NE13 ....141 A4
High Spen NE39 ....173 F3
Hipsburn NE66 ....42 A6
Mickley Square NE43 ...169 E8
Newcastle u T NE5 ....169 E8
Pegswood NE61 ....115 F3
Prudhoe NE42 ....166 B2
Wearhead DL13 ....111 B2
South View Gdns NE46 ...161 A4
South View Pl NE23 ....133 B6
South Waterside NE18 ...55 D4

South Wellfield Fst Sch
NE25 ....144 B4
Southcliff NE26 ....145 C4
Southend Ave NE24 ...128 C6
Southern Cl NE63 ....118 B3
Southern Way NE40 ...168 C4
Southernwood DH8 ...177 A2
Southfield Ave NE68 ....17 E2
Southfield La NE39 ....175 F3
Southfields NE23 ....142 A8
Southfork NE15 ....169 C6
Southgate NE12 ....142 D3
Southgate Wood NE61 ...120 A5
Southlands
 Hexham NE46 ....160 D4
Tynemouth NE30 ....145 B1
Southlands Mid Sch
NE23 ....133 B3
Southlands NE30 ....145 A1
Southleigh NE26 ....145 B5
Southmead NE65 ....183 D4
Southridge Fst Sch
NE25 ....144 D6
Southside Matfen NE20 ...93 B6
Widdrington Sta NE61 ...65 E4
Southward NE26 ....135 D5
Southward Cl NE26 ...135 D5
Southward Way NE25 ...134 E1
Southway NE15 ....169 E7
Southwell Pl NE23 ....132 E6
Spa Dr DH8 ....176 C7
Spawell Dr TD12 ....179 B7
Speedwell Ct NE63 ...117 B1
Spelvit La NE61 ....119 F7
Spen La NE39,NE40 ...173 F7
Spen Rd NE39 ....173 F7
Spencer Ct NE24 ....123 B1
Spencer Dr NE61 ....115 E3
Spencer Rd DH8 ....123 B1
Spencer Terr NE15 ...149 B1
Spetchells NE42 ....166 D3
Spinney The
 Annitsford NE23 ....133 C1
Killingworth NE12 ....142 E2
Morpeth NE61 ....120 A6
Spital Cres NE64 ....118 D3
Spital La NE46 ....160 F7
Spital Rd NE64 ....118 D3
Spital Villas NE15 ....146 A3
Spittal Fst Sch TD15 ...178 D2
Spittal Hall Pl TD15 ...178 C2
Spittal Hall Rd TD15 ...178 C2
Spittal Terr NE46 ....161 A5
Splitty La NE47 ....97 F5
Splitty La End NE47 ....97 F5
Spoutwell La NE65 ....163 A5
Spring Cl DH8 ....174 E2
Spring Ville NE22 ....122 F4
Springdale TD15 ....178 A1
Springfield
 Longhoughton NE66 ....32 B1
Ovington NE42 ....165 D4
Springfield Cl NE42 ...165 D4
Springfield Gr NE25 ...144 E3
Springfield Mdws NE66 ...181 E5
Springfield Pk
 Alnwick NE66 ....181 D5
NE66 ....3 E6
Springfield Rd NE66 ...169 C1
Springfield Terr NE47 ...155 E6
Springhill La TD15 ....3 F5
Springhill Wlk NE61 ...119 E7
Springhouse La DH8 ...175 C8
Springwell Cl NE21 ...169 D1
Springwell Dr NE61 ...112 E4
Springwood NE65 ....52 C6
Square The
 Chillingham NE66 ....21 D5
Guide Post NE62 ....121 F7
Horncliffe TD15 ....4 E4
Lesbury NE66 ....42 A6
Ponteland NE20 ....139 C5
Powburn NE66 ....29 B3
Riding Mill NE44 ....170 A8
Swarland NE65 ....52 C6
Stable Block NE45 ...163 F5
Stable Cl NE61 ....115 E7
Stable Cott NE61 ....65 C1
Stable Dr NE65 ....65 A8
Stable Yard Cotts NE48 ...81 B2
Stables The NE70 ....10 A2
Stagshaw NE12 ....142 C5
Stagshaw Rd NE45 ...162 F6
Stamfordham CE Fst Sch NE18 ...91 A1
Staith La NE21 ....169 A4
Staithes La NE15 ....115 A1
Stakeford Cres NE62 ...122 B8
Stakeford Fst Sch NE62 ...122 C8
Stakeford La NE62 ....122 A7
Stakeford Rd NE62 ....122 C3
Stakes Rd NE13 ....141 B6
Stamford NE12 ....142 D4
Stamfordham Rd
 Newcastle u T NE5 ...149 C4
Newcastle u T NE15,NE5 ...148 D7
Stancley Rd NE42 ....166 E2
Stanegate
 Haydon Bridge NE47 ...89 D2
Newbrough NE47 ....90 D2
Stanegate Cotts NE47 ...90 E2
Stanhope St NE4 ....167 F1
Stanley Cl [7] TD15 ....3 E6
Stanley Cres Gilsland CA8 ...86 D1

Stanley Cres continued
Prudhoe NE42 ....166 E3
[5] Whitley Bay NE26 ...145 B4
Stanley Gdns
 Consett DH8 ....177 A3
Seghill NE23 ....133 F1
Stanley Gr NE22 ....122 B1
Stanley St Blyth NE24 ...128 F7
[16] Consett DH8 ....177 A3
Stannerford Rd NE40 ...167 F6
Stanners The [6] NE65 ...42 B1
Stannington Fst Sch
NE61 ....125 B4
Stannington Pl NE20 ...138 E8
Stannington St NE24 ...128 F7
Stannington Station Rd
NE61 ....125 B1
Stannington Vale NE61 ...125 D1
Stanton Ave NE24 ...128 B5
Stanton Cl NE61 ....115 E3
Stanton Gr NE30 ....145 A1
Stanton Rd
 Shiremoor NE27 ....143 E3
Tynemouth NE30 ....145 A1
Staple Ct NE68 ....17 E2
Star of the Sea RC Prim Sch
NE25 ....144 E2
Stardale Ave NE24 ...128 B5
Stargate Ind Est NE40 ...168 E3
Stargate La NE40 ...168 E4
Starlight Cres NE25 ...134 C3
Station Bank
 Mickley Square NE43 ...165 E2
Ryton NE40 ....168 C6
Station Cl NE44 ....100 F8
Station Cotts Belford NE70 ...16 B4
Bolton NE66 ....39 D7
Cornhill on T TD12 ....6 B2
Greenhead CA8 ....151 F7
Haydon Bridge NE47 ...158 A5
Hipsburn NE66 ....42 A5
Longhirst NE61 ....116 B7
Morpeth NE61 ....120 A7
Ponteland NE20 ....138 E6
Seghill NE23 ....134 A1
Warkworth NE65 ....42 A1
Station Cn NE49 ....153 C4
Station First Sch The
NE22 ....122 D3
Station Gdns TD12 ....6 B2
Station Ind Est NE42 ...166 B3
Station Rd Alston CA9 ...185 D4
Ashington NE63 ....117 B4
Backworth NE27 ....143 D3
Bardon Mill NE47 ....155 F6
Bedlington NE22 ....122 C2
Belford NE70 ....16 B4
Broomhill NE65 ....53 E4
Consett DH8 ....177 A2
Corbridge NE45 ....163 A7
Cramlington NE23 ....133 A7
Crawcrook NE41 ....167 C5
Dudley NE23 ....141 E8
Embleton NE66 ....24 C1
Haltwhistle NE49 ....153 C4
Haydon Bridge NE47 ...158 B6
Heddon-on-t-W NE15 ...148 A1
Hexham NE46 ....161 C5
Killingworth NE12 ....142 B3
Longhoughton NE66 ....32 B1
Newburn NE15 ....168 F7
Prudhoe NE42 ....166 C3
Rothbury NE65 ....182 B3
Stannington NE61 ....134 A1
Warkworth NE65 ....42 B1
Whitley Bay NE26 ....145 B4
Wooler NE71 ....180 C6
Wylam NE41 ....167 B5
Station Sr [1] NE26 ...145 B4
Station St
 [4] Bedlington NE22 ...122 D3
Blyth NE24 ....128 E8
Station Terr
 Choppington NE62 ....121 F3
Consett DH8 ....177 A2
Staward Ave NE25 ...134 D2
Stead La NE22 ....122 C1
Stead Lane Fst Sch
NE22 ....122 C1
Steadings The
 Ashington NE63 ....117 A2
Embleton NE66 ....24 B1
Steadlands Sq NE22 ...122 C1
Steads The NE46 ....120 A6
Steel St DH8 ....176 F3
Steelhaven [12] DH8 ...176 F3
Stella Bank NE21 ....168 F5
Stella Hall Dr NE21 ...169 A4
Stella La NE21 ....169 B4
Stella Rd Blaydon NE21 ...169 B4
Ryton NE21 ....169 B4
Stephen St Blyth NE24 ...128 E8
Consett DH8 ....176 F3
East Hartford NE23 ....127 B3
Stephenson Ct
 Berwick-u-T TD15 ....3 F5
Wylam NE41 ....167 C6
Bedlington NE22 ....122 A3
Stephenson Ind Est [18] NE46 ...161 A5
Stephenson Pl NE12 ...142 C2
Stephenson Rd NE65 ...183 E5

Stephenson Terr
Newcastle u T NE15 . . . . . .149 B1
Rothbury NE65 . . . . .182 B5
Throckley NE15 . . . . .148 D2
Wylam NE41 . . . . .167 B6
Stephenson Way NE22 .122 A4
Steppy La NE66 . . . . .42 A6
Stirling Dr NE22 . . . . .122 C2
Stobhill Villas NE61 . . . . .120 A7
Stockerley Rd DH8 . . . . . .177 B1
Stocksfield Hall NE43 . . .171 A8
Stocksfield Sta NE43 . . . .171 A7
Stokoe Dr NE63 . . . . .118 A3
Stokoe St DH8 . . . . .176 E4
Stone Cl NE68 . . . . .17 E2
Stone Row NE65 . . . . .53 E4
Stonechat Mount NE21 .169 A4
Stonecross NE63 . . . . .117 C2
Stonegate NE15 . . . . .146 D1
Stonehaugh Way NE20 .138 B2
Stonelaw Mid Sch NE23 .133 A4
Stoneleigh NE16 . . . . .120 E4
Stoneycroft E NE12 . . . . .142 E2
Stoneycroft W NE12 . . . .142 E2
Stoneylea Cl NE40 . . . . . .167 E3
Stoneylea Rd NE15 . . . . .169 F8
Stoneyrigg Cl NE49 . . . . .153 B3
Stoneywaites NE40 . . . . .173 E8
Stony Path DL13 . . . . . . .111 C1
Stonybank Way NE43 . . . .171 E8
Stonyflat Bank NE42 . . . .166 E2
Store Farm Rd NE64 . . . .118 C5
Store St Blaydon NE21 . . .169 B1
Consett DH8 . . . . .176 F3
Newcastle u T NE15 . . . . . .169 C6
Storey Cres NE64 . . . . . . .118 C5
Storey La NE22 . . . . .169 A4
Storey St NE23 . . . . .133 C5
Stott Cl TD15 . . . . .3 F5
Stott St NE6 . . . . .181 C4
Stowe Gdns NE61 . . . . . . .115 E4
Straffen Ct ☑ NE65 . . . . .183 D5
Straker Dr NE46 . . . . .160 E3
Stratford Cl
Cramlington NE23 . . . . .132 E7
Killingworth NE12 . . . . .142 E3
Stratford Gdns ☑ DH8 .176 F4
Strawberry Ave NE23 . . .142 C5
Strawberry Cotts NE62 .122 B8
Strawberry Terr NE13 . .140 F4
Stretton Way NE27 . . . . .143 C5
Striker's Bank NE20 . . . . .85 C1
Strother Cl NE47 . . . . .158 A5
Strothers Bank NE47 . . .100 B4
Strothers Rd NE39 . . . . . .173 F5
Strothers Terr NE39 . . . .173 F4
Struddars Farm Ct
NE21 . . . . .169 F2
Stuart Gdns NE13 . . . . . .148 D2
Studland Cl NE29 . . . . . . .144 F1
Studley Dr NE65 . . . . .52 C6
Studley Gdns NE25 . . . . .145 A4
Sturton Grange Cotts
NE65 . . . . .41 E2
Styan Ave NE26 . . . . .145 B5
Styford Gdns NE15 . . . . .169 E7
Sudbury Way NE23 . . . . .132 E6
Suffolk Cl NE63 . . . . .117 A4
Sugley Dr NE15 . . . . .169 D6
Sugley St NE15 . . . . .169 D6
Sugley Villas NE15 . . . . .169 D6
Summerdale DH8 . . . . . . .176 D7
Summerfield NE17 . . . . . .175 A5
Summerhill
Blaydon NE21 . . . . .169 B3
Consett DH8 . . . . .176 E7
Summerhill Ave NE3 . . . .141 D1
Summerhill Ct NE66 . . . .181 F4
Summerhouse La
Ashington,North Seaton
NE63 . . . . .118 B3
Ashington,Woodbridge
NE63 . . . . .118 A4
Summers St ☑ NE24 . . .128 E8
Summerson Way NE22 .122 D2
Sunderland St DH8 . . . . .177 D4
Sunlea Ave NE30 . . . . . . .145 C2
Sunningdale NE25 . . . . . .144 D5
Sunny Brae
Embleton NE66 . . . . .24 D1
Greenside NE40 . . . . .173 F8
Sunnygill Terr NE40 . . . .167 F2
Sunnyside
Cornhill on T TD12 . . . . .6 C4
Cramlington NE23 . . . . .133 A6
Sunnyside Cres TD15 . . .178 B2
Sunnyside Cut TD15 . . . .178 B1
Sunnyside Mews TD15 . .178 B1
Surrey Cl NE63 . . . . .117 A4
Surtees Pl DH8 . . . . .176 C5
Sussex St ☑ NE24 . . . . . .128 E8
Sutherland Ave NE64 . . .118 D4
Swaledale Ave NE24 . . .128 A7
Swaledale Ct NE24 . . . . .128 A7
Swallow Cl NE63 . . . . . . .122 E8
Swallow Ct NE12 . . . . . . .142 C4
Swalwell Cl NE42 . . . . . . .166 C2
Swansfield NE15 . . . . . . .119 E7
Swansfield Park Rd
NE66 . . . . .181 C4
Swarland Fst Sch NE65 . . .52 C6
Swarland Rd NE25 . . . . . .134 D2
Swarland Terr NE61 . . . . .53 F2
Sweetbriar NE61 . . . . . . .114 E2
Sweetbriar Way NE24 . .128 C4

Sweethope Ave
Ashington NE63 . . . . .117 F2
Blyth NE24 . . . . .128 D8
Sweethope Dene NE61 .120 A6
Swiftdale Cl NE22 . . . . . .121 F1
Swinbourne Gdns NE26 .144 F6
Swinburn Rd NE25 . . . . . .134 D2
Swindale Cotts NE41 . . . .167 B6
Swindale Dr NE12 . . . . . .142 C3
Swinhoe Farm NE70 . . . . .15 D5
Swinhoe Gdns NE13 . . . .141 B6
Swinhoe Rd NE67 . . . . .24 C8
Swinley Gdns NE15 . . . . .169 F6
Swinton Cl NE61 . . . . .120 B6
Sycamore Ave
Alnwick NE66 . . . . .181 A4
Blyth NE24 . . . . .123 D1
Dinnington NE13 . . . . .140 C7
Guide Post NE62 . . . . .121 E7
Ponteland NE20 . . . . .138 D4
Whitley Bay NE25 . . . . .144 F4
Sycamore Cl ☑ NE61 . . . .65 C5
Sycamore Gr NE22 . . . . . .166 A2
Sycamore Pl NE12 . . . . . .142 C4
Sycamore Rd NE21 . . . . .169 C2
Sycamore St
Ashington NE63 . . . . .117 D3
Haltwhistle NE49 . . . . .153 D4
Throckley NE15 . . . . .148 D3
Sycamores The NE62 . . .121 E7
Sylvan Cl NE61 . . . . .119 D7
Sylvia's Cl NE65 . . . . .143 B4
Symon Terr NE17 . . . . . . .175 B8
Synclen Ave NE45 . . . . . .163 A6
Synclen Rd NE45 . . . . .163 A6
Synclen Terr NE45 . . . . . .163 A6

T

Taberna Cl NE15 . . . . . . .147 E2
Talbot Gn NE5 . . . . .169 F8
Talbot House Sch NE15 .148 F2
Tangmere Cl NE23 . . . . . .133 C7
Tankerville Terr NE1 . . .180 C6
Tanners Garth NE66 . . . .181 D3
Tanners Row ☑ NE46 . . .161 A5
Tarset Dr NE42 . . . . .166 D2
Tarset Rd NE25 . . . . .144 B5
Tate St ☑ NE24 . . . . .128 F8
Taunton Ave NE29 . . . . . .144 F1
Taunton Pl NE23 . . . . .133 B8
Tavistock Wlk NE23 . . . . .133 B8
Tay St NE17 . . . . .173 C1
Taylor Ave
Ashington NE63 . . . . .118 B3
Wideopen NE13 . . . . .141 C6
Taylor Gdns NE16 . . . . . .135 D6
Taylor St Blyth NE24 . . . .128 A6
Consett DH8 . . . . .176 F2
☑ Seahouses NE68 . . . . . . .17 F2
Taylor Terr ☑ NE27 . . . . .143 E1
Taylor's Bldgs NE22 . . . .122 D2
Taylor's Terr DH8 . . . . . . .176 C1
Taynton Gr NE23 . . . . .133 F2
Teal Ave NE24 . . . . .128 F4
Teasdale St DH8 . . . . .177 A3
Tebay Dr NE15 . . . . .169 F8
Tedder Pl NE66 . . . . .32 B2
Tedham Rd NE15 . . . . .169 C7
Tees Gr DH8 . . . . .177 D5
Tees St NE17 . . . . .173 C1
Teesdale Pl ☑ NE24 . . . .127 F8
Telford Cl NE17 . . . . .143 C5
Telford Ct NE61 . . . . .119 F5
Temperance Terr ☑
TD15 . . . . .178 B5
Temperley Pl NE46 . . . . . .161 A4
Tempest St NE21 . . . . . . .169 A4
Templar St ☑ NE15 . . . . .178 D4
Temple Ave NE24 . . . . . . .128 C8
Temple Gdns DH8 . . . . . .176 F1
Temple Hos NE47 . . . . . . .113 B8
Temple of Mithras*
NE46 . . . . .90 B6
Temple Thornton NE61 . .75 F4
Tenbury Cres NE29 . . . . .144 E1
Tenby Sq NE23 . . . . .133 C8
Tennyson Ct NE42 . . . . . .166 B1
Tenter Garth NE15 . . . . .148 C2
Tenter Hill NE71 . . . . .180 C6
Tenter Terr NE61 . . . . . . .120 A8
Tenth Ave Blyth NE24 . . .128 E6
Morpeth NE61 . . . . .120 B6
Tern Cl NE24 . . . . .128 C4
Terrace The
Consett DH8 . . . . .176 C6
Harlow Hill NE15 . . . . .93 F3
Ovingham NE42 . . . . .166 A4
Terrier Cl NE22 . . . . .122 C1
Tewkesbury NE12 . . . . . .142 D4
Tewkesbury Rd NE15 . . .169 C7
Thames St NE17 . . . . .173 C1
Theresa St NE21 . . . . . . .169 C3
Thieves Bank NE61 . . . . .116 C1
Third Ave
Ashington NE63 . . . . .117 E3
Blyth NE24 . . . . .128 D6
Morpeth NE61 . . . . .120 B7
Third Row Ellington NE61 .112 E4
Linton NE61 . . . . .112 A3
Third St Consett DH8 . . . .177 B2
Leadgate DH8 . . . . .177 C5
Leadgate DH8 . . . . .177 D6
Thirlmere Ave NE30 . . . .145 A2
Thirlmere Cl NE12 . . . . . .142 E1
Thirlmere Terr NE64 . . . .118 E4
Thirlmere Way NE24 . . . .123 A1

Thirlmoor Pl NE62 . . . . . .122 A8
Thirlwall View CA8 . . . . .151 F8
Thirston Dr NE23 . . . . . . .133 C6
Thistle Ave NE40 . . . . . . .168 A4
Thomas Bewick Sch
NE5 . . . . .149 C2
Thomas Holliday Homes ⑩
NE22 . . . . .122 D3
Thomas Percy RC Mid Sch
NE66 . . . . .181 C3
Thomas St
☑ Consett DH8 . . . . .176 F2
Consett,Blackhill DH8 . . . . .176 D4
Newcastle u T NE1 . . . . . . .149 F2
Thomas Taylor Cotts
NE27 . . . . .143 C5
Thompson Ave NE12 . . . .142 C4
Thompson St
☑ Bedlington NE22 . . . . . .122 D3
Blyth NE21 . . . . .123 D1
Blyth NE24 . . . . .123 E1
Thorn Cl NE13 . . . . .141 A5
Thorn Tree Dr NE22 . . . .121 F2
Thornbury ⑧ NE21 . . . . .169 B1
Thornbury Ave NE23 . . . .134 B7
Thornbury Cl NE25 . . . . .144 C6
Thorndale Pl NE24 . . . . . .128 A8
Thorndale Rd NE15 . . . . .169 F5
Thornehill Gdns NE62 . . .122 A8
Thorneyburn Ave NE25 .144 B5
Thorneyburn Way NE24 .128 C7
Thorneyfield Dr NE12 . . .142 B2
Thorneyford Pl NE20 . . .138 E7
Thornfield Rd DH8 . . . . . .176 C1
Thornhill Cl NE25 . . . . . . .134 D2
Thornhill Pk NE20 . . . . . .138 E7
Thornhill Rd NE20 . . . . . .138 E7
Thornlea NE61 . . . . .129 C6
Thornley Ave NE23 . . . . .133 C6
Thornley Rd NE5 . . . . .169 F8
Thornley Terr NE62 . . . . .122 C6
Thornton Cl NE61 . . . . . . .120 B6
Thornton Cotts NE40 . . .168 C6
Thornton Cres NE21 . . . .169 C3
Thornton Gate ④ TD15 . . . .3 E6
Thornton Mains Cotts
TD15 .3 C2
Thornton Terr NE12 . . . . .143 A1
Thorntree Ave NE13 . . . .132 B1
Thorntree Cl NE25 . . . . . .144 B4
Thorntree Cotts NE13 . .132 B1
Thorntree Dr NE25 . . . . . .144 C4
Thorntree Gdns NE63 . . .118 A2
Thorntree Way NE24 . . . .127 F7
Thoroton St NE24 . . . . . . .128 E8
Thorp Ave NE61 . . . . .115 A2
Thorp Cl NE24 . . . . .128 B5
Thorp Cotts NE40 . . . . . . .168 A5
Thorpe Dr NE40 . . . . .168 C5
Three Tuns La ⑫ NE66 .181 C5
Threefords NE71 . . . . .13 A4
Throckley Fst Sch NE15 .148 C2
Thropton Ave NE24 . . . . .128 C5
Thropton Cl NE24 . . . . . . .128 C7
Thropton Village Fst Sch
NE65 . . . . .50 B5
Thrunton Wood* NE66 . . . .39 C4
Thumbtree Cl NE47 . . . . .155 E6
Thursby Ave NE30 . . . . . .145 B2
Tilbury Gr NE30 . . . . .145 A2
Till Ave NE21 . . . . .169 B2
Till Gr NE61 . . . . .112 E5
Tilley Cres NE42 . . . . .166 B2
Tillmouth Ave NE25 . . . .134 C2
Tillmouth Park Rd
NE15 . . . . .178 D1
Tindale Ave NE23 . . . . . . .133 C6
Tindale Dr DH8 . . . . .177 C4
TindaleTerr CA8 . . . . .94 B6
Tindle St DH8 . . . . .176 E4
Tinkler's Bank NE45 . . . .162 F3
Tinmill Pl DH8 . . . . .176 D3
Tintagel Cl NE23 . . . . .133 B8
Tintagel Ho ④ TD15 . . . .178 B4
Titchfield Terr
Ashington NE63 . . . . .117 D2
Pegswood NE61 . . . . .115 F4
Tithe Cotts NE20 . . . . . . .138 E7
Tiverton Ave NE29 . . . . . .144 C1
Tiverton Pl NE23 . . . . .133 B8
Tofthouse Rd NE19 . . . . . .47 C4
Tofts Bank NE47 . . . . .157 F6
Tofts La TD15 . . . . .2 E4
Top Row Cotts TD12 . . . . .11 F8
Torcross Way NE23 . . . . .133 B8
Torver Cl NE13 . . . . .141 B5
Torver Way NE30 . . . . . . .145 A5
Tosson Cl NE22 . . . . .122 B1
Tosson Pl NE13 . . . . .117 E3
Totnes Dr NE23 . . . . .133 B8
Tower Dr NE66 . . . . .30 E1
Tower Gdns NE40 . . . . . . .168 C5
Tower Knowe* NE48 . . . . . .69 A5
Tower Knowe Forest Wlks*
NE48 . . . . .69 A5
Tower La NE66 . . . . .181 B5

Tower Rd TD15 . . . . .178 B3
Towers Cl NE22 . . . . .127 A8
Towerside NE66 . . . . .39 B6
Towhouse Gn NE47 . . . . .155 D5
Town Farm Cl NE46 . . . . .91 B3
Town Farm Field NE45 .162 F6
Town Foot NE65 . . . . .182 B5
Towne Gate The NE15 . . .147 E2
Towneley Cotts NE40 . . .168 A4
Towneley Ct NE42 . . . . . .166 E3
Towneley Terr NE39 . . . .173 E4
Townfield Gdns NE15 . . .168 F8
Townfoot Steading NE66 .42 A6
Townhead NE47 . . . . .100 B4
Townsend Cres NE61 . . .119 D6
Townsend Ct NE65 . . . . . . .53 D4
Townsville Ave NE25 . . . .144 D3
Tows Bank NE49 . . . . .95 C3
Trafalgar Rd NE12 . . . . . .142 D4
Trafalgar St ☑ DH8 . . . . .176 F2
Trafford Wlk NE5 . . . . . . .149 E3
Trajan Wlk NE15 . . . . .147 D2
Transbritannia Ct NE21 .169 E4
Tranwell Cl NE61 . . . . . . .115 E3
Tranwell Cotts NE61 . . . .119 B6
Tranwell Dr NE25 . . . . . . .144 C6
Tranwell Dr NE25 . . . . . . .134 E2
Treaty Pk TD12 . . . . .5 A2
Trench The Hartburn NE61 .75 E8
Trenchard Way NE66 . . . . .32 B2
Trent Dale DH8 . . . . .177 D5
Trent St NE17 . . . . .173 C1
Trentham Gdns NE61 . . .115 F4
Trevelyan Ave
Bedlington NE22 . . . . .122 B1
Blyth NE24 . . . . .128 C6
Trevelyan Dr NE5 . . . . . . .149 F4
Trevone Pl NE23 . . . . .134 A2
Trewit Rd NE26 . . . . .145 B5
Trinity Ct NE45 . . . . .162 F6
Trinity Gr NE23 . . . . .134 A2
Trinity Terr NE45 . . . . . . .162 F6
Tripping Chare TD15 . . . . .10 D4
Trillington CE Fst Sch
NE61 . . . . .64 E3
Troon Cl DH8 . . . . .176 E5
Trotter Gr NE22 . . . . .122 C1
Trysting Tree Dr NE66 . . .31 A2
Tudor Cl NE20 . . . . .138 C4
Tudor Terr DH8 . . . . .176 E3
Tughall Rd NE67 . . . . .24 B5
Tulip Cl NE21 . . . . .169 B2
Tulip St NE42 . . . . .166 B2
Tundry Way NE21 . . . . . . .169 F4
Tunstall Gr DH8 . . . . .177 D4
Turn The NE61 . . . . .119 F5
Turnberry NE25 . . . . .144 C5
Turnberry Cl DH8 . . . . . . .176 E5
Turnberry Way NE23 . . . .133 C6
Turner Cl NE40 . . . . .168 D4
Turner St Amble NE65 . . .183 D6
Consett DH8 . . . . .176 D6
Shiremoor NE27 . . . . .143 E1
Turners Way NE61 . . . . . .119 D7
Turnstone Gdns NE66 . . . .24 D1
Turret Gdns TD15 . . . . . . .178 A2
Turret Rd NE15 . . . . .169 F7
Turvelaws Farm Cotts
NE71 . . . . .180 D8
Tute Hill NE61 . . . . .65 E3
Tweed Ave
Ellington NE61 . . . . .112 E5
Leadgate DH8 . . . . .177 D5
Tweed Dr NE61 . . . . .120 B6
Tweed Gr NE15 . . . . .169 C7
Tweed Rd TD12 . . . . .179 C6
Tweed St Ashington NE63 .117 E4
Berwick-u-T TD15 . . . . .178 B5
Chopwell NE17 . . . . .173 C1
Tweed Terr TD12 . . . . .179 D6
Tweedmouth Mid Sch
TD15 . . . . .178 B2
Tweedmouth Prior Park Fst
Sch TD15 . . . . .178 B1
Tweedmouth West Fst Sch
TD15 . . . . .178 A3
Tweedside Trad Est
Berwick-u-T TD15 . . . . .3 E7
Tweedmouth TD15 . . . . . . .178 A3
Tweedy St NE24 . . . . .128 A8
Tweedy's Bldgs NE40 . . .168 B5
Twelfth Ave NE24 . . . . . . .128 D6
Twentieth Ave NE24 . . . .128 C5
Twentyfifth Ave NE24 . .128 D5
Twentysecond Ave
NE24 . . . . .128 C5
Twentysixth Ave NE24 . .128 C5
Twentythird Ave NE24 . .128 C5
Twickenham Ct NE23 . . .133 F2
Twizell Ave NE21 . . . . . . .169 B2
Twizell Pl NE20 . . . . .138 E7
Twizell St NE24 . . . . .128 C5
Twyford Cl NE23 . . . . .133 B8
Tyelaw Mdws NE65 . . . . . .41 C3
Tyne Ave DH8 . . . . .177 D5
Tyne Ct NE46 . . . . .161 A6
Tyne Gdns
Ovingham NE42 . . . . .166 B4
Ryton NE40 . . . . .168 E4
Tyne Gn NE46 . . . . .161 A6
Tyne Green Ctry Pk*
NE46 . . . . .161 B6
Tyne Green Rd
Hexham NE46 . . . . .161 A6
Hexham NE46 . . . . .161 B6
Tyne Mills Ind Est NE46 .161 C5

Tyne Riverside Ctry Pk*
Prudhoe NE42 . . . . .166 B2
* Throckley NE15 . . . . .168 D4
Tyne St Ashington NE63 . .117 F3
Blaydon NE21 . . . . .169 A2
Chopwell NE17 . . . . .173 C1
Consett DH8 . . . . .177 A2
Tyne Terr NE48 . . . . .80 A2
Tyne Valley Gdns NE40 .168 D3
Tyne View Blaydon NE21 .169 A2
Crawcrook NE40 . . . . .167 B1
Newcastle u T NE15 . . . . . .169 D6
Wylam NE41 . . . . .169 A2
Tyne View Rd NE49 . . . . .153 A4
Tyne View Terr
Prudhoe NE42 . . . . .166 A1
Stocksfield NE43 . . . . .171 A4
Tyne Wlk NE15 . . . . .148 B6
Tynebank NE21 . . . . .169 A2
Tynedale Ave NE26 . . . . .144 F5
Tynedale Cl NE41 . . . . . . .167 A1
Tynedale Ct NE49 . . . . . . .153 A4
Tynedale Dr NE24 . . . . . . .128 A8
Tynedale Gdns NE43 . . . .171 B5
Tynedale Mews NE45 . . .163 A6
Tynedale Mid Sch NE24 .128 A8
Tynedale Ret Pk NE46 . .161 C5
Tynedale Terr
Acomb NE46 . . . . .91 A1
Hexham NE46 . . . . .160 F1
Tynedale Terr ☑ NE49 . .153 A4
Tyneley Cotts NE67 . . . . . .23 F5
Tynevale Ave NE21 . . . . .169 B2
Tyneview Terr NE15 . . . .169 D6
Tyneview Terr NE46 . . . .161 A6

U

Ubbanford TD15 2
Ulgham Grange Farm Cotts
NE61 65
Ullswater Cl NE24 127
Ullswater Dr NE12 142
Ullswater Rd NE64 118
Umfraville Dene NE42 . . .166
Underhill Dr NE62 122
Underwood Gr NE23 127
Union Brae TD15 178
Union Hall Rd NE15 169
Union Park Rd TD15 178
Union St Blyth NE24 128
☑ Seahouses NE68 17
Unity Terr NE24 123
Unsworth Gdns ☑ DH8 .176
Unsworth St ☑ DH8 176
Unthank Rd
Haltwhistle NE49 153
Melkridge NE49 151
Uplands NE25 144
Upper Barresdale NE66 .181
Upper Crone St NE27 143
Upper Dodds La ⑬
NE66 181
Upper Fenwick Gr NE15 .115
Upper Howick St NE66 . .181
Upper Precinct The
NE21 169

V

Valebrook NE46 160
Valehead NE25 144
Valerian Ave NE46 147
Valerian Ct NE63 117
Valeside NE15 148
Valley Cres NE21 169
Valley Ct NE46 91
Valley Dene NE17 175
Valley Gardens Mid Sch
NE25 144
Valley Gdns Consett DH8 .176
Whitley Bay NE25 144
Valley Gr NE40 167
Valley Rd NE25 134
Valley View
Consett,Bridgehill DH8 176
☑ East Ord TD15 3
Hexham NE46 161
Leadgate DH8 161
Newcastle u T,Lemington
NE15 169
Prudhoe NE42 166
Vallum Rd NE15 148
Vanborough Ct NE25 134
Vanburgh Gdns NE61 . . .119
Vance Ct NE21 169
Vedra Cl DL13 111
Ventnor Gdns NE26 145
Vera St NE40 172
Vernon Dr NE25 144
Vernon Pl NE64 118
Vicarage Terr
Bedlington NE22 122
Nenthead CA9 127
Victoria Ave NE46 161
Victoria Cl NE25 134
Victoria Cres
Alnwick NE66 181
Hexham NE46 145
Victoria Ct
☑ Consett DH8 176
Longbenton NE12 142
Tynemouth NE30 145
Victoria Gr NE42 166
Victoria Mews
Blyth NE24 128

oria Mews continued
itley Bay NE26 ....145 B5
dstream TD12 ....179 C6
itley Bay NE26 ....9 A4
oria Pl Amble NE65 ..183 C5
oria Rd Consett DH8 .176 F2
der NE71 ....180 C6
oria Sq CA9 ....185 D3
oria St
dstream TD12 ....179 C6
nsett DH8 ....176 E3
wcrook NE40 ....167 F4
oria Terr
wick NE66 ....181 D4
llington NE22 ....122 C1
ton NE65 ....52 E3
msterley NE17 .....175 B6
wbiggin-by-t-S NE64 .118 E4
dhoe NE42 ....166 D2
Throckley NE15 .....148 D2
itley Bay NE26 ......145 B5
oria Villas NE22 ....122 B1
tory Cotts NE23 ....133 A1
tory Dr NE65 ....52 C6
wlands NE63 ....117 D4
a La NE65 ....51 E3
a Real Bglws DH8 ...177 B4
a Real Ct DH8 ......177 A4
a Real Ct DH8 ......177 A4
a Real Est DH8 .....177 A4
a Real Rd DH8 ......177 A4
a Real Sch DH8 .....177 B4
age Ct NE26 ....144 F5
age E NE40 ....168 C6
age Farm
ropton NE65 ....50 A5
albottle NE15 ....149 A1
age Rd NE23 ....133 C6
age View NE65 ......50 B5
as The
amington NE61 ......124 C7
deopen NE13 ....141 C5
ers Gdns NE70 .....16 E1
dolanda Roman Fort*
.....................88 E1
domora Roman Fort*
48 ....174 E4
domora Villas DH8 ..174 E4
e Ct NE46 ....161 B4
e Terr NE46 ....161 B4
en Terr TD15 ....178 B5
can Pl NE22 ....127 A8
can Terr NE12 ......142 E1

Stead Rd NE66 ......24 C1
de Ave NE15 ....93 F4
ggonway The NE42 ..166 D3
gon Way Rd NE66 ..181 D4
gtail Ct NE15 ....182 C4
gtail Rd NE65 ......182 C5
bottle Campus Tech Coll
15 ....148 F2
bottle Hall Gdns
15 ....149 A1
bottle Rd
ewburn NE15 ....168 F8
bottle NE15 ....148 F1
bottle Village Fst Sch
15 ....148 F1
ikerbank NE65 .....182 B5
ikerburn NE23 .....133 B3
llkergate
nwick NE66 ....181 B6
erwick-u-T TD15 ...178 B6
llace Gn TD15 .....178 B5
llace Terr NE40 ....168 C4
llington Ave
unswick Village NE13 .141 A6
nemouth Village NE30 .145 A1
llington Ct NE22 ...122 C2
llington Ct
llingworth NE12 ...142 C3
aton Delaval NE25 ..134 D3
nemouth NE30 ....145 B1
llington Ctyd NE61 ..74 D3
llington Dr NE15 ...169 E8
llington Hall Walled Gdn*
61 ....74 D3
llington Rd NE63 ..117 F2
llish Walls Rd DH8 .109 E5
llridge Cotts NE20 ..84 A3
llridge Dr NE25 ...134 E1
lltown Quarry Wlks*

alsham Cl NE24 ....152 B8
alsh Cl NE13 ......141 A6
alton Ave NE24 ....128 C8
alton Dr NE62 .....121 F8
alton Terr Consett DH8 .177 A4
ochester DH8 ......174 E4
alwick Rd NE25 ....144 F5
ames The NE67 .....24 D7
ames La NE46 .....161 B4
anley St NE24 .....128 E8
anlock Cl NE23 ....133 C3
anny Rd NE22 .....122 B1
ansbeck Ave
yth NE24 ....128 E5
akeford NE12 ......122 A8
nemouth NE30 .....145 A1
ansbeck Bsns Pk
E63 ....117 B5
ansbeck Cl NE61 ..112 E5
ansbeck Cres NE61 .115 E3
ansbeck Ct NE23 ..127 A8

Wansbeck General Hospl
NE63 ....117 F4
Wansbeck Gr
Leadgate DH8 ......177 D5
New Hartley NE25 ..134 D6
Wansbeck Ho NE15 .169 C6
Wansbeck Mews NE15 .117 B4
Wansbeck Pl NE61 ..114 E1
Wansbeck Rd
Ashington NE63 ....117 B2
Dudley NE23 ....141 F8
Wansbeck Riverside Pk*
NE63 ....116 F1
Wansbeck Sq NE63 .117 C4
Wansbeck St
Ashington NE63 ....123 A8
Chopwell NE17 .....173 C1
Morpeth NE61 ......120 A8
Wansbeck Terr NE62 .122 D7
Wansbeck View NE62 .122 B8
Wansdyke NE61 ....114 D1
Wapping 1 NE24 ...128 F8
Ward La Stonehaugh NE48 .79 F2
Wark NE48 ....80 D2
Ward Way NE47 ....156 B2
Wark View NE46 ....91 A3
Wardle Dr NE23 ....142 B8
Wardle Terr
Crawcrook NE40 ...167 F4
Longframlington NE65 .51 F4
Wardway The CA9 ..185 C1
Warenford Cl NE23 .133 C4
Warenmill Cl NE15 .169 B7
Warenton Pl NE29 ..144 B1
Waring Ave NE26 ...135 B7
Wark Ave NE27 .....143 F4
Wark CE Fst Sch NE48 .80 F3
Wark Common Farm
TD12 ....11 A7
Warkburn Forest Walks*
NE48 ....79 D2
Warkdale Ave NE24 .128 A6
Warkworth Ave
Blyth NE24 ....128 E5
Newsham NE65 .....53 E8
Whitley Bay NE26 ..145 A5
Warkworth Castle*
NE65 ....53 E8
Warkworth Cres
Ashington NE63 ....117 C3
Newburn NE15 .....168 F7
Warkworth Dr
Ellington NE61 .....112 E5
Pegswood NE61 ....115 F3
Wideopen NE13 ....141 C6
Warkworth Hermitage*
NE65 ....53 E8
Warkworth La NE65 .112 C6
Warkworth St NE15 .169 C6
Warkworth Terr
Berwick-u-T TD15 ..178 B6
Broomhill NE65 .....53 E4
Warkworth Woods NE13 .141 B2
Warnhead Rd NE22 .122 B1
Warren Ct NE63 ....117 C2
Warrens Wlk NE21 .169 A1
Warton Farm Cotts NE65 .49 E5
Warwick Cl NE23 ...133 E1
Warwick Gr NE22 ..121 D1
Warwick Rd NE5 ...169 E8
Warwick St NE4 ....128 C4
Wasdale Cl NE23 ..133 C3
Water Row NE15 ...168 E7
Waterbeck Cl NE23 .133 C3
Waterbury Rd NE24 .141 B1
Waterfield Rd NE22 .122 B7
Waterford Cl NE26 .135 D6
Waterford Cres 6 NE26 .145 B4
Waterford Gn NE63 .122 D8
Waterford Pk NE13 .140 F6
Watergate Rd NE8 .109 F3
Waterloo Pl TD15 ..178 C2
Waterloo Rd Blyth NE24 .128 E7
Earsdon NE25 ......144 A5
Waterloo St NE21 ..169 A1
Watermill NE40 ....168 C5
Watershaugh Cl NE65 .53 E8
Watershaugh Rd NE65 .53 D8
Waterside NE61 ....119 F8
Watling St
Corbridge NE45 ....162 F5
Leadgate DH8 ......177 D4
Watling Street Bglws
DH8 ....177 C5
Watson Ave NE23 ..142 A8
Watson St DH8 .....176 E4
Watson Terr 17 NE61 .120 A8
Watt's La NE61 .....118 E5
Watt's Rd NE26 ....145 A6
Waverley Ave
Bedlington NE22 ...122 B1
Bedlington NE22 ...122 C2
Whitley Bay NE25 ..144 F4
Waverley Cres NE15 .169 B7
Waverley Ct NE12 ..122 C2
Waverley Dr NE22 .122 C2
Waverley Pl NE24 ..118 E5
Waverley Prim Sch
NE15 ....169 B6
Waverly Dr NE22 ...122 D2
Waverton Cl NE23 .133 B3
Wayn Riggs NE46 ..91 C6
Wayn Riggs Terr NE46 .91 C6
Wealleans Cl NE63 .118 B3
Wear Ave DH8 .....177 D5
Wear St Chopwell NE17 .173 B1

Wear St continued
Consett DH8 ....177 A2
Weardale Ave NE24 .128 A8
Weardale Folk Mus*
DL13 ....111 D1
Wearhead Prim Sch
DL13 ....111 B2
Weatherley St 3 NE68 .17 F2
Weatherside NE21 ..169 B1
Weavers Way NE66 .181 C2
Weddells Ct 15 TD15 .178 B4
Weddells La 12 TD15 .178 B4
Wedder Law NE23 ..133 B3
Wedderburn Sq NE63 .117 C3
Wedgewood Cotts
NE15 ....169 D6
Wedmore Rd NE5 ..169 D6
Weetslade Cres NE23 .142 A7
Weetslade Rd NE23 .142 A7
Weetslade Terr NE23 .142 C5
Weetwood Ave NE71 .180 B6
Weetwood Rd
Cramlington NE23 ..133 C4
Wooler NE71 ....180 C6
Welbeck Com Fst Sch
NE63 ....118 A2
Welbeck Rd NE62 ..121 E7
Welbeck Terr
Ashington NE63 ....117 D2
Pegswood NE61 ....115 F4
Welburn Cl NE42 ...166 C5
Welbury Way NE23 .133 B3
Weldon Rd NE23 ...133 E5
Welfare Cres
Ashington NE63 ....117 F3
Newbiggin-by-t-S NE64 .118 C4
Welford Rd NE15 ..176 C1
Well Bank
Corbridge NE45 ....162 F5
Henshaw NE47 .....155 C6
Wearhead DL13 .....111 D1
Well Cl TD15 ....8 E2
Well Close Sq TD15 .178 B5
Well Dean NE42 ....166 D3
Well La Tynemouth NE27 .144 B2
Tynemouth NE27 ...144 C2
Well Rd Stocksfield NE43 .171 B5
Tweedmouth TD15 .178 C6
Well Ridge Cl NE25 .144 C3
Well Ridge Pk NE25 .144 C7
Well Sq TD15 ......178 C6
Well Strand NE65 ..182 B5
Well Way NE61 .....114 F1
Wellfield NE65 ......53 E8
Wellfield Cl
4 Alnmouth NE66 ...42 B5
Throckley NE15 .....148 C1
Wellfield NE40 .....167 E3
Wellfield Mid Sch NE25 .144 B4
Wellhead Dean Rd
NE62 ....116 F2
Wellhead Terr NE63 .117 A4
Wellington Ave NE25 .144 A5
Wellington Rd NE62 .122 A7
Wellington St Blyth NE24 .128 F7
Newcastle u T,Lemington
NE15 ....169 D6
Wellington St E 10
NE24 ....128 F8
Wellington Terr TD15 .178 B4
Wellway Ct 6 NE61 .114 F1
Wellway Ct NE65 ..115 A1
Wellwood St NE15 .183 C5
Welton Cl NE43 ....171 D6
Welwyn Ave NE22 .122 D3
Wembley Ave NE25 .144 E4
Wembley Gdns NE24 .123 B6
Wembley Gr NE24 ..123 C6
Wenlock NE64 ......128 F6
Wensleydale Mid Sch
NE24 ....128 F6
Wensleydale Terr NE24 .128 F6
Wentworth Cl NE20 .138 C4
Wentworth Gdns NE25 .144 C4
Wentworth Pl
Allendale Town NE47 .97 F2
Hexham NE46 ......161 B5
Wentworth Terr NE47 .97 F2
Werdohl Way DH8 .177 B4
Wesley Cl NE21 ....169 D3
Wesley Dr NE12 ...143 B1
Wesley Gr NE40 ...167 E3
Wesley Mount NE40 .167 E3
Wesley St Consett DH8 .176 F2
Consett,Blackhill DH8 .176 D4
Prudhoe NE42 .....166 D2
Wesley Terr NE42 ..166 D2
Wesley Way
Longbenton NE12 ..143 B1
Throckley NE15 .....148 D2
West Acre DH8 .....176 C5
West Acres Alnwick NE66 .181 E4
Blaydon NE21 ......169 D2
Dinnington NE13 ...140 B8
West Ave Amble NE65 .183 C5
Guide Post NE62 ...121 D7
Longbenton,Forest Hall
NE12 ....142 F1
Newcastle u T NE5 .149 F2
Scremerston TD15 ..4 A4
Whitley Bay NE25 ..144 E5
West Bailey NE12 ..142 B3
West Blackdene DL13 .111 C1
West Bridge St NE24 .123 D3
West Brizlee Dr NE66 .30 D2
West Brunton Farm Cotts
NE13 ....140 D2
West Chevington NE61 .65 C8
West Cl NE65 ....53 E8

West Clifton NE12 ..142 C4
West Copperas NE15 .169 F7
West Cotts NE67 ....23 E3
West Cres Amble NE65 .183 C5
Chopwell NE17 .....175 B7
Gunnerton NE48 ....81 D2
West Ct 7 Amble NE65 .183 C5
Blyth NE24 ....128 C6
West Denton Cl NE15 .169 D8
West Denton Prim Sch
NE5 ....149 D1
West Denton Rd NE15 .169 D8
West Denton Way NE5 .149 E1
West Dr Amble NE65 .183 B5
Berwick-u-T TD15 ...3 B4
Blyth NE24 ....128 C4
West End Chatton NE66 .21 D7
Craster NE66 ....32 C6
Seaton Sluice NE26 .135 D4
Shilbottle NE66 .....51 C3
Tweedmouth TD15 .178 A4
West End Pl TD15 ..178 A4
West End Rd TD15 .178 A4
West End Terr 1 NE46 .161 A4
West Fall DL13 .....111 B2
West Falldon Cotts
NE67 ....23 F1
West Farm DH8 ....175 C2
West Farm Ct
Cramlington NE23 ..133 B7
Killingworth NE12 ..142 E2
West Farm La DH8 .175 C2
West Fishwick Cvn Site
TD15 ....2 C5
West Ford Rd NE62 .122 B8
West Gns 11 NE12 .120 A8
West Haven DH8 ...175 C2
West Hextol NE46 ..160 F4
West Hextol Cl NE46 .160 F4
West Hill NE61 .....119 E7
West Horton NE71 ..14 D1
West La
Killingworth NE12 ..142 D2
Medomsley NE17 ...175 B4
West Lane Cotts NE65 .51 E3
West Lane Cvn Pk NE65 .51 E3
West Law NE65 ....176 D8
West Lea NE65 .....50 A5
West Learmouth TD12 .179 E2
West Mains TD15 ...3 A4
West Market St NE61 .113 B3
West Mdws NE5 ...149 D4
West Monkseaton Sta
NE25 ....144 D4
West Moor Ct NE12 .142 B1
West Mount NE12 ..142 C3
West Newbiggin TD12 .6 E8
West Par
4 Alnwick NE66 ...181 D4
Consett DH8 ....177 A2
Leadgate DH8 .....177 C4
West Park Gdns NE21 .169 C1
West Park View NE23 .141 F8
West Pastures NE63 .117 B2
West Pk NE61 ......119 E7
West Quarter NE46 .160 F5
West Rd Bedlington NE22 .122 D2
Consett DH8 ....176 C4
Haltwhistle NE49 ..153 C4
Longhorsley NE65 ..64 A5
Ponteland NE20 ....138 E6
Prudhoe NE42 .....166 B2
Newcastle u T NE15 .169 F8
West Riggs NE62 ..126 F8
West Salisbury St 4
NE24 ....128 D8
West Sleekburn Ind Est
NE22 ....122 D6
West Sleekburn Mid Sch
NE62 ....121 F6
West Spencer Terr
NE15 ....149 B1
West St Belford NE70 .15 F4
Berwick-u-T TD15 ..178 B6
High Spen NE39 ...173 F4
Leadgate DH8 .....177 C4
Norham TD15 ......2 D8
Shiremoor NE27 ...143 D1
Spittal TD15 ....178 C2
West Terr
Corbridge NE45 ....162 F6
Seaton Sluice NE26 .135 D6
Stakeford NE62 ....122 C7
West Thorp NE5 ...149 F5
West Turnpike NE66 .29 B1
West Vallum NE15 .169 F7
West View
Ashington NE63 ....117 D3
Bedlington NE22 ...122 C3
Blaydon NE21 ......169 C3
Cambois NE24 .....123 C6
Consett DH8 ....176 D5
Crawcrook NE40 ...167 E6
Dudley NE23 ....144 A5
Earsdon NE25 .....153 C4
Haltwhistle NE49 ..153 A4
Medomsley NE17 ..177 A8
Morpeth NE61 .....114 C5
Newbiggin-by-t-S NE64 .118 E5
NE15 ....169 C6
Pegswood NE61 ...115 E3
Seahouses NE68 ...17 E2
Seghill NE23 ....133 F1
Wideopen NE13 ...141 B7
Wylam NE41 ....167 B6
West View Bldgs NE30 .145 C3

West View Terr NE46 .161 C3
West Weetwood NE71 .180 F7
West Woodburn Fst Sch
NE48 ....72 C5
West Wylam Dr NE42 .166 E3
West Wynd NE12 ...142 D3
Westacres NE48 ....80 E4
Westbourne Ave NE62 .117 A1
Westbourne Gr NE46 .160 F5
Westbourne Terr NE25 .134 E3
Westbourne Mews NE41 .167 E3
Westerhope Prim Sch
NE5 ....149 E3
Westerkirk NE23 ...133 C3
Westerley Terr NE49 .153 C4
Western Ave
Newcastle u T NE5 .149 D1
Prudhoe NE42 .....166 B2
Seaton Delaval NE25 .134 C3
Western Cl 5 NE26 .144 F8
Western Hill DH8 ..176 C5
Western Terr NE23 .141 F8
Western Way
Blaydon NE21 .....169 E2
Ponteland NE20 ...138 A2
Ryton NE40 ....168 C4
Whitley Bay NE26 .144 F8
Westfield 9 Amble NE65 .183 C5
Dudley NE23 ......141 F8
Morpeth NE61 .....119 E7
Westfield Ave
Berwick-u-T TD15 .178 B7
Brunswick Village NE13 .141 A6
Crawcrook NE40 ...167 F3
Whitley Bay NE25 .144 D4
Westfield Cl NE46 .160 F5
Westfield Cres
Crawcrook NE40 ..167 F3
Newbiggin-by-t-S NE64 .118 C4
Westfield La NE40 .168 B6
Westfield Rd TD15 .178 B7
Westfield Terr NE46 .160 F5
Westgarth NE5 ....149 F4
Westgate
Haltwhistle NE49 ..153 D4
Morpeth NE61 .....119 D7
Westgate Cl NE25 .144 C6
Westgate Ho NE61 .181 B5
Westgreen NE62 ...121 F5
Westlands
Bellingham NE48 ..184 B5
Haltwhistle NE49 ..153 A4
Newcastle u T NE5 .149 C1
Seaton Sluice NE26 .135 C6
Tynemouth NE30 ..143 B1
Westlea NE22 .....126 D8
Westley Ave NE26 .135 F1
Westley Cl NE26 ...135 F1
Westloch Rd NE23 .133 B3
Westmacott St
Newburn NE15 .....168 E8
Newcastle u T NE48 .72 D3
Westminster Ave NE24 .144 B1
Westminster Cl NE26 .145 C4
Westmoor Dr NE12 .142 B1
Westmoor Prim Sch
NE12 ....142 C2
Westmorland Ave
Bedlington NE22 ...121 E1
Newbiggin-by-t-S NE64 .118 D4
Westmorland Way
NE23 ....133 A6
Westnewton NE71 .12 D1
Westsyde NE20 ...138 B3
Westvale NE15 ....148 B2
Westview NE15 ....24 C1
Westward Ct NE5 .149 E3
Westward Gn NE25 .144 C4
Westway Blaydon NE21 .169 B2
Throckley NE15 ....148 E3
Westway Ind Est NE15 .148 D3
Westwood Cotts NE47 .163 A4
Westwood Gn NE65 .116 F1
Westwood La NE17 .175 B5
Westwood Rd NE15 .141 C1
Westwood View NE40 .167 F3
Wetherby Cl
Ashington NE63 ....117 C2
Consett DH8 ....176 D7
Wettondale Ave NE24 .128 A7
Whalebone La NE61 .119 F8
Whalton CE Fst Sch
NE61 ....85 C8
Whalton Cl NE63 ..120 B5
Whalton Pk NE61 ..75 F1
Wharfedale Gdns NE24 .128 A6
Wharmlands Gr NE15 .169 F7
Wharmlands Rd NE15 .169 F7
Wharton St NE24 ..128 C5
Wheat Cl DH8 ......176 E7
Wheatfield Cl NE42 .149 F3
Wheatfield Rd NE5 .149 F3
Wheatfields NE23 ..134 B4
Wheatridge NE26 ..134 B4
Wheatriggs NE71 ..13 A4
Wheatriggs Ave NE71 .13 A4
Whernside Ct NE23 .133 B3
Whernside Pl NE23 .133 B3
Whernside Wlk NE48 .168 D4
Whetstone Bridge Rd
NE46 ....160 F4
Whetstone Gn NE46 .160 F4
Whin Hill NE71 .....32 C6

Whinbank NE20 ....138 D2
Whinfell Cl NE23 ....133 C3
Whinfell Rd NE20 ....138 D3
Whinham Way NE61 ....120 B5

Whinny La
 Ebchester DH8 ....174 E1
 Mitford NE61 ....76 F8
Whinshield Side NE47 ..155 F1
Whitbeck Rd NE15 .....169 F8
Whitburn Pl NE23 ....133 B3
Whitby Ave NE46 ....160 F5
Whitdale Ave NE24 .....128 A6
White Cotts NE65 ....51 F3
White Cross NE46 ......161 C4
White Gates NE65 ....64 A5
White House Cotts NE66 . 30 F4
White House Dr NE66 ...30 F3
Whiteacre NE48 ....72 C6
Whiteacres NE61 ....120 A7
Whiteadder Cl **13** TD15 ..3 E6
Whiteburn NE42 ....166 B1
Whitecroft Rd NE12 ....142 B2

Whitefield Cres
 Broomhill NE65 ....53 F3
 Pegswood NE61 ....115 E3
Whitefield Farm Cotts
 NE61 ....116 A2
Whitefield Gdns NE40 ..173 F8
Whiteford Pl NE23 ......134 A2
Whitehall Cotts CA9 ....110 A7
Whitehall La DH8 ....177 F1
Whitehall Rd NE15 .....148 F2
Whitehill Rd NE23 ......127 A1

Whitehouse Farm Ctr*
 NE61 ....124 E8
Whitehouses NE47 ......90 D2
Whiteley Cl NE40 ......168 A1
Whiteley Rd NE21 ......169 E4
Whitesand Cl **13** TD15 ..3 E6
Whiteside NE44 ....100 F8
Whitewell Cl NE40 .....168 C5
Whitewell La NE40 .....168 C5
Whitewell Rd NE21 .....169 C2

Whitfield CE Fst Sch
 NE47 ....96 F5
Whitfield Rd
 Newcastle u T NE15 ...169 F5
 Seaton Delaval NE25 ..134 D3
Whitfield St DH8 ....177 A3
Whithorn Ct NE24 .....128 C7

Whitley Bay High Sch
 NE26 ....144 E6
Whitley Bay Sta NE26 ..145 B4

Whitley Chapel CE Fst Sch
 NE47 ....99 C4
Whitley Lodge Fst Sch
 NE26 ....144 E8
Whitley Meml CE Fst Sch
 NE22 ....127 A8
Whitley Pl NE25 ....134 E2
Whitley Rd Earsdon NE25 .144 A5
 Longbenton NE12,NE27 ..143 C1
 Whitley Bay NE26 .....145 B4

Whitley Terr
 5 Bedlington NE22 ..122 D3
 Seaton Delaval NE25 ..134 E2
Whitmore Rd NE21 .....169 C3
Whitsun Ave NE22 .....122 A2
Whitsun Gdns NE22 ....122 A1
Whitsun Gr NE22 ......122 A1
Whitsun View NE71 ....180 C5

Whittingham CE Fst Sch
 NE66 ....39 B7
Whittington Cl
 Ashington NE63 ....117 A2
 Tynemouth NE30 ......145 C2
Whittingham Rd
 6 Glanton NE66 ......29 C1
 Newcastle u T NE5 ....149 F4
 Tynemouth NE30 ......145 C2
Whittis Cres NE47 .....158 B5
Whittis Hill NE47 ......158 B5

Whittis Rd NE47 ....158 B5
Whitton Ave NE24 .....128 B5
Whitton Bank Rd NE65 .182 B4
Whitton Pk NE71 ....13 A4
Whitton Pl NE25 ....134 D3
Whitton Terr NE65 .....182 C5

Whittonstall Fst Sch
 DH8 ....101 F4
Whittonstall Rd NE17 ..173 A1
Whittonstall Terr NE17 ..173 A1
Whitwell Terr NE40 ....168 C6

Whorlton Grange Cotts
 NE5 ....149 E4
Whorlton La NE5 ......149 D5
Whorlton Pl **1** NE5 ..149 E3
Whorlton Terr NE5 ....149 B4
Whorral Bank NE61 ...115 B2

Whytrig Com Mid Sch
 NE25 ....134 C4
Whytrigg Cl NE25 .....134 B3
Wicklow Cl NE62 ......122 D8
Widdrington Cotts NE66 ..41 D3
Widdrington Dr NE18 ..136 A4
Widdrington Gdns
 NE13 ....141 C6
Widdrington Rd NE21 ..169 C2
Widdrington Sta NE61 ..65 E5
Widdrington Terr NE21 ..169 A4
Widow's Row NE46 .....41 C3
Wildshaw Cl NE23 .....133 C3
Wilkes Cl NE5 ....149 F2
Wilkwood Cl NE23 .....133 C4
Willia Rd NE49 ....153 D6

William Allan Homes
 NE22 ....126 D8
William Roberts Ct
 NE12 ....142 D1
William St Blyth NE24 ..128 E6
 Chopwell NE17 ....173 B1
 Pegswood NE61 ......115 F3
William Whiteley Homes
 NE40 ....168 A1
William's Cl NE65 .....183 B4
William's Way **5** NE70 ..15 F4
Willoughby Dr NE36 ...144 E7
Willoughby Way NE26 ..144 E7
Willow Ave NE47 ......123 D1
Willow Cl Broomhill NE65 ..53 F3
 Hipsburn NE66 ....42 A6
 Morpeth NE61 ....120 B8
Willow Cres Blyth NE24 .128 C4
 Leadgate DH8 ....177 D3
Willow Ct Ryton NE40 ..168 D6
 Stakeford NE62 ....122 B7
Willow Dyke NE45 ....163 A6
Willow Gdns NE12 ....142 C4
Willow Pk NE61 ....74 E5
Willow Pl NE20 ....138 E4
Willow Rd NE20 ....169 D2
Willow Way NE20 ....138 E3
Willowburn Ave NE66 ..181 D3
Willowburn Trad Est
 NE66 ....181 E3
Willowdene NE12 .....142 E2
Willows Cl NE13 ......141 A5
Willows The
 Morpeth NE61 ....120 A8
 Seaton Burn NE13 ....132 B1
 Throckley NE15 ......148 D1
Willowtree Ind Est
 NE66 ....181 E2
Wilson Ave NE22 .....144 B4
Wilson Terr NE12 .....142 D1
Wilsway NE15 ....148 C2

Wilton Cl
 Cramlington NE23 ....133 C3
 Whitley Bay NE25 ....144 C5
Wilton Dr NE25 ......144 B5
Wilton Manse NE25 ...144 B4
Wimbourne Gn **1** NE5 .149 F3
Winchester Ave NE24 ..128 E7
Winchester Cl **6** NE63 .117 F2
Winchester Way NE21 ..121 F2
Winchester Wlk NE13 ..141 B6
Windburgh Dr NE23 ...133 B3
Windermere Cl NE23 ..133 B3

Windermere Dr NE12 ..142 C3
Windermere Rd NE64 ..118 C3
Winding The NE13 .....140 B7
Windmill Gr NE24 .....128 A8
Windmill Hill
 Ellington NE61 ....112 E5
 Hexham NE46 ....161 A5
Windmill Hill Cl NE61 ..112 E6
Windmill Hts NE61 ....112 E6
Windmill Ind Est NE23 .126 C2
Windmill Way NE61 ...120 B8
Windshields Wall* NE47 ..88 C2
Windsor Cres
 Berwick-u-T TD15 ....178 A6
 Ovingham NE42 ......166 B5
 Whitley Bay NE26 ....145 C4
Windsor Ct
 Bedlington NE22 .....126 F8
 Corbridge NE45 ......163 A6
 Cramlington NE23 ....127 A1
Windsor Dr NE24 .....128 D3
Windsor Fst Sch NE64 .118 D3
Windsor Gdns
 Alnwick NE66 ....181 B5
 Bedlington NE22 .....126 F8
 Consett DH8 ....177 A2
 Whitley Bay NE26 ....144 F6
Windsor Gdns W NE26 .144 F6
Windsor Pl
 Longbenton NE27 ....143 C1
 Ponteland NE20 .....138 B4
Windsor Rd
 Newbiggin-by-t-S NE64 .118 D4
 Whitley Bay NE26 ....144 E5
Windsor Terr
 5 Amble NE65 ......183 D6
 Choppington NE62 ...121 F4
 Corbridge NE45 .....163 A6
 Crawcrook NE40 .....168 A4
 Hexham NE46 ....160 F5
 Leadgate DH8 ....177 D4
 Newbiggin-by-t-S NE64 .118 D4
 Whitley Bay NE26 ....145 C4
Windsor Villas NE62 ...122 A7
Windsor Wlk NE63 ....118 A2
Windt St NE13 ....141 A5
Windy Gyle NE63 .....117 E4
Windyside Hill
 Longhoughton NE66 ...32 A5
 Rennington NE66 ......31 F4
Winfield TD15 ....2 B5
Wingate Cl NE15 .....169 E6
Wingrove Terr DH8 ...177 D4
Winsford Ave **1** NE29 ..144 F1
Winshields NE23 ......133 C4
Winship St NE24 ......128 C4
Winster Pl NE23 ......133 B3
Winston Way NE43 ...171 C3
Winter Shaft Cotts NE47 ..90 A3
Winter's Gibbet* NE61 ..61 A1
Winton Cl NE23 ....134 A2
Wishart Terr NE39 ....173 F4
Wishaw Cl NE23 ......133 C4
Wishaw Rise NE15 ....169 E7
Witton Rd NE27 ......143 F3
Woburn Cl NE23 ......127 A1
Woburn Dr NE22 .....122 C2
Wolmer Rd NE24 .....128 F5
Wolsingham Ct NE23 ..132 F7
Wolsley Rd NE4 ......128 E7
Wood Fields NE20 ....138 F6
Wood Gr NE15 ....169 E7
Wood La NE22 ....122 B1
Wood Rd NE48 ....55 D4
Wood St DH8 ....176 C6
Woodbine Cotts NE40 ..168 B5
Woodbine Terr **10** NE65 ..183 C5

Woodburn Sq NE26 ...144 D7
Woodburn St
 Newcastle u T NE15 ..169 C7
 Widdrington Sta NE61 ..65 D5
Woodburn Terr NE42 ..166 B2
Woodburn Way NE26 ..144 E7
Woodcroft Cl NE23 ...133 B1
Woodcroft Rd NE41 ...167 A6
Woodend NE20 ....138 D2
Woodhall Ct NE25 ....134 C3
Woodhead Ct NE49 ...153 C5
Woodhead La NE49 ...153 C5
Woodhead Pk NE49 ...153 C5
Woodhead Rd NE42 ..166 F3
Woodhead Villas NE49 .153 C5
Woodhill Dr NE61 ....119 E8
Woodhill Rd NE23 ....133 C4

Woodhorn Colliery Mus*
 NE63 ....117 F5
Woodhorn Cotts NE63 .117 F5
Woodhorn Cres NE64 ..118 D5
Woodhorn Ct NE63 ...117 E4
Woodhorn Dr NE62 ...121 F8
Woodhorn Farm NE64 .118 D6
Woodhorn Gdns NE13 .141 B6
Woodhorn La NE64 ...118 E5
Woodhorn Pk NE63 ...117 D4
Woodhorn Rd
 Ashington NE63 ......117 E4
 Newbiggin-by-t-S NE64 .118 D5
Woodhorn Villas NE63 .117 F5
Woodkirk Cl NE23 ....134 A2
Woodland Ct DH8 ....176 D6
Woodlands
 Hexham NE46 ....161 D4
 Ponteland NE20 .....138 D3
 Rothbury NE65 ......182 B5
 Throckley NE15 .....148 C2
 Ulgham NE61 ....65 D3
 Warkworth NE65 ......53 E8
Woodlands Cl NE25 ...144 A5
Woodlands Cres DH8 ..176 D6
Woodlands Ct NE15 ..148 C2
Woodlands Grange
 NE12 ....142 E1
Woodlands Ho NE24 ..128 B8
Woodlands Park Dr
 NE21 ....169 D2
Woodlands Park Villas
 NE13 ....141 C4
Woodlands Pk
 Coldstream TD12 .....179 B6
 Widaopen NE13 .....141 C5
Woodlands Rd
 Ashington NE63 ......118 A2
 Consett DH8 ....176 D6
 Newcastle u T NE15 ..169 D7
Woodlands Terr NE12 .142 E1
Woodlands Sch NE25 ..144 D3
Woodlea
 Longbenton NE12 ....142 D1
 Newbiggin-by-t-S NE64 .118 E5
Woodlea Cres NE46 ..161 C4
Woodleigh Rd NE25 ..144 E4
Woodman Cl NE61 ....119 E7
Woodside
 Bedlington NE22 .....122 C1
 Blyth NE24 ....128 F6
 Broomhill NE61 ....53 E2
 Hexham NE46 ....161 D4
 Morpeth NE61 ......119 D7
 Ponteland NE20 .....138 C2
 Prudhoe NE42 ......166 F2
Woodside Ave
 Corbridge NE45 .....163 B6
 Seaton Delaval NE25 .134 D2
 Throckley NE15 .....148 E2
Woodside Cl NE40 ...168 C5
Woodside Cres NE65 ..53 F2
Woodside La
 Greenside NE40 .....168 B3
 Ryton NE40 ....168 B4
Woodside Pk TD15 .....2 E5
Woodside Rd NE40 ...168 B5
Woodside Terr NE17 ..175 B8
Woodside Villas NE46 .161 D4

Woodside Way NE40 ..168
Woodstead NE66 24
Woodstock Rd NE15 ..169
Woodvale NE20 138
Woodvale Gdns
 Newcastle u T NE15 ..169
 Wylam NE41 167
Woodvale Rd
 Blaydon NE21 169
 Killingworth NE12 142
Woodville Rd NE15 ...169
Woody Cl DH8 177
Wooler Fst Sch NE71 ..180
Wooler Gn NE15 149
Wooler Sq NE13 141
Woolerton Dr NE15 ..169
Wooley Grange NE46 .100
Woolmarket TD15 178
Woolsington Ct NE22 ..122
Woolsington Gdns NE13 .141
Woolsington Pk S NE13 .141
Worcester Way NE13 ..141
Wordsworth Ave NE24 .123
Worsdell St NE24 123
Wreay Wlk NE23 133
Wreigh Burn Fields NE65 .50
Wright Dr NE23 142
Wright St NE24 128
Wrightson St NE23 ...127
Wych Elm Cl NE61 ...112
Wydon Ave NE49 153
Wydon Pk NE46 161
Wydon Terr NE46 153
Wylam Ave NE25 134
Wylam Fst Sch NE41 ..167
Wylam Mill NE41 167
Wylam Sta NE41 167
Wylam View NE21 ...169
Wylam Wood Rd NE41 .167
Wynd The
 5 Alnmouth NE66 42
 Amble NE65 183
 Longbenton NE12 ...142
 Throckley NE15 148
Wynde The NE20 138
Wynding The
 Annitsford NE23 133
 Bamburgh NE69 17
 Beadnell NE67 24
 Bedlington NE22 121
Wyndon La NE49 153
Wynyard Dr NE22 ...122

Y

Yard Heads TD15 178
Yardley Gr NE23 133
Yarmouth Dr NE23 ...133
Yarrow Cl **9** TD15 3
Yatesfield Rd NE19 59
Yearle Steading NE71 .180
Yelverton Ct NE23 ...133
Yeovil Cl NE23 133
Yew Tree Dr NE22 ...121
Yewcroft Ave NE15 ..169
York Cl NE23 133
York Cres NE66 181
York Gr NE22 121
York Rd Alnwick NE66 .181
 Consett DH8 176
 Whitley Bay NE26 ...145
York St NE24 128
Young Rd NE12 142
Youngers Terr **7** NE65 ..42
Younghall Cl NE40 ...168

Z

Zetland Dr NE25 144
Zion Terr NE21 169